The Sunkist Case

The Sunkist Case

A Study in Legal-Economic Analysis

Willard F. Mueller
University of Wisconsin-Madison

Peter G. Helmberger
University of Wisconsin-Madison

Thomas W. Paterson
Susman, Godfrey and McGowan
Houston, Texas

Lexington Books
D.C. Heath and Company/Lexington, Massachusetts/Toronto

Library of Congress Cataloging-in-Publication Data

Mueller, Willard Fritz.
   The Sunkist case.

   Bibliography: p.
   Includes index.
   1. Citrus fruit industry—Law and legislation—
United States.   2. Antitrust law—United States.
3. Monopolies—United States.   4. Sunkist Growers,
Inc.   5. Citrus fruit industry—United States.
I. Helmberger, Peter G.   II. Paterson, Thomas W.
III. Title.
KF1909.C57M84 1987 343.73'076435 86-46242
                    347.30376435
ISBN 0-669-15189-0 (alk. paper)

Published simultaneously in Canada
Printed in the United States of America
Casebound International Standard Book Number: 0-669-15189-0
Library of Congress Catalog Card Number: 86-46242

The paper used in this publication meets the minimum requirements
of American National Standard for Information Sciences—
Permanence of Paper for Printed Library Materials, ANSI
Z39.48-1984. ⊗ ™

87 88 89 90 91 8 7 6 5 4 3 2 1

Contents

Figures and Tables

Figures

Tables

Preface and Acknowledgments

I n 1977, the Federal Trade Commission issued a complaint charging Sunkist Growers, Inc., with monopolizing the California-Arizona citrus industry. After four years of litigation, the case was settled with a consent agreement without trial or adjudication of any issue of fact or law.

We would like at the very outset to state our interest in this case. During 1979–80, the two senior authors served as consultants to Sunkist on matters relating to the FTC litigation and necessarily draw upon that experience. In writing this book, we have striven to maintain objectivity. Whether we have succeeded is for others to decide. We emphasize, however, that Sunkist did not impose any restraints on our analyses or conclusions.

Several considerations have led us to proceed with this book notwithstanding the risk of bias in our inquiry. Easily the most important of these was the rare opportunity to study the operations of a large cooperative concern with virtually free access to all internal documents, data collections, market analyses, and the like plus access to Sunkist personnel for personal interviews. We cannot recall a single instance in which we were denied information, except where the cost of statistical tabulations would have been prohibitively high, or in which a Sunkist official refused to see us or answer forthrightly whatever questions we might have. The resulting rich body of publishable data and evidence formed the basis not only for the study of the structure and performance of the California-Arizona citrus industry but also for what we hope is an insightful investigation of the pricing and marketing policies that lie at the core of market conduct. We believe this is of some considerable importance in that market conduct is often the neglected link in industrial organization research based on the structure-conduct-performance paradigm.

The origins of this book go well beyond the FTC–Sunkist case, however. We have had for many years a keen interest in the nature and role of cooperative enterprise in determining market performance, an interest on the part of the two senior authors that goes back over a quarter of a century. The junior author's interest in the subject, as reflected in chapter 2, is an outgrowth of his studies in legal-economic analysis at the University of Wisconsin.

We have also been aware along with other students of cooperative enterprise that the theory of the profit-seeking firm can and must be seriously modified if that theory is to serve as a useful framework for empirical research on cooperative marketing. This awareness on our part has become even more acute in the course of preparing this book for we have come to believe the FTC case against Sunkist was consummately in error for the simple, basic reason that it sought to apply the wrong theory in the organization of its case.

Obviously, we owe a debt of gratitude to the entire Sunkist organization. We are particularly grateful to the following officials and former officials of Sunkist who gave freely of their time and expert knowledge: the late Robert H. Autenrieth, Richard S. Bylin, Dale V. Cunningham, William A. Delaney, Russell L. Hanlin, J. Gordon Henderson, and Darlene V. Ohnemus.

We were fortunate also to have had the opportunity in an early stage of our research to discuss the issues raised by the FTC–Sunkist case with Andrew Schmitz (University of California-Berkeley) and James G. Youde (Northwest Economic Associates). We wish to offer our sincere thanks to both. We also thank our colleagues Bruce M. Marion and Peter C. Carstensen for reviewing our legal and economic analyses and helping us avoid foolish errors, and Charles A. Stull, who served as a research assistant on parts of the project. Ann Mennell has painstakingly edited the entire manuscript, correcting grammatical errors, misspelled words, misplaced footnotes, and fulfilling all the other "little" tasks required to get a manuscript off to the publisher on time. We appreciate the assistance of all of the above people and rightly take the blame for the mistakes that remain. We also thank Karen Denk for converting our wretched longhand into clean copy and typing most of the several drafts of each chapter.

Finally, there is the question of research funding. In this regard, we gratefully acknowledge the support of the College of Agricultural and Life Sciences, University of Wisconsin-Madison and the Agricultural Cooperative Service, U.S. Dept. of Agriculture.

1
Introduction

The Nature of Legal-Economic Analysis

Simply put, legal-economic analysis involves a marriage of the disciplines of law and economics. It is a marriage borne of necessity. When public-policy makers design legal rules to govern complex economic activity, economic concepts inevitably become the handmaidens of those drafting and enforcing the rules.

Not all practitioners of legal-economic analysis hold the same view regarding the appropriate roles of the participants in the marriage. Some students of legal-economic analysis would rely exclusively on economic theory in fashioning legal rules guiding human and corporate behavior. The leading contemporary legal scholar expounding this approach is Richard A. Posner, now a federal judge, who argues for applying economic analysis to all areas of law in the belief that "it may be possible to deduce the basic formal characteristics of law itself from economic theory."[1] To many legal and economic scholars, this is an overly ambitious goal, one that promises more for economics than it can deliver. But even legal scholars who are somewhat skeptical about the utility of economic theory believe that law and economics can make "common cause" in developing sensible legal rules.[2]

While economics played a small role, and economists an even smaller one, in the formulation of the Sherman Antitrust Act of 1890, the invaluable use of each soon became evident to those enforcing the law. Although economists initially were reluctant to endorse the law, they soon saw it as essential to the preservation of competitive capitalism. J.M. Clark's conversion to supporting antitrust law perhaps typifies the experience of many economists at the beginning of the twentieth century. As William Baldwin observed, "He [Clark] was opposed to the antitrust laws until they proved effective, and then he supported them on the grounds that they worked."[3]

Antitrust practitioners soon came to realize that developing operational rules on such matters as monopoly and other restraints of trade was the peculiar domain of economics. Initially quite modest, the contributions of economists increased with each passing decade as the economic theory of industrial organization developed and became more relevant to twentieth-century industrial markets and corporate behavior. Empirical verification of theory often has lagged badly, with even some of the most tested hypotheses not verified beyond reasonable doubt. Despite the acknowledged shortcoming of microeconomic theories and empirical testing of them, few would argue that economic counsel not be sought in resolving public policy matters in antitrust. In recent decades, it has become commonplace to employ economic analysis in the formulation of new antitrust laws and the enforcement of existing ones. Despite the shortcomings of economics, no other social science offers more reliable knowledge about competition and monopoly. The antitrust laws are in great part like empty sacks until economic meaning is given to them.

Economics is most useful in promulgating, interpreting, and enforcing laws that have as their sole objective an economic purpose. When this is not so, economists may be forced to yield to other disciplines or may provide only part of the input needed to reach a decision. This is also true with the antitrust laws. Those responsible for enacting these laws had in mind noneconomic as well as economic goals. In a recent comprehensive analysis of this subject, Robert Lande shows that the main objectives behind the antitrust laws included (1) a hostility toward aggregations of economic, social, and political power, (2) the prevention of price enhancement that harmed consumers, (3) the misallocation of economic resources, and (4) a desire to promote a fair opportunity to compete.[4]

Does the existence of multiple, sometimes conflicting, goals limit the relevance of economic analysis? Only partially. First, economists still have much to offer—certainly more than experts in any other discipline—in determining whether the articulated goals of antitrust are being frustrated by particular conduct and, if so, whether there exist less objectionable alternatives. Second, economics is useful in measuring the economic cost of trading off one conflicting goal for another.

The unique contribution of economics in analyzing potential violations of the antitrust laws is that it permits a more rigorous analysis of the issues involved. Economic analysis of a problem begins with building models (verbally, graphically, or mathematically) intended to capture the essence of reality. Such models are used to predict economic events. Testing the predictions of a model involves hypothesis testing, the domain of empirical economic analysis. Until a model has been tested empirically, it provides only a theoretical explanation of reality. Some economic concepts are so well accepted (e.g., downward-sloping demand curves) that observed exceptions to them are viewed as paradoxes. Even when a theory has not been or cannot be adequately tested, it may still provide valuable insights into economic relationships. Applied to the antitrust laws, the legal-economic approach involves, among other things, using economic theory to develop empirically testable hypotheses that will show whether a particular antitrust law has been violated. For example, many antitrust issues concern the existence or use of market power. The first step in such analyses invariably requires defining the relevant economic market within which market power is allegedly held or used. The problem of market definition is, in the words of Justice Fortas, "an economic task put to the use of the law."[5] Today, it is inconceivable to analyze this question without resort to economic theory and empirical analysis. So it is with many other matters such as the source, extent, and consequences of market power. In what follows, we endeavor to heed Lawrence Sullivan's admonition that those employing legal-economic analysis "understand the power of economics and its potential, but also its limits—to draw upon it not as one who borrows or imposes, but as one possessing a tool; to use it selectively, both wisely and well."[6]

Objectives of the Book

This is a legal-economic analysis of the application of the antitrust laws to agricultural cooperatives. It examines in depth an antitrust case involving one of the nation's oldest and largest agricultural cooperatives, Sunkist Growers, Inc. Sunkist has been the leading factor in the California/Arizona citrus industry almost from its inception in the latter part of the nineteenth century. The book analyzes an antitrust case brought by the Federal Trade Commission charging Sunkist with monopolizing the California/Arizona citrus industry. Although the case was ultimately settled with a consent agreement in 1980, considerable information was made public in pretrial pleadings regarding the nature of the California/Arizona citrus industry and the central place of Sunkist in the industry. The Federal Trade Commission prepared an extensive 167-page Trial Brief discussing the legal-economic theory of its case and the evidence that it believed supported this theory. Sunkist prepared a comprehensive statement of its defense to the FTC charges. Sunkist Growers, Inc., also generously made available to the authors the nonpublic record developed during the four years of investigation and pretrial adjudication as well as information about Sunkist's activities that appeared in the FTC's Trial Brief but was excised for confidentiality reasons from the public version of the brief. Sunkist also generously made available information of its shipments for several years since the case was settled. Without the cooperation of Sunkist, it would not have been possible to conduct the research reported here.

The objective of the book is to analyze the legal-economic basis of the FTC's charges. At the more general level, the book provides insight into the circumstances in which large agricultural cooperatives such as Sunkist risk violating the antitrust laws. It also provides some insight into the manner in which the public interest is affected in the application of these laws to cooperatives.

The book proceeds as follows:

1. It begins by describing briefly the salient issues in the Federal Trade Commission case charging Sunkist with violating certain antitrust laws.

2. It next identifies the legal rules that are to be used in evaluating the issues in the *Sunkist* case. Since these rules are embodied in court precedents, an analysis is made of key decisions that interpret the relevant antitrust statutes. The relevant legal rules will be used, in turn, to identify the kinds of economic and noneconomic analysis helpful in determining whether Sunkist violated the antitrust laws.

3. Attention is then focused on the analytical framework to be used in making the economic analysis. This framework aids in formulating relevant hypotheses that need to be tested before a judgment can be made as to whether the legal rules have been violated.

4. Most of the remainder of the book involves testing these hypotheses. Specifically, this includes analysis of the structure, conduct, and performance of the California/Arizona citrus industry, with special attention given to Sunkist's role in the industry.

5. Finally, we summarize the significance of our findings for determining whether Sunkist violated the antitrust laws and whether the relief ordered by the Federal Trade Commission was appropriate.

We begin by describing briefly the nature of the Federal Trade Commission's case charging Sunkist Growers, Inc., with monopolizing the California/Arizona citrus industry.

The Sunkist Case

In December 1976, Sunkist Growers, Inc., was informed that the staff of the Federal Trade Commission intended to recommend that Sunkist be charged with actual and attempted monopolization of the California/Arizona citrus industry.[7] A formal complaint was issued May 31, 1977.[8] We begin our examination with an overview of the *Sunkist* case as viewed by the FTC staff.[9]

The Sunkist case was brought under section 5 of the Federal Trade Commission Act, which prohibits "unfair" methods of competition, and section 7 of the Clayton Act, which prohibits mergers that may substantially lessen competition or tend to create a monopoly. The section 7 charge was subsequently dismissed. Although section 5 of the Federal Trade Commission Act has a potentially broader reach than the Sherman Act, the FTC case was based almost exclusively on the legal precedents interpreting section 2 of the Sherman Act.[10] The Supreme Court has held that "The offense of monopoly under section 2 of the Sherman Act has two elements: (1) the possession of monopoly power in the relevant product market and (2) the willful acquisition or maintenance of that power as distinguished from growth or development as a consequence of a superior product, business acumen, or historic accident."[11] The Court has, in turn, defined monopoly power to consist of "the power to control prices or exclude competition."[12]

In the FTC's view, the facts that Sunkist was an agricultural cooperative and that fresh California/Arizona oranges and lemons were subject to federal marketing orders were not a defense to the antitrust charges in the complaint.[13] The Capper-Volstead Act gives cooperatives only a limited antitrust exemption. In the FTC's view, the act did not exempt cooperatives from prohibition of the sort of practices alleged in the complaint. On the other hand, the FTC staff believed that the existence of federal orders was irrelevant because the complaint did not challenge growers' or Sunkist's participation in these marketing orders; the FTC therefore considered the existence of the orders entirely unrelated to the question of whether or not Sunkist had violated the antitrust laws.

The FTC's case was based on three kinds of alleged evidence: (1) the existence of a monopolistic market structure, (2) market conduct demonstrating that Sunkist already possessed monopoly power, and (3) market conduct designed to achieve, maintain, and enhance Sunkist's monopoly position.

The structural evidence was Sunkist's alleged 70 percent share of fresh domestic lemon and California/Arizona orange shipments since 1960 or earlier. This, said the FTC staff, was "clear inferential evidence of monopoly power."[14] Moreover, it could be inferred that Sunkist already possessed monopoly power from its alleged "persistent price leadership in all the relevant markets, and its price premium, resulting primarily from deliberate differentiation of a homogeneous product."[15] The FTC further asserted that there existed evidence that Sunkist withheld fresh citrus from the market to raise or stabilize prices. Sunkist also allegedly withheld supplies and held large inventories of lemon juice to raise or stabilize prices.

While acknowledging that the "mere possession of monopoly might not violate the antitrust laws," the FTC asserted that Sunkist had pursued various "deliberate" acts to perpetuate that monopoly. Among these alleged acts were the following:

1. A deliberate corporate policy to control 65 to 75 percent of each variety of citrus produced in California/Arizona.

2. The implementation of this goal by combining with numerous commercial packing houses.

3. The use of exclusive dealing arrangements with its grower-members' packing houses, about one-half of which were commercial, noncooperative houses. The agreements with the latter houses (1) prohibited the houses from packing citrus from non-Sunkist growers and (2) foreclosed competing marketers and processors from access to these supplies of citrus.

4. In 1974, Sunkist acquired Growers Citrus Products, the only processor of oranges and lemons in Arizona, thereby increasing Sunkist's already dominant processing capacity by about 15 percent.

5. Sunkist required commercial packinghouses to affiliate with it on an "all-or-nothing" basis, thereby preventing a packinghouse from disaffiliating from Sunkist.

Adequate relief for Sunkist's alleged monopolization, in the FTC staff's view, could only be achieved by putting an end to Sunkist's monopoly position and "break[ing] up or render[ing] impotent the monopoly power found to have been preserved and maintained in violation of law."[16] The FTC staff said that in these circumstances, it was the Commission's duty to use its wide latitude in fashioning relief "to pry open to competition the markets which have been closed by Sunkist's unlawful monopolization."[17]

On August 15, 1980, after more than four years of investigation and pretrial litigation, Sunkist Growers, Inc., entered into a consent agreement, which the commission approved.[18] The primary substantive provision of the consent order was the requirement that Sunkist divest itself of its Arizona Products Division, which consisted of the Growers Citrus Products properties acquired by Sunkist in 1974. In a related provision, Sunkist agreed not to acquire for ten years any commercial citrus-processing plants in California or Arizona without prior approval of the FTC. The second substantive provision ordered that for a period of five years from the time the order became final, Sunkist was to have not more than thirty-nine affiliated commercial packinghouses unless prior approval of the FTC was obtained. Finally, for a period of five years, Sunkist was prohibited from acquiring, without prior FTC approval, any citrus packinghouse.

These, then, are the key elements of the FTC's case, as viewed by the FTC's staff, and the relief ultimately agreed to by the FTC to remedy the alleged violations of law. Not surprisingly, Sunkist Growers, Inc., disagreed with both issues of fact and law as set forth by the FTC complaint and the staff's subsequent pleadings.[19]

The remainder of this book entails a legal-economic analysis of the FTC charges. The analysis proceeds as follows. In chapters 2 and 3, we identify the law and economic theory of monopolization as they apply to agricultural cooperatives. Chapter 4 analyzes the structure of the California/Arizona citrus industry and determines the extent of market power this structure confers on Sunkist. Chapters 5 and 6 examine the various patterns of price and nonprice conduct that Sunkist allegedly engaged in to achieve and maintain a monopoly position. Chapter 7 summarizes our findings and conclusions regarding the FTC allegations. In chapter 8, we examine the nature and merits of the 1981 agreement between Sunkist and the FTC settling the antitrust litigation. Appendixes provide various FTC and Sunkist documents.

Notes

1. Richard Posner, *Antitrust Law: An Economic Perspective* (Chicago: University of Chicago Press, 1976), 1.

2. Derek Bok, "Section 7 of the Clayton Act and the Merging of Law and Economics," *Harvard Law Review* 74(December 1960):227.

3. William L. Baldwin, *Antitrust and the Changing Corporation* (Durham, N.C.: Duke University Press, 1961), 65.

4. Robert H. Lande, "Wealth Transfers as the Original and Primary Concern of Antitrust: The Efficiency Interpretation Challenged," *Hastings Law Journal* 34(September 1982):34.

5. *United States v. Grinnell Corp.*, 384 U.S. 563 (1966).

6. Lawrence Sullivan, *Handbook of the Law of Antitrust* (St. Paul: West, 1977), 9.

7. Letter from Sunkist counsel to the Federal Trade Commission, December 8, 1976. A draft of the proposed complaint dated September 9, 1976, was attached to this correspondence.

8. Federal Trade Commission, *In the Matter of Sunkist Growers, Inc.*, FTC Docket 9100 (Washington, D.C.: FTC, May 31, 1977). The complaint appears in appendix A.

9. The following discussion is based largely on statements and facts appearing in the FTC staff's Trial Brief. The views expressed are those of the FTC staff and do not necessarily reflect the views of the five FTC commissioners who approved issuance of the complaint and ultimately would have decided, after a trial on the merits, whether Sunkist violated the antitrust laws as alleged in the complaint.

10. FTC Brief, 107.

11. *United States v. Grinnell Corp.*, 384 U.S. 563, 570–71 (1966).

12. *United States v. E.I. du Pont de Nemours & Co.*, 351 U.S. 377, 391 (1956).

13. *United States v. Borden Co.*, 308 U.S. 188 (1939); *Maryland & Virginia Milk Producers Association, Inc. v. United States*, 362 U.S. 458 (1960).

14. FTC Brief, 3.

15. Ibid., 3–4.

16. Ibid., 150. Quoting from *United States v. Grinnell Corp.*, 384 U.S. 563, 577 (1966).

17. FTC Brief, 150.

18. Federal Trade Commission, *In the Matter of Sunkist Growers, Inc.*, FTC Docket 9100, "Agreement Containing Order to Divest and Other Relief" (Washington, D.C.: FTC, August 15, 1980).

19. Sunkist Growers, Inc., "Statement of the Defense," FTC Docket 9100 (March 22, 1979).

2
Law of Monopolization for Agricultural Cooperatives

An Overview of Monopolization under Section 2 of the Sherman Act

The Federal Trade Commission's complaint charged Sunkist with violating section 7 of the Clayton Act as well as section 5 of the Federal Trade Commission Act. The staff brief did not pursue the section 7 charge. Instead, it treated the acquisition of Growers Citrus Products as evidence of Sunkist's monopolizing conduct rather than as an illegal merger under section 7. For this reason, the legal analysis here and elsewhere examines the alleged monopolization violation of section 5. Because today the law of monopolization under section 5 of the Federal Tade Commission Act relies almost exclusively on precedent under section 2 of the Sherman Act, this chapter necessarily focuses on these precedents.

Unlawful monopolization under section 2 of the Sherman Act[1] addresses market dominance and exclusionary conduct or intent.[2] According to the Supreme Court in *United States v. Grinnell Corp.*,[3] a person who has unlawfully monopolized in restraint of trade satisfies two tests. First, the person must have monopoly power. Second, the person must have willfully acquired or maintained that power as opposed to achieving it from "growth or development as a consequence of a superior product, business acumen, or historic accident."[4]

The monopoly power element in *Grinnell* is the power to control prices or to exclude competitors in the relevant market.[5] By tradition, the first step in evaluating the presence of this power is to define the relevant product and geographic market. The relevant market is the "narrowest market which is wide enough so that products from adjacent areas or from other producers in the same area cannot compete on substantial parity with those included in the market."[6] The power to control price or exclude competitors in this market does not, as Sullivan points out, imply that there are two separate standards for determining monopoly power.[7] Because price and competition are intimately related, "the usual formulation is merely a convenient way to suggest a single test—whether a firm has sufficient power to raise prices, and whether it could, by lowering prices, exclude competitors from the market."[8] Accordingly, monopoly power does not require that prices be set at a profit-maximizing level or that competition actually be excluded. As the Supreme Court stressed in *American Tobacco*, the material consideration is whether the firm has the power to do these things.[9]

In addition to proving monopoly power, the plaintiff in a section 2 action must establish that the monopolist has engaged or intended to engage in certain conduct. Specifically, the plaintiff must show that the alleged monopolist intended or actually acquired or maintained the monopoly power through unlawfully predatory or exclusionary conduct in contrast to doing so by means of a superior product, historic accident, or business acumen. Conduct that is exclusionary in purpose or function tends to erect barriers to new-firm entry or to deter incumbent-firm expansion.[10]

In this chapter, we evaluate Sherman section 2 monopolization for agricultural marketing cooperatives. After restating *Grinnell* for application to agricultural marketing cooperatives, we consider evidence that may support a finding of monopoly power and exclusionary intent. We then assess the monopolization case law for cooperatives. Here we identify instances where courts have not adequately modified their monopolization analysis for a cooperative and consider the corresponding implications for liability.

Agricultural Marketing Cooperatives and Sherman Section 2 Monopolization

The Standard

An agricultural marketing cooperative is a business association operating primarily to market farm products for its members.[11] Some cooperatives are involved in the first stages of processing and marketing farm commodities,[12] others only represent producers in sales negotiations with buyers, seeking to enhance terms of sale for member-farmers.[13] In either case, the cooperative is a combination of farmers and is engaged in trade or commerce.

The prospect that a marketing cooperative might represent an unlawful combination under the Sherman Act[14] prompted Congress to pass section 6 of the Clayton Act[15] and later to pass the Capper-Volstead Act of 1922.[16] In *National Broiler Marketing Association v. United States*,[17] the Supreme Court identified the congressional purpose in passing Capper-Volstead.[18] According to the Court, in Capper-Volstead Congress expressed its concern with both the nature of production agriculture—perishability, bulky products, uncertainty, production cycles—and the organization of the markets in which farmers compete—competitively organized farmers as price takers and imperfectly organized buyers with power to control price and nonprice terms of sale.[19] Congress expected that, through cooperatives, individual farmers could respond to the factors that might otherwise contribute to lower farm incomes. With Capper-Volstead, eligible cooperatives would not be subject to the antitrust proscriptions on combinations in restraint of trade.[20]

Case law on Capper-Volstead has largely focused on the extent of protection Capper-Volstead provides from antitrust charges. In this regard, courts have soundly rejected various claims that the Capper-Volstead Act entirely removes cooperatives from the reach of the antitrust laws. In *United States v. Borden Co.*,[21] the Supreme Court reversed a district court holding that the only cooperative-related restraints of trade prohibited were those leading to unduly enhanced prices and, for these, the secretary of agriculture was to have exclusive jurisdiction.[22] The Supreme Court found that the Capper-Volstead authorization for collective action is limited and that the secretary's responsibility is auxiliary.[23] Faced with similar arguments in *Maryland and Virginia Milk Producers Association v. United States*,[24] the Supreme Court held that section 2 of Capper-Volstead does not give the secretary of agriculture exclusive jurisdiction over cooperatives responsible for restraints of trade or over cooperatives engaged in monopolization.[25] And, because *Borden* made clear that cooperatives are subject to Sherman section 1, the Court reasoned that Congress could not have intended section 1 of Capper-Volstead to exempt cooperatives from Sherman section 2.[26] The Court observed that the "sections closely overlap, and the same kinds of predatory practices may show violations of all."[27]

Besides establishing that Capper-Volstead does not put cooperatives entirely beyond the reach of the antitrust laws, *Borden* and *Maryland and Virginia* demonstrate alternative bases for finding that a cooperative is not entitled to any protection. In *Borden*, the Court ruled that Capper-Volstead does not protect combinations with nonproducers, an organizational analysis.[28] In *Maryland and Virginia*, the cooperative was validly organized, but it had allegedly engaged in activity which, if proved, was beyond what section 1 of Capper-Volstead authorizes.[29] Subsequent case law on Capper-Volstead has continued to develop both types of limitations.

As in *Borden*, one line of case law has addressed the organizational requirements that a cooperative must satisfy to be eligible for Capper-Volstead protection. In these cases, courts have evaluated who is a Capper-Volstead person,[30] who is a Capper-Volstead agricultural producer, and which activities[31] must a Capper-Volstead cooperative perform.[32] A cooperative is not entitled to protection if it has violated section 1 voting, dividend, or operating requirements, if it is not comprised of business organizations each directly engaged in farm-level production, or if it does not undertake any function that might be characterized as being within processing or preparing for market, handling, or marketing.[33] A cooperative might also be ineligible for protection if any members are among those whom policy indicates Congress did not intend for Capper-Volstead to protect.[34]

In a second line of cases, courts have held that a cooperative organizationally compatible with Capper-Volstead may still be ineligible for protection from antitrust charges if it has engaged in activity as a cooperative that goes beyond the scope of the Capper-Volstead exemption. The classic statement is from *Maryland and Virginia*, where Justice Black observed that the general philosophy of Clayton section 6 and the Capper-Volstead Act is that "individual farmers should be given, through agricultural cooperatives acting as entities, the same unified competitive advantage—and responsibility—available to businessmen acting through corporations as entities."[35] That is, in matters going beyond the Capper-Volstead section 1 requirements for protection from antitrust charges, the cooperative is to have the same opportunities and liabilities as does a proprietary firm. In the context of Sherman section 2 monopolization, the *Maryland and Virginia* line of case law has attempted to distinguish between the market power and exclusionary activities Capper-Volstead authorizes and situations when a cooperative has gone so far beyond what Capper-Volstead may allow that it is ineligible for protection and may indeed have violated section 2.[36]

One possibility, of course, is that Capper-Volstead does not modify application of section 2 to agricultural marketing cooperatives. The district court in *Fairdale Farms, Inc. v. Yankee Milk, Inc. (Fairdale I)*[37] took essentially this view. The court held that a plaintiff alleging that a cooperative has engaged in monopolization has no greater burden than if the plaintiff were charging a proprietary firm with monopolization.[38] According to the district court, a cooperative with monopoly power violates section 2 if it willfully acquired this power.[39] Presumably, registering new farmer members would be willful acquisition.[40] As the district court saw it, while Capper-Volstead does not proscribe the formation of a cooperative, courts are to draw the line on a cooperative's market power at the point where the cooperative acquires monopoly power.[41] Of course, if a cooperative acquires or exercises its power through predatory means, this could also satisfy *Grinnell*.[42]

On appeal, the U.S. Court of Appeals for the Second Circuit reversed the district court holding in *Fairdale I*.[43] The court found that Capper-Volstead modifies *Grinnell*; a cooperative can undertake some activity willfully to acquire or to maintain monopoly power.[44] Unlike the district court, the court of appeals could not find anything in section 1 of Capper-Volstead limiting farmers' collective market power to something less than that associated with monopoly power.[45] Moreover, the court was unwilling to assume responsibility for divining the point at which the collective formation and growth of a cooperative becomes unlawful monopolization.[46] Limits on a cooperative's monopoly cannot be tied solely to market power acquired or maintained by normal growth or by voluntary restriction of new members—willful acts not expressly within a *Grinnell* exception.[47] For a cooperative, Capper-Volstead means that unlawfully acquired monopoly power or legitimate monopoly power unlawfully maintained must refer to conduct that is predatory or that stifles or smothers competition.[48]

The Second Circuit's decision in *Fairdale I* has considerable case law support[49] and has received broad endorsement. The United States Courts of Appeals for the Sixth,[50] Eighth,[51] Tenth,[52] and Eleventh[53] Circuits have expressed approval of *Fairdale I*.[54] Restated for agricultural marketing cooperatives, the second element in *Grinnell* has a fourth exception. A plaintiff charging a cooperative with Sherman section 2 monopolization must prove that the cooperative has monopoly power and that the cooperative willfully acquired or maintained this power as opposed to achieving it from growth or development as a consequence of a superior product, business acumen, or historic accident or, in addition, conduct compatible with what Congress authorized in the Capper-Volstead Act.[55]

Conduct going beyond Capper-Volstead has been loosely referred to as "predatory."[56] But in "cases construing the Capper-Volstead Act, ['predatory practices'] is intended to distinguish monopolies acquired through anticompetitive practices from lawful accretions of market power willfully created through the voluntary enrollment of members of cooperatives."[57] Predatory practices are not restricted to "anticompetitive practices without business justification."[58] "An anticompetitive practice may have economic justification but its use may be taken with unlawful intent and in the desire to achieve an unlawful goal."[59] Objectionableness in these instances may depend on the cooperative's market power.

As Judge Wyzanski recognized in *Cape Cod*, an assessment should be made of the cooperative's strength in a particular market and how it achieved that strength. In a monopolization case, "an increasing percentage and a very high percentage of the market may invite much more careful scrutiny than a small percentage."[60] When a firm with some market power undertakes conduct identical to that by a firm with considerably more market power, they may not share the same results or motivation. The more dominant firm, by definition, has more influence on the market. Accordingly, "even lawful contracts and business activities may help to make up a pattern of conduct unlawful under the Sherman Act."[61]

Identifying Monopoly Power and Conduct

Market Power and Agricultural Marketing Cooperatives. Market power for an agricultural marketing cooperative or for any firm refers to control over price. If a firm has market power, it must lower price to sell more. When firms are atomistically organized, as is usually the case in agricultural production, each firm faces a horizontal demand curve for its output. Individually, a producer has no market power, but instead is a price taker. One potential avenue to market power is collective action through a cooperative.

The Capper-Volstead modification of *Grinnell* is relevant for two types of agricultural marketing cooperatives, operating and bargaining cooperatives. In an operating cooperative, producers collectively undertake activities occurring past the farm level. This may involve "product procurement, sorting, preparing for market, storage, sales, transportation, and processing."[62] The underlying motive for organizing an operating cooperative is to increase farmers' returns. The cooperative might accomplish this by earning some of the profits involved in marketing, by organizing or performing marketing functions more efficiently, by exercising market power over terms of trade, or by ensuring that the producer has an outlet for its product.[63] Through a bargaining cooperative, farmers join together to influence their terms of sale with the buyers each farmer would otherwise face on his own.[64] Sales terms include price or a price-determination formula as well as such things as quality standards, grading procedures, or handling allowances.[65] Bargaining cooperatives attempt to influence terms of trade in different ways. Some take title to members' production and negotiate sales terms with buyers.[66] In other bargaining cooperatives, members designate the cooperative as the exclusive bargaining or selling agent for their production.[67] Some bargaining cooperatives do not negotiate with buyers, but gather information and provide members with a forum for determining the common sales terms that each will individually require from buyers.[68]

When an operating cooperative assembles or processes farm output, the producer will receive a price reflecting the value of his output and his share of any net margins from the marketing activities. Mighell and Jones observe that any long-run ability to return higher prices will depend on the cooperative developing a differentiated product with a special brand name and monitoring the quantity it permits to flow into the processed product.[69] Youde and Helmberger add that this market power is more available to a cooperative handling consumer products because "product identification and differentiation are easier to attain at that level."[70]

In only certain circumstances will a bargaining cooperative have the potential for improving farmers' prices and incomes, and these circumstances will not be satisfied for all commodities.[71] A principal requirement for a cooperative to raise price above the competitive level will be the coopera-tive's ability to control output.[72] Because the cooperative qua cooperative generally only controls the disposition of output among outlets,[73] this con-dition must be satisfied with some other mechanism—especially if there are a large number of producers and production occurs over a broad geograph-ic area.[74] Without control over supply, the potential for price enhance-ment largely depends on the degree of competition among buyers for producers' output.[75] As competition among buyers "approaches the limit of perfect competition, the potential for farmer gains erodes away and disappears in the long run."[76]

Monopoly Power in the Relevant Market. That a cooperative has some control over price does not mean that it has monopoly power. The distinc-tion between market power and monopoly power is the degree of control over price. Both the monopolist and the monopolistically competitive firm may perceive that each one's demand curve slopes downward and, hence, to sell more, each must charge a lower price. But unlike the monopolistically competitive firm, the monopolist has a substantial "degree of power to control price, to be inefficient, or to exclude competitors."[77]

Monopoly power can be assessed directly and indirectly. Absent evi-dence of actual control or exclusion, however, the assessment must be indi-rect. Whether a firm has monopoly power may be evaluated looking at market structure, the firm's conduct, and the firm's performance.

Market share, a structural variable, is a principal indicator of power in the relevant market.[78] If a firm cannot control quantity supplied, it cannot control price. Market share is not the only determinant of monopoly power, though. The number of other firms in the market and the distribu-tion of market shares among these firms influence the significance of a given market share.[79] A given market share in a market with a number of small rivals may suggest greater power than would the same share in a market with only one or two other firms. Likewise, a seller with a large market share has no long-run power over price unless there are barriers to new entry or to the expansion of incumbent rival firms. These barriers will be specific to the industry, but might include technological or pecuniary economies of scale, large capital requirements, patent rights, a highly differentiated product,[80] or access to resources such as labor, land, trans-portation, or energy. Finally, a given market share in a contracting industry—where new entrants' sales must come at the expense of incum-bent firms—suggests greater power over price than would the same share in a rapidly growing industry.

Monopoly power might be inferred from a firm's conduct or perfor-mance as well as from structural variables. To the extent that it would not be effective or practical for a less powerful firm to engage in certain activity, conduct is an indicator of monopoly power.[81] This may include either pricing so as to deter new entry or fringe-firm expansion[82] or else threatening to stop buying or selling unless a party modifies its behavior. If a firm is able to undertake certain marketing strategies, this might also support a finding of monopoly power.[83]

From economic theory, monopoly is associated with certain performance. A profit-maximizing monopolist will have higher prices, lower outputs, and greater profits relative to performance in an atomistically organized market. Profit and price levels in relationship to product costs, absent X-inefficiency[84] or strategic pricing, may indicate monopoly power. This evidence will be more convincing if the levels have persisted over time despite changes in supply or demand conditions.[85] Taken with structural evidence, the conduct and performance indicators may provide sufficient circumstantial evidence to establish that a firm has the substantial power over price necessary to constitute monopoly power.

Applied to the agricultural marketing cooperative, some otherwise generally valid indicators of monopoly power may prove to be misleading. This might be particularly the case with evidence of a large share in the relevant market, a structural variable. Even if an operating or a bargaining cooperative controls the distribution of 100 percent of the raw commodity, it will not necessarily have monopoly power. Economists have shown that a cooperative's potential for controlling price depends, among other things, on its ability to control the quantity supplied by its members and on the market organization of buyers.[86]

Other indicators of monopoly power may be equally if not more convincing with a cooperative than a proprietary firm. Monopoly power may be inferred from price as well as from structure or conduct.[87] A monopoly price is one that is high relative to costs and persists over time despite changes in supply or demand. Because a dominant firm may engage in strategic pricing or long-run profit maximization or because it may have higher costs, price-cost margins may be of dubious value as an indicator of monopoly power. But unlike a proprietary firm where ownership is separate from patronage, a cooperative seeking Capper-Volstead protection must conduct at least one-half of its business with its owners.[88] If, and to the extent that, this involvement puts further pressure on management to maximize revenues by manipulating quantity, price becomes an important indicator of the degree of the cooperative's market power. A relevant issue with respect to monopoly power is how to identify a monopoly price for a cooperative.

The basic guideline on what is a monopoly price comes straight from the case law on monopolization. In *Maryland and Virginia*, the majority specified that an agricultural cooperative is to have the same advantages and responsibilities as do businesspeople acting through corporate entities.[89]

The characteristics of a monopoly price for a cooperative are, accordingly, the characteristics of a monopoly price that a proprietary firm charges.[90] If the cooperative maximizes revenues, this price will likely be high relative to costs or to comparable products and will persist over the long run.[91]

Exclusionary Conduct. If a cooperative is shown to have monopoly power, the plaintiff must further establish that the cooperative has engaged or intended to engage in exclusionary conduct. Evidence of objectionable intent or conduct is necessary to distinguish intent consistent with competitive processes from exclusionary intent. The evidence may provide conclusive, presumptive, or supportive proof of the requisite general exclusionary intent. An analysis of exclusionary conduct is not wholly independent from a finding of monopoly power. The conduct of firms with monopoly power is more open to scrutiny than the conduct of firms with relatively less market power.[92] Moreover, some decisons indicate that exclusionary conduct must reflect the use of monopoly power.[93] Exclusionary conduct might include merger, marketing strategies designed to tie up input supplies or sales outlets, advertising-induced product differentiation, and, certainly, predation.

Sullivan defines predatory conduct as "conduct which has the purpose and effect of advancing the actor's competitive position, not by improving the actor's market performance, but by threatening to injure or injuring actual or potential competitors, so as to drive or keep them out of the market, or force them to compete less effectively."[94] Also according to Sullivan, this conduct will have two identifying features. First, "there will be something odd, something jarring or unnatural seeming about it. It will not strike the informed observer as normal business conduct, as honestly industrial."[95] Second, "it will be aimed at a target, at an identifiable competitor or potential competitor or an identifiable group of them."[96]

Recent scholarship has focused on legal-economic rules that courts can use to identify predatory pricing designed to discipline or exclude rivals. Areeda and Turner associate predatory pricing with eliminating equally efficient rivals by selling at nonremunerative prices.[97] Under their rule, price below short-run average variable cost is presumptive evidence of predation.[98] Scherer expresses a basic suspicion of the Areeda-Turner short-run price-cost rule. According to him, the rule is wrong and may lead to economically unsound decisions.[99] Appropriate analysis of pricing conduct requires assessing the

> Relative cost positions of the monopolist and fringe firms, the scale of entry required to secure minimum costs, whether fringe firms are driven out entirely or merely suppressed, whether the monopolist expands its output to replace the output of excluded rivals or restricts suppl; again

when the rivals withdraw, and whether any long-run compensatory expansion by the monopolist entails investment in scale-embodying new plant.[100]

Despite these concerns, other commentators and courts generally accept the Areeda-Turner formulation as *a* rule for identifying predatory pricing.[101] As *the* rule, though, there is considerable disagreement, especially among commentators.[102] Mueller summarizes the recent scholarship, concluding that prices above average variable cost and even average total cost can be evidence of predation when accompanied with further proof of a design to prey upon incumbent firms or to exclude potential rivals.[103] Critical to this analysis will be market structure and the alleged predator's market or extramarket resources and economic or noneconomic evidence of exclusionary conduct or intent.[104]

Case Law Evidence of Sherman Section 2 Monopolization

Case law lends support to the Helmberger and Hoos' observation that market power is likely, if at all, with cooperatives dealing in only certain commodities.[105] The application of section 2 monopoly to agricultural marketing cooperatives has largely involved fluid milk and Arizona/California citrus. In this section, we review the principal section 2 monopolization cases, including some where a conspiracy or an attempt to monopolize was charged.[106] Cases are presented in the context of *Grinnell* and essentially in chronological order. While we recognize that case law on section 2 monopolization is not static, our purpose is to identify, first, the evidence that courts have found persuasive or unpersuasive with respect to monopoly power and exclusionary purpose or conduct and, second, how court findings have changed over time. With some exceptions, it will be seen that the decisions do not extensively analyze monopoly power. And, until some of the most recent cases, the courts have tended to require evidence of conduct that is clearly predatory to satisfy the exclusionary purpose or conduct requirement.

Although one of the first cases to deal with section 2 made a blanket association between market share and market dominance, it did not confine the jury to clearly predatory conduct in order to find unlawful monopoly. In *Cape Cod Food Products v. National Cranberry Association*,[107] Judge Wyzanski advised the jury that monopolizing under Sherman section 2 means acquiring a dominant position in a relevant market "so as to exclude actual or potential competition."[108] The court did not ask the jury to consider whether the defendant cooperative had such a dominant position, however. Instead, the court indicated that a cooperative with a large market share is in a dominant position, but this is unlawful only if it achieved this position through a prohibited restraint of trade, a predatory practice, or the bad faith use of otherwise legitimate devices.[109] The court instructed the jury that it would be prohibited monopolization if "a group of persons used their power to lend money and their power to foreclose on loans, not with the intent of forwarding their banking or credit or like interests, but with the purpose of stifling actual or potential competition."[110]

As in *Cape Cod*, the Supreme Court recognized in *Maryland and Virginia* that "lawful contracts and business activities may help to make up a pattern of conduct unlawful under the Sherman Act."[111] Addressing alleged attempt and monopolization charges, the Court observed that the cooperative controlled 86 percent of the milk purchased by all dealers in the Washington, D.C., metropolitan area.[112] The Court did not assess whether this was the relevant market for monopoly power, whether its high market share allowed the cooperative to charge monopoly prices, or whether the cooperative controlled supply. Instead the Court stressed that if on remand the government proved its conduct allegations, this would clearly establish that the cooperative had violated section 2.[113] The alleged conduct included excluding, eliminating, and attempting to eliminate milk producers and nonaffiliated producer associations by interfering with nonmember truck shipments, inducing a dairy to switch its nonassociation members' milk to another outlet, boycotting a feed supplier that also ran a dairy in order to compel purchases from the association, and using a dairy's indebtedness to the association to force it to buy association milk.[114]

Bergjans Farm Dairy Company v. Sanitary Milk Producers involved an alleged attempt to monopolize milk processing.[115] The defendant cooperative's power in the distribution of raw milk was relevant because it was alleged that it used this power to further its designs on controlling milk processing.[116] The court found that in the St. Louis market order area, the cooperative controlled the distribution of 55 to 60 percent of the raw milk.[117] The district court found that the cooperative had monopoly or near monopoly power as evidenced by its market share, its ability to raise funds in a short time by withholding partial payment to members, its bargaining power with financial institutions for nonsecured loans, and its dual position as a raw milk supplier and a processor.[118] The court further found that while the cooperative had lawfully obtained its power in raw milk distribution,[119] it had used this power unlawfully to attempt to monopolize milk processing. The objectionable conduct[120] included driving down the wholesale price for milk, selling milk at prices below cost, deceptive bookkeeping, using revenues from higher prices in certain areas to subsidize lower prices in areas where the cooperative sought to control competition, cutting prices and later raising them after eliminating a competitor, conspiring with retailers to fix resale prices and giving them secret rebates, and threatening processors with cutting off their access to raw milk.[121]

In *North Texas Producers Association v. Metzger Dairies, Inc.*,[122] a jury found that the defendant cooperative either had monopolized or had attempted to monopolize raw milk marketing in the Dallas-Fort Worth area.[123] On appeal, the Fifth Circuit did not expressly examine market power or the presence of monopoly power in a relevant market. The court simply indicated that the cooperative supplied 85 to 90 percent of the raw milk in the Dallas-Fort Worth area.[124] Moreover, the cooperative had successfully imposed a 30 cent per hundredweight increase in the price of milk to processors.[125] In determining that there was sufficient evidence for the jury to find for a plaintiff processor, the court primarily considered the cooperative's activities toward the plaintiff.[126] The court noted that the cooperative had attempted to impose various conditions for sales to the processor and, when the processor refused to comply with the conditions, the cooperative tried to disrupt its access to alternative sources and to buy the processor for the purpose of then controlling price. There was also evidence that the cooperative instigated a boycott of the processor's milk.[127]

The alleged section 2 violation in *Otto Milk Company v. United Dairy Farmers Cooperative Association*[128] was "endeavoring to monopolize the marketing of milk" in an area of southwestern Pennsylvania.[129] The Third Circuit did not expressly indicate the relevant product, but it apparently was raw milk for fluid consumption. Nor did the court dispute that there were alternative sources of raw milk.[130] The court affirmed a district court finding that the defendant cooperative violated Sherman section 2 based on evidence of the cooperatives's response to the plaintiff. Specifically, when the plaintiff-processor refused to drop its supplier in favor of the defendant, the defendant picketed retailers selling the plaintiff's milk and urged buyers to boycott the plaintiff.[131]

The plaintiffs in *Knuth v. Erie-Crawford Dairy Cooperative Association*[132] were milk producers in Pennsylvania furnishing milk under contract to the defendant cooperative. The plaintiffs alleged that the cooperative conspired with processors to restrain trade in raw milk and to monopolize its distribution.[133] The district court dismissed the action for failure to state a claim. The Third Circuit reversed, finding that the plaintiffs had sufficiently alleged a violation of Sherman sections 1 and 2.[134] The alleged conduct included a conspiracy to fix the price of cheaper milk shipped into Pennsylvania by giving processors rebates for purchasing milk produced in Pennsylvania. It also included manipulating milk shipments to circumvent operation of a Pennsylvania minimum-price schedule for milk produced in Pennsylvania.[135]

The first alleged monopolization case specifically to consider monopoly power and conduct came on the heels of *Grinnell* in *Case-Swayne Co., Inc. v. Sunkist Growers, Inc.*[136] in 1966.[137] In that case, the Ninth Circuit discussed market power in alternative relevant markets. In reviewing the basis for the district court's grant of Sunkist's motion for a directed verdict, the court found that there was sufficient evidence for the jury to determine that the relevant market was product oranges grown in California and Arizona.[138] Sunkist's share of this market was about 67 percent; this, together with evidence of Sunkist's ability to control by-product price, convinced the court that there was sufficient evidence for a jury to have found that Sunkist had monopoly power.[139] On the conduct element of *Grinnell,* the Ninth Circuit observed that while individual instances of the alleged misconduct might be insufficient to establish the wrongful use of monopoly power, the jury must look at the evidence as a whole.[140] Seen this way, the court found that the plaintiff had established a prima facie case for the wrongful use of monopoly power and held that the district court erred in granting the motion for a directed verdict.[141] The alleged misconduct included boycotting the plaintiff while selling to other processors, preventing supplier deliveries, controlling orange prices, and eliminating competitors by manipulating price and supply. More specifically, these acts included Sunkist's admitted purpose of controlling all the oranges it could and utilizing them in its own manufacturing facilities, preventing a dealer from fulfilling a commitment to sell oranges to the plaintiff, policing the Sunkist System and imposing sanctions on members selling fruit contrary to contract provisions with Sunkist, manipulating prices on fruit and juice, and using consignment contracts and low bidding to secure a government contract.[142]

Nine years after *Case-Swayne,* the Ninth Circuit decided another monopolization case involving Sunkist. In *Pacific Coast Agricultural Export Association v. Sunkist Growers, Inc.,* [143] an association of fresh fruit exporters charged Sunkist with monopolizing oranges grown in Arizona and California for export to Hong Kong. On appeal from a jury verdict for the plaintiff, the Ninth Circuit evaluated the evidence before the jury on Sunkist's power in the relevant market and the asserted acts of monopolization. The court found that Sunkist had used its lawful dominance over the distribution of California/Arizona oranges[144] to secure 70 percent of the Hong Kong market within six months of entering that market directly.[145] Over the relevant time period, Sunkist's share of this market ranged from 45 to 70 percent.[146] The court recognized that Sunkist's share was less than had been required in some monopolization decisions,[147] but noted that while market share is perhaps the most important factor in gauging monopoly power, it "does not alone determine the presence or absence of monopoly power."[148] Instead of considering Sunkist's ability to control price, though, the court looked solely at the relative size and change in market shares after Sunkist's entry. Because no competitor had controlled more than 18 percent of the market prior to Sunkist's entry or more than 12 percent after Sunkist's entry, the court was convinced that with its control over initial distribution, Sunkist had monopoly power.[149] Turning to whether there was significant evidence of acts of monopolization, the court found that the jury was justified in finding that Sunkist engaged in monopolization.[150] Among the acts were Sunkist's attempting to restrict the supply of oranges available to plaintiff, attempting to divert fruit from plaintiff for direct sale to Hong Kong, fraudulently persuading plaintiff to surrender lists of Hong Kong customers and then giving these lists to Sunkist's exclusive sales agent in Hong Kong, and demanding shipping privileges for export operations exceeding its market share and thereby denying shipping space to rivals.[151]

In five decisions since *Fairdale I*, courts have applied *Grinnell* with varying degrees of thoroughness. Despite expectations to the contrary in *Fairdale I* and regardless of its correctness, *Fairdale II*[152] is an inartful treatment of *Grinnell*. On appeal, the Second Circuit affirmed the district court order granting the cooperative's motion on remand for summary judgment based on an application of the principles from *Fairdale I*.[153] Rather than beginning with an assessment of monopoly power in a relevant market, however, the court leaped to an assessment of "predatory" acts independent of any relation to the cooperative's market power or to one another. At no point in *Fairdale I* or *Fairdale II* is there an analysis of market power. Nor is there an evaluation of a relevant market, conduct, or performance as evidence of monopoly power.[154] The court was solely interested in whether the evidence satisfied the threshold for unlawful acts. The first of these was the plaintiff's allegation that the cooperative set so high a price on milk for sale to processors that this constituted a predatory policy. The Second Circuit said this could not stifle competition with other cooperatives or farmers. Moreover, because the plaintiff had alleged that it was predatory with respect to consumers, the court did not consider the impact on buyers.[155] The court likewise found that setting different premiums in different milk marketing areas was not predatory; the prices were not below cost[156] and prices reflected varying degrees of bargaining power.[157] Finally, the Second Circuit found that because the cooperative did not control all supplies of raw milk, it could refuse to deal with those who would not meet its sale terms. Hence, its refusal to deal with the plaintiff was not predatory.[158] After looking at the acts individually and independently of market power, the Second Circuit found none was a "predatory practice."[159]

A clear misreading of *Fairdale I* and a misapplication of *Grinnell* occurred in *GVF Cannery, Inc. v. California Tomato Growers Association, Inc.*[160] The district court in that case observed that *Fairdale I* modified the application of *Grinnell* to cases involving a cooperative.[161] Without considering monopoly power in any relevant market, though, the court found for the cooperative on a monopolization and attempt claim because there was no allegation of predatory conduct. That is, there was no allegation of picketing, boycotts, coercion, forced membership, price discrimination, or secret rebates.[162] The court did not consider whether, in the context of the relevant degree of market power, less egregious conduct could satisfy the second element in *Grinnell* on the monopolization claim.

Three decisions involving monopolization in the supply of raw milk followed *Fairdale I*. In *Kinnett Dairies, Inc. v. Dairymen, Inc.*,[163] a dairy processor alleged that the cooperative (Dairymen, Inc.) acting alone and with others had monopolized the supply of raw Grade A milk in the Southeast.[164] The district court took a two-pronged approach in its analysis. First, the court assumed that even if the cooperative had monopoly power, this was compatible with Capper-Volstead. Hence, if there were no "predatory practices," the section 2 claim would fail. In this regard, the district court evaluated the various activities that Dairymen, Inc., undertook. The court began by observing what would generally be lawful for the cooperative to do. By fair and legitimate means, Dairymen, Inc., could recruit as many farmer members as existed. As agent for its members, the cooperative could collect milk at member farms, test it, haul it, process it, and sell it at a price the cooperative fixed. So long as Dairymen, Inc., did not control all supply, it could refuse to sell to one or more customers on reasonable terms.[165] The cooperative could also allocate territories for the sale of different members' milk. The cooperative could join with other cooperatives satisfying the basic Capper-Volstead requirements for protection from antitrust charges or it could become a member of a cooperative having only cooperatives as members.[166] Also, it was reasonable for the cooperative to have one-year written supply contracts with members.[167] The alleged predatory conduct the court next reviewed included Dairymen, Inc.'s unilaterally announcing nonnegotiable premium prices, cutting off the plaintiff's profitable hauling operation, cutting off customers who tried to substitute part of their purchases from the cooperative with alternative sources, warding off a potential competitor by cutting off or threatening to cut off a buyer's supply, insisting on committed volume contracts with processors, and cutting off the plaintiff's milk supply and then threatening not to deal with the plaintiff or to sell only at supplemental prices.[168] Assessing these acts alone and in conjunction, the court found that they neither stifled competition nor were predatory in any sense of the word.[169]

The second prong to the court's analysis was to consider—assuming the alleged acts were indeed "predatory" under section 2 so that Dairymen, Inc. was not entitled to Capper-Volstead protection—whether Dairymen, Inc. had monopoly power. Here the court considered the relevant market and the cooperative's power in this market. The court determined that the relevant product was raw Grade A milk and that the geographic market included Georgia and parts of twelve nearby states.[170] The cooperative's share in this market was less than 30.2 percent during the relevant time period.[171] Without explaining why, but apparently on the basis of the low market share, the court concluded that at no time did the cooperative have the power to control prices or to exclude competition on its own or in combination with others.[172] For this reason, even if the cooperative was not entitled to Capper-Volstead treatment, the cooperative had not engaged in unlawful monopolization and judgment was accordingly to be entered in its favor.[173]

Regardless of the apparent thoroughness of the district court decision, the court avoided the substance of the plaintiff's allegations. The plaintiff conceded that the Dairymen, Inc. conduct did not satisfy any traditional notion of predation.[174] Instead, the plaintiff contended that the cooperative had engaged in monopolization through its involvement in a network of arrangements with other cooperatives supplying milk in the relevant market.[175] The court never expressly assessed whether Dairymen, Inc. had monopoly power in combination with others or due to its conduct in the context of this potentially enhanced market power.[176]

Unlike *Kinnett*, the Eighth Circuit in *Alexander v. National Farmers Organization*[177] expressly considered the various arrangements among cooperatives that might support a finding of monopoly power.[178] On a review of the district court record, the court found that the district court had erred in holding that the National Farmers Organization (NFO) had not sufficiently proved that the relevant product was Grade A milk.[179] The court was also convinced that the defendant cooperatives were major marketers of milk produced in the Midwest, having 70 to 90 percent of all milk pooled in various of the major federal order markets at issue and controlling over 85 percent of Grade A milk in a number of strategic metropolitan markets.[180] But the court was uncertain as to "monopoly power in a properly defined market or submarkets."[181] Hence, the court found that it was not clear error for the district court to dismiss the monopolization claim for lack of monopoly power.[182]

The Eighth Circuit did find, though, that the district court erred in holding that the defendant cooperatives had not conspired to monopolize. The alleged conduct that the court found to demonstrate an intent to eliminate competition in general and the NFO in particular[183] included attempting to block the NFO from qualifying to market milk in various federal market orders;[184] coercing processor buyers to stop purchasing from suppliers not affiliated with the cooperatives, doing so by short shipping, making late deliveries, soliciting the buyer's customers, and offering to sell processed milk at close to the buyer's cost of production; engaging in discriminatory pricing between buyers to force an uncooperative buyer away from the NFO; threatening an NFO-supplied processor with litigation and other harassment; terminating members and haulers; making certain acquisitions and mergers; and destroying relevant evidence.[185] Based on its findings, the court held that the district court erred in holding for the defendant cooperatives.[186]

The preceding discussion of case law evidence of section 2 violations reveals certain categories of cases. There are several cases in which the court only evaluated a claim of attempt or a conspiracy to monopolize. The conduct needed in these cases must demonstrate a specific exclusionary intent.[187] Included here are *Bergjans Farms* (below-cost pricing, secret rebates, and coercion), *Otto Milk* (picketing and boycotting), and *Knuth* (price discrimination). There are other cases where the court's discussion does not make clear whether it analyzed an attempt claim or a monopolization claim, but it would appear to have been the former. Included here are *Maryland and Virginia* (boycotting and eliminating competitors) and *North-Texas Producers* (secret rebates and price discrimination). There are also several cases where monopolization was clearly at issue. In some of these, the court casually observed that the cooperative had a large market share. It would then indicate that because a cooperative is entitled to law-fully obtained monopoly power, alleged misconduct is the key to a violation. Included here are *Cape Cod, Fairdale II,* and *GVF Cannery.* Finally, there are cases where the court followed the *Grinnell* two-part analysis in assessing the monopolization claim. These cases view market share as the basic indicator of market power. They do not require egregiously predatory conduct to establish a general exclusionary intent. Included here are *Case-Swayne,*[188] *Pacific Coast Export, Kinnett Dairies,* and *Alexander.*

A pervasive tendency throughout the section 2 cases is to equate monopoly power with market share. As noted, in some decisions, courts indicate that if a cooperative has monopoly power this is compatible with Capper-Volstead. Hence, the only relevant inquiry is with respect to monopoly conduct. Absent monopoly conduct, there is no section 2 violation. But looking at conduct independently of market power means that these courts, as in *GVF Cannery,* are more inclined to look for predatory conduct evincing the specific intent necessary for attempt claims and sufficient but not necessary for monopolization claims. This approach tends to extend to cooperatives an immunity that goes beyond Capper-Volstead. The *Fairdale II* and *Cape Cod* approaches go the other way. The cavalier use of market share as evidence of monopoly power would seem to expose coopera-tives to an enhanced likelihood of section 2 liability.[189] And even in cases where courts evaluated market share in a clearly specified relevant market, there was still little if any scrutiny of market share as a valid indicator of market power. That is, the decisions do not consider the ability to control supply. Nor do they often assess market share relative to other firms' shares, whether control was shared through marketing agreements, or the presence of barriers to entry or incumbent firm expansion. Only very rarely do the decisions expressly review performance indicators of monopoly power.

Summary and Conclusions

The Capper-Volstead authorization for collective action among agricultural producers modifies the application of *Grinnell* to agricultural marketing cooperatives. A plaintiff charging a cooperative with unlawful monopoly under Sherman section 2 must first establish that the cooperative has monopoly power. The plaintiff must further establish that the cooperative willfully acquired or maintained this power as opposed to achieving it from growth or development as a consequence of (1) a superior product, (2) business acumen, (3) historic accident, or (4) conduct compatible with what Congress authorized in section 1 of the Capper-Volstead Act.

Monopoly power within relevant product and geographic markets depends on more than a high market share. Economic theory indicates that market share is relevant if the cooperative can control supply with restricted membership agreements, long-term supply contracts, quality restrictions, price discrimination, dumping, or failing to return higher revenues to producers. If the cooperative can influence supply, a high market share is more meaningful when it is high relative to the combined market share of its leading rivals, when the cooperative is able to enhance its control through marketing agreements with other cooperatives, and when there are substantial barriers to entry or incumbent firm expansion in the form of technological or pecuniary economies of scale, capital requirements, patents, access to production resources, advertising, or a differentiated product.

If the finder of fact determines that there is a monopoly power, it must consider whether the proffered intent or conduct evidence demonstrates a general exclusionary purpose that is outside the scope of acceptable conduct under the restated version of *Grinnell*. Sufficient exclusionary evidence will be clearly predatory acts: picketing, boycotts, coercion, secret rebates, sabotage, and pricing below average variable cost. Other evidence satisfies this element as well. Exclusionary conduct, looked at as a whole and with or without evidence of price greater than average variable cost, may include unreasonably tying up supply; interfering with producers', rivals', or buyers' access to alternative outlets or sources of supply; undermining their ability to sell; exploiting their vulnerability to the cooperative; or discriminating against certain members in a given class of producers, rivals, or buyers. As indicated in *Dairymen, Inc.*, this conduct may have had a business justification but, viewed as a whole, it could still be undertaken with the intent to achieve or maintain a monopoly position.

Inadvertently, some courts have used Capper-Volstead to make cooperative concerns more vulnerable to challenge for monopolizing than similarly situated proprietary concerns. These courts often begin their analysis with an observation that the cooperative has a large market share but that this is permissible because of the Capper-Volstead exemption. The only issue, then, is whether the cooperative has engaged in predatory conduct. This seemingly benign approach has led some of these courts implicitly to assume that cooperatives with large shares must have monopoly power because of their privileged treatment under Capper-Volstead. This leads to the critical omission of an examination of whether there exist sufficient barriers to entry to permit the exercise of monopoly power. Such examinations have become increasingly central in both attempt-to-monopolize and monopolization cases involving proprietary corporations.[190] Such examinations also are essential in cooperative cases if farmers are to be given, "through agricultural cooperatives acting as entities, the same unified competitive advantage—and responsibility—available to businessmen acting through corporations as entities."[191]

Notes

1. 15 U.S.C. § 2 (1982).

2. Section 2 also proscribes attempts and combinations or conspiracies to monopolize any part of trade or commerce. Id. These prohibitions are outside the scope of this chapter except as otherwise represented.

3. *United States v. Grinnell Corp.* 384 U.S. 563 (1966).

4. Id., 570–71.

5. Id., 571.

6. L. Sullivan, *Handbook of the Law of Antitrust* (St. Paul: West, 1977), 41.

7. Id., 76–77.

8. Id.

9. *American Tobacco Co. v. United States*, 328 U.S. 781, 811 (1946).

10. Sullivan, *Handbook of the Law of Antitrust*, 99–101. Sullivan points out that this is the modern test of exclusionary conduct, deriving from Judge Wyzanski's interpretation of *Alcoa* in *United States v. United Shoe Machinery Corp.*, 110 F. Supp. 295 (D. Mass. 1953), *aff'd per curiam*, 347 U.S. 521 (1954).

11. Agricultural Cooperative Service, *Farmer Cooperative Statistics, 1982* 2 U.S. Dept. of Agriculture, Cooperative Info. Report no. 1 sec. 27 (Washington, D.C.: U.S. Dept. of Agriculture, 1984).

12. These are referred to as operating cooperatives. R. Knutson, "What Is a Producer?" in *Proceedings of the National Symposium on Cooperatives and the Law* (University of Wisconsin Center for Cooperatives, 1974), 142–43.

13. These are referred to as bargaining cooperatives.

14. For early cases against agricultural marketing cooperatives proceeding on a Sherman Act theory, see *Burns v. Wray Farmer's Grain Co.*, 65 Colo. 425, 176 P. 407 (1918) (holding unlawful an agreement among farmer-stockholders in a grain cooperative not to sell their products to competitors of the cooperative); *Reeves v. Decorah Farmers' Cooperative Society*, 160 Iowa 194, 140 N.W. 844 (1913) (holding unlawful an agreement among member hog producers to sell their marketable stock only to the cooperative).

15. 15 U.S.C. § 17 (1982). The House and Senate Reports on section 6—H.R. Report 627, 63d Cong., 2d sess. (1914) and S. Report 698, 63d Cong., 2d sess. (1914)—evidence Congress's intent (1) to remove all doubt as to the propriety of the existence of the agricultural associations meeting statutory requirements and (2) to prevent the courts from using the antitrust laws to interfere with cooperative operations or force their dissolution. See "Agricultural Cooperatives—The Clayton Act and the Capper-Volstead Act Immunize the Concerted Price-Bargaining Activities of Two Agricultural Cooperatives from Antitrust Liability," *Texas Law Review* 53 (1975): 840–42.

16. 7 U.S.C. §§ 291–92 (1982). Capper-Volstead Act proponents represented the act as designed to give farmers a fair opportunity to respond to business conditions by combining together to equalize the disparity in the market power between themselves acting singly and corporate middlemen, without fear of antitrust prosecution. H.R. Report 24, 67th Cong., 1st sess. (1921).

The discussion here will be in terms of the Capper-Volstead Act although section 6 of the Clayton Act is also relevant. The major difference between the two statutes is in terms of who is protected. Section 6 provides for a limited antitrust exemption for agricultural cooperatives not having capital stock. Capper-Volstead provides for limited antitrust protection regardless of whether the cooperative has capital stock. Though not synonymous, the two are treated similarly with respect to what are legitimate cooperative activities. *Northern California Supermarkets, Inc. v. Central California Lettuce Producers Coop.*, 413 F. Supp. 984, 991 (N.D. Cal. 1976), *aff'd*, 580 F.2d 369 (9th Cir. 1978), *cert. denied*, 439 U.S. 1090 (1979).

17. 436 U.S. 816 (1978).

18. This section relies extensively on T.W. Paterson and W.F. Mueller, "Agricultural Marketing Cooperatives and Section 1 of the Capper-Volstead Act: Conditioning (Limited) Antitrust Immunity on Capper-Volstead Policy," Working Paper no. 84 (Food Systems Research Group, University of Wisconsin-Madison, December 1984).

19. 436 U.S. at 824–27.

20. To be eligible for Capper-Volstead protection from antitrust charges, a cooperative must satisfy section 1 of the Capper-Volstead Act, 7 U.S.C. § 291 (1982). Section 1 provides that:

> Persons engaged in the production of agricultural products as farmers, planters, ranchmen, dairymen, nut or fruit growers may act together in associations, corporate or otherwise, with or without capital stock, in collectively processing, preparing for market, handling, and marketing in interstate and foreign commerce, such products of persons so engaged. Such associations may have marketing agencies in common; and such associations and their members may make the necessary contracts and agreements to effect such purposes: *Provided, however,* that such associations are operated for the mutual benefit of the members thereof, as such producers, and conform to one or both of the following requirements:
>
> First. That no member of the association is allowed more than one vote because of the amount of stock or membership capital he may own therein, or,
>
> Second. That the association does not pay dividends on stock or membership capital in excess of 8 per centum per annum.
>
> And in any case to the following:
>
> Third. That the association shall not deal in the products of nonmembers to an amount greater in value than such as are handled by it for members.

21. 308 U.S. 188 (1939).

22. Id., 203–04. Section 2 of Capper-Volstead, 7 U.S.C. § 292 (1982), provides in part that if

> Upon [specified notice and hearing] . . . the Secretary . . . shall be of the opinion that such association monopolizes or restrains trade in interstate or foreign commerce to such an extent that the price of any agricultural product is unduly enhanced thereby, he shall issue . . . an order . . . directing such association to cease and desist from monopolization or restraint of trade.

The cooperative's argument was that the Capper-Volstead section 2 provision for the secretary's action on restraints of trade leading to unduly enhanced prices evidenced Congress's intent that the authority be exclusive. 308 U.S. at 205 (1939).

23. 308 U.S. at 206.

24. 362 U.S. 458 (1960).

25. Id., 462–63. Sherman section 2 monopolization was not charged in *Borden*. Id., 463.

26. Id., 463.

27. Id. In *Sunkist Growers, Inc. v. Federal Trade Commission*, 464 F. Supp. 302, 308–12 (C.D. Cal. 1979), the district court held, similarly to *Borden* and *Maryland and Virginia*, that Congress did not intend for the Capper-Volstead Act to exempt cooperatives from section 5 of the Federal Trade Commission Act, 15 U.S.C. § 45 (1982).

28. 308 U.S. at 206.

29. 362 U.S. at 468.

30. In *Northern California Supermarkets, Inc. v. Central California Lettuce Producers Cooperative*, 413 F. Supp. 984 (N.D. Cal. 1976), *aff'd*, 580 F. 2d 369 (9th Cir. 1978), *cert. denied*, 439 U.S. 1090 (1979), the plaintiff argued that Capper-Volstead only applies to "small struggling farmers," not big corporate businesses. Id., 991. The district court rejected this, noting that nowhere in the Capper-Volstead Act is there a restriction on the size of Capper-Volstead growers. Id., 993–94 n.11. But see *National Broiler Marketing Ass'n v. United States*, 436 U.S. 816 (1978), for the view that Capper-Volstead protects small, nonintegrated farmers, id., 847 (White, J., dissenting), and certainly not the behemoths of agribusiness, id., 834–35 (Brennan, J., concurring).

31. In *Case-Swayne Co. v. Sunkist Growers, Inc.*, 389 U.S. 384 (1967), the Supreme Court rejected Sunkist's argument that Capper-Volstead protects any organizational structure provided growers receive the benefits of the collective activity. The Court held that Capper-Volstead benefits only actual farmers and the associations they operate for their mutual help as producers. Id., 384, 390. See also *National Broiler Marketing Association v. United States*, 436 U.S. 816 (1978).

32. The principal cases here include *Maryland and Virginia*, 362 U.S. at 466; *Treasure Valley Potato Bargaining Association v. Ore-Ida Foods, Inc.*, 497 F.2d 203 (9th Cir. 1974), *cert. denied*, 419 U.S. 999 (1974); *Northern California Supermarkets, Inc. v. Central California Lettuce Producers Cooperative*, 413 F. Supp. 984 (N.D. Cal. 1976), *aff'd*, 580 F.2d 369 (9th Cir. 1978), *cert. denied*, 439 U.S. 1090 (1979); and *Fairdale Farms, Inc. v. Yankee Milk, Inc.*, 635 F.2d 1037 (2d Cir. 1980), *cert. denied*, 454 U.S. 818 (1981).

33. Paterson and Mueller, op. cit., note 18.

34. Id.

35. 362 U.S. at 466.

36. Just because a cooperative is not eligible for Capper-Volstead protection does not mean that it has violated the monopolization proscription of the Sherman Act.

37. 1980-1 Trade Cas., (CCH) ¶ 63,029 (D. Vt. 1979), *aff'd in part, vacated in part, and remanded,* 635 F.2d 1037 (2d Cir. 1980), *cert. denied,* 454 U.S. 818 (1981).

38. 1980-1 Trade Cas., at 77,115 and 77,119.

39. Id., 77,116.

40. Id., 77,116-19.

41. Id.

42. Id., 77,116 ("We do not doubt that proof of predatory practices adds substantial weight to a plaintiff's monopoly claim, but we refuse to hold that it is a necessary element.")

43. 635 F.2d 1037 (2d Cir. 1980), *cert. denied,* 454 U.S. 818 (1981).

44. Id., 1040-43, 1045.

45. Id., 1040, 1043-44.

46. Id., 1040.

47. Id., 1045.

48. Id., 1044.

49. While *Fairdale I* is the first case to hold expressly that "cooperatives may grow into monopolies," 635 F.2d 1037, 1040 (2d Cir. 1980), earlier cases had indicated this. For instance, in *Cape Cod Food Products, Inc. v. National Cranberry Association,* 119 F. Supp. 900 (D. Mass. 1954), Judge Wyzanski—who authored *United Shoe Machinery*—advised the jury that a cooperative may achieve "100 percent of the market through skill, efficiency, superiority of product," or through the marketing agreements Capper-Volstead authorizes. Id., 907. Justice White indicated the same thing in *National Broiler,* noting that it is with Capper-Volstead that Congress allows farmers lawfully to transform monopsony into bilateral monopoly. 436 U.S. at 842 (White and Stewart, JJ., dissenting) (dicta). Other cases provide similar support for the proposition that a cooperative can have monopoly power, e.g., *Bergjans Farm Dairy Co. v. Sanitary Milk Producers,* 241 F. Supp. 476, 483 (E.D. Mo. 1965); *Shoenberg Farms, Inc. v. Denver Milk Producers, Inc.,* 231 F. Supp. 260, 268 (D. Colo. 1964). In *Sunkist Growers, Inc. v. Winckler & Smith Citrus Products Co.,* 370 U.S. 19 (1962), the Supreme Court observed without comment that the jury had been instructed that Sunkist could lawfully have a monopoly. Id., 24. Because the only issue before the Court was interorganizational conspiracy, however, this provides only limited support for the proposition of lawful cooperative monopoly power. Id., 21.

50. *United States v. Dairymen, Inc.* 660 F.2d 192, 194 (6th Cir. 1981), *cert. denied,* 106 S. Ct. 73 (1985).

51. *Alexander v. National Farmers Organization, Inc.,* 687 F.2d 1173, 1182 (8th Cir. 1982), *cert. denied,* 461 U.S. 937 (1983).

52. *Holly Sugar Corporation v. Goshen County Cooperative Beet Growers Association,* 725 F.2d 564, 569 (10th Cir. 1984).

53. *Kinnett Dairies, Inc., v. Dairymen, Inc.,* 512 F. Supp. 608, 642 (M.D. Ga. 1981), *aff'd,* 715 F.2d 520-21 (11th Cir. 1983), *cert. denied,* 465 U.S. 1051 (1984).

54. *GVF Cannery, Inc. v. California Tomato Growers Association, Inc.*, 511 F. Supp. 711, 714-15 (N.D. Cal. 1981), also endorses *Fairdale I*. The holding in *Fairdale I* is anticipated in *Pacific Coast Agricultural Export Association v. Sunkist Growers, Inc.*, 526 F.2d 1196, 1203-04 (9th Cir. 1975), *cert. denied*, 425 U.S. 959 (1976); *Treasure Valley Potato Bargaining Association v. Ore-Ida Foods, Inc.*, 497 F.2d 203, 209-17 (9th Cir. 1974), *cert. denied*, 419 U.S. 999 (1974); *Case-Swayne Co., Inc. v. Sunkist Growers, Inc.*, 369 F.2d 449, 451-52, 459 (9th Cir. 1966).

55. If a plaintiff does not satisfy his burden of proof, the cooperative with monopoly power is still subject to monitoring for undue price enhancement under section 2 of Capper-Volstead. See *Fairdale II*, 715 F.2d at 32; *Dairymen, Inc.*, 660 F.2d at 194 n.4. The enforcement record under section 2 indicates that this monitoring may not be very stringent. See R.H. Folsom, "Antitrust Enforcement Under the Secretaries of Agriculture and Commerce," *Columbia Law Review* 80 (1980): 1623, 1634-35.

56. Commentators and at least one district court appear to read *Fairdale I* narrowly on what is predatory. Despite repeated references in *Fairdale I* to conduct less egregious than picketing, harassment, boycotts, coerced membership, and discriminatory pricing, 635 F.2d at 1044, they have confined *Fairdale I* to this conduct. See, e.g., Note, "The Agricultural Cooperative Antitrust Exemption—*Fairdale Farms, Inc. v. Yankee Milk, Inc.*," *Cornell Law Review* 67 (January 1982): 396-98 (Under *Fairdale I*, "An agricultural cooperative is liable for monopoly only if it commits predatory acts. The court's holding ignores numerous pronouncements" to the contrary.); *GVF Cannery, Inc. v. California Tomato Growers Association, Inc.*, 511 F. Supp. 711, 715-16 (N.D. Cal. 1981) (enumerating predatory acts that would satisfy Sherman section 2). One explanation that has not been used as a justification for reading *Fairdale I* narrowly is the Second Circuit's narrow application of "predatory" in *Fairdale II*. 715 F.2d 30-34 (2d Cir. 1983), *cert. denied*, 464 U.S. 1043 (1984).

57. *United States v. Dairymen, Inc.*, 660 F.2d 192, 194 (6th Cir. 1981), *cert. denied*, 106 S. Ct. 73 (1985).

58. Id.

59. Id., 195.

60. 119 F. Supp. at 908.

61. *Maryland and Virginia*, 362 U.S. at 472, citing *Schine Chain Theatres, Inc. v. United States*, 334 U.S. 110 (1948).

62. Knutson, "What Is a Producer?" 143.

63. Id.

64. P.G. Helmberger and S. Hoos, *Cooperative Bargaining in Agriculture: Grower-Processor Markets for Fruits and Vegetables* (Berkeley: University of California-Berkeley, Division of Agricultural Sciences, 1965), 28.

65. Id.

66. Bunje refers to this type of bargaining cooperative as the marketing type. R. Bunje, *Cooperative Farm Bargaining and Price Negotiations*. Cooperative Information Report 26, (Washington, D.C.: U.S. Dept. of Agriculture, July 1980), 45-46.

67. Id., 46-47.

68. Id., 48–51. Bunje identifies two additional types of bargaining cooperatives. One corresponds to the National Farmers Organization (NFO) model, where a producer designates the NFO as an exclusive agent in collective bargaining with buyers. Id., 47–48. The other type refers to state-supported bargaining arrangements with provisions for arbitration. Id., 51–52.

69. R. Mighell and L. Jones, *Vertical Coordination in Agriculture*, Agricultural Economics Report no. 19 (Washington, D.C.: U.S. Dept. of Agriculture, Feb. 1963): 39.

70. J.G. Youde and P.G. Helmberger, "Marketing Cooperatives in the U.S.: Membership Policies, Market Power, and Antitrust Policy," *Journal of Farm Economics* 48 (1966): 23, 30.

71. S. Hoos, "Economic Possibilities and Limitations of Cooperative Bargaining Associations," in *Cooperative Bargaining* (Farmer Cooperative Service Report no. 113 (Washington, D.C.: U.S. Dept. of Agriculture, August 1970), 12, 24.

72. If there is no output control, a higher price will stimulate a larger supply, thereby lowering the market-clearing price.

73. P.G. Helmberger and S. Hoos, "Economic Theory of Bargaining in Agriculture," *Journal of Farm Economics* 45 (December 1963): 1272–73.

74. Hoos, "Economic Possibilities," 20.

75. Helmberger and Hoos, "Economic Theory of Bargaining," 1272–73.

76. Id., 1277.

77. D.F. Turner, "Antitrust Policy and the Cellophane Case," *Harvard Law Review* 70 (1956): 281, 304.

78. *United States v. Grinnell Corp.*, 384 U.S. 563, 571 (1966).

79. This accounts for the popularity of the Herfindahl-Hirschman (Herfindahl) Index of market concentration. The Herfindahl Index is a summary concentration measure reflecting market share and dispersion of market share among firms. The market Herfindahl is the sum of each firm's squared market share. For the largest four firms, the Herfindahl is the sum of each's market share squared. If there were five firms in a market, with one firm having 40 percent of sales and each of the other firms 15 percent, the market Herfindahl would be 2500. If the same five firms each had 20 percent of the market, the Herfindahl would be 2000. The difference reflects the disparity of market power in the first example. See F.M. Scherer, *Industrial Market Structure and Economic Performance*, 2d ed. (Chicago: Rand McNally, 1980), 58–59.

80. E.g., *Borden, Inc.*, 92 FTC 669 (1978) (reconstituted lemon juice).

81. G.W. Stocking and W.F. Mueller, "The Cellophane Case and the New Competition," *American Economic Review* 45 (March 1955): 29.

82. This is limit pricing. Scherer, *Industrial Market Structure*, 234 note 79.

83. For example, in *United Shoe*, United Shoe Machinery Corporation refused to sell to shoe manufacturers the machinery generating the most revenue. It offered only a leasing option. 110 F. Supp. at 314, 340.

84. Leibenstein refers to the relationship between actual productive performance and technically efficient performance as "X-efficiency." A firm may be X-inefficient due to incomplete knowledge of available techniques, motivation, learning, and psychological factors. H. Leibenstein, "Allocative Efficiency vs. 'X-Efficiency'," *American Economic Review* 56 (1966): 392. For an extensive survey of

productive efficiency in agriculture, see B.C. French, "The Analysis of Productive Efficiency in Agricultural Marketing: Models, Methods, and Progress," in *A Survey of Agricultural Economics Literature* 1, ed. L. Martin (Minneapolis: University of Minnesota Press, 1977), 93.

85. If a firm does not adjust price to account for changes in costs or demand, this indicates that the firm, insulated from market conditions, is more powerful.

86. E.V. Jesse and A.C. Johnson, "Defining and Identifying Undue Price Enhancement," in *Antitrust Treatment of Agricultural Marketing Cooperatives*, ed. E.V. Jesse, Monograph 15 (Food Systems Research Group, University of Wisconsin-Madison, September 1983): 61, 92–98; E.V. Jesse and A.C. Johnson, "Marketing Cooperatives and Undue Price Enhancement: A Theoretical Perspective," Working Paper no. 46 (Food Systems Research Group, University of Wisconsin-Madison, October 1980); P.G. Helmberger, "Cooperative Enterprise as a Structural Dimension of Farm Markets," *Journal of Farm Economics* 46 (1964): 603; J.G. Youde and P.G. Helmberger, "Marketing Cooperatives in the U.S.: Membership Policies, Market Power, and Antitrust Policy," *Journal of Farm Economics* 48 (1966): 23.

87. See supra text corresponding to notes 84–85.

88. See supra note 20.

89. 362 U.S. at 466.

90. From this it would seem to follow readily that this is also an unduly enhanced price under section 2 of Capper-Volstead. See W.F. Mueller, "The Enforcement of Section 2 of the Capper-Volstead Act," in *Antitrust Treatment of Agricultural Marketing Cooperatives*, ed. E.V. Jesse, Monograph 15 (Food Systems Research Group, University of Wisconsin-Madison, September 1983). Seen this way, Capper-Volstead section 2 reaches a subclass of prices that may be attributable to monopoly. It reaches the unduly enhanced price but not the price that is, say, strategically set to deter new entry. Strategic pricing may support a finding of monopolization under the Sherman Act.

91. An example of a monopoly price is suggested in the Federal Trade Commission's action against Borden on its lemon juice. *Borden, Inc.*, 92 FTC 669 (1978). Evidence in that case revealed that ReaLemon Lemon Juice commanded a premium of as high as 25 to 30 cents per unit or 30 percent over competitive offerings, even though reconstituted lemon juice is basically reconstituted lemon juice. Id., 789–90.

92. Id., 794 (citing *United States v. Griffith*, 334 U.S. 100 (1948); *American Tobacco Co. v. United States*, 328 U.S. 781 (1946); *United States v. Aluminum Co. of America*, 148 F.2d 416 (2d Cir. 1945).

93. E.g., *Borden*, 92 FTC at 802–3; *Telex Corp. v. IBM*, 510 F.2d 894, 925–26 (10th Cir. 1975).

94. Sullivan, *Handbook of the Law of Antitrust*, 108.

95. Id., 111–12.

96. Id.

97. P. Areeda and D.F. Turner, "Predatory Pricing and Related Practices under Section 2 of the Sherman Act," *Harvard Law Review* 88 (1975): 697, 709.

98. Id., 732–33. Areeda and Turner use average variable cost as a surrogate for marginal cost. Id., 716–18. They recognize an exception to their rule when average total cost is less than price which is less than marginal cost. Id., 712.

99. F.M. Scherer, "Predatory Pricing and the Sherman Act: A Comment," *Harvard Law Review* 89 (1976): 868, 890.

100. Id. (footnote omitted).

101. Most courts have now agreed that sustained sales at prices below average variable cost—the proxy for marginal cost—should be rebuttably presumed to be predatory. Prices equal to or greater than average variable cost are not necessarily predatory. E.g., *D.E. Rogers Associates, Inc. v. Gardner-Denver Co.*, 718 F.2d 1431, 1437 (6th Cir. 1983), *cert. denied*, 104 S. Ct. 3513 (1984); *William Inglis & Sons Baking Co. v. ITT Continental Baking Co.*, 668 F.2d 1014, 1035-36 (9th Cir. 1981), *cert. denied*, 459 U.S. 825 (1982); *Northeastern Tel. Co. v. AT&T Co.*, 651 F.2d 76, 88 (2d Cir. 1981), *cert. denied*, 455 U.S. 943 (1982); *International Air Industries, Inc. v. American Excelsior Co.*, 517 F.2d 714, 724 (5th Cir. 1975), *cert. denied*, 424 U.S. 943 (1976). The FTC announced its similar rule in *International Telephone & Telegraph* [July-December] *Antitrust & Trade Reg. Rep.* (BNA) no. 117 (August 9, 1984), 283, 286.

102. E.g., R.A. Posner, *Antitrust Law: An Economic Perspective* (Chicago: University of Chicago Press, 1976), 188-93; P.L. Joskow and A.K. Klevorick, "A Framework for Analyzing Predatory Pricing Policy," *Yale Law Journal* 89 (December 1979): 213, 252; D.F. Greer, "A Critique of Areeda and Turner's Standard for Predatory Practices," *Antitrust Bulletin* 24 (1979): 233, 261.

103. W.F. Mueller, "Alleged Predatory Conduct in Food Retailing," Working Paper no. 78 (Food Systems Research Group, University of Wisconsin-Madison, September 1984): 9-10.

104. When associated with price below even average total cost, Greer identifies the following as predatory conduct or evidence of predatory intent: threatening phone calls; internal memoranda or letters expressing intent; long-term business plans of injurious price-cutting activity; recorded appreciation of the consequences of such activities; penetrating studies of the victim's financial weaknesses and staying power under adverse price circumstances; bribing distributors to refuse service to victims; bribing government officials to harass the victims or block their use of public facilities such as ports; directly harassing victims with needless and unfounded patent infringement suits or other costly legal actions; and sabotage. Greer, "A Critique of Areeda and Turner's Standard," 233, 247-48. Mueller illustrates the use of financial studies in a predatory pricing action, "Alleged Predatory Conduct in Food Retailing."

105. Helmberger and Hoos, "Economic Theory of Bargaining," 1280.

106. A conspiracy to monopolize and an attempt to monopolize both require proof of specific exclusionary intent. Conduct demonstrating a specific intent is sufficient evidence of general exclusionary conduct in a monopolization charge, *United States v. Griffith*, 334 U.S. 100, 105 (1948), and is therefore relevant for our purposes. Power in a relevant market may be indicative of intent or of the probability of success in a conspiracy or an attempt case. Circuits are divided on whether evidence of a relevant market is necessary. Sullivan, *Handbook of the Law of Antitrust*, 132-40.

107. 119 F. Supp. 900 (D. Mass. 1954).

108. Id., 906.

109. Id., 907.

110. Id. This charge related to an alleged conspiracy to monopolize between a cooperative, several individuals, and a trust company. The instruction is significant because it includes conduct that would be legitimate if used in good faith.

111. *Maryland and Virginia Milk Producers Association v. United States*, 362 U.S. 458, 472 (1960). The observation was made in the context of an alleged restraint of trade unlawful under Sherman section 1. Earlier in the opinion, the Court indicated that practices unlawful under section 1 may support a violation of section 2. Id., 463.

112. Id., 460.

113. Id., 468.

114. Id.

115. 241 F. Supp. 476 (E.D. Mo. 1965).

116. Id., 483.

117. There was no discussion of whether the milk was Grade A or Grade B. Grade A milk can be used for fluid consumption or for processing. Because of sanitation requirements, Grade B milk generally cannot be used for fluid consumption.

118. 241 F. Supp. at 483.

119. Id.

120. Conduct satisfying the requisite threshold of specific intent for a claim of an alleged attempt to monopolize also satisfies the general intent necessary for such a claim. *United States v. Griffith*, 334 U.S. 100, 105 (1948).

121. 241 F. Supp. at 479–85.

122. 348 F.2d 189 (5th Cir. 1965).

123. The plaintiff alleged monopolization or attempted monopolization. The Fifth Circuit could not discern on which claim the jury returned its verdict. Id., 196.

124. Id., 194.

125. Id. The price before the increase was $5.30 per hundredweight.

126. Id., 195–96.

127. Id.

128. 388 F.2d 789 (3d Cir. 1967).

129. The decision refers to monopolizing and endeavoring to monopolize.

130. These factors indicate a theory of attempt to monopolize.

131. 388 F.2d at 797.

132. 395 F.2d 420 (3d Cir. 1968).

133. This case reveals that conduct that may lead to a cooperative losing its eligibility for Capper-Volstead protection—joining with nonproducers—may also represent conduct supporting a finding of the specific intent that is necessary for a monopolization claim.

134. 395 F.2d at 424.

135. Id., 423–24.

136. 369 F.2d 449 (9th Cir. 1966).

137. While *Grinnell*, 384 U.S. 563 (1966), clearly presents the elements in a monopolization claim, Judge Hand indicated these in *Alcoa*, 148 F.2d 416 (2d Cir. 1945), and the test received subsequent explication in *United States v. United Shoe Machinery Corp.*, 110 F. Supp. 295 (D. Mass. 1953), *aff'd per curiam*, 347 U.S. 521 (1954), and in *United States v. E.I. du Pont de Nemours & Co.*, 351 U.S. 377 (1956).

138. 369 F.2d 449, 458 (9th Cir. 1966).

139. Id., 457-58 and n.15.

140. Id., 459.

141. Id., 459, 462.

142. Id., 459. The latter acts were offered in support of plaintiff's claim that Sunkist attempted to monopolize. Hence, they are relevant in establishing the exclusionary element in a monopolization claim.

143. 526 F.2d 1196 (9th Cir. 1975).

144. Sunkist growers produced about 75 percent of all California/Arizona oranges during the relevant time period. Id., 1201.

145. Prior to selling directly, Sunkist had relied on numerous export companies, including the plaintiff, to serve the Hong Kong market. Id.

146. Id., 1204.

147. Id., citing *Alcoa*, 148 F.2d 416, 424 (2d Cir. 1945).

148. Id.

149. Id.

150. Id.

151. Id.

152. 715 F.2d 30 (2d Cir. 1983), *cert. denied*, 464 U.S. 1043 (1984). Judge Van Graafeiland authored *Fairdale I* and *Fairdale II*.

153. 715 F.2d at 34.

154. It would seem that, to a considerable measure, the inartfulness of *Fairdale II* reflects the plaintiff's presentation and the instruction given in *Fairdale I* for the district court to consider "predatory practices" in deciding whether to grant the defendant's motion for summary judgment. 635 F.2d at 1045.

155. 715 F.2d at 32.

156. The court apparently followed the Areeda-Turner marginal-cost test for predatory pricing. Id., 33 (citing Areeda and Turner, III *Antitrust Law* ¶ 710, 149). (The rule is actually presented in ¶ 711, 153-54.)

157. 715 F.2d at 32-33.

158. Id., 33-34.

159. Absent monopoly power, a finding of predatory practices is not sufficient to satisfy Sherman section 2. It would also seem that without a prior assessment of market power, a court is confined to looking only at the truly predatory acts evident in attempt and conspiracy cases.

160. 511 F. Supp. 711 (N.D. Cal. 1981).

161. Id., 715.

162. Id., 715-16. The district court never cited *Pacific Coast Agricultural Export Association v. Sunkist Growers, Inc.*, 526 F.2d 1196, 1204 (9th Cir. 1975), *cert. denied*, 425 U.S. 959 (1976), where less egregious conduct was held to be sufficient evidence of acts of monopolization. Moreover, the district court's analysis of the Ninth Circuit decision in *Case-Swayne Co. v. Sunkist Growers, Inc.*, 369 F.2d 449 (9th Cir. 1966), is too narrow. 511 F. Supp. at 715-16.

163. 512 F. Supp. 608 (M.D. Ga. 1981), *aff'd*, 715 F.2d 520 (11th Cir. 1983).

164. 512 F. Supp. at 612.

165. The cooperative with monopoly power cannot refuse to deal on reasonable nondiscriminatory terms with rivals or buyers. Id., 632; see also *Fairdale II*, 715 F.2d at 33-34; *Pacific Coast Export*, 526 F.2d 1196, 1209 (9th Cir. 1975).

166. This would be a federated cooperative.

167. 512 F. Supp. at 632–33.

168. Id., 633.

169. Id.

170. Id., 639.

171. Id., 624, 629.

172. Id., 640–41.

173. Id., 643.

174. Id.

175. Id.

176. In a separate government case against Dairymen, Inc., charging an attempt to monopolize, the Sixth Circuit held that the district court had used too stringent a test of predation and had improperly rejected proposed submarkets. *United States v. Dairymen, Inc.*, 660 F.2d 192 (6th Cir. 1981), *cert. denied*, 106 S. Ct. 73 (1985). Presented with similar arguments on appeal in *Kinnett Dairies*, the Sixth Circuit affirmed the district court holding. The court found that the district court did not use an overly stringent test of predation to evaluate the cooperative's conduct and that the district court adequately considered proposed submarkets in its evaluation of monopoly power. 715 F.2d 520–21 (11th Cir. 1983). Neither appeals court made a distinction between the conduct satisfying the requisite intent for an attempt to monopolize charge and a monopolization charge.

177. 687 F.2d 1173 (8th Cir. 1982), *cert. denied*, 461 U.S. 937 (1983).

178. 687 F.2d at 1192. In the context of a charge of conspiracy to monopolize, the court elaborated on the network of arrangements the cooperatives used to enhance their overall control. The cooperatives allocated territories, shared control, and met jointly to discuss certain threats to their market power. Id., 1194–95.

179. Id., 1191.

180. Id., 1192. See supra, note 178.

181. Id., 1192.

182. Id.

183. Evidence of specific intent to monopolize would also be evidence of a general intent to monopolize in a monopolization claim. *United States v. Griffith*, 334 U.S. 100, 105 (1948).

184. In *Marketing Assistance Plan, Inc. v. Associated Milk Producers, Inc.*, 338 F. Supp. 1019 (S.D. Tex. 1972), the district court indicated that a firm is not "entitled to abuse regulatory schemes through the persistent filing of complaints and appeals to harass competitors and to keep them from securing operating permits." Accordingly, "activities under the cover of a federal milk order designed to achieve a monopoly position . . . can violate the antitrust laws." Id., 1023.

185. 687 F.2d at 1194–207.

186. Id., 1208.

187. *United States v. Aluminum Co. of America*, 148 F.2d 416, 431–32 (2d Cir. 1945).

188. 369 F.2d 449 (9th Cir. 1966).

189. Commentators also casually associate a high cooperative market share with monopoly power, treating it the same as a high market share for a proprietary firm. E.g., Note, "Establishing Bargaining Units in Agricultural Marketing," *Virginia Law Review* 68 (September 1982): 1293–94, 1299; Note, "Antitrust Law, *Fairdale*

Farms, Inc. v. Yankee Milk, Inc.: The Right of Agricultural Cooperatives to Possess Monopoly Power," *Journal of Corporation Law* 7 (1982): 339, 351 ("Obviously, a cooperative will almost always possess monopoly power soon after it is formed."); E.M. Warlich and R.S. Brill, "Cooperatives vis-a-vis Corporations: Size, Antitrust and Immunity," *South Dakota Law Review* 23 (Summer 1978): 561, 566–68.

190. See, e.g., *American Standard, Inc. v. Bendix Corp.*, 487 F. Supp. 265, 269 (W.D. Mo. 1980) ("The nature and existence of entry barriers, barriers to expansion, potential competition, scale economies, homogeneity of products and the competitive performance of firms in the industry . . . are all factors, among others, which may affect the defendant's ability to exert monopoly power in the relevant market."); *United States v. American Telephone & Telegraph Co.*, 524 F. Supp. 1336, 1347–48 (D.D.C. 1981) (The district court found that the United States had made a persuasive showing of monopoly power through evidence of "barriers to entry, such as the creation of bottlenecks, entrenched customer preferences, the regulatory process, large capital requirements, access to technical information, and disparities in risk"). In Sherman section 2 attempt cases based on predatory pricing, courts have held that price above average variable cost may be predatory when barriers to entry are high. See, e.g., *International Air Industries, Inc. v. American Excelsior Co.*, 517 F.2d 714, 724–25 n.31 (5th Cir. 1975), *cert. denied*, 424 U.S. 943 (1976). See also *ILC Peripherals Leasing Corp. v. IBM*, 458 F. Supp. 423, 432 (N.D. Cal. 1978), *aff'd sub. nom.*; *Memorex Corp. v. IBM*, 636 F.2d 1188 (9th Cir. 1980), *cert. denied*, 452 U.S. 972 (1981).

191. *Maryland and Virginia*, 362 U.S. at 466.

3

Economics of Monopolization for Agricultural Cooperatives

The preceding chapter detailed the legal requirements for finding monopolization under section 2 of the Sherman Act. The major issues involve such economic matters as defining relevant markets, determining the structural characteristics of a market, and identifying conduct that may influence market structure (e.g., strategic conduct that creates entry barriers) or facilitate monopoly performance (e.g., conduct that results in collusive behavior). All of these concepts are central to the theory of industrial organization.

According to the framework of industrial organization, the determinants of the conduct and performance of business enterprises can be grouped into three categories, two pertaining to environmental conditions and another pertaining to the economic nature of the agents involved (buyers and sellers). One set of environmental conditions is that of market structure. Principal dimensions of market structure include the levels of concentration for buyers and sellers, the extent of product differentiation, and the nature of barriers to entry. Other market characteristics may be relevant depending on particular cases. The accuracy of available information on supply and demand conditions is of considerable importance, for example, in the wholesale pricing of fresh fruits and vegetables.

A second set of environmental conditions that determine conduct and performance consists of the legal framework that establishes boundaries of acceptable behavior and/or that seeks to determine performance directly in one or more dimensions. Laws against monopolization exemplify rules governing acceptable modes of behavior. For example, laws that regulate public utilities and programs requiring farmers to abide by acreage allotments seek to control certain aspects of market performance directly. It will be seen presently that federal marketing orders, which determine maximum weekly shipments of fresh oranges and lemons to the domestic market (United States and Canada), may be crucial in determining performance in the California/Arizona citrus sector.

A third set of determinants, as noted above, concerns the economic nature of the agents (buyers and sellers) whose decisions determine performance. The literature on industrial organization gives short shrift to what we shall call the organizational characteristics of economic agents. This is largely because economists have been concerned mainly with profit-seeking firms and households, while placing great reliance on a theory that supposes that business enterprises (consumers or input suppliers) use marginal analysis in seeking to maximize profit (utility). There are numerous examples, however, where researchers have had to extend theory to cover special cases and to attach great significance to the organizational characteristics of economic agents in order to further understanding of competitive behavior and performance. The role of hospitals in health-care–delivery systems and of labor unions in labor markets are striking examples. Of profound and basic importance in this book is the literature that seeks to establish the relationships between the organizational characteristics of a farmer cooperative and their implications for the nature of market conduct and performance.

An important role of the theory of price is the development of hypotheses concerning relationships between the determinants of performance and performance itself. In what follows, we adapt and extend price theory to cover the California/Arizona citrus sector as a special case, giving special attention to the Sunkist System and drawing upon previous developments in the theory of cooperation.[1] The resulting hypotheses as to the impact of Sunkist operations on the performance of the California/Arizona citrus sector constitute the analytical framework for this book. As a preliminary to the modeling of the California/Arizona citrus sector, it is helpful to consider in some detail the nature of the Sunkist System.

Organizational Characteristics of the Sunkist System

The first citrus cooperatives in California were organized in the 1880s. In 1893, a predecessor to the present organization was established, creating essentially the same organizational format that exists today. By the late 1970s, the organization consisted of 6,500 citrus growers, 73 packinghouses, 17 district exchanges, and Sunkist Growers, Inc.[2] These entities are organized as a federated cooperative and are collectively referred to as the Sunkist System. The legal organization of the Sunkist System is illustrated in figure 3–1. See chapter 6 for a more detailed discussion of Sunkist's legal organization.

Citrus growers may become members of the Sunkist System in two ways. They may join through simultaneous application for membership in a local nonprofit cooperative and in Sunkist Growers, Inc. (hereafter referred to as Sunkist Central). The local cooperatives provide harvesting

The Sunkist System

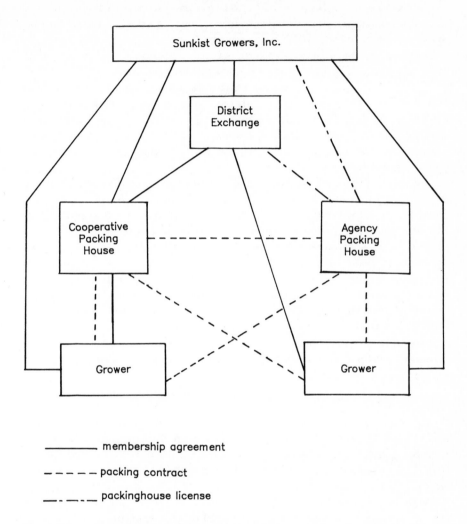

Figure 3-1. **Membership and Contractual Relationships among Participants in the Sunkist System**

and packing services; often, locals also provide orchard services for growers, including pruning, frost protection, fumigating, and spraying. Some growers choose to use commercial packinghouses (also called licensed or agency packinghouses) to provide the services otherwise provided by local cooperatives. These growers are members of a district exchange and Sunkist Growers, Inc. The commercial packinghouses have no voting or other membership rights or privileges in the Sunkist System.

Growers and local cooperative packinghouses usually delegate to a district exchange the final decision on price (except auction sales), destination, and transportation. The exchange relies to a considerable extent on market information obtained from Sunkist Central.

Within the Sunkist System, citrus fruit is produced and marketed in fresh or processed form in both domestic and foreign markets. As stated in Section 2.1 of the bylaws of Sunkist Growers, Inc. (reprinted in entirety in appendix B), "The fundamental purpose of the Sunkist System is to market the Growers' citrus fruit in the form received, or in processed, or other form at the highest return to such Growers, consistent with their long-term interests. In carrying out such purpose, Sunkist shall act as a nonprofit cooperative marketing association."

What are the major decisions made within the Sunkist System and who has the authority to make these decisions? The answers to these questions constitute what we will refer to as the organizational structure of the Sunkist System. Description of this structure is basic to our analysis for two reasons. First, such a description will reveal significant differences between the Sunkist System and the typical profit-seeking corporation. These differences will help explain why economic theory of the profit-seeking firm is, in the absence of important modification, not applicable to Sunkist. Second, understanding the nature of the system's organizational structure will be important in developing that part of the theory of cooperation that is most relevant to an explanation of Sunkist's role in determining the economic performance of the California/Arizona citrus sector.

Member-Growers Determine Level of Citrus Production

The member-grower has the exclusive right to decide how much to produce and what cultural practices to use in production. The output of the typical member-grower is small relative to the total California/Arizona citrus output. The grower therefore views the per carton return from the packinghouse as independent of the level of his or her output. Packinghouses, exchanges, and Sunkist Central could only influence the production of member-growers through altering the level of grower returns.

Grower membership agreements are of an indefinite duration, but may be terminated at the end of each year. Because of Sunkist's open-membership policy, any qualified grower can join Sunkist and take advantage of Sunkist's marketing services. Not only is membership open to any qualified grower, but the new grower can gain access to Sunkist without making any initial capital outlay, since Sunkist's revolving-fund method of financing does not require a capital investment when joining. As shown below, there is considerable movement of citrus growers into and out of the Sunkist System over time.

Membership agreements specify that the member-grower must market all of the citrus produced on acreage designated in the agreement through a packinghouse affiliated with Sunkist. The member-grower may market fruit from acreage not designated in the agreement outside the system, however, if he or she so desires. This provides the grower with an opportunity to compare returns from the Sunkist System with returns from alternative marketing outlets, and it facilitates mobility of fruit among outlets as growers strive to achieve the highest return possible for their fruit.

Marketing Sunkist Citrus

Packinghouses are responsible for preparing growers' fruit for either the fresh market or product market. Packinghouse management normally decides when fruit will be harvested, often takes charge of harvest operations, and makes arrangements for hauling fruit from orchard to packinghouse. There, under the direction of packinghouse managers, citrus for the fresh market goes through numerous operations including washing, drying, grading, sizing, packing, and brief storage. Fruit for "products" (fruit used in processed products) is segregated in bins for subsequent hauling to one of three Sunkist processing plants.

According to Section 9.1 of Sunkist's bylaws, "Each Local Association [packinghouse] shall market all of the fresh fruit subject to its control through the District Exchange with which it is affiliated. Each District Exchange shall market through Sunkist all of the fruit subject to its control." (District exchanges do not handle the physical product, which is shipped directly from packinghouses to wholesale customers.) Local packinghouses must deliver to Sunkist all of their products fruit. Sunkist, in turn, is obligated to market all such fruit.[3] In this marketing arrangement, each local association and district exchange designates Sunkist Central as its agent, granting to Sunkist authority to conduct its marketing activities in such manner as it determines is in the best interests of its members. All membership agreements of local cooperative associations and of district exchanges with Sunkist Central may be terminated during a specified period each year. The agreements are of one-year duration.[4]

As regards marketing fresh fruit, Sunkist Central's bylaws set forth several important regulations. According to one of these regulations, each member-grower and local association delegates to its district exchange the right to determine to what markets it shall ship, where its fruit will be sold, and, with the exception of auctions, what price it is willing to receive. Importantly, this delegation is not made to Sunkist Central. Moreover, local associations "reserve the right from time to time to terminate this delegation and to exercise said rights for such period as they may deem proper or to redelegate said reserved rights to said district exchange."

Another regulation states that local associations and district exchanges are not permitted to solicit business from the trade or correspond with any buyer for the purpose of promoting the sale of their fresh fruit. The selling function is to be performed exclusively by Sunkist Central. Other regulations pertain to Sunkist Central's authority in matters relating to transportation, losses, customer claims, pooling, obligation to distribute proceeds, and establishing shipping quotas and allocations which are mainly relevant in export sales. Sunkist Central may process products fruit or sell such fruit to other processors, and it may establish pools and quality standards. Sunkist Central is obligated to return proceeds of sales minus necessary marketing costs to packinghouses in proportion to their contributions of products fruit.

License Agreement between Sunkist and Licensed Commercial Packinghouses

Since the *Case-Swayne* decision in 1967, licensed commercial packinghouses no longer are members of Sunkist.[5] However, Sunkist's member-growers may enter into license agreements with commercial packinghouses that pack for such growers. The fruit so packed is, in turn, marketed through the Sunkist System in behalf of Sunkist's members. The licensed commercial houses agree to pack exclusively the fruit of Sunkist members. The licensed commercial packer has an agreement with Sunkist Central that obligates the packer to return to such grower the net proceeds from the marketing of growers' fruit by Sunkist Central, after deducting the packer's costs and agreed reasonable charges.

These and other provisions spell out explicitly the licensed commercial packer's obligation to Sunkist and the growers for whom it packs under license. The contracts between commercial licensed houses and Sunkist Central are for one year.

The licensed commercial houses also perform most of the harvesting and related matters that are performed for growers by cooperative packinghouses. The compensation they receive from growers reflects the performance of these essential services as well as those relating to packing the growers' fruit.

Summary and Implications

The Sunkist System is an open-membership, federated cooperative with highly decentralized decision making and with component parts bound together through one-year contracts. Member-growers decide how much to produce and agree to market through packinghouses affiliated with Sunkist through either membership or license. Packinghouse managers organize harvesting and packing operations and, although agreeing to market all fresh fruit through affiliated district exchanges, maintain important reserve rights as regards pricing of fruit. Packinghouse managers have the ultimate authority as to quantity and destination of fresh fruit shipments subject to citrus marketing orders and Sunkist's export program (both of which are described later in this book). District exchanges play important roles in determining prices buyers must pay for fresh citrus, except where fruit is sold at auction. Sunkist Central assumes responsibility for selling fresh citrus, maintaining contracts with domestic and foreign buyers, receiving and distributing to exchanges the receipts from fruit sales, establishing grades, organizing advertising and promotional programs, and regulating use of trademarks, trade names, and patents. Sunkist also assumes responsibility for processing and marketing products fruit and for marketing products made therefrom.

The organizational structure of the Sunkist System sets it apart from profit-seeking, proprietary firms. An important difference is that Sunkist's marketing services are organized on a nonprofit basis and are provided to members at cost. Another important difference is that Sunkist has no control over the output it must market, controlling neither the output nor the number of members.

The decentralized nature of the Sunkist System sets it apart from centralized cooperatives as well as proprietary firms. A plant owned and operated by a multiplant, centralized firm would ordinarily accept orders from top management as to prices as well as levels and destinations of shipments. A centralized cooperative might have no control over production, but would at least control the disposition of whatever its members elected to produce. In contrast, Sunkist does not have control, for example, over what prices are acceptable to its grower-members in selling fresh fruit. It does not have control, to take another example, over how much will be sold in one part of the country and how much will be sold somewhere else. (See chapter 5 for further explanation.) What this means is that Sunkist's control over the marketing of whatever its members elect to produce is severely constrained by the distribution of authority for making important decisions among district exchanges and packinghouses.

The looseness with which its component parts are bound together also has an implication for the manner in which the Sunkist System affects market performance. If ownership constitutes the hoops of steel that bind together the plants of a multiplant, proprietary firm, then the license and membership agreements that bind Sunkist together are little more than glue, a glue that may be dissolved by the currents of competition within a single season. Every packinghouse that is affiliated with Sunkist is a potential competitor in that it may drop its affiliation and market outside the Sunkist System, as many have done through the years. The same could surely not be said for a plant owned and operated by either a proprietary firm or a centralized cooperative.

The differences between Sunkist and the proprietary firm have important implications for an analysis of competitive behavior. The theory of the profit-seeking firm mainly assumes that the firm strives to maximize its profit. Such an assumption can hardly be expected to explain the behavior and performance of a firm organized on a nonprofit basis. Clearly, modifications of theory of the firm are required if that theory is to be made applicable to the cooperative form of enterprise. These modifications are taken up in the next section.

Before taking up the relevant theory of this case, we note here that the FTC's Trial Brief identifies the exclusive dealing contracts between local packinghouses and Sunkist as a key factor in Sunkist's "obtaining and maintaining market power in the California/Arizona industry." While this allegation will be critically analyzed in detail later, we simply note here that if Sunkist were a centralized, vertically integrated cooperative, rather than a federated cooperative, such contracts would be superfluous.

In conclusion, it is important to acknowledge that the Sunkist System has operated in essentially the same fashion since its inception over eighty years ago. Throughout this period, there existed contracts between members and among the packinghouses making up the federated system. As the Federal Trade Commission said in 1937, "Thus, prior to 1900, the essential features of the present cooperative organization and marketing plan were developed."[6] The FTC reported the existence in 1937 of such important characteristics as open membership, the presence of noncooperative packinghouses among Sunkist members as early as the 1890s, the local association's right (through the reserve clause) to control its own shipments, the right of free competition among local associations, and the practice of packing only member fruit.[7] No fundamental changes have been made in Sunkist's federated structure and its contractual agreements since 1937. One change occured in 1968, following the U.S. Supreme Court decision in *Case-Swayne Co., Inc. v. Sunkist Growers, Inc.,* 389 U.S. 384 (1967). As a result of that decision, Sunkist reorganized so that commercial packinghouses were no longer members of Sunkist. Such houses may be licensed by Sunkist to pack grower-members' fruit, but the growers using such packinghouses must be members of Sunkist and of a district exchange or a local association that does not have its own packing facility.

Models of the California/Arizona Citrus Industries with Special Attention Given to Sunkist

In order to derive the main theoretical relationships used in this book, we examine first the performance of markets in vertical sequence under conditions of perfect competition. We then consider, in turn, pure monopoly, dominant-firm theory, a farmer cooperative marketing 100 percent of the output, and a cooperative marketing a relatively large percentage of the output, over 50 percent, for example. A final topic concerns the role of cooperative marketing in the presence of federal marketing order programs.

Perfect Competition in the Marketing of Fresh Citrus

Consider the marketing of a farm product such as a variety of fresh citrus. Beyond the farm gate, the product is packed in a packing industry and then sold to the wholesale-retail sector for distribution to ultimate consumers. For the moment, we abstract from export sales and a processing outlet.

In figure 3–2 let the demand for the citrus fruit at the retail level be represented by the line labelled *D*. The demand relationship is negatively

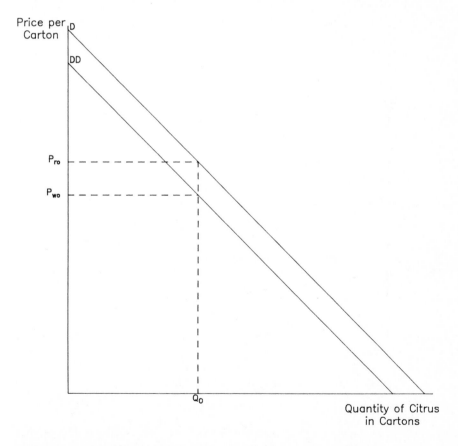

Figure 3–2. Retail-Level and Packinghouse-Level Demands for Fresh Citrus

inclined so that the quantity demanded increases as the price falls. For simplicity, assume that the necessary per-carton cost of wholesaling and retailing the product beyond the packing stage, hereafter referred to as the wholesale-retail margin, is constant for all levels of retail sales. In figure 3–2, this margin is represented by the distance $(P_{ro} - P_{wo})$. Subtracting the wholesale-retail margin from the demand curve for all levels of output yields the derived demand for packed fruit represented by DD in figure 3–2. If, for example, the packing industry produced output equal to Q_o, then, in perfectly competitive equilibrium, the wholesale retail trade would pay packers a price equal to P_{wo} and consumers would pay retailers a price equal to P_{ro}.

In figure 3–3 the long-run supply for citrus fruit at the farm level is represented by the line labelled S. The supply relationship is upward sloping,

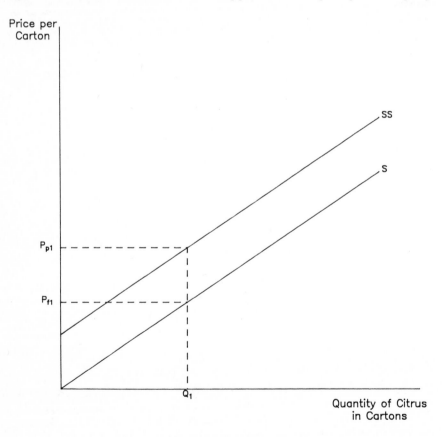

Figure 3–3. Farm-Level and Packinghouse-Level Supplies, Fresh Citrus

indicating that an increase in price would induce growers to increase production. For simplicity, assume that the necessary per-carton cost of packing the fruit, hereafter referred to as the packing margin, is constant for all levels of production. In figure 3-3, the packing margin is represented by the distance $(P_{p1} - P_{f1})$. Adding the packing margin to the supply curve for all levels of output yields the supply for packed fruit represented by SS. If, for example, citrus growers produced a level of output equal to Q_1, then, in perfectly competitive equilibrium, they would receive a price equal to P_{f1} and the packing industry would receive a price equal to P_{p1}.

In order to derive competitive equilibrium in the vertical sequence of markets through which citrus must pass on its way from producer to ultimate consumer, we superimpose figure 3-2 onto figure 3-3. This yields figure 3-4.

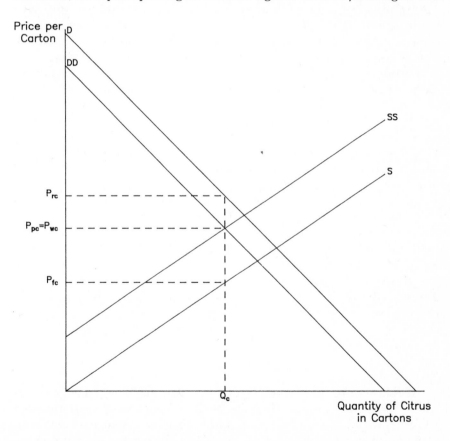

Figure 3-4. Retail-Level and Packinghouse-Level Demands and Farm-Level and Packinghouse-Level Supplies, Fresh Citrus

Competitive equilibrium is given by the intersection of the demand and supply for packed citrus represented by DD and SS, respectively. Farm output of citrus equals Q_c and farm price equals P_{fc}. Packinghouses receive the price P_{pc} and ultimate consumers pay P_{rc}. The crucial aspect of competitive marketing is that $(P_{rc} - P_{wc})$, the wholesale-retail margin, plus $(P_{pc} - P_{fc})$, the marketing margin for packinghouses, just covers the necessary costs of marketing. The resulting marketing costs are as low as possible, consistent with providing the necessary marketing services for the equilibrium level of output.

Monopolization of the Packing Industry

The competitive outcome may be compared and contrasted with that resulting from monopolization at the packinghouse level. For this purpose, we assume that all packinghouses are owned and operated by a single profit-maximizing concern and that entry of firms into the packing business is not possible. The D, DD, SS, and S curves as previously explained are given in figure 3–5. Under present assumptions, the SS curve shows the average cost of producing packed citrus by the monopolist. Profit maximization implies equating the marginal cost of production given by MC in figure 3–5 to the marginal revenue from sales given by MR. Equilibrium output equals Q_m, farm producers receive P_{fm}, and consumers pay P_{rm}. The wholesale-retail sector pays a price equal to P_{wm}. The monopolist's excess profit per carton of packed fruit equals $(P_{wm} - AC_{pm})$. (It is purely coincidental that P_{fm} equals AC_{pm}.) For convenience, the competitive values of the assorted variables are also given in figure 3–5. Monopoly at the packinghouse level restricts output from Q_c to Q_m. Price received by farmers falls from P_{fc} to P_{fm}. Price paid by consumers rises from P_{rc} to P_{rm}. The wholesale-retail marketing margin $(P_{rm} - P_{wm})$ remains the same as before, but the margin for packing fruit increases from $(P_{pc} - P_{fc})$ to $(P_{wm} - P_{fm})$. The crucial point is that, relative to competitive equilibrium, monopoly restricts output and lowers price to farm producers at the same time that price to consumers is increased. The total marketing margin is no longer the minimum required to provide all marketing services, in that one component of that margin represents monopoly profit at the packinghouse level.

It is of utmost importance to recognize that the monopolist is able to control prices and gain excess profit because it has exclusive control over packinghouse facilities. The monopolistic firm can limit the amount of fruit packed and sold to the wholesale-retail trade. It therefore controls and, relative to competition, limits the level of production at the farm level. The

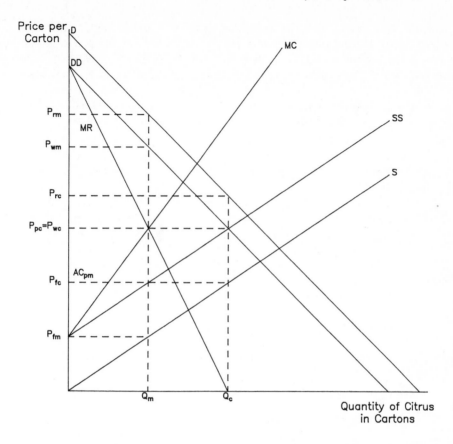

Figure 3–5. A Monopolistic Seller of Fresh Citrus

monopolistic firm has control over prices *because* it has control over the level of production.

We turn next to the theory of the dominant firm. We do so for two reasons. First, by comparing the pure-monopoly outcome with the dominant-firm outcome, it can be shown how loosening the control over production loosens the control that a relatively large firm has over prices. Second, in its Trial Brief, the FTC implicitly adopts as its model of Sunkist the model of the profit-seeking dominant firm.

Applying dominant-firm theory to the California/Arizona citrus sector, we assume the existence of a fringe of relatively small packers and one relatively large or dominant packer accounting for more than 50 percent, say, of industry sales. Entry of new packing firms is assumed to be impossible. To avoid unnecessary complications, it is further assumed that the large firm enjoys lower costs because of patented processes, superior managerial ability, or whatever. The dominant firm sets both the price received by citrus growers and the price paid by the wholesale-retail sector. Clearly, the higher the price to growers, the more they would be willing to produce and the lower must be the wholesale price if all fruit is to be marketed. In figure 3-6, let SS_n show how much the competitive fringe of small packers would be willing to sell to the wholesale-retail sector at various wholesale prices, given that for each wholesale price, there is a corresponding price that must be paid to citrus growers. (The DD and S curves are the same as before.) Subtracting laterally the SS_n curve from the demand curve given by DD yields the demand relationship confronting the dominant firm. This relationship is labelled DD_d in figure 3-6. If, for

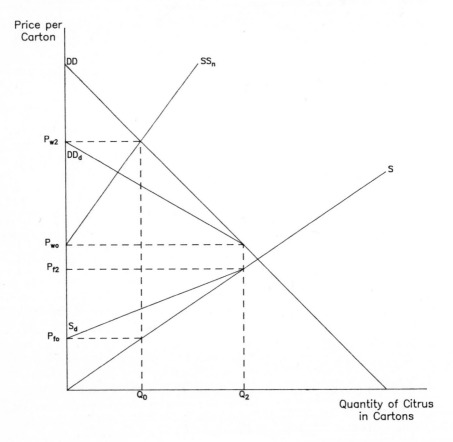

Figure 3-6. A Dominant-Firm Seller of Fresh Citrus

example, the dominant firm sets the wholesale price equal to P_{wo}, the fringe would not pack fruit because normal profit could not be earned at such a low wholesale price. Thus, by construction, if fringe packers pack fruit, the packing cost per carton must exceed $(P_{wo} - P_{f2})$, the difference between the grower price and the wholesale price for total industry output equal to Q_2. If the dominant firm sets the wholesale price at P_{w2}, on the other hand, the fringe of small firns would supply Q_0, which is all that wholesale-retail buyers would be willing to buy at the high price. The dominant firm would have no market at all.

Under these circumstances, it might well be profitable for the dominant firm to price the fringe out of the market. In this case, the model reverts to a pure-monopoly model discussed above. The alternative analyzed here involves the setting of the wholesale price by the dominant firm so as to allow the competitive fringe to survive.

It is also possible to derive a relationship between the price at the grower level and the quantity that growers would make available to the dominant firm, given the requirements of the competitive fringe. This relationship is given by S_d in figure 3-6. The grower price corresponding to the wholesale price P_{w2} is P_{fo}; nothing is supplied to the dominant firm at this set of prices. As the dominant firm lowers the wholesale price, total quantity demanded will increase and a higher price must be paid to growers. If the dominant firm sets the wholesale price at P_{wo}, the corresponding grower price is P_{f2}; the total quantity supplied by growers is available to the dominant firm. The supply curve to the dominant firm, S_d, is more elastic than the normal supply because as the dominant firm expands its production, the production of the competitive fringe contracts.

The wholesale demand and the grower supply confronting the dominant firm (given by DD_d and S_d, respectively, in figure 3-6) are reproduced in figure 3-7. We assume that the dominant firm's packing cost per carton, its packing margin, increases as its size of operations expand over the relevant range, because of diseconomies of size. (Diseconomies of size are also assumed for the fringe of competitive firms.) The packing margin is subtracted from DD_d in figure 3-7 for all relevant levels of output, yielding an average revenue product curve for the dominant firm given by ARP_d. This curve shows the maximum price the dominant firm could pay growers for various levels of output and still cover all its costs plus a normal rate of return on its investment. The MRP_d curve shows the marginal revenue product for various levels of output; the MC_d shows the marginal cost of acquiring citrus at the grower level. Profit maximization by the dominant firm implies equating the marginal revenue product to the marginal cost of citrus. Grower price equals P_{f1}, the wholesale price equals P_{w1}, output equals Q_1, and the dominant firm's profit is represented by the area $(ARP_{d1} - P_{f1}) Q_1$. Under the assumed conditions, the competitive fringe also earns

Figure 3–7. A Profit-Maximizing Dominant Firm Selling Fresh Citrus

excess profit. The amount supplied by the fringe could be deduced by introducing the price P_{w1} into figure 3–6.

Using the analytical apparatus developed in figures 3–6 and 3–7, it can be shown that as the slope of the SS_n curve is decreased, the profit-maximizing price set by the dominant firm declines as does its profit-maximizing share of industry output. The slope of SS_n would be less, the more easily small competitive firms are able to expand capacity.

In both the case of pure monopoly and that of the dominant firm, entry of new firms into the packing industry was disallowed by assumption. If this assumption is relaxed, then profit maximization by the monopolistic firm, of either the pure-monopoly or dominant-firm variety, becomes more complex. If entry is possible, then in the short run, the monopolistic firm might find it advantageous to maximize short-run profit, running the risk of encouraging entry and losing market share in the long run. The entry of new relatively small firms in the dominant-firm model, for example, would cause SS_n to shift to the right, thus lowering the dominant firm's market share and excess profit. Alternatively, the monopolistic firm might practice limit pricing, keeping price below the short-run maximizing level in order to forestall entry of new firms and decline of market share. Broadly speaking, the easier entry of new capacity or firms is, the less the monopoly power of the monopolistic firm.

Marketing of Fresh Citrus through a Large Cooperative

The objective of the following analysis is to examine market conditions that might bestow market power on a farmer cooperative. We assume throughout that the cooperative is owned and controlled by citrus growers and operates on a nonprofit basis, providing packing services at cost to its member-growers. Unless otherwise stated, we also assume that the cooperative neither restricts membership nor controls the production of its members. Such a cooperative will be characterized hereafter as being open-ended. Considered in turn are cases in which the cooperative packs 100 percent of the citrus and over 50 percent of the citrus. The results are compared with the previous results of a pure monopoly and of a dominant profit-seeking firm. We assume in the first two cases that the cooperative neither differentiates its product nor practices price discrimination, but change these assumptions in the final two cases in this section.

A Cooperative Packing 100 Percent of Citrus with No Product Differentiation or Price Discrimination. Assume that the cooperative packs all of the citrus produced and that entry of new packing firms is not possible. Then the *DD* curve in figure 3–2 shows the maximum price the cooperative can obtain from wholesale-retail buyers for all possible levels of output. If for each level of output we subtract the packing cost per carton from the *DD* curve, again assuming constant costs, we will then have a new relationship given by *CAR* (cooperative average revenue) in figure 3–8. This relationship shows the maximum price the cooperative can return to its members for whatever level of output they produce. Equilibrium is given by the intersection of *CAR* and *S* and is exactly the same as under perfect competition. Consider any output less than Q_c. In that case, the cooperative is withholding a profit from growers and/or members are not producing as much as they would like at the price returned to them by their cooperative. The result is disequilibrium. Consider any output larger than Q_c. In that case, either the cooperative is incurring a loss and/or the growers are producing more than they would like to produce for the price received. Again, we have disequilibrium. At Q_c, the cooperative operates on a nonprofit basis and is able to return to growers a price equal to P_{fc}; at P_{fc}, growers are

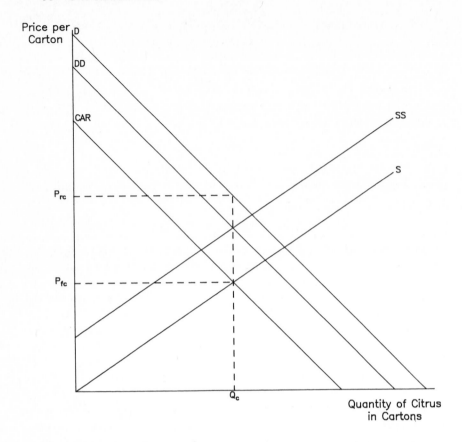

Figure 3–8. A Cooperative Marketing the Entire Market Output of Fresh Citrus

willing to produce Q_c. Finally, we note that by construction, the intersection of *CAR* and *S* occurs at exactly the same output as does the intersection of *SS* and *DD*. Thus, competitive equilibrium and cooperative equilibrium are exactly the same.

From another point of view, the *CAR* curve in figure 3–8 may be viewed as the derived demand on the part of perfectly competitive packers for farm output of citrus. The intersection of supply, *S*, and derived demand for farm citrus, given by *CAR* in this case, would yield perfectly competitive equilibrium. Cooperative marketing and perfect competition lead to the same market outcome because only at Q_c is marketing cost per carton minimized with no excess profit accruing to any marketing firms.

It is worth stressing that the market conduct of the cooperative is not the same as the conduct of any one of the many, relatively small packing-houses that constitute a competitive packing industry. In the model of perfect competition, each packinghouse manager views the price as a given, adjusting his or her output so as to maximize profit. The cooperative marketing 100 percent of the citrus output takes the output as *given* and quotes a price to wholesale-retail buyers that allows the sale of all of its packed fruit. In vigorous competition, packinghouses take price as given and adjust output accordingly. A marketing cooperative takes output as given and adjusts selling price accordingly. The resulting market conduct may be referred to as quantity-taking behavior. Thus, although the conduct of the cooperative differs from that of the perfectly competitive packinghouse, the market performance is exactly the same in either case. We have stressed this point because, if quantity-taking behavior characterizes the pricing of citrus within the Sunkist System, then we have an important piece of conduct evidence that supports the empirical validity of the theory. Moreover, the FTC in its Trial Brief seems to hold that only if price-taking behavior exists at the packinghouse level will the competitive outcome be achieved. We have shown this position to be false, however, because quantity-taking behavior on the part of a cooperative leads to the same result. It may be noted parenthetically that the monopolist in figure 3–5 does not take output as given. On the contrary, the monopolist sets prices in order to assure a particular level of output, Q_m, which equates marginal cost and marginal revenue.

A Cooperative Packing a Dominant Share with No Product Differentiation or Price Discrimination. Turning to theory of a dominant cooperative, we retain all of the assumptions made in our previous analysis of the dominant firm except that the dominant firm is now assumed to be a cooperative. In the model of the profit-maximizing dominant firm, the ARP_d curve, as derived, showed the maximim price the dominant firm could pay citrus growers and still cover all packing costs. In theory of the profit-maximizing firm, the ARP_d curve is the same as the CAR curve in cooperative theory. For present purposes, we may therefore think of the ARP_d curve in figure 3–7 as the CAR_d curve for a cooperative.

Cooperative equilibrium is given by the intersection of CAR_d and S_d. Equilibrium output and grower price are Q_s and P_{fs}, respectively. Clearly, open-ended cooperation expands output, increases price to growers, and lowers the wholesale-retail price, all relative to the market outcome of a dominant, profit-maximizing firm. Importantly, the cooperative's share of the marketings greatly exceeds the share of the dominant, profit-maximizing firm under equivalent cost conditions. Far from being an indication of market power, the cooperative's large market share reflects the cooperative's drive to provide packing services at cost and its low wholesale-pricing policy that shrinks the excess profits and scale of operations of the high-cost, relatively small firms. It can indeed be shown that if the cooperative's packing cost per carton is both constant beyond some minimum efficient scale of operation and below the lowest per-carton cost of the small packers, then the cooperative will drive all high-cost packers out of business, achieving, perhaps unwittingly, competitive equilibrium in the process.

The above analysis of cooperation rests on certain assumptions about the mode of operations of the cooperative. Specifically, it was assumed that the cooperative did not restrict membership, control production of members, differentiate its product, or practice price discrimination. The conclusion that cooperation leads to vigorous competition regardless of the cooperative's market share rests squarely on these assumptions. It is imperative, therefore, that the modifications of the above theory required by the relaxation of these assumptions be further developed.

As a slight digression, it may be noted that a marketing cooperative that restricts membership and/or controls the production of its members in order to raise the price received from the wholesale-retail sector, at the same time avoiding a surplus of production, is exercising market power. This case is not explored further here because it will become clear that Sunkist neither restricts membership for the above purpose nor controls the production of its members. On the contrary, Sunkist has a long history of encouraging affiliated packinghouses to sign up new members and of providing Sunkist member-growers with field services designed to increase their efficiency and production.

We therefore turn to the possibility that the cooperative differentiates its product and/or practices price discrimination, taking up the issue of differentiation first.

An Open-Ended Cooperative with Product Differentiation but No Price Discrimination. Consider an initial situation in which the cooperative markets a large percentage of the citrus crop with the remainder of the crop marketed through a fringe of relatively small packinghouses. Equal packinghouse efficiency is assumed with no attempt on the part of the cooperative initially to differentiate its product. Free entry is also assumed. It is also supposed that growers align themselves among cooperative and noncooperative packinghouses in quest of the highest perceived returns for their fruit, with no intrinsic like or dislike for cooperative marketing. Under these conditions, market performance will be that associated with perfect competition.

The objective in what follows is to ascertain how market performance would change if the cooperative initiated a program to differentiate its product. Suppose, therefore, that the cooperative launches an advertising program.

The objective of the program is to increase the price that can be returned to its member-growers. Let P_{ws} and P_{wn} equal, respectively, the prices paid to the cooperative and to other packinghouses by the wholesale-retail trade for packed citrus. Let AC equal the packing cost per carton as given by the vertical distance between S and SS in figure 3-3. Let AD equal the cooperative's advertising cost per carton.

Three alternative conditions might prevail under a new equilibrium in which all adjustments have been made to the cooperative's advertising program. First, consider the possibility that

$$P_{ws} - AC - AD < P_{wn} - AC. \tag{3.1}$$

Under this condition, the price premium, $P_{ws} - P_{wn}$, if any, is less than AD. In this situation, all growers benefit from the advertising program in terms of a greater demand for the product. In this case, the effect of the advertising is a generic increase in demand for California/Arizona citrus rather than the differentiation of Sunkist members' citrus. Despite this, Sunkist member-growers must pay all the costs. Adherence to the advertising program by the cooperative would under these circumstances cause a continuing decline in membership as growers seek out the highest return for their fruit. Thus, in equilibrium, the inequality given by equation 3.1 does not appear feasible. This theoretical possibility may be important in understanding why cooperatives with large shares of industry marketings might not choose to engage in advertising.

A second possibility is that

$$P_{ws} - AC - AD > P_{wn} - AC. \tag{3.2}$$

Here the price premium, $P_{ws} - P_{wn}$, exceeds the advertising cost per carton. In this case, the advertising program is sufficiently effective as to attract all growers to the cooperative, driving all noncooperative packinghouses out of business. The price P_{wn} is to be construed as the highest price obtainable by the most-favored potential entrant. This case is certainly feasible from a theoretical point of view and, since it would appear to be the most likely case in which advertising might give the cooperative monopoly power, further analysis is of interest.

If the cooperative's objective is to increase the price received by member-growers, and if an advertising program is in effect, then, in the new equilibrium, the grower price must exceed P_{fc} in figure 3-8. (Here and hereafter, we ignore the highly unlikely case where advertising has no effect on price paid to member-growers.) What this means is that the new derived demand for packed fruit is shifted to the right by a sufficiently large margin so that when both packing and advertising costs per carton are subtracted from it, the resulting CAR curve lies to the right of that given in figure 3-8. In fact, to maximize the per-carton returns to growers, the cooperative would choose that level of advertising that shifts the *CAR* relationship to the right as far as possible. As an illustration, see CAR_a in figure 3-9. Here, relative to competitive equilibrium, the output of citrus is increased, from Q_c to Q_a, and the price to consumers is raised by the amount of advertising cost per unit. It is clear that if the inequality given by equation 3.2 holds, then cooperative marketing does not lead to competitive equilibrium even though the cooperative is open-ended and does not practice price discrimination.

It would be absurd to conclude from this result, however, that cooperation leads to monopolization in the same sense as this term is used in the analysis of a profit-seeking firm. First, the price quoted by the cooperative to the wholesale-retail sector rises and falls with whatever level of output its

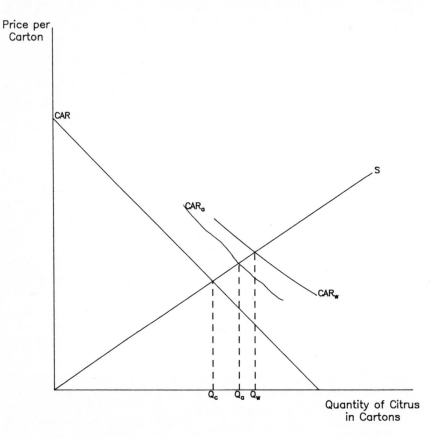

Figure 3-9. A Cooperative Marketing Entire Market Output of Fresh Citrus with Advertising but No Price Discrimination, and with Both Advertising and Price Discrimination

member-growers choose to produce; the cooperative has no more control over price than it had before advertising occurred. The important implication of our assumption, which asserts quantity-taking behavior still applies, is still subject to empirical test. Second, for any given advertising expenditure, a profit-maximizing monopolist would choose the level of output (or that price) at which marginal cost of production and marginal revenue from sales are equated. It is entirely possible that the monopolist's output is less than competitive output whereas the cooperative output, as we have already seen, must exceed competitive output. Finally, the total expenditures by the wholesale-retail sector on packed fruit, given cooperation, just equal the total cost of packing (including advertising) plus the cost of producing the fruit. Under monopoly, substantial excess profit could exist.

A third possible condition might hold in a new equilibrium:

$$P_{ws} - AC - AD = P_{wn} - AC. \tag{3.3}$$

Here the price premium received by the cooperative $(P_{ws} - P_{wn})$ equals the advertising cost per unit. Growers align themselves between the cooperative and noncooperative packinghouses so as to equate prices received. In light of the cooperative's objective, it appears very likely that the price received by the member-grower is higher than it would have been in the absence of advertising. (Otherwise, why undertake the program?) It follows, then, from equation 3.3, that price to nonmember-growers has also been increased. Since there is no production control and all growers receive higher prices, we can be sure that total output of citrus will exceed the competitive output. Consumer prices will also rise above the perfectly competitive level because, in part, the average cost of producing citrus increases as citrus production increases. Although it is not inevitable that the cooperative's share of industry marketings will increase, such a result seems likely. As to the view that advertising could be used by the cooperative to monopolize the packing industry, the conclusions reached above in connection with inequality (3.2) are applicable here as well.

To sum up the above discussion of product differentiation, consider a marketing cooperative that does not restrict membership or production of members and does not practice price discrimination. Could advertising be used by such a cooperative to achieve monopolization, allowing the controlling of prices and the impeding of the flow of resources into citrus production? Our answer is an emphatic no. Even in the extreme case where advertising is sufficiently effective as to cause all growers to affiliate with the cooperative, there are critical differences between the cooperative outcome and the monopoly outcome.[8] It is true that cooperative advertising destroys the equivalence between the cooperative and the perfectly competitive outcome because in the model of perfect competition, advertising is disallowed. The importance of this latter result from the viewpoint of public welfare and antitrust policy will be considered in more detail later in this book. Suffice it here to say that in a world of imperfect competition and imperfect information, a world in which advertising is commonplace, it is by no means certain that the performance of the citrus sector as described under conditions of perfect competition in figure 3-4 is to be preferred on welfare grounds to the performance of the citrus sector resulting from an open-ended cooperative that markets all the industry output and also engages in advertising as in figure 3-9, where $Q = Q_a$.[9] Moreover, to embrace the view that cooperatives are in violation of antitrust laws whenever it can be shown that their operations are not consistent with perfect competition is to hold cooperatives up against a standard far more severe and demanding than that applied to profit-seeking firms. As shown in chapter 2, monopolizing under section 2 of the Sherman Act requires evidence of monopoly power, which implies power well in excess of that resulting from minor departures from perfect competition that are commonplace in many segments of the economy.

An Open-Ended Cooperative with Price Discrimination. We turn next to the issue of price discrimination, which we here interpret to include the possibility of physical destruction of citrus. For the purpose of analyzing the implications of price discrimination by a marketing cooperative, we reconsider the nature of the *DD* curve in figure 3-8, again assuming that the cooperative markets 100 percent of the crop, but does not restrict membership or members' output. Advertising is allowed, however. For our present purpose, the *DD* curve is to be interpreted as the aggregate demand for several groups of buyers. Domestic and export buyers of fresh citrus and buyers of citrus for processing are relevant possibilities. Under these assumed conditions, the cooperative may be able to practice price discrimination, equating the marginal revenues among markets and charging different prices to different buyers for the same product. Physical destruction of citrus might also be used to avoid negative marginal revenues.

Assuming that price discrimination is feasible, the sale proceeds from all markets may be pooled and the average pool returns to growers for any given level of production will exceed the corresponding cooperative average return associated with no price discrimination. In figure 3-9 is reproduced *CAR* from figure 3-8. Recall that in the model analyzed with the aid of figure 3-8, neither product differentiation nor price discrimination was allowed. The curve labelled CAR_a gives the relationship between cooperative average receipts and output on the assumption that advertising is both permissible and effective in shifting *CAR* to the right. The new curve given by CAR_w shows that average pool return to member-growers for all levels of production on the assumption that advertising is effective and price discrimination is feasible. It may be noted parenthetically that without effective advertising, the CAR_w curve would be further to the left but still above CAR.

The impact of price discrimination on market performance may now be compared with earlier results obtained on the assumption that price discrimination did not exist. First, as indicated earlier, effective advertising causes output to increase from Q_c to Q_a in figure 3–9. With price discrimination, output increases still further, from Q_a to Q_w. Second, in previous models, with or without advertising, the cooperative had no control over price. The independent production decisions of member-growers determined total output which, in turn, determined prices at the grower level as well as at higher levels in the marketing channel. Feasible price discrimination, on the other hand, does provide the cooperative with latitude in pricing in that prices in different markets may be moved up or down at the cooperative's discretion. Moreover, if product destruction is allowed, it is no longer necessarily true that the level of output passing through the marketing channel is determined by the decisions of member-growers. Third, a myriad of theoretical possibilities exist as to the consequences of price discrimination and advertising on the levels of prices paid by different groups of buyers. The prices to some groups of buyers will likely rise while the prices to others might fall.

Although feasible price discrimination provides the marketing cooperative with some modicum of market power, it nonetheless remains true, as in the previous case where differentiation but not discrimination was allowed, that substantial differences exist between the resulting market performance and the performance associated with monopolization by a profit-maximizing handler. It remains true, for example, that the total receipts from the sale of the cooperative's products are, after deduction of all costs incurred, returned to growers in the form of pooled returns. There is no excess profit in the marketing margins. Thus, the effect of price discrimination by an open-ended cooperative is to increase output beyond that associated with monopolization. Within the confines of a comparative static model, a cooperative might engage in physical destruction of some of the citrus crop, but a profit-seeking monopolist would price the crop so as never to encounter nonpositive marginal returns in the first place. Physical destruction is very inefficient and it is possible that the welfare implications of monopoly are less objectionable than those associated with open-ended cooperation and persistent product destruction.

The above analysis of price discrimination on the part of a marketing cooperative assumes that price discrimination is feasible. The conditions under which this assumption might or might not be appropriate must be examined if the sources of market power open to a cooperative are to be understood.

Several conditions must exist before price discrimination becomes feasible. First, the cooperative must be in a position to separate the markets for its output in that arbitrage between any two buyers representing different buyer groups must be forestalled. Second, the demands must exhibit differing price elasticities when marginal revenues are equated or else prices will also be equated and discrimination will not occur. A third requirement arises in the case where the cooperative does not market 100 percent of the crop. This requirement entails further restrictions in demand and supply elasticities and necessitates some elaboration.

Price discrimination in its most simple version involves charging a higher price to one group of buyers than to another. Ordinarily, the highest price is quoted to that group of buyers with the least elasticity of demand. There will be an obvious incentive, however, for a fringe of small competing packinghouses to ship exclusively to the highest-price market. This tendency may thwart the cooperative's effort to practice price discrimination even on the assumption that the cooperative's share of growers in the industry remains constant and aside from the free-rider problem to be discussed momentarily. We will not pause here to give a rigorous, mathematical treatment of this problem. Broadly speaking, (1) the more similar the demands for different groups of buyers, (2) the more elastic the supply response, and (3) the greater the share of production handled by the fringe of small packinghouses, then the more unlikely is the feasibility of price discrimination on the part of a relatively large cooperative and the less is the potential for cooperative market power. It should be apparent that the incentive for a fringe of packinghouses to market all of their output in the highest-priced market could easily undermine any market power that a dominant cooperative might otherwise be able to acquire through practicing price discrimination. The theoretical issues here identified could have great practical significance.

Finally, and perhaps most important of all, in order for the cooperative to practice price discrimination, it must somehow be able to solve the free-rider problem. If price discrimination is practiced, then cooperative members will have an incentive to break away from the cooperative and sell their output at the highest price possible rather than receive a pool return reflecting a price spectrum. If the cooperative is federated, there will be an incentive for local packinghouses to leave the association and undertake their own marketing. Nonaffiliated packinghouses will be able to pay their growers a higher price than the average pool return from the cooperative. In a word, price discrimination creates incentives for the expansion of production on the part of noncooperative growers, at the same time encouraging members to leave the association. The cooperative that practices price discrimination after having established a dominant position in the market is sowing the seeds of its own destruction unless it can somehow solve the free-rider problem.

How can the free-rider problem be avoided? First, the marketing cooperative might obtain substantial economies of size. Such cost economies could be sufficient to offset the price advantage that other packinghouses might otherwise have. Second, the cooperative might use long-term membership agreements with growers and/or long-term full-supply contracts with buyers so as to foreclose cooperative defections and retard output growth for the typical nonmember. Full-supply contracts would appear to be particularly effective where only a few large buyers are involved and where buyers are mainly concerned that all pay the same price.

Finally, the cooperative association may strive to create new products and processes and to develop new markets so as to gain an advantage over nonaffiliated packinghouses. Clearly, however, cooperative innovation and progressiveness would tend to offset any welfare loss due to price discrimination. While other alternative solutions to the free-rider problem may be open to the cooperative, perhaps enough has been said to suggest the nature of factors requiring investigation in empirical analysis.

Some Theoretical Implications of Federal Marketing Order Programs

In order to understand the determination of the performance of California/Arizona citrus markets, it is imperative that the nature and role of federal orders are taken into consideration. The three orders of most relevance here are Federal Order (FO) 910 for California/Arizona lemons. FO 907 for California/Arizona navel oranges, and FO 908 for California/Arizona valencia oranges. (Our discussion is limited to the operation of these marketing orders as they existed prior to 1980, the period in which Sunkist was charged with monopolizing.)[10] These three orders regulate the permissible sizes and maximum weekly quantities of fresh-grade fruit that may be shipped to the domestic market defined to include Canada. The maximum allowable shipments are prorated among growers according to their levels of expected production. For administrative ease, the prorate is assigned to packinghouses. The three prorate orders permit the handler in a given week to overship the allotted quantity by 20 percent, but the overshipment must be deducted from the next week's allotment. Undershipments may be carried forward and added to the handler's allotment for the following week only.[11] Allotment loans are also permitted between handlers within each prorate district. Administrative committees appointed by the U.S. Secretary of Agriculture make recommendations to the Secretary as regards weekly shipments. It should be emphasized that the Sunkist System does not have a majority control over any of the three administrative committees.

In order to appreciate the importance of these programs, let DD be the weekly demand for fresh citrus in figure 3–10 and let A_0 be the maximum

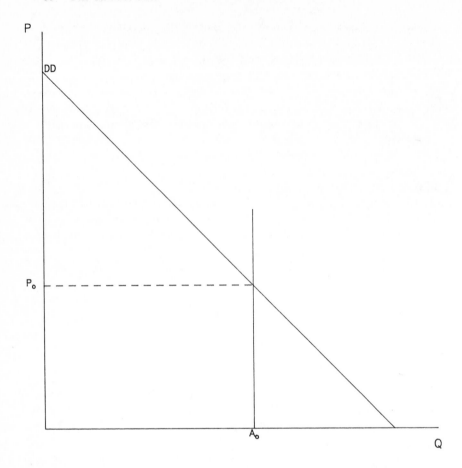

**Figure 3–10. Weekly Demand for Fresh Citrus with Weekly Allotment
under a Federal Order**

quantity that packers may ship to the market. Several possibilities need to
be recognized. First, various factors such as weather may interfere with the
movement of fresh fruit to the market, so that a quantity less than A_0 is
actually shipped. Second, because of the flexibility of order regulations,
actual shipments somewhat larger than or less than A_0 would be permissible. Third, allotments represent maximum allowable shipments and would
not be binding constraints if packinghouses preferred to ship less. For
example, if export prices tend to rise above domestic prices, as happens on
occasion, shippers could switch fruit from domestic to export markets and
experience the loss of prorate for the season.

    If competition in procurement is less than pure or perfect, setting Q
equal to A_0 need not imply that buyers pay P_0 for fruit shipped to the fresh

market. In particular, if there is market power in procurement, then a price less than P_O might be paid for fruit for the fresh market. Under these circumstances, citrus production would fall and some program benefits might accrue to fruit handlers. Where marketing orders limit shipments to markets, it is necessary that competition in marketing be keen if marketing firms are to be denied benefits. An important role for cooperative marketing in the presence of marketing orders that limit shipments is to assure effective competition in marketing the product. An effective cooperative ensures that *all* growers receive a competitive price by paying its growers price P_O. If the cooperative is a significant factor in the market, other handlers must meet the competitive price; if other handlers fail to pay the competitive price, their growers have a strong incentive to join the cooperative in succeeding years. By preventing grower prices from going below the competitive price P_O, cooperatives prevent the market instability created when market prices send out inaccurate signals to growers. In this way, cooperatives contribute to the effective functioning of marketing orders and enhance grower returns.

What implications do marketing orders have in regard to the question of whether a relatively large cooperative has monopoly power? We have already seen that the main source of monopoly power for an open-ended cooperative is the possibility of price discrimination. Further, a major obstacle to practicing price discrimination is the free-rider problem. Although an open-member cooperative is virtually impotent in solving the free-rider problem, with many agricultural products, farmers may use marketing orders administered by the federal or state governments to accomplish price discrimination with no fear of free-riding. It is important to bear in mind, however, that in this case, the ultimate source of market power would be a legislatively authorized federal or state marketing order, not the cooperative. Moreover, whether price discrimination actually is achieved by a federal order depends on the provisions of the order. Marketing orders may be instituted for a variety of purposes; price discrimination need not be one of them.

The use and effects of marketing orders are clearly separable from the question of unlawful monopolization by agricultural cooperatives.[12] It should be recognized, however, that cooperatives often play a key role in representing their members in marketing orders. The legislation authorizing federal orders contemplated that cooperatives would represent producers in the initiation, operation, and termination of marketing orders.[13] Indeed, it is difficult to visualize the effective functioning of marketing orders unless farmers rely on a cooperative association to represent their interests.[14] Because of this, through the years, many cooperatives were organized, where they did not already exist, for the primary purpose of representing growers in the implementation and more effective functioning of orders. Without cooperatives to represent them, individual growers lack the time and resources to monitor orders effectively.

As to the application of the above analysis to the role of Sunkist in the California/Arizona citrus sector, we note two major possibilities of attaining market power beyond that resulting from the order alone. First, the marketing order may result in price discrimination as between the fresh market and all other markets that is not optimal in terms of returning the highest price possible to the growers of whatever citrus is involved. In this case, Sunkist could theoretically strive to keep shipments of its packing-houses below levels permissible under the orders. Second, since the orders do not regulate shipments as between the processing and export outlets, Sunkist could theoretically strive to practice price discrimination between those two outlets. Of course, the restraints imposed by the free-rider problem apply to both of the above cases. Below we examine whether Sunkist engaged in either of these practices.

The reader should keep in mind that the FTC did not challenge the effects of California/Arizona marketing orders nor did it claim that Sunkist used these orders in its alleged monopolization of the California/Arizona citrus industry. Rather, the FTC alleged that Sunkist possessed and exercised monopoly power independently of any power that may have been conferred on growers by marketing orders. Because the FTC acknowledged the above, the analysis in chapters 4 through 7 focuses on whether Sunkist restricted supply in some markets with the intent and effect of raising prices above those that would have resulted under the marketing orders alone.

Conclusions and Implications for Antitrust Analysis

The nonprofit nature of a marketing cooperative coupled with open-ended operations disallow monopolization. In the absence of product differentiation and price discrimination, open-ended cooperation leads to perfectly competitive equilibrium.[15] The cooperative marketing 100 percent of the crop could only restrict production below the competitive level by keeping price to growers below the competitive level and by keeping the price to wholesale-retail buyers above the competitive level. The inevitable consequence of such a pricing policy would be excess profit, which is inimical to the interests of member-growers and incompatible with the objective of providing marketing services at cost on a nonprofit basis.

Product differentiation as a result of advertising destroys the equivalence between the perfectly competitive outcome and the cooperative outcome. If cooperative operations are nonprofit and open-ended, however, then the role of the cooperative in pricing is still passive. Price is set in order to clear the market rather than to equate marginal cost of production and marginal revenue from sales, as in the case of a profit-maximizing monopolist. Cooperative output exceeds both the perfectly competitive output and the output associated with monopolization.

An open-ended cooperative that is able continually to practice price discrimination, with or without advertising, does possess some market power. Even so, nonprofit and open-ended operations cause output to exceed that associated with monopolization. Certain conditions must be met if price discrimination is to be feasible, however, and these conditions become increasingly stringent as the cooperative's share of marketings falls below 100 percent. Moreover, price discrimination gives rise to a free-rider problem in that cooperative members have an incentive to leave the cooperative and nonmember growers have an incentive to expand output. If this problem is not circumvented, so that the cooperative can at least maintain its share of the marketings, then price discrimination becomes infeasible.

Because a detailed critique of the FTC allegations is reserved until later, we will be brief in pointing out here that the FTC uses the theory of the profit-maximizing firm rather than the theory of cooperation as the economic framework for its case. When the theory of the firm is extended to include the nonprofit cooperative as a special case, then it is clear that for an open-ended cooperative, large market share and product differentiation are, in and of themselves, unable to provide the cooperative with even a modicum of market power. The FTC's emphasis on market share and product differentiation is misplaced, reflecting as it does an inappropriate theory. The remainder of this book is devoted to examining each of the FTC's charges within the theoretical framework set forth above. In chapter 7, we summarize our findings and conclusions. In chapter 8, we analyze the nature and significance of the 1981 agreement between Sunkist and the FTC which settled the antitrust litigation.

Notes

1. P.G. Helmberger and S. Hoos, "Cooperative Enterprise and Organization Theory," *Journal of Farm Economics* 44(May 1962):275–290; P.G. Helmberger, "Cooperative Enterprise as a Structural Dimension of Farm Markets," *Journal of Farm Economics* 46(August 1964):603–617; P. Vitaliano, "The Theory of Cooperative Enterprise: Its Development and Present Status," in *Agricultural Cooperatives and the Public Interest,* ed. B.W. Marion, Monograph 4 (Food Systems Research Group, University of Wisconsin-Madison, September 1978), 21–42.

2. Sunkist Growers, Inc., "Statement of Its Defense," FTC Docket 9100 (March 22, 1979), 12; memorandum from the secretary's office to staff officers, Sunkist Growers, Inc., Circ. 579–12 (February 7, 1979).

3. About 20 percent of all California cooperatives other than citrus cooperatives had "limited acceptance" provisions in their contracts in the 1950s. W.F. Mueller and J.M. Tinley, *Membership Marketing Contracts of Agricultural Cooperatives in California,* California Agricultural Experiment Station Bulletin 760 (University of California-Davis, College of Agriculture, March 1958), 36. See chapter 6 for a comprehensive treatment of Sunkist's marketing contracts.

4. Over 20 percent of all California cooperatives other than citrus cooperatives had contracts exceeding one year in the 1950s. Ibid., 9a–12.

5. *Case-Swayne Co. v. Sunkist Growers, Inc.,* 389 U.S. 384 (1967).

6. Federal Trade Commission, *Agricultural Income Inquiry, Part II, Fruits, Vegetables, and Grapes* (Washington, D.C.: GPO, 1937), 678.

7. Ibid., 678–89.

8. This prediction of economic theory is borne out by the empirical findings of Wills that cooperatives advertising their brands receive lower prices than like-situated proprietary firms. R.L. Wills, "Evaluating Price Enhancement by Processing Cooperatives," *American Journal of Agricultural Economics* 67(May 1985):182–192.

9. There are two especially relevant questions to be answered in an empirical evaluation of a cooperative's advertising effort: (1) Does the advertising have a generic effect on industry demand rather than a purely product-differentiating effect? (2) Is the product sold under the cooperative brand superior in quality to products sold under other brands?

10. Some changes have occurred in the California citrus orders in recent years, but none of these changes are relevant to the analysis presented here.

11. U.S. Dept. of Agriculture, Farmer Cooperative Service, Special Report 12 (Washington, D.C.: U.S. Dept. of Agriculture), 39.

12. A possible exception is where a cooperative engages in practices that tend to manipulate for anticompetitive purpose and effect the functioning of an order program. For example, the Dept. of Justice's monopolization case against the Associated Milk Producers, Inc., charged the cooperative with "loading the pool," a practice that allegedly injured competitors. The charge was not proven, as the case was settled with a consent decree. *United States v. Associated Milk Producers, Inc.,* 394 F. Supp. 29 (W.D. Mo. 1975).

13. Among other things, federal orders limit the number of members that a cooperative may have on the administrative committees of marketing orders. For example, the federal order for California/Arizona navel oranges permits a cooperative organization that handles more than 50 percent of the total oranges to have no more than three grower members and two handler members on the eleven-member Navel Orange Administrative Committee. As a result, while Sunkist members market over 60 percent of the navel oranges, they are not permitted to elect a majority of administrative committee members. These rules were designed to limit the power of cooperatives in the administration of marketing orders.

14. In the FTC's 1937 study of cooperatives, it recognized and applauded the central role cooperatives could play in carrying out federal agricultural programs. FTC, *Agricultural Income Inquiry,* 891.

15. The conclusions reached here are in accord with those of Masson and Eisenstat. They conclude that if it does not practice price discrimination, an "open

ended cooperative, even with a 100% market share, would have no deleterious monopoly effects but could fully countervail monopsony power." Robert T. Masson and Philip Eisenstat, "Capper-Volstead and Milk Cooperative Market Power: Some Theoretical Issues," in *Agricultural Cooperatives and the Public Interest,* ed. B.W. Marion, Monograph 4 (Food Systems Research Group, University of Wisconsin-Madison, September 1978), 62–63.

4
Structure of Domestic Markets for Fresh Citrus Fruit

S unkist sells its members' citrus products in three types of markets: fresh domestic markets, the fresh export markets, and the processed products markets. The discussion of market structure in this chapter is limited primarily to California/Arizona lemons, valencia oranges, and navel oranges sold in their domestic fresh markets. Although the fresh export and the "products" (products used in processed citrus products) markets are important to Sunkist (and are discussed in succeeding chapters), we have not included an extensive analysis of their market structures below for the following reasons. First, the FTC Trial Brief did not allege that Sunkist monopolized the fresh citrus sold in export markets. Second, Sunkist's conduct in the products and export markets is disciplined by the same basic conditions that influence so importantly its conduct in the fresh domestic market, i.e., an open-membership policy and the potential development of a free-rider problem should Sunkist enhance prices to members significantly by schemes restricting members' supplies. Thus, the lessons taught by the findings regarding competition in the domestic fresh market are instructive as to the state of competition in the other markets as well.

Market Concentration

Relevant Product Markets

A necessary predicate to the analysis of an industry's structure is the determination of the relevant economic market within which prices are determined. The Federal Trade Commission's Trial Brief[1] lists a number of reasons for restricting the relevant product market to fresh oranges grown in California/Arizona and fresh lemons grown in California, Arizona, and Florida. The brief also defines the relevant geographic market as the U.S. and Canada.[2]

For purposes of the following analysis, we shall accept these definitions of the relevant product and geographic markets. We do so to simplify our exposition. In fact, however, there does exist evidence demonstrating that significant amounts of fresh Florida oranges are sold in competition with California/Arizona oranges, thereby influencing significantly the prices at which California/Arizona oranges are sold. Also, distinct markets can be identified for the two orange varieties grown in California/Arizona. Navel oranges are picked and marketed over the period from late November through April or May. Valencia oranges are marketed from March until October or November. As a result, each variety is subject to unique supply and demand conditions.

Fresh Domestic Orange Shipments

In 1980, about 50 percent of all California/Arizona oranges were sold in the domestic fresh orange market, with the remainder sold in the fresh export market (15 percent) and processed product market (35 percent). About 53 percent of these oranges were navels and the remaining 47 percent were valencias. Between 1962/63 and 1982/83, total consumption of domestic fresh California/Arizona oranges rose by nearly 50 percent, whereas the products market grew by over 200 percent and the fresh exports market grew by nearly 400 percent.

For about nine decades, most California/Arizona citrus sold in the domestic market has been marketed by two nonprofit agricultural cooperatives: Sunkist Growers, Inc. (formerly the California Fruit Growers Exchange)[3] and Pure Gold, Inc. (formerly Mutual Orange Distributors).[4]

As early as 1920/21, these two cooperatives marketed 72.9 percent of all California/Arizona citrus fruit; thereafter, their share grew rather steadily, reaching 95.0 percent in 1933/34. (See table 4-1.) Sunkist's share was about

Table 4-1
Percentage of Citrus Fruit Handled by Cooperative Associations in California and Arizona, 1920/21 through 1934/35

Marketing Season	Boxes Handled by Cooperative Associations	Ratio of Cooperative Handling to Production
1920/21	20,402,043	72.9%
1921/22	13,304,219	72.1
1922/23	19,868,556	78.8
1923/24	22,979,820	72.7
1924/25	18,495,076	78.4
1925/26	24,315,573	76.1
1926/27	27,860,039	76.3
1927/28	22,431,624	75.3
1928/29	35,949,993	75.3
1929/30	23,846,772	75.3
1930/31	38,156,246	85.3
1931/32	35,717,964	79.7
1932/33	34,172,536	79.6
1933/34	35,330,130	95.0
1934/35	48,016,334	92.1

85 percent and Pure Gold's share 10 percent.[5] It is not possible to determine for this early period the respective market shares of these two cooperatives in fresh oranges and fresh lemons. (At the time, California producers grew about 87 percent of all U.S. citrus fruit and 99.3 percent of all U.S. lemons.)[6]

Since 1954/55, Sunkist's share of total fresh valencia and navel orange shipments has averaged 70 percent. Sunkist's share of valencia oranges sold in the fresh market has ranged from a high of 85.1 percent in 1965/66 to a low of 64.4 percent in 1980/81. (See table 4-2.) Sunkist's share of navel oranges sold in the fresh market ranged from a high of 80.8 percent in 1965/66 to a low of 53.2 percent in 1982/83 (See table 4-3.)

Table 4-2
Sunkist's Share of Valencia Orange Production, Domestic Fresh Market, Export Fresh Market, and Processed Product Market, 1954/55 through 1982/83

Year	Total Production	Domestic Fresh Market	Export Fresh Market	Processed Production Market
1954/55	73.7%	74.6%	70.3%	73.4%
1955/56	72.8	76.6	66.4	71.4
1956/57	72.4	74.1	71.2	70.2
1957/58	74.8	79.5	62.4	63.7
1958/59	74.2	77.2	74.9	69.6
1959/60	71.4	72.4	65.6	71.3
1960/61	75.4	78.3	73.7	71.0
1961/62	71.5	74.3	65.1	69.7
1962/63	72.3	77.8	69.2	67.2
1963/64	70.5	71.6	78.7	67.2
1964/65	73.3	72.7	75.4	73.5
1965/66	86.1	85.1	86.9	87.1
1966/67	84.6	83.0	83.9	86.7
1967/68	82.7	83.1	79.8	82.6
1968/69	81.5	77.2	80.8	84.7
1969/70	76.3	73.3	81.5	77.7
1970/71	83.7	82.7	82.6	84.8
1971/72	71.0	79.2	84.5	78.0
1972/73	85.0	84.5	87.2	84.9
1973/74	73.0	78.5	76.9	84.7
1974/75	81.7	81.4	80.2	82.7
1975/76	78.3	79.8	77.0	77.8
1976/77	74.7	75.8	72.8	74.5
1977/78	75.5	72.9	73.0	79.3
1978/79	66.0	68.2	57.3	67.6
1979/80	68.9	73.3	63.9	67.5
1980/81	62.7	64.4	61.4	62.1
1981/82	61.8	66.5	57.9	56.3
1982/83	60.7	65.9	59.2	58.6
Average	74.4	76.0	73.1	74.0

Source: Sunkist Growers, Inc.

Table 4-3

Sunkist's Share of Naval Orange Production, Domestic Fresh Market, Export Fresh Market, and Processed Product Market, 1954/55 through 1982/83

Year	Total Production	Domestic Fresh Market	Export Fresh Market	Processed Production Market
1954/55	70.8%	70.4%	65.2%	75.5%
1955/56	68.6	68.4	55.5	74.1
1956/57	68.3	68.2	63.4	71.5
1957/58	72.5	72.8	55.6	76.1
1958/59	69.2	69.4	71.4	67.1
1959/60	66.0	65.9	63.4	67.9
1960/61	67.7	68.0	50.1	72.0
1961/62	68.6	69.8	44.6	71.2
1962/63	67.1	69.1	38.7	64.8
1963/64	69.0	69.9	63.0	65.9
1964/65	73.1	73.2	59.2	76.0
1965/66	81.4	80.8	70.4	84.9
1966/67	79.5	78.8	68.3	85.1
1967/68	76.9	77.3	66.8	77.2
1968/69	73.6	72.3	75.1	76.8
1969/70	72.8	70.8	70.9	78.1
1970/71	72.0	70.7	75.6	76.4
1971/72	69.0	67.2	74.5	72.6
1972/73	71.9	69.6	64.4	76.5
1973/74	67.1	65.6	72.0	71.0
1974/75	67.6	65.6	75.2	70.3
1975/76	65.9	64.9	64.5	73.3
1976/77	59.7	59.5	62.1	59.7
1977/78	57.5	57.2	58.5	57.7
1978/79	57.0	59.2	63.7	51.5
1979/80	55.3	55.7	58.4	54.3
1980/81	53.7	55.6	55.8	50.3
1981/82	54.9	54.3	57.8	55.8
1982/83	52.8	53.2	54.8	51.6
Average	67.2	67.0	62.7	69.1

Source: Sunkist Growers, Inc.

Public information is not available on the volume of shipments by other marketers of California/Arizona fresh oranges in the domestic market. The FTC Brief reported that there were about twenty marketers competing with Sunkist. The largest of these was another open-membership cooperative association, Pure Gold, Inc., whose market share had declined to less than 5 percent by the mid-1980s. Other competitors included Sun World Citrus Inc., Paramount Citrus Association, Riverbend Farms, Airdrome Express Company, Mendelson-Zeller Company, Nash de Camp, Southland Produce Company, Suntreat Company, Transwest, Valdora Produce Company, and Wileman Bros. & Elliot, Inc.[7] Thus, expressed solely in terms of the number and size distribution of firms, the California/Arizona fresh orange industry consisted of a dominant firm with a fringe of relatively small firms.

Fresh Domestic Lemon Shipments

In 1979/80, 27 percent of all California/Arizona lemons were sold as fresh lemons in the domestic market. Most lemons (52 percent) were sold as processed products and another 20 percent were sold as fresh lemons in the export market. Between 1962/63 and 1982/83, total consumption of fresh lemons remained essentially unchanged, whereas processed lemon product

Table 4-4
Sunkist's Share of Lemon Production, Domestic Fresh Market, Export Fresh Market, and Processed Product Market, 1954/55 through 1982/83

Year	Total Production	Domestic Fresh Market	Export Fresh Market	Processed Production Market
1954/55	80.6%	83.7%	70.4%	79.0%
1955/56	79.2	82.7	74.6	74.8
1956/57	75.8	79.2	69.5	73.6
1957/58	76.4	79.7	70.9	75.5
1958/59	76.5	79.8	74.2	74.1
1959/60	73.3	76.7	77.4	69.5
1960/61	73.1	77.1	78.1	64.6
1961/62	71.0	76.2	76.9	64.5
1962/63	69.0	73.9	72.7	58.6
1963/64	66.5	71.7	74.0	60.8
1964/65	70.5	73.0	76.7	59.6
1965/66	79.3	86.2	84.3	70.6
1966/67	83.9	89.2	81.9	80.8
1967/68	80.6	85.1	79.4	77.8
1968/69	82.4	85.5	85.3	78.3
1969/70	83.0	85.2	83.7	80.6
1970/71	83.2	85.8	85.6	79.7
1971/72	83.2	84.1	86.4	80.7
1972/73	81.8	82.6	85.8	79.5
1973/74	83.5	84.6	83.7	82.5
1974/75	86.0	88.2	84.2	85.8
1975/76	78.8	78.7	81.5	76.8
1976/77	75.5	80.8	80.5	70.2
1977/78	73.5	75.6	76.8	71.2
1978/79	65.1	69.5	71.4	56.5
1979/80	71.1	72.9	70.2	70.5
1980/81	66.1	69.2	65.7	65.2
1981/82	60.8	66.9	63.4	57.3
1982/83	59.3	60.2	60.7	58.4
Average	75.5	78.8	76.8	71.6

Source: Sunkist Growers, Inc.

sales grew by about 200 percent and fresh export sales grew by about 75 percent.

Sunkist has been the leading marketer of fresh lemons in the domestic market as well as of fresh oranges since around the turn of the century.[8] Its share of fresh lemon shipments in 1954/55 was 83.7 percent. Sunkist's share subsequently reached a high of 89.2 percent in 1966/67; thereafter, it declined, reaching a low of 60.2 percent in 1982/83. (See table 4–4.)

As with fresh oranges, in the late 1970s, the second largest marketer of fresh lemons sold domestically was another open-membership cooperative association, Pure Gold. Other lemon marketers in the late 1970s were Airdrome, Mendelson-Zeller Company, Nash de Camp, Paramount Citrus Association, Southland Produce Company, Suntreat Company, Transwest (all of California), and various Florida marketers.[9] By the mid-1980s, Pure Gold had lost market position and was outranked by at least two other lemon marketers, Sun World Inc. and Coastal Lemon Company.

The Condition of Entry

The condition of entry measures the advantages in terms of costs or selling price that established firms have over potential entrant firms. This advantage can be measured by the degree to which established firms can persistently elevate prices above costs without making it attractive for new firms to enter the industry. There are four categories of entry barriers: (1) economies of scale, (2) absolute cost advantages, (3) product differentiation, and (4) strategic behavior by established firms.

Economies of Scale

Scale economies are measured by the minimum optimum scale of operations required to realize all unit cost savings. There are several types of such economies, some associated with the size of plant and others (so-called multiplant economies) with the size of the firm. Both kinds of scale economies exist in this industry.

Plant Economies of Scale. Various factors determine the minimum optimum size (MOS) citrus packinghouse. Not only are various technical considerations relating to packing operations important, but the effective MOS packinghouse is critically influenced by the density of its procurement area (the distance a packinghouse must reach out to obtain various volumes of fruit). If a packer must travel great distances to obtain sufficient volumes of fruit, it may have to trade off some packing economies resulting from large volume operations in order to keep procurement costs from skyrocketing.

This explains in part the wide range in size of packinghouses that operate successfully.

Based on various sources, we estimate that in the late 1970s, orange packinghouses had a MOS in the range of one to two thousand cars annually.[10] A packinghouse of one thousand cars would have accounted for 1.1 percent of sales in 1976/77; a house with two thousand cars would have accounted for 2.2 percent of the total California/Arizona shipments in that year.

In fact, some recently built plants are smaller than this. For example, a recently built packinghouse has a rated annual capacity of only three-hundred cars. Several successful proprietary concerns also operate relatively small plants.

In specialized lemon packinghouses, scale economies (as measured by a MOS plant's percentage of the market) are higher than in the orange industry because the size of the lemon industry is smaller. However, packers in many areas need not operate a specialized lemon packinghouse. Most proprietary concerns apparently pack both oranges and lemons in the same packinghouse. When this is done, the scale requirements are lower than the above estimates for oranges.

In 1979/80, there were sixty-three packinghouses affiliated with Sunkist compared with 116 in 1960/61. Whereas in 1960/61, Sunkist houses packed an average of 500 cars each, by 1979/80 they packed 1,764 cars each, more than tripling their volume over the period. Nonetheless, the average-size Sunkist packinghouse in 1979/80 still handled only about 1 percent of total California/Arizona citrus shipments; this was well below the average MOS plant found by Scherer et al., in their study of twelve industries.[11] Only two of the industries studied, cotton fabrics and nonrubber shoes, had MOS plants of 1 percent or less. Both of these were competitively structured industries and classified by Scherer as having low entry barriers.

Multiplant Economies of Scale. Although no significant economies of scale exist at the packinghouse level, there appear to exist certain multiplant economies of scale that only Sunkist is large enough to enjoy. The most apparent of these involve national brand advertising, research and development, and the special requirements of developing and operating in foreign markets. We consider briefly each of these.

For many food products, potentially large and significant multiplant scale economies relate to advertising, a major source of increasing concentration in consumer goods industries.[12] Sunkist initiated its first advertising efforts in 1907. Like other agricultural cooperatives representing a large part of an industry about which consumers are poorly informed of product quality and other characteristics, Sunkist's early advertising efforts were aimed mainly at increasing consumer demand.[13]

The 1907 advertising campaign, which had a $6 thousand budget, was undertaken in conjunction with the Southern Pacific Railroad and targeted the state of Iowa.[14] Fruit was shipped in special, bannered trains and the railroad company billboarded the entire state with such slogans as "Oranges for Health—California for Wealth."[15] During the advertising campaign, orange consumption in Iowa rose 50 percent whereas country-wide consumption went up 17.7 percent.[16]

This successful campaign persuaded Sunkist that advertising could increase significantly the demand for oranges. Whereas the 1907 effort involved generic advertising, in 1908, Sunkist received the now famous Sunkist trademark, laying the basis for brand advertising. In the following years, it spent large amounts promoting the Sunkist brand as a badge of quality fresh citrus. From 1907/08 through 1983/84, Sunkist spent $274 million for advertising, merchandising, and sales promotion. (See table 4–5.) These expenditures averaged 1.5 percent of fresh citrus sales over the 19-year period 1915/16 through 1933/34. Expenditures rose in succeeding

Table 4–5
Advertising, Merchandising, and Sales Promotion of Fresh Citrus Products Sold by Sunkist Growers, Inc., 1907/08 through 1983/84
($ thousands)

Period	Average Annual Advertising, Merchandising, and Sales Promotion	Average Annual Total Sales of Fresh Citrus	Advertising as a Percent of Sales
1907/08–1914/15[a]	$ 118	N.A.	N.A.
1915/16–1933/34[a]	980	$ 64,430	1.52%
1934/35–1959/60[a]	2,469	122,407	2.02
1960/61–1964/65	3,281	139,120	2.36
1965/66–1969/70	7,258	187,260	3.88
1970/71–1974/75	8,604	270,657	3.18
1975/76–1979/80[b]	9,662	361,351	2.67
1980/81–1983/84	13,435	469,226	2.86
Average 1915/16–1983/84	3,577[b]	157,562	2.21

Source: Sunkist Growers, Inc.

Note: Sunkist fresh citrus products included lemons, navel and valencia oranges, grapefruit, and tangerines. Oranges and lemons have accounted for well over 90 percent of Sunkist fresh citrus sales over the period. It was not possible to break out advertising expenditures by these categories in all years. Total sales include exports because advertising and related expenses include those made on fresh export sales.

NA = not available.

[a]Periods of this length are used for these years because data are not available for shorter periods.

[b]Total advertising outlays and sales for the 1978/79 crop were excluded because advertising expenditures were reduced substantially due to a severe freeze. If the 1978/79 outlays are included, the total for 1907/08 through 1983/84 is $274 million.

years, reaching a peak of 3.9 percent for the period 1965/66 through 1969/70. During the 1970s, expenditures as a percentage of sales declined to less than 3 percent of sales. The accumulated advertising and related expenditures of $274 million over a 77–year period has created one of the United States's best-known brands. The average annual outlays of $11 million during 1975-84 represented less than 3 percent of sales because Sunkist was able to spread the outlays over an increasingly large absolute volume of sales. This, coupled with the fact that smaller marketers have not developed comparable brands, indicates that Sunkist enjoys substantial economies of scale in advertising.

Both economic theory and empirical evidence are equivocal with respect to economies of scale in the areas of research and development (R&D). Simply put, there are conflicting economic theories and the empirical evidence is mixed, revealing a great diversity of experience.[17] An examination of the available evidence indicates that Sunkist Central's size has enabled it to engage in more extensive research than can the smaller citrus marketers. Sunkist research efforts, which began in the 1920s, currently are centered in laboratories at Ontario, California. In 1978-79, Sunkist devoted $1,700,000 to research and development. Personnel conducting these efforts included engineers, physicists, industrial designers, economists, horticulturalists, entomologists, mycologists, and physiologists.[18] Among the tasks performed by these researchers are studying problems of precooling and air conditioning fruit; improving refrigeration in cold storage and in transit; testing materials and processes for handling and preparing fruit after harvesting; supervising the manufacture of waxes to maintain fruit quality; cooperating with entomologists to determine effects of pest control programs on fruit's keeping quality; studying improvements in ocean, rail, and truck transportation; and developing new processes for economical preparation and marketing of fruit.[19] Through the years, Sunkist engineers have made notable improvements in packinghouse equipment, including development of rapid pack devices, bulk-handling and storage systems, frost separators, and conveyor belt systems. Sunkist industrial engineers and economists have conducted feasibility studies leading to efficient plant design and machinery usage.

Sunkist received its first patents in the early 1920s. In 1934, it formed a patent division within the research department.[20] Among its early accomplishments was the discovery of basic processes permitting the preparation of a pectin powder of superior purity and utility than was otherwise available.[21]

Reflecting the relatively large role that Sunkist Central plays in research and development in the California/Arizona citrus industry is the number of patents it received from 1950 to 1978.[22] As shown in table 4-6, Sunkist received 79 patents (95 percent of the industry total) during the

Table 4-6
Number of U.S. Patents Awarded to Sunkist and Its Leading Competitors, 1950–78

	Sunkist	Di Giorgio Corp.	Mendelson-Zeller Co.	Paramount Citrus	Pure Gold Inc.	Seald-sweet	Southland Produce Co.	Sun World Inc.	Ventura Coastal Corp.[a]
1950		1							
1951									
1952	3								
1953	2								
1954	2								
1955	1								
1956	5								
1957	2								
1958	1								
1959	2								
1960	1								
1961	5				1				
1962	3								1
1963	1								
1964	5								
1965	1								
1966	3								
1967	2								1
1968	3								
1969	5								
1970	1								
1971	6								
1972	5								
1973	5								
1974	4								
1975	4								
1976	4								
1977	2								
1978	1								
Total	79	1	0	0	1	0	0	0	2

Source: Records of Sunkist Growers, Inc.

Note: All blank spaces denote no U.S. patents issued.

[a]Including Ventura Processors, Inc.

29–year period 1950–78. Between 1968 and 1978, it received 40 patents, whereas the other 8 firms received none.

Although Sunkist marketed about 75 percent of all citrus over this twenty–nine–year period, it accounted for nearly all patents received by corporations in the California/Arizona citrus industry. This performance by the industry's largest enterprise differs from that typically found in the food industry. Large food–manufacturing corporations generally receive proportionately fewer patents than medium–size and smaller companies.[23] In addition, Sunkist has a long history of cooperating with university and government researchers involved in horticultural and other research important to the citrus industry.

Sunkist's record supports the hypothesis that it enjoys some economies of scale in research and development. However, we found no evidence that in recent years Sunkist held patents that significantly impeded entry in citrus marketing or processing, even in the short run. This may reflect conditions common to many food–processing industries today. Despite Sunkist's acknowledged leadership in technological improvement, many Sunkist–inspired innovations were rapidly adopted by the industry. In addition, many innovations originated with public and private researchers outside the citrus industry and were available to all citrus packers. As a result, new entrants in citrus face no difficulty purchasing technologically efficient equipment.[24]

Sunkist may enjoy certain advantages from its superior R&D in other areas. Although it is not possible to quantify the magnitude of such economies, it is possible to assess the implications for competitive behavior and performance. Such an assessment is made below.

Finally, there seem to exist economies of scale in penetrating new foreign markets. Small citrus packers may find it too costly to undertake programs required to enter a new foreign market. This likely explains why Sunkist has been the leading force in expanding the demand for California/Arizona citrus. This has included R&D aimed at creating new products and conducting informational advertising that explains the nutritional attributes of citrus, as discussed elsewhere. In addition, Sunkist has actively pursued the development of new markets abroad. Two accomplishments in the latter area deserve special attention.

Commencing in the late 1950s, Sunkist initiated extensive efforts to open the Japanese market to U.S. citrus growers. This involved extensive negotiations and other efforts to break down the barriers confronting foreigners wishing to sell in Japan, as well as undertaking substantial promotional efforts. These efforts first paid off when, in 1964, Japan liberalized the quotas of lemon shipments from the United States. By 1984/85, Sunkist recorded sales of $160 million to Japan, where the Sunkist brand had become one of the best-known food product brands.

Another important and successful undertaking by Sunkist in the foreign market was the development of a complex barter arrangement to sell citrus to Eastern Bloc nations. These sales totaled $8 million in 1978/79. At that time, Sunkist was the only U.S. marketer selling citrus in the Eastern Bloc market.

The development of the Japanese and Eastern European markets has benefited all citrus growers by increasing total demand, and all Americans by expanding their international trade. It is highly doubtful that a smaller marketer would have had the incentive and ability to accomplish these results. In any event, Sunkist must be credited as the innovator in both instances.

Any advantages Sunkist gains in opening and developing new markets abroad are likely to be short lived, however, since once a foreign country begins buying California/Arizona fruit, other packinghouses will find it much easier to enter than did the first entrant. Such free riding by others on Sunkist's efforts probably prevent it from maintaining a significant long-term advantage from this source. This expectation is borne out by the data in tables 4-2, 4-3, and 4-4, which show that Sunkist was unable to maintain a higher market share in the export market than in the domestic fresh market.

Absolute Cost Advantages

Absolute cost advantages arise whenever an established firm can obtain resources at a lower cost than can new firms. Two types of absolute-cost entry barriers are potentially relevant in the citrus-packing industry: the cost of capital and access to resources, in this case, fresh citrus supplies.

The capital investment required in a new packinghouse is about $1 million to $3 million.[25] Although this amount may be beyond the means of most individual citrus growers or other individual investors, this is a very modest amount of capital compared to that required by new entrants in most moderate to highly concentrated modern industries.[26] Even if several packinghouses were required to achieve all significant multiplant economies of scale, the capital barrier would not be formidable in fresh citrus marketing by modern-day standards.[27]

Another potential absolute cost barrier in the citrus industry is access to citrus supplies. Two factors tend to minimize this as a potential barrier: the high degree of grower mobility and packinghouse mobility.

California/Arizona citrus growers are free to move from one packinghouse to another at the beginning of each marketing season. The formal and informal marketing contracts of Sunkist and Pure Gold, as well as those of proprietary marketers, are of only one-year duration. Thus, there are no long-term marketing contracts to forestall the new entrant from gaining access to growers. There is much evidence of considerable mobility among grower-members of the largest cooperative marketer, Sunkist. Sunkist's experience very likely is not unique.

There also exists considerable mobility among citrus packinghouses. Rather than build a new packinghouse, a new marketer of citrus may persuade an established proprietary or cooperative packinghouse (and its grower-suppliers) to affiliate or merge with it. This could involve independent proprietary houses, a house affiliated with another proprietary marketer, a proprietary packinghouse operating as a licensed packer for Sunkist or Pure Gold, or a local cooperative packinghouse that is a member of Sunkist or Pure Gold. The latter two types of houses are fair game for a new entrant or an expanding existing marketer because Sunkist and Pure Gold have only one-year contracts with licensed proprietary houses and with local cooperative packinghouses.

The freedom of a new entrant or established company to affiliate with or acquire houses that are affilitated with Sunkist or Pure Gold is without precedent outside those industries in which federated cooperatives participate. The significance of this for entry conditions is enormous. It is analogous to giving a new entrant into an industry freedom to buy one of the established firms' plants without requiring the firm's approval.

One result of this is to reduce the capital cost otherwise required to build a new packinghouse, since a packinghouse may affiliate with a new marketer at no cost. But most importantly, this makes it possible for the new entrant to avoid the "capacity effect" otherwise experienced by new entrants. Otherwise, when an entrant builds new capacity, it creates some excess capacity in the industry, at least for a short time (unless it enters an entirely new production area).

Thus, the federated structure of Sunkist lowers entry barriers in fresh citrus marketing. Were Sunkist a proprietary concern or a centralized cooperative, entry of new marketers would be much more difficult. The extent of packinghouse mobility is analyzed in detail below.

Product Differentiation

Advertising-created or other types of product differentiation may erect entry barriers if established firms have strong brands that command substantial price premiums over the brands of new entrants. Sunkist's advertising efforts extending back to 1907 were aimed partly at differentiating the Sunkist brand, although much of its advertising, particularly in early decades, had the purpose and effect of increasing the total demand for quality, fresh California/Arizona citrus. In evaluating Sunkist's advertising effort and its effects, it is important to note the advertising outlays were very modest compared to the advertising push given many differentiated food products. Table 4–7 shows the measured media advertising outlays as a percentage of sales for the four leading firms in twenty-eight food industries. The median expenditure is 3 percent of sales, with one-fourth of all industries exceeding 5 percent.

Table 4–8 shows for 1979 the measured media advertising expenditures for various brands of soft drinks, beer, coffee, and snack foods.[28] Advertising outlays of each of these brands exceeded $8 million and many exceeded $20

Table 4–7
Measured Media Advertising by Top Four Advertisers of Branded Products Expressed as a Percentage of Estimated Domestic Sales to Consumers of Four Largest Companies, 1975

Product Class SIC Number	Title	Percentage
20670	Chewing gum	12.10%
20860	Soft drinks	9.47
20430	Breakfast cereals	8.36
20516	Pastries, especially refrigerated	7.51
20653	Packaged candies, excluding chocolate	6.58
20991	Ready-to-mix desserts	5.53
20334	Canned fruit juices	5.29 (PL)
20662	Chocolate candies and bars	4.89
20980	Pasta products	4.09 (PL)
20651	Candy bars, excluding chocolate	4.03
20264	Yogurt and flavored milks	3.70
20371	Frozen juices and fruits	3.73 (PL)
20992	Chips	3.61
20514	Soft cakes	3.04
20381	Frozen pies and other baked goods	2.88
20335	Canned vegetable juices	2.85
20521	Crackers	2.48
20338	Jams, jellies, and preserves	2.40 (PL)
20652	5-cent and 10-cent candies	2.23
20322	Canned soups	2.16
20658	Salted nuts	2.08 (PL)
20522	Cookies	1.56
20512	Rolls and muffins, especially refrigerated	1.51 (PL)
20511	Bread	1.31 (PL)
20515	Pies	0.85
20262	Fluid milk	0.75 (PL)
20240	Ice cream	0.74 (PL)
20654	Bulk candies	0.32 (PL)

Source: J.M. Connor, *Competition and the Role of the Largest Firms in the U.S. Food and Tobacco Industries,* Working Paper no. 29 (Madison, Wis.: Food Systems Research Group, University of Wisconsin-Madison, February 1979).

Note: The symbol "PL" designates product classes that contain items marketed under "private" or store labels in supermarkets. Specifically, at least 10 percent of national supermarket sales were private label sales according to a special study by Selling Areas-Marketing, Inc. (SAMI). To the extent that the four leading manufacturers produce both national brand as well as private label items, the advertising-to-sales ratios are biased downward to an unknown extent. Thus, the figures in the table measure the minimum advertising-to-sales ratio for the top four advertisers.

Table 4–8
Measured Media Advertising Expenditures for
Selected Products, 1979
($ thousands)

Products	Advertising Expenditures
Soft Drinks	
Pepsi Cola	$43,891
Coca-Cola	41,851
7-Up	26,119
Kool Aid	23,229
Minute Maid Ades & Juices	12,848
Hawaiian Canned Punch	9,110
Countrytime Drinks	8,166
Sunkist Orange Soda	8,031
Beer	
Budweiser	36,517
Miller High Life	31,386
Schlitz	29,807
Miller Lite	27,740
Lowenbrau	18,828
Natural Light	17,617
Michelob	17,191
Bush Bavarian	16,732
Michelob Light	16,575
Coors	14,114
Coffee	
Maxwell House	36,071
Folger	32,961
Sanka	20,701
Snack Foods and Appetizers	
Wrigley's Gums	40,715
Jello Desserts, etc.	27,525
Doritos Tortilla Chips	12,733
Hostess Baked Goods & Cakes	9,653
Fritos	8,991

Source: Leading National Advertisers, Inc., *Company/ Brand$* 1979 (New York: Leading National Advertisers); *The Impact American Beer Market, Review and Forecast* (M. Shanken Communications, 1981).

million. Few of these brands had total sales as large as Sunkist's sales of fresh citrus products ($423 million in 1978/79). Yet, even the smallest of those listed, Fritos, spent more ($9.0 million) on measured media advertising alone than Sunkist spent on advertising, promotion, and merchandising. General Cinema Corp., which is licensed to use the Sunkist trademark for soft drinks, spent over $8 million on measured media advertising of Sunkist orange soda;[29] this was about equal to Sunkist Growers, Inc.'s, total annual expenditures for advertising, promotion, and merchandising during 1975/76 through 1979/80, as shown in table 4–5. Sunkist Growers,

Inc.'s, measured media advertising expenditures during 1981 were $3.3 million, making it the 514th largest advertiser.[30] In contrast, Sunkist ranked among the top seventy-five advertisers in the mid-1930s.[31]

Even though Sunkist's advertising outlays are relatively modest, however measured, it is conceivable that Sunkist's long history of advertising has differentiated its products sufficiently to permit it to command substantial price premiums relative to existing and potential entrants. There are occasionally instances when, for various reasons including first-mover advantages, firms that spend little for advertising possess powerful brands. Hershey chocolate and Coors beer at one time held such unique status.

No precise estimates are available of the size of price premiums, if any, that the Sunkist brand commands in the sales of fresh citrus. And insofar as such premiums exist, there is a problem in determining how much of the premium is attributable to the brand as opposed to other product and service characteristics offered buyers by Sunkist. Sunkist and trade sources indicate that Sunkist often gets a premium of 25 cents per carton and, in some instances, a premium of as much as 50 cents per carton. There remains the question of why buyers pay such premiums. First, there is evidence that buyers often prefer to deal with Sunkist because it provides a dependable source of good-quality fruit over an entire season and that buyers are willing to pay Sunkist a premium because of this. Industry sources further acknowledge that the quality of Sunkist's first-grade fruit exceeds the top quality of fruit packed by other houses. A survey of packers found that only Sunkist used standards exceeding the top USDA grade.[32] In this case, the Sunkist brand serves as a badge of superior quality.

So what exactly do the trade buyers, as well as some Sunkist personnel, mean when they refer to a 25–cent premium for Sunkist fruit? The most plausible inference is that they are referring to paying premiums for fruit sold under the Sunkist trademark in contrast to prices paid for top-quality fruit packed under non-Sunkist trademarks. If so, at least part of the price difference is attributable to a recognition that the brand represents real differences in product quality, since Sunkist's top-grade fruit generally is of higher quality than the fruit of other packers. This raises the issue, just how large is the alleged price premium received by Sunkist? The accepted method of measuring price premiums as a proxy for the height of a product-differentiation–created barrier to entry, as it affects potential entrants or existing firms not enjoying this advantage, is to measure the price premium as a percentage of the selling price.[33] Using Sunkist's price premium as a percentage of the sale price for first-grade Sunkist oranges sold in the late 1970s, a price premium of 25 cents per case is equal to about 5 percent for the lowest-price and 2.5 percent for the highest-price fruit.

For purposes of argument, we shall assume that the Sunkist brand results in a price premium of 5 percent. Since Sunkist spends nearly 3 percent of sales on advertising and promoting oranges and lemons, a firm without a premium brand and not engaging in advertising would have a price disadvantage of only 2 percent, assuming that Sunkist's entire 5 percent difference was due solely to advertising-achieved product differentiation.

To place Sunkist's price premiums in perspective, they must be compared with price premiums commonly found in other differentiated consumer products. Table 4–9 shows the price premiums received for the leading brands of various consumer products. The greatest premium shown was received for the ReaLemon processed lemon juice brand. It enjoyed a price premium of about 30 percentage points over its leading competitive brand. As revealed in the record of an FTC case involving ReaLemon juice, it was physically identical to other brands.[34] Although ReaLemon commands the highest price premium of the brands shown in table 4–9, others also command significant premiums. Clorox brand of household bleach commands a 9–percentage-point premium over other leading advertised brands, a 13–point premium over regional brands of bleaches, and a 28–point premium over private label brands of bleach. As

Table 4–9
Wholesale Prices of Various Brand Categories of Selected Grocery Products Expressed as a Percentage of the Leading Brand's Price, 1979/1980

		Price as Percentage of the Leading Brand's Price		
Product	Leading Brand	Private Label	Regional Label	Other Leading National Brands
Lemon Juice	ReaLemon[a]	NA	70%	NA
Catsup	Heinz	70%	88	81%
Bleach	Clorox	72	87	91
Frozen Orange Juice	Minute Maid	77	77	95
Green Beans	Del Monte	80	91	101
Tomato Sauce	Hunt's	84	NA	93
Corn	Green Giant	84	87	96
Salt	Morton	84	100	NA
Pears	Del Monte	90	95	99
Peaches	Del Monte	94	NA	102
Raisins	Sun Maid	90	NA	99

Source: W.F. Mueller, "The Enforcement of Section 2 of the Capper-Volstead Act," in *Antitrust Treatment of Agricultural Marketing Cooperatives,* ed. E.V. Jesse, N.C. Project 117, Monograph 15 (Food Systems Research Group, University of Wisconsin-Madison, September 1984), 135–146.

NA = Not available.

[a]The ReaLemon price is based on *Borden, Inc.,* 92 FTC 669 (1976) initial decision. The 70 percent figure is the average wholesale price premium over its leading competitive brand for the period April–July 1973. The figure was 65 percent for April/May 1973 before a price cut of 20 percent; in June/July 1973, ReaLemon's price was 30 percent above its nearest competitor's.

revealed in the FTC's *Proctor & Gamble* case, all household bleaches are virtually identical in chemical composition. Thus, Clorox's large price premium is due entirely to advertising-created product differentiation rather than any significant real differences in product quality.

Even in such competitive industries as canned fruits and vegetables, the leading brands command significant price premiums over regional brands. Some of these differences may be attributable to real cost differences of producing products of different quality.

Although table 4–9 compared only 11 products, it is fairly representative of the average price premiums common to advertised grocery products. Table 4–10 expresses the average prices of various categories of brands as a percentage of the price of the leading brands of 145 food products. On average, the second- to fourth-ranked brands were priced 6 percent below the top-priced brand, regional brands were 11 percent lower, and private labels were 17 percent lower.

The price premium for the Sunkist brand is modest compared with most other leading brands of food products. Clearly, the price premium received by Sunkist is very small compared to those received for powerful brands like ReaLemon, Heinz catsup, or Clorox bleach. Sunkist's premiums are even smaller than those received for such relatively low-premium items as canned fruits and vegetables, which are generally recognized as being sold in quite competitively structured markets. Therefore, when viewed in the context of industrial experience elsewhere in the food industry,

Table 4–10
Average Relative Retail Prices of Various Brand Categories of Processed Food Products Expressed as a Percentage of the Leading Brand's Price, 1979/80

		Average Prices as a Percentage of Leading Brand Price			
Advertising of Leading Brand ($ thousands)[a]	Number of Product Categories	Second to Fourth Ranked Brands' Relative Price	Other Brands' Relative Price	Private Labels' Relative Price	Generics' Relative Price
0	27	93%	94%	84%	76%
0–$500	37	94	90	86	70
$500–$1,000	14	97	92	82	68
$1,000–$2,000	20	95	89	81	67
$2,000–$4,000	18	90	82	80	66
$4,000–$8,000	17	92	86	80	68
$8,000 +	12	96	85	81	66
Total Average	145	94	89	82	69

Source: J.M. Connor, R.T. Rogers, B.W. Marion, and W.F. Mueller, *The Food Manufacturing Industries: Structure, Strategies, Performance and Policy* (Lexington, Mass.: Lexington Books, 1984), 293.

Note: Relative prices are averages for April/May 1979 and 1980, based on selected items from Nielsen Early Intelligence System data.

[a]Advertising values are total major expenditures measured by Leading National Advertisers, Inc. (1978).

it is proper to infer that Sunkist's product differentiation does not give it a significant price advantage relative to other existing firms or prospective entrants.

This finding reflects the competitive significance of an open-membership cooperative. Sunkist's organizational structure undermines large price premiums created by advertising or other means. The conduct and performance effects often associated with product differentiation of profit-seeking corporations do not apply to the California/Arizona citrus sector. Because the Sunkist System is an open-membership, highly decentralized organization, any significant price premiums resulting from its advertising would attract new members and the expansion of existing ones. Thus, an open-membership, nonprofit cooperative inevitably erodes price premiums created by product differentiation.[35] For example, a cooperative such as Sunkist would quickly dissipate the "monopolistic" price premium received for ReaLemon, which the FTC staff and administrative law Judge sought to erode through an order requiring compulsory licensing of the ReaLemon trademark. Ironically, though the Commission judged compulsory licensing as "too severe" a remedy, such licensing would not necessarily have resulted in as low a price as would have occurred if the brand had been held by an open-membership cooperative.[36]

Strategic Behavior by Established Firms

In addition to the barriers to entry described above, barriers may be erected as the result of strategic behavior by incumbent firms. Salop differentiates "strategic" entry barriers from "innocent" entry barriers: "An *innocent* entry barrier is unintentionally erected as a side effect of innocent profit maximizing. In contrast, a *strategic* entry barrier is purposely erected to reduce the possibility of entry."[37] Strategically erected barriers may take such forms as predatory pricing and advertising, tying contracts, exclusive dealing arrangements, and other entry-forestalling strategies adopted by incumbents that make it more difficult for new entry to occur.

Central to the FTC case was that Sunkist attained and maintained a monopoly with strategic behavior involving, among other alleged practices, exclusive dealing arrangements with its grower members' packinghouses. We discuss these practices in chapter 6.

Sunkist Reduces Entry Barriers for Growers and Packinghouses

The Significance of Open Membership

Sunkist's unique organizational structure has the effect of virtually eliminating entry barriers as a source of market power in the citrus industry.

Sunkist's open-membership policy enables the new citrus grower to find a ready home for its citrus by the simple act of becoming a grower-member of Sunkist. Hence, if Sunkist is able to obtain a price premium for its products—whether by greater efficiency, advertising-enhanced demand, or other ways—other California/Arizona citrus growers are free to participate in these premiums.

Perhaps the full significance of this fact for competitive performance can best be appreciated by contrasting Sunkist's policy with the more familiar situation involving a proprietary concern with a strong trademark and a large, efficient distribution system. Let us consider the case of the Borden Company's ReaLemon processed lemon juice operations.[38] Given the great value of the ReaLemon trademark and Borden's extensive distribution system, a small lemon juice processor without a brand would gladly market its product under the ReaLemon trademark and through Borden's extensive distribution system if it could do so at a nominal charge. Should Borden behave like an open-membership cooperative and permit all comers to use its brand for a fee equal to Borden's advertising outlays per dollar of sales, virtually all barriers to entry in the ReaLemon brand market would be eliminated and supply would increase until prices were pushed down to average costs.

This example may seem unreal to students of modern industrial markets because they probably would never have studied open-membership cooperatives. Yet, this is precisely the competitive significance of Sunkist's open-membership policy. At virtually no initial costs, a new grower can reap the full benefits of Sunkist's over eighty years of experience in citrus marketing. The grower need remain a Sunkist member only so long as he desires. Thus, because Sunkist's open membership prevents it from controlling the supply of citrus marketed through it, the idea that entry barriers confer power on Sunkist is without meaning or substance. Entry barriers confer power in setting prices only if the business shielded by them is able to exercise control over its own output. Its open-membership policy deprives Sunkist of the power to control its supply and, therefore, its output.

Sunkist also lowers entry barriers confronting proprietary or commercial packinghouses. An entrepreneur contemplating entering the citrus-packing business may offer to serve as a licensed commercial Sunkist packinghouse. Such an arrangement benefits actual or would-be Sunkist members because use of a licensed commercial packinghouse makes it unnecessary for the grower to provide the capital for a new packinghouse, nor need the grower assume the risks associated with owning such a business. The proprietary firm operating the packinghouse benefits as well, since it need initially restrict itself solely to the fruit-packing business, leaving to Sunkist the job of marketing the member-grower's citrus. If, after a time, the proprietary concern becomes successful in the packing part of the fresh citrus business, it may at any time discontinue, on one year's notice, as a licensed commercial Sunkist house and become a licensed commercial house to growers belonging to another citrus cooperative or it may strike out on its own in the marketing phase of the business as well. Thus, the use of licensed commercial houses by Sunkist growers makes it easier for proprietary firms to enter the industry than if Sunkist were either a proprietary business or a federated cooperative relying solely on grower-owned cooperative packinghouses.

Mobility of Packinghouse Affiliations

The impact of open membership is not mere speculation and conjecture. Proprietary citrus packers and marketers have followed this kind of phased entry via initial affiliation with the Sunkist System. Nothing better illustrates the absence of significant entry barriers in the California/Arizona fresh citrus industry than the ease and frequency with which packinghouses affiliate and disaffiliate with Sunkist and other California/Arizona marketing agents. We shall refer to this process as packinghouse mobility.

Table 4-11 summarizes for 1960/61 to 1979/80 the total number of packinghouses affiliated with, joining, and disaffiliating with the Sunkist System. The persistent decline in the number affiliated with Sunkist reflects the continuing increase in the minimum–efficient-size packinghouses.

Over the 20-year period, 53 packinghouses previously operating independently or affiliated with others joined the Sunkist System as did another 8 houses that had built new facilities.[39] (See table 4-12.) On the other hand, 44 packinghouses left Sunkist to join another organization. (See table 4-13.) All but one of the packinghouses joining Sunkist were licensed commercial concerns that served Sunkist's grower-members.

The largest single source of packinghouses affiliating with the Sunkist System was the affiliation in 1966 of 13 packinghouses of Blue Goose Growers, Inc.[40] One Blue Goose packinghouse did not affiliate with Sunkist in 1966 and one that did disaffiliated the following year.[41] Since 1980, all of the former Blue Goose packinghouses have disaffiliated with Sunkist. The second major source of newly affiliating licensed commercial packinghouses (five affiliations) was Pure Gold, Inc., the other California/Arizona citrus-marketing cooperative. The remaining packinghouses came from a variety of sources, with fifteen involving independent commercial houses, eight involving newly constructed commercial houses, and 5 originating with unidentified sources.

Whereas 61 packinghouses affiliated with Sunkist from 1960/61 to 1979/80, 114 packinghouses disaffiliated with Sunkist, including 26 that

Table 4-11
Number of Total Sunkist Packinghouses and Packinghouses Joining and Departing Sunkist, 1960/61 through 1979/80

| Year | Total Sunkist Packinghouses | | | Number of Packinghouses | | | | | |
| | Cooperative[a] | Commercial[a] | Total | Joining Sunkist | | | Departing Sunkist | | |
				Cooperative	Commercial	Total	Cooperative	Commercial	Total
1960/61	83	33	116		1	1	2	1	3
1961/62	83	33	116		3	3	5[b]	1	6
1962/63	75	35	110		5	5	5[b]	2	7
1963/64	69	38	107		2	2	4[b]	1	5
1964/65	67	40	107		5	5	7	2	9
1965/66	63	43	106		16	16	1	3	4
1966/67	61	57	118		3	3	0	5	5
1967/68	61	53	114		1	1	4[b]	3	7
1968/69	56	50	106		2	2	1	2	3
1969/70	53	50	103		5	5	3[b]	5	8
1970/71	51	54	105		3	3	4[b]	3	7
1971/72	45	53	98		2	2	3[b]	5	8
1972/73	44	51	95		4	4	1[b]	2	3
1973/74	43	52	95		2	2	0	3	3
1974/75	43	50	93		0	0	2	6	8
1975/76	41	45	86		1	1	1	6	7
1976/77	40	36	76	1[c]	0	1	2[b]	4	6
1977/78	39	31	70		4	4	5	8[b]	13
1978/79	35	31	66		1	1	0	2	2
1979/80	33	30	63		0	0	0	0	0
Total				1	60	61	50(26[d])	64	114(83[d])

Source: Developed from the records of Sunkist Growers, Inc.

Note: Total Sunkist packinghouses data are based on a report issued each February. Joining and departing figures are based on November–October season.

[a]Does not include Arizona voting units, Butte-Glenn Citrus Association, Redlands Associates, or Ventura County Independents Association.

[b]Merger(s), with new entity remaining in Sunkist.

[c]Reorganized from a licensed commercial packinghouse to a local cooperative packinghouse.

[d]Excluding mergers.

Table 4-12
Origins of Packinghouses Joining Sunkist, 1960/61 through 1979/80

Year	Types of Joining Houses					Newly Con-structed Facilities	Purchased Existing Facilities[a]	Inde-pendent	Miscel-laneous	Unknown
	Cooper-ative Houses	Comm-ercial Houses	Pure Gold Inc.	Blue Goose Growers	Southland Produce Company					
1960/61	0	1	0	0	0	0	0	1	0	0
1961/62	0	3	0	1	0	0	0	1	0	1
1962/63	0	5	0	0	0	1	1	2	0	1
1963/64	0	2	1	0	0	2	0	0	1	0
1964/65	0	5	1	0	0	1	0	1	0	1
1965/66	0	16	0	13	0	0	1	2	0	0
1966/67	0	3	0	0	0	1	0	1	0	0
1967/68	0	1	0	0	0	0	0	1	0	1
1968/69	0	2	2	0	0	0	2	0	0	0
1969/70	0	5	0	0	0	1	0	1	2	0
1970/71	0	3	0	0	0	0	0	1	1	1
1971/72	0	2	0	0	0	0	2	1	0	0
1972/73	0	4	0	0	0	1	0	2	0	0
1973/74	0	2	0	0	0	0	0	0	0	0
1974/75	0	0	0	0	0	0	0	0	1	0
1975/76	1[b]	1	0	0	0	0	0	0	0	0
1976/77	0	0	1	0	0	0	0	0	1	0
1977/78	0	4	0	0	1	1	0	1	0	0
1978/79	0	1	0	0	0	0	0	0	0	0
1979/80	0	0	0	0	0	0	0	0	0	0
Total	1	60	5	14	1	8	6	15	6	5

Source: Developed from the records of Sunkist Growers, Inc.

[a] This represented situations where a licensed proprietary house or the members of a local cooperative purchased a facility that could be used to pack citrus. None of these facilities was acquired by Sunkist Growers, Inc.

[b] Reorganized from commercial to cooperative house.

Table 4-13
Subsequent Marketing Affiliations of Packinghouses Departing Sunkist, 1960/61 through 1979/80

Year	Departing Houses			Pure Gold	Para-mount	Mendel-son-Zeller	Sun World	Nash de Camp	Inde-pen-dent	Merged with another Sunkist House	Purchased by another Sunkist House	Closed	Miscel-laneous
	Cooper-ative	Comm-ercial	Total										
1960/61	2	1	3	0	0	0	0	0	0	0	1	2	0
1961/62	5	1	6	1	1	0	0	0	0	2	1	1	0
1962/63	5	2	7	0	2	0	0	0	0	2	0	2	0
1963/64	4	1	5	0	0	0	0	0	0	3	0	2	0
1964/65	7	2	9	0	0	0	0	0	2	0	0	7	0
1965/66	1	3	4	1	0	0	0	0	1	0	0	2	0
1966/67	0	5	5	0	0	0	0	1	2	1	0	1	0
1967/68	4	3	7	0	0	0	0	0	1	0	0	5	0
1968/69	1	2	3	0	0	0	0	0	0	0	0	3	0
1969/70	3	5	8	1	0	0	0	0	0	1	3	3	0
1970/71	4	3	7	0	0	2	0	0	0	0	0	2	2
1971/72	3	5	8	1	0	0	0	0	1	1	1	4	1
1972/73	1	2	3	0	0	0	0	0	0	1	0	1	0
1973/74	0	3	3	2	0	0	0	0	0	0	0	1	2
1974/75	2	6	8	2	0	0	0	0	2	0	0	3	0
1975/76	1	6	7	0	0	0	0	0	2	0	1	3	1
1976/77	2	4	6	1	1	0	0	0	0	1	1	1	0
1977/78	5	8	13	1	0	0	2	0	3	1	2	1	3
1978/79	0	2	2	0	0	0	1	0	0	0	0	1	0
1979/80	0	0	0	0	0	0	0	0	0	0	0	0	0
Total	50[a]	64	114	9	4	2	3	1	15	14	12	45	10

Source: Developed from the records of Sunkist Growers, Inc.

[a]Twenty-six of the fifty involved mergers or acquisitions among Sunkist cooperatives. All others were closed.

merged with or were acquired by other Sunkist packinghouses, as seen in table 4–13. Although the largest number of departures (45) involved the closing of packinghouses, significant numbers were acquired by proprietary competitors (10) or else became independent packinghouses (15). The affiliations and disaffiliations involving the Pure Gold cooperative are particularly interesting. During the period, 5 packinghouses left Pure Gold to join Sunkist (table 4–12) and 9 left Sunkist to join Pure Gold (table 4–13).

This experience highlights the high degree of mobility among packinghouses. The two-way mobility between these two citrus cooperatives indicates that neither had a substantial advantage over the other. Nor did independent commercial houses face serious entry or exit barriers: 15 independent commercial houses affiliated with Sunkist as licensed commercial packinghouses (table 4–12) and 15 disaffiliated (table 4–13). Further attesting to the high degree of mobility is the fact that 60 proprietary packinghouses affiliated and 64 disaffiliated with Sunkist during the 20-year period whereas there remained only 30 licensed commercial houses affiliated with Sunkist in 1979/80. Moreover, of the 60 packinghouses that affiliated with Sunkist during this period, 34 had disaffiliated by the end of the period. Eighteen left within 1 to 5 years; 12 left within 6 to 10 years; and 4 left within 11 to 15 years.[42]

Finally, further evidence that the Sunkist System reduces entry barriers for competing citrus marketers is that it served as the major source of packinghouses for its competitors. In 1979/80, fully 24 of the 43 packinghouses affiliated with Sunkist's competitors either were acquired from Sunkist or voluntarily disaffiliated with Sunkist and joined another cooperative or proprietary citrus marketer. (See table 4–14). For example, 7 of the 12 houses packing for Pure Gold, Inc., in 1979/80 originally were affiliated with the Sunkist System.

Table 4–14
Origins of Packinghouses Affiliated with Leading Non-Sunkist Citrus Marketing Organizations, 1979/80

			Previous Affiliation of Packinghouse			
Marketer	*Total*	*Sunkist*	*Newly Built*	*Pure Gold*	*Miscellaneous*	*Unknown*
Pure Gold	12	7	4	0	1	0
Paramount	4	2	1	0	0	1
Mendelson-Zeller	3	1	0	1	1	0
Nash de Camp	1	1	0	0	0	0
Sun World Marketing	4	3	1	0	0	0
Other Independents	19	10	4	0	4	1
Total	43	24	10	1	6	2

Source: Developed from the records of Sunkist Growers, Inc.

The record of mobility among Sunkist packinghouses demonstrates an absence of significant entry and exit barriers of packinghouses affiliated with Sunkist. When a licensed commercial packinghouse affiliates with Sunkist by packing grower-members' fruit, the licensed house need not possess any of the multiplant economies of scale in the California/Arizona citrus industry. If such packinghouses subsequently discover more profitable marketing arrangements, they may readily disaffiliate with Sunkist. While the mobility pattern depicted above illustrates how Sunkist facilitates entry, this pattern also demonstrates why Sunkist is not able to exercise control over the supply of fruit marketed through it. For, should Sunkist attempt to raise prices by withholding part of its members' fruit, nonmembers would get a free ride on Sunkist's actions. Growers and packinghouses affiliated with Sunkist could also enjoy the free ride by leaving Sunkist. This structural characteristic of the Sunkist System compels it to compete vigorously with rival marketing organizations. It can only accomplish this by getting the best possible market-clearing price for its members' fruit at the lowest possible marketing cost. Simply put, it is subject to the same competitive pressures as any firm operating in a keenly competitive market.

How, then, should the mobility observed above be interpreted? Is it evidence of Sunkist's efficiency or inefficiency? The packinghouse leaving Sunkist obviously believes it is better off by doing so. The packinghouse affiliating with Sunkist believes the opposite. Could both be correct? Yes, to the extent that each faces different circumstances. The continuing mobility (which also had been common before 1960/61) indicates that as perceptions and circumstances change, individual growers and packinghouses seek their preferred alternative. To a large extent, the numerous disaffiliations from Sunkist result from Sunkist's open-membership policy. Whenever grower returns rise because of a Sunkist handling or marketing innovation, this attracts new growers and/or packinghouses until Sunkist returns are driven back in line with those of other California/Arizona marketers. The end result is that prices tend toward the long-run competitive equilibrium price.

Comparison of Entry Barriers in Citrus and Other Industries Charged with Monopolization

The various entry barriers in the California/Arizona fresh citrus markets represent a sharp contrast to those in other industries charged with dominant-firm monopoly. Consider first the structure of the general purpose electronic digital computer systems industry, which IBM was charged with monopolizing in 1968. IBM held a market share of about 60–70 percent; the fringe consisted of a half-dozen firms; several very large firms had been unsuccessful and forced to exit the industry; a minimum-optimum–size firm represented about 10–15 percent of the market; capital costs of a new entrant were in excess of $500 million (larger than Sunkist's total assets); practically no successful entry had recently occurred; IBM enjoyed a substantial product differentiation advantage; and IBM earned large supracompetitive profits.[43] The Dept. of Justice withdrew the case in 1982.

As already discussed above, Borden was able to dominate the processed lemon juice market in part because it held a 90 percent market share and had in Borden's words, "one of the greatest brand names in the history of the supermarket."[44] However, in addition to its large market share in processed lemon juice and its powerful ReaLemon brand which commanded a 30 percent price premium, it engaged in predatory pricing to destroy its leading rival.

Clearly, Sunkist has nothing in common with these two cases except its large market share. Large market share never confers lasting market power when entry barriers are very low. Moreover, as spelled out in chapter 3, because Sunkist is an open-membership, decentralized cooperative, it would be unable to benefit (as would a profit-seeking firm) from any entry barriers that did exist.

Critique of FTC's Structural Analysis

The FTC Brief began its analysis of market structure of the California/Arizona citrus industry by defining the relevant product and geographic markets Sunkist allegedly monopolized. It defined three relevant product markets: fresh-grade California/Arizona oranges; fresh-grade California/Arizona lemons; and lemon juice processed from California/Arizona lemons. The relevant geographic market was defined as consisting of the United States and Canada.

Sunkist Growers, Inc.'s, "Statement of Its Defense" argued that because navel oranges and valencia oranges were picked and marketed during two distinct seasons, "the two varieties face different market conditions in competing for a share of the consumer's food dollar."[45] The Sunkist statement further argued that competition also existed with citrus produced in Florida and Texas, as well as with imports from Morocco, South Africa, Israel, and Mexico. California/Arizona oranges competed with other fruits, including peaches, apples, bananas, and other citrus.[46] As to the FTC definition of the lemon products market, Sunkist argued that there were three distinct product categories: lemon juice, lemon oil, and pectin. As noted above, for purposes of this analysis, we have used the FTC's market definitions except that we, as did the FTC, treated navel oranges and valencia orange varieties separately when analyzing Sunkist's market shares in California/Arizona oranges.

FTC counsel's structural analysis of Sunkist's alleged monopoly power consisted of two kinds of evidence: Sunkist's market shares in the various relevant markets and practices designed to acquire and maintain Sunkist's dominant share.[47] As shown in tables 4-2, 4-3, and 4-4, Sunkist had average market shares exceeding 60 percent in each of the relevant markets. Economists generally agree that if the other conditions necessary for monopoly are present, a share above 40 percent confers monopoly power.[48] But, while the FTC Brief lavishes the reader with pages of market share statistics, it sheds no light on the all-important issue of the condition of entry in the relevant markets. Economists are unanimous that substantial monopoly power cannot persist in the absence of significant entry barriers.[49] Not an iota of evidence is presented as to the significance of economies-of-scale entry barriers in any stage of processing and marketing in the relevant markets.[50] Nor does the brief mention the existence of any capital or technological barriers to entry. The only structural variable in addition to market share mentioned in the brief is product differentiation; the brief makes some general claims regarding Sunkist's successful efforts to differentiate the Sunkist brand. But this subject is not examined in an appropriate theoretical framework (product differentiation by a nonprofit, open-membership cooperative), nor is any effort made to measure empirically the size of the price premium resulting from the differentiation.

The greatest flaw in the FTC analysis of the market structure of the California/Arizona industry is the failure to use the appropriate conceptual framework for analyzing whether a cooperative has monopoly power. Chapter 3 deals extensively with the appropriate theory of monopolization by cooperatives. For a cooperative to monopolize, certain necessary conditions must be met. Neglecting to analyze whether these conditions are met constitutes the fatal flaw in FTC counsel's treatment of Sunkist's alleged monopoly power, a flaw that permeates those parts of the brief dealing with conduct as well as structure. Certain nonprice practices that might conceivably be viewed as strategic behavior creating entry barriers when engaged in by a proprietary firm are not anticompetitive when engaged in by an open-membership cooperative. We return to these matters in the discussion of nonprice conduct in chapter 6.

Notes

1. FTC Brief, 24-25.
2. Ibid., 39-41.

3. California Fruit Growers Exchange was organized in 1905 as a successor to the first California citrus cooperative, Southern California Fruit Exchange. Federal Trade Commission, *Agricultural Income Inquiry, Part II. Fruits, Vegetables, and Grapes* (Washington, D.C.: GPO 1937), 678.

4. Ibid, 684. Mutual Orange Distributors was organized in 1906.

5. Ibid., 684.

6. Ibid., 667–68.

7. FTC Brief, 48.

8. Federal Trade Commission, *Agricultural Income Inquiry*, 667.

9. FTC Brief, 53.

10. J.B. Holtman, "Orange Packinghouse Costs, California/Arizona," study prepared for Sunkist Growers, Inc.

11. F.M. Scherer, A.B. Beckenstein, E. Kaufer, and R.D. Murphy, *The Economics of Multi-Plant Operation*, Harvard Economic Studies 145 (Cambridge, Mass.: Harvard University Press, 1975), 30, 94.

12. W.F. Mueller and R.T. Rogers, "Changes in Market Concentration of Manufacturing Industries," *Review of Industrial Organization* 1(Spring 1984):1–14.

13. Land O'Lakes Creameries, Inc., also developed in the 1920s its advertised trademark as a standard for high-quality butter.

14. A.W. McKay and W.H. Stevens, *Organization and Development of a Cooperative Citrus-Fruit Marketing Agency*, USDA Bulletin no. 1237 (Washington, D.C.: U.S. Dept. of Agriculture, May 1924), 28.

15. K.B. Gardner and A.W. McKay, *The Citrus Industry and the California Fruit Growers Exchange*, Farm Credit Administration Circular C-121 (Washington, D.C.: U.S. Dept. of Agriculture, June 1940), 65.

16. Ibid.

17. W.F. Mueller, J. Culbertson, and B. Peckham, *Market Structure and Technological Performance in the Food Manufacturing Industries*, Monograph 11 (Food Systems Research Group, University of Wisconsin-Madison, February 1982), 11–18.

18. C.H. Kirkman, *The Sunkist Adventure*, Farmer Cooperative Service, Cooperative Information Report no. 94 (Washington, D.C.: U.S. Dept. of Agriculture, 1975), 59–60.

19. Ibid.

20. Gardner and McKay, *Citrus Industry*, 74.

21. Ibid.

22. Industrial organization researchers have found that patents provide a convenient and meaningful index of the relative research output of firms. See M.I. Kamien and N.L. Schwartz, "Market Structure and Innovation: A Survey," *Journal of Economic Literature* 13(March 1975):4–5.

23. Mueller, Culbertson, and Peckham, *Market Structure and Technological Performance*.

24. Interviews by the authors revealed that there was a greater need for technical research by Sunkist in the early decades of the industry than there is today. For example, when it entered the citrus-processing business, Sunkist was forced to develop new equipment or aid equipment manufacturers in doing so. In succeeding decades, the food machinery industry developed improved equipment and related services, thereby reducing the need for engineering work by Sunkist. This is similar to what has happened elsewhere in the food-processing industry.

25. Sunkist sources.

26. Scherer et al., *Economics of Multi-Plant Operation*.

27. Ibid., 104–8.

28. Measured media is limited to television, magazines, network radio, newspaper supplements, and outdoor billboards. Excluded are newspaper advertising and nonadvertising promotional expenditures such as point-of-sales merchandising efforts. The latter kinds of advertising (promotion and merchandising), which are included in the Sunkist expenditures shown in table 4–5, often greatly exceed measured media advertising.

29. In 1980, Sunkist soft drink accounted for only 1.5 percent of the total soft drink market. *Beverage World,* May 1981.

30. Leading National Advertisers, Inc., *Ad $ Summary* (January–December 1981):22.

31. H.H. Bakken and M.A. Schaars, *The Economics of Cooperative Marketing* (New York: McGraw-Hill, 1937), 522. In 1981, the seventy-fifth largest advertiser, based on measured media expenditures, alone, spent $41 million. Leading National Advertisers, Inc., *Ad $ Summary,* (January–December 1981):12.

32. Peter Bronsteen, "Allegations of Monopoly and Anticompetitive Practices in the Domestic Lemon Industry" (Ph.D. diss., University of California-Los Angeles, 1981): 157–58.

33. J.S. Bain, *Industrial Organization* (New York: Wiley, 1959), 255–69.

34. Federal Trade Commission, *In the Matter of Borden, Inc.* FTC Docket 8978, Initial Decision, Finding 83 (Washington, D.C.: FTC, 1976).

35. This expectation is supported by Wills's empirical study of the effect of advertising. He found that cooperatives that engage in brand advertising generally receive lower price premiums than do proprietary food firms that engage in similar amounts of advertising and have similar market shares. R.L. Wills, "Evaluating Price Enhancement by Processing Cooperatives," *American Journal of Agricultural Economics* 67(May 1985):183.

36. Only if there were *no* barriers to entry (including zero license fees) would compulsory licensing result in the same prices as an open-membership cooperative.

37. S.C. Salop, "Strategic Entry Deterrence," *American Economic Review* 69 (May 1979):35.

38. As shown in table 4–9, Borden's ReaLemon brand enjoyed a large price premium over its largest competitor.

39. The forty-one figure excludes newly constructed, "miscellaneous," and "unknown" facilities.

40. Sunkist gave as the explanation of this affiliation an announcement by Minute Maid, which until then had been Blue Goose's outlet for product-grade fruit, that it would no longer guarantee the return on Blue Goose's product fruits, a financial commitment that had caused Minute Maid serious problems in large crop years. Sunkist's returns on product fruit had been improving steadily. Sunkist Growers, Inc., "Statement of Its Defense," FTC Docket 9100 (March 22, 1979), 40.

41. Ibid.

42. Reported in Sunkist records.

43. L.W. Weiss, "The Structure-Conduct Performance Paradigm and Antitrust," *Pennsylvania Law Review* 127(1979):1124–39; L.E. Preston, "Predatory

Marketing," in *Regulation of Marketing and the Public Interest,* Frederick Balderston, J.M. Carmen, and F.M. Nicosia (Pergamon, 1981).

44. Federal Trade Commission, *In the Matter of Borden, Inc.,* FTC Docket 8978, Initial Decision, Finding 83 (Washington, D.C.: FTC, 1976).

45. Sunkist Growers, Inc., "Statement of Its Defense," FTC Docket 9100 (March 22, 1979), 29.

46. Ibid., 29–30.

47. FTC Brief, 24–56 deals with defining the relevant markets and with measuring Sunkist's shares in various markets. Many pages in the remainder of the brief make some reference to Sunkist's large market share.

48. See for example, W.G. Shepherd, *The Economics of Industrial Organization,* 2d ed. (Englewood Cliffs, N.J.: Prentice-Hall, 1985), 28.

49. Bain, *Industrial Organization;* Scherer, *Industrial Market Structure;* Shepherd, *The Economics of Industrial Organization.*

50. At one point the brief implies that Sunkist enjoys certain advantages, presumably resulting from economies of scale, in exporting fresh fruit. However, it does not charge Sunkist with monopolizing this market. See infra, chapter 5.

5
Market Conduct:
Pricing Practices

Industrial organization theory posits that market structure determines in large part the conduct available to firms. But, as Greer has emphasized, it is the "combination of structural conditions and firm motivation" that determines conduct.[1] One aspect of firm motivation that becomes particularly relevant in this book is the fact that the Sunkist System is a nonprofit cooperative association operated for the benefit of its farmer members. The significance of this organizational characteristic has already been demonstrated by the theoretical discussion in chapter 3. Most importantly, absent some effective method of controlling the supply of its existing and potential members, as well as nonmembers, a cooperative usually is compelled to price in ways that lead to a competitive market price. Here we shall determine whether the predictions of the theory of cooperation regarding pricing conduct are borne out in the relevant markets in which Sunkist operates: fresh oranges and lemons sold in domestic markets, fresh oranges and lemons sold in foreign markets, and lemons and oranges sold as processed products.

After our review of the Sunkist System's pricing practices in each of the relevant markets, we shall report the conduct evidence relied upon by the FTC in arriving at its conclusion that the Sunkist System behaved like a monopolist. We then shall analyze the FTC's facts and arguments.

The chapter deals only with the pricing conduct of Sunkist in its various markets. Other dimensions of conduct not dealt with explicitly in cooperative theory are discussed in the following chapter. Specifically, the theory of cooperation teaches us little as to whether cooperatives differ from proprietary firms in their desire to achieve market power through the use of exclusionary predatory practices. Empirical studies have identified instances where cooperatives have used such strategies.[2] Hence, whether the Sunkist System has used such practices is not a theoretical issue but an empirical issue, a subject we address in chapter 6.

Pricing Fresh Oranges and Lemons in the Domestic Market

The objective of the Sunkist System in pricing fresh citrus in the domestic market is to obtain the highest price possible subject to the constraint that each Sunkist packinghouse is able to ship as much as it desires. In deciding how much to ship to the domestic market, the packinghouse manager is bound, under normal market conditions, by marketing orders and shipping allotments. The economic nature of marketing orders was explained earlier. It may be worth emphasizing once again, however, that the allotment for a packinghouse is dependent on the allotments of its growers, which, in turn, depend on the independent production decisions of growers. Decisions to ship less than allotments are made by the packinghouse manager, not Sunkist Central. An individual packinghouse has an incentive in normal seasons to sell the full prorate of its member growers. To do otherwise reduces the growers' returns. The only way in which individual houses would benefit from selling under prorate would be if all houses did so.[3] (Industry people refer to a packinghouse's maximum allowable weekly shipments under a federal citrus order as the packinghouse's prorate.) This would require collective action among all houses, which, as noted above, would invite free riding by nonmembers.[4] Despite the problems inherent in such action, the FTC alleged that Sunkist did take such actions.

To help achieve its pricing objective, the Sunkist System maintains thirty-seven district sales offices. Buyers place orders for fresh citrus with the appropriate district sales office. All orders are relayed by the district sales office through high-speed teletype to Sunkist Central and to all district exchanges simultaneously. Typically, an order identifies fruit from a particular packinghouse. The appropriate district exchange relays the order to the specified house. The house decides whether or not to fill the order and whether to make a counter offer. Offers and counteroffers are at scale prices, as defined below. Packinghouse replies are relayed to Sunkist Central's sales department through the district exchange. If an order is open (if it does not specify a particular house), then the order is communicated to all houses and is awarded to the first to accept. Some offers are neither house-specific nor completely open-ended. Here, the district exchanges play a more active role in allocating in an equitable manner the sales opportunities among the various houses.

A key step in the pricing of fresh oranges and lemons is the development of the *scale offer* by the Sunkist System. The scale offer is a statement of FOB prices buyers must pay, with exceptions to be noted later, in order to obtain fresh citrus from Sunkist packinghouses. This statement provides a matrix of prices for sizes and grades of each variety of fruit. Special quotations are given for oranges packed in polyethylene bags. Scale prices

need not be the same among various districts within the California/
Arizona area. Consider, for example, the scale prices for first-grade Sunkist
navel oranges, size eighty-eight as of December 4, 1978. The prices per
carton were $8.00, $6.75, and $6.50, respectively, for Southern California,
Central California, and Arizona. Different prices for different areas reflect
significant variation in fruit quality as a result of variation in weather
patterns and soil conditions.

Sunkist Central plays an important role in setting scale prices in that it
brings together information on (1) demand conditions, (2) the supplies of
fruit available for shipment in its many packinghouses, and (3) supplies of
competing fruits including apples, bananas, soft fruit during summer
months, and Florida, Texas, and imported citrus. Conference phone calls
between personnel from Sunkist Central and the district exchanges are a
vital part of the process whereby scale prices are determined. Of prime
importance in setting scale prices is the information on floor counts. Each
packinghouse indicates to its exchange the amount of fruit by variety, size,
and grade that it will have available for shipment in the domestic market
on the following day. This information is passed along to Sunkist Central
by telephone. Scale prices must be adjusted over time to assure that fresh
fruit ready for shipment is in fact shipped within a short period of time.
The fruit cannot be held back for any significant period. A Sunkist vice
president of fresh fruit marketing explained the pricing process as follows:

> One of the principal considerations would be reports and the information
> that we receive daily from the district exchanges describing the inventory
> on hand. And when that inventory began to become uncomfortable on any
> particular variety or any particular size or on any particular grade, this is
> an indication that something needs to be done. On the other side of the
> picture, the communications from district exchanges indicating that they
> are generally receiving more orders than they could handle of any particu-
> lar variety, size, or grade, is also a symptom that some kind of a price
> change or change in supply is imminent.[5]

In response to a question as to whether other reports than floor counts
affect the final price, this official responded: "No. I think those are the
principal elements. The reports with respect to the inventory position describe our supply situation. Those with information with respect to orders
describe the demand situation, and that is what makes pricing."[6]

It would be a mistake to suppose that Sunkist Central has the capacity
to set scale prices independently of market forces. The district exchange or
several exchanges in any particular area have the authority to set their own
scales, although all price quotations must be issued through Sunkist Central. Moreover, a district exchange or one or more houses within any
exchange may decide to offer fruit at off-scale prices. Off-scale prices could

contain premiums reflecting high-quality fruit. More often than not, however, off-scale pricing entails discounting. Off-scale offers are ordinarily open for a twenty-four–hour period and specify price, size, grade, and a packinghouse label. Such offers are also issued through Sunkist Central. While we have no systematic figures on quantities of fruit sold off-scale, apparently such quantities may on occasion be quite substantial. For example, the manager of sales operation at Sunkist Central judged that as much as 10 percent of valencia oranges during the 1979 season were sold off-scale. This percentage excludes auction sales as discussed below.

Local packinghouses also have the authority to decide to sell fruit on a "roller basis" or at any one of several eastern auction markets. A "roller" is a railroad car loaded with citrus and shipped east with the ultimate destination left to later negotiations between potential buyers and Sunkist district sales offices. If a sale is not made during transit, a roller is sent to auction. According to a Sunkist official, roller fruit is mostly distressed fruit which has not moved at scale prices and has aged to the point where if it is not sold in the fresh market very soon, it will need to be shipped to processed products.[7] The decision as to an acceptable price of roller fruit is ordinarily made by the district exchange.[8]

Local packinghouses also have the authority to send fruit direct to eastern auctions. Sunkist Central may provide advice and suggestions as to timing and which auction is likely to yield highest returns. Fruit sent to auction is mostly distressed fruit similar to that sold via rollers.

The continuous problem that must be solved in the pricing of western fresh citrus is finding the demand price such that all the fruit that packinghouses want to sell can in fact be sold. There is little doubt that the Sunkist System plays a leadership role in the pricing mechanism. This is so not because Sunkist has market power arising out of the control of production or sales, but through its operation as clearinghouse for numerous largely independent packinghouses and through its ability to assess demand and supply conditions in order to *discover* market-clearing prices. If Sunkist Central together with the district exchanges set the Sunkist price too high, packinghouse inventories will accumulate and new scales will be issued and/or off-scale offers, auctions, and rollers will be used to move fruit. If the Sunkist price is too low, orders will go unfilled and/or buyers will obtain allotted fruit at prices that may allow excess profit in retail-wholesale distribution.

The above discussion of pricing in the domestic market is subject to a few qualifications arising out of the opportunity for exports and promotional activities. Some Sunkist houses pack a special quality of navel oranges that is in great demand in Hong Kong and fetches a price premium above domestic prices. The houses frequently choose to ship less than quantities allotted under the order. In addition, export prices occasionally rise above domestic prices and allotted shipments occasionally exceed available supplies. Under such circumstances, allotted shipments tend to become inoperative and domestic prices reflect general supply and demand conditions including export demand. Even here, however, Sunkist price scales are determined mainly by floor counts and orders for fruit. Finally, reference has already been made to Sunkist's trade incentive program. For example, a buyer, usually a retailer, might receive cash payments from Sunkist Central for performing advertising activities. This program is appropriately viewed as an aspect of Sunkist's advertising and promotion.

At this juncture, it is convenient to consider two charges made by the FTC and a pricing implication of a third. The first charge concerns geographic price discrimination and the second, manipulation of auction market prices. The pricing implication has to do with Sunkist's advertising program.

In discussing the determinants of conduct and performance, it was noted that Sunkist has no way of preventing arbitrage so that geographic price discrimination within the domestic market would appear unlikely if not impossible. In terms of actual pricing policy, scale prices are FOB so that effective buying prices between any two spatial points (between Denver and Chicago, say) differ exactly by the differences in transportation costs. The spatial pattern of effective scale prices (scale plus transfer cost per unit) corresponds to the performance of a perfect market in space. The major deviations from this pattern are caused by off-scale sales and by the sales of non-Sunkist houses. Such deviations are the inevitable consequences of a competitive process among independent houses and the largely independent houses within the Sunkist System.

Finally, it is not possible to document with any precision the magnitude of price premiums received by Sunkist as a result of its advertising program. Good data on prices received by non-Sunkist houses are not available. Price comparisons in the case of citrus are hazardous in any event because fruit quality varies continuously. Moreover, large chain companies that specialize in selling high-quality products find dealing with Sunkist advantageous because Sunkist offers assurance of large volumes of uniformly high-quality fruit at reliable prices. How to split any price premium into that part due to advertising and that part due to assurance of supply is a difficult if not impossible task. In any event, even assuming that all of the price premium for Sunkist brand citrus is due to advertising, the premium is very modest compared to that commonly found for other highly advertised food products.[9]

FTC Allegations Regarding Sunkist Practices in Fresh Markets

The FTC's Trial Brief alleged that the Sunkist System engaged in five monopolistic pricing practices in the sale of fresh California/Arizona citrus.[10]

1. Sunkist practiced price leadership (pp. 75–76).
2. Sunkist withheld fresh fruit supplies to control prices (pp. 57–58).
3. Sunkist manipulated prices by engaging in a practice called "switching the trade" (changing the relative prices among different sizes or grades of a product) (pp. 59–60).
4. Sunkist received a price premium for the fresh oranges and lemons sold under the Sunkist brand primarily as a result of advertising (pp. 76–78).
5. A Sunkist consultant's report proved that Sunkist had monopoly power in setting lemon prices (pp. 76–78).

Sunkist's Alleged Price Leadership

Sunkist's dominant market share, says the FTC Brief, "enables it to set the price for the industry in all three relevant product markets."[11] As evidence of this practice, the FTC cites the fact that Sunkist Central:

> Publishes and circulates to its packinghouses, district exchanges, and salesmen, a current price list called "Sunkist scale" or "Sunkist quotes." Competing California-Arizona fresh citrus marketers follow Sunkist's prices, regarding Sunkist as the price leader, and rarely, if ever, establish their own price independently of Sunkist. Moreover when Sunkist adjusts or changes its price scale, its competitors change their prices.[12]

No evidence was presented as to whether Sunkist led the industry to a monopolistic or a competitive price level.

Sunkist's Alleged Withholding of Supplies

The FTC cited several instances in which Sunkist officials made statements indicative of withholding supplies. Because of the limited amount of evidence reported, we shall reproduce in full the evidentiary statements quoted in the FTC Brief.

In late 1974, in a weekly status report to the president of Sunkist Central, an assistant vice president for fresh fruit marketing noted: "Shippers this past week undershipped their prorate allotments about 20% or around 150 cars *in order to help stabilize the market* and establish buyer confidence in the market" (emphasis added by FTC counsel).[13]

The FTC further alleged that the following statement was evidence that, in March 1975, the orange sales manager of Sunkist Central told Sunkist's district managers that withholding navel shipments had raised prices:

> At times in recent weeks we have had a few more navels available than could be utilized at satisfactory values. In order to correct this situation it

became necessary to make some adjustments in quotations, *as well as to curtail weekly shipments. We believe our objective has now been accomplished* as interest on navels is once again increasing and the outlook appears much brighter (emphasis added by FTC counsel).[14]

In February 1976, the domestic fresh fruit sales manager reported to other Sunkist personnel in very similar language:

At times in recent weeks we have been shipping more navels than could be utilized at satisfactory values. Because of these lower values, shipper resistance to ship has prevailed and current shipments now reflect basic demand. *We believe our immediate objective has now been accomplished*, as interest in navels is once again increasing and the promotional outlook is considerably brighter (emphasis added by FTC counsel).[15]

A week later this manager reported that "Utilization of current prorate allotments by Sunkist shippers now is approaching 100% in contrast to the 70–80% experienced the past several weeks."[16]

In late 1975, a Sunkist director pointed out, as the FTC characterized it, "that Sunkist's price control potentially involves million of dollars. . . . What can *we do to decrease volume* [of valencia oranges] by the small percentage needed *to maintain price levels? Failure to do so costs us millions. Occasionally we succeed, proving it can be done*" (emphasis added by FTC counsel).[17]

Sunkist's Alleged Practice of Switching the Trade

Sunkist "manipulated" price, according to FTC counsel's Brief, by employing a practice it called "switching the trade." FTC counsel explained this practice as follows. If Sunkist had a surplus of one size of a fruit variety, Sunkist would raise the price of the variety's "other sizes to induce buyers to switch to the surplus citrus."[18] Such changes in relative prices causes customers to change the volumes of purchases of various sizes. FTC counsel argued that this practice permitted Sunkist to artificially raise price because "Sunkist knows that with its monopoly share buyers cannot practicably go elsewhere, because competitors do not have sufficient supplies."[19]

Sunkist's Price Premium

The final behavioral evidence cited by the FTC is the charge that "Sunkist is able to extract a price premium for its fresh orange and lemons, despite the fact that California-Arizona citrus of like grade and size is homogeneous."[20] To support this charge, FTC counsel cited a report to the membership committee in 1966 from the grower relations manager which noted that, "Sunkist fruit continues to sell at a *premium.*"[21]

FTC counsel also cited a 1971 survey of Sunkist's five sales division managers which disclosed that Sunkist fruit received a fifteen to seventy-five cents per carton FOB premium above comparable industry competition.[22] Furthermore, in 1970, the Sunkist District Exchange Managers Club was told to use discretion lest they charge an excessive premium, thereby causing chain store buyers to switch suppliers.[23]

FTC counsel argued that Sunkist's premiums, as documented above, were not attributable to differences in quality or service. Rather, the premium was due to "artificial product differentiation resulting from advertising and its strong export market. . . ."[24] To support its allegation that Sunkist's domestic price premium was due primarily to its advertising program, the FTC Brief quoted a Sunkist official's statement that, "We do receive a premium, not because of quality, but because of our presold name at retail."[25]

The FTC put forth evidence allegedly showing that Sunkist recognized that its brand advertising contributed to its size. First, when in the early 1970s, other industry members sought an industrywide generic advertising program for oranges, Sunkist did not participate. Among its reasons for declining to participate was that a generic advertising program would eliminate the Sunkist price premium.[26] Second, in 1971, Sunkist's grower relations manager recognized the Sunkist premium as being important in attracting and maintaining membership.[27] Thus, Sunkist considered the price premiums "valuable grower assets which the corporation is obligated to preserve and increase if possible."[28]

Sunkist's Consultant's Report

FTC counsel relied heavily on a study by a Sunkist consultant to support the conclusion that Sunkist had monopoly control over price.[29] In the 1950s, Sunkist commissioned a study by the late Dr. R.G. Bressler, a professor of agricultural economics at the University of California-Berkeley. Bressler analyzed the nature and importance of short-term price and sales fluctuations, the effects of temperature and prices on sales, and the role of the auction markets in the total market. The study also made "proposals to improve stability and grower incomes through modifications in the prorate procedures and by actual removal of surplus stocks from eastern markets."[30]

Because the demand for lemons was very price inelastic (-0.3), small changes in the supply or demand of fresh lemons resulted in sharp changes in price. Although the federal lemon marketing order sought to adjust supply to changing demand conditions, Bressler's analysis showed that the order often failed to accomplish this objective. When the order resulted in excessive shipments, the oversupply tended to be diverted to markets in the East. Thus, "much of the oversupply finds its way to the auction markets and these extra quantities react with the local demands and result in relatively pronounced price decreases."[31]

Bressler devised a scheme for dealing with this problem, which he believed had resulted in excessive costs to growers. As the FTC Brief put it:

> Dr. Bressler suggested, among other things, that if pursuant to the federal marketing order the industry as a whole purchased lemons in auction markets whenever prices fell below some predetermined level, industry revenue gains would exceed the cost of operating the program. Such a program would, in effect, fine tune the marketing order which by itself was too unresponsive to determine consistently the profit maximizing shipment schedule.[32]

Importantly, as this characterization by the FTC explained, Bressler's scheme was devised primarily as a way of improving, from the vantage point of farmers, the functioning of the lemon marketing order. Bressler added, however, that if the plan did not become a part of the marketing order, "Sunkist may have to consider carrying the program alone."[33] The FTC Brief focused on this part of Bressler's report, citing the following statements:

> In this event, only 77 percent of the increase in gross revenue resulting from the price-support activity would come to Sunkist growers while they would bear the entire cost. *Because Sunkist has such a substantial share of the total market, even this program would be quite profitable. . . .*
>
> These calculations make clear that supporting prices at a moderate level through surplus purchase and removal could add substantially to the net returns to lemon growers in the industry as a whole, *and even that the program would be feasible for Sunkist without industry-wide participation.*[34]

Based on the above statements, the FTC Brief concluded that "Sunkist possessed the power to control the price of fresh lemons in the domestic market. . . . Thus Sunkist's own economic analysis clearly establishes the existence of monopoly power in this relevant product market."[35]

Analysis of FTC's Allegations Concerning Sunkist's Conduct in Fresh Markets

What, then, are we to make of this evidence of Sunkist's alleged monopolistic pricing practices? In sum, the FTC argument ran as follows. Sunkist allegedly exercised monopolistic control over prices because its large market share enabled it to play the role of industry price leader. In this role, it raised prices by restricting supply through systematic undershipment of its members' marketing order prorate. It also forced customers to pay higher prices through "switching the trade." The price it was able to set as the industry price leader was enhanced by its advertising-created product differentiation. Finally, Sunkist's own analysis, as reflected in a report prepared for it by an economic consultant, proved that Sunkist had monopoly power over price.

Sunkist as a Price Leader

Complaint counsel did not spell out any well-articulated theory of price leadership. In counsel's view, evidence indicating that someone is a price leader is sufficient to warrant an inference of monopoly power; complaint counsel drew no distinctions between types of price leadership.

FTC counsel rested its price leadership case almost exclusively on selected statements of Sunkist personnel. Statements made by responsible officials of a defendant in the normal course of business often provide insight into such matters as the nature and use of market power. But such business commentary must be used judiciously. Statements by business-people often may be based more on hope than on reality, reflecting an "expression of excessive zeal" or simply "a purpose to prevail over competitors by lawful means."[36] They also may lend themselves to alternative explanations of intent and, therefore, may support conflicting hypotheses. Because of this, businesspeople's statements must be tested against alternative hypotheses and, whenever possible, supplemented by hard quantitative evidence. Let us, therefore, examine the evidence presented within the conceptual framework set forth in chapter 3.

The Sunkist System's objective is to obtain the best possible returns for its members consistent with the constraints imposed by its organizational characteristics and by market forces. Because of its large market share and its superior knowledge of the market, Sunkist Central necessarily must take some initiatives in the price discovery process; it cannot act passively. In practice, Sunkist does indeed play the role of a price leader. But, economists recognize that merely identifying a seller as a price leader does not answer the question of whether the seller leads the industry to a monopolistic price, a competitive price, or something in between. As Stigler notes, a price leader may command "adherence of rivals to his price only because, and to the extent that, his price reflects market conditions with tolerable promptness."[37] Stigler has labeled such a seller a "barometric" price leader. Markham has extended this concept by distinguishing between two sorts of barometric price leadership, competitive and monopolistic, and has developed criteria for identifying each type.[38]

Markham reasons that a price leader will be unable to lead the industry to a monopolistic price unless there exist certain necessary conditions, particularly high market concentration and "severely restricted" entry.[39] Especially relevant in the case of Sunkist's price leadership is the requirement that entry must be severely restricted. In the absence of the necessary structural conditions, "The barometric firm possesses no power to coerce the rest of the industry into accepting its price and . . . proceeds with initiating price increases in a market . . . only so rapidly as supply and demand conditions dictate."[40]

Which of these two types of barometric price leader does the Sunkist System most closely approximate? Based on market structure criteria, Sunkist meets only one of the two necessary conditions. While Sunkist has a large market share, Sunkist is unable to restrict entry. Indeed, as shown above, in practice the Sunkist System actually facilitates entry of both growers and packinghouses.[41] Thus, there is a fatal flaw in FTC counsel's argument. The brief makes no reference to the conditions of entry in the California/Arizona fresh citrus market.

Our analysis of Sunkist's pricing conduct supports Markham's theory of a competitive barometric price leader. Sunkist Central, together with the district exchanges, seeks to *discover* the market-clearing prices.[42] If the Sunkist "scale" price is set too high, packinghouse inventories will accumulate and new scales will be issued and/or off-scale offers, auctions, and rollers will be used to move more fruit. If the Sunkist price is too low, orders will go unfilled and/or buyers will obtain fruit at prices that may allow excess profit in retail-wholesale distribution. As to allegations that the Sunkist System sells under its prorate, one should note at the outset that the Sunkist System lacks any mechanism for allocating sales among growers and its federation of packinghouses, as would be necessary if it were to systematically sell below prorate.

What, then, is the relevance of the evidence cited in the FTC Brief? It is entirely consistent with the theory that Sunkist was acting as a competitive barometric price leader. The key evidence cited by the FTC related to a few selected statements of Sunkist officials which demonstrated that the Sunkist System was very much concerned with short-run prices. The most conclusive evidence, in the FTC counsel's view, that Sunkist was exercising control over supply "by the systematic undershipment of prorate" were the following two previously quoted statements.

Shippers this past week undershipped their prorate allotments about 20% . . . in order to help stabilize the market and establish buyer confidence in the market.

At times in recent weeks we have had a few more navels than could be utilized at satisfactory values. In order to correct this situation it became necessary to make some adjustments in quotations, *as well as to curtail weekly shipments.* We believe our objective has now been accomplished (emphasis added by FTC counsel).[43]

FTC counsel argued that failure to ship one's prorate is evidence of curtailing supply beyond that contemplated by the citrus marketing order.[44] This is wrong. The citrus marketing orders permit a handler to undership or overship in a given week. A grower may overship the allotment by 20 percent, but the overshipment must be deducted from the next week's allotment. On the other hand, underships may be carried forward and added to the handler's allotment for the following week. Additionally, allotment loans are also permitted among handlers within each prorate district.

Thus, in discovering the appropriate competitive market-clearing price, the Sunkist System, as well as other citrus shippers, do not necessarily sell their entire allotment every week of the marketing year. It is possible and appropriate that the Sunkist System concern itself with short-run efforts to "stabilize" the market and seek to "establish buyer confidence in the market." Such short-run "stabilization," which evens out shipments over the marketing season, does not constitute monopolization but, rather, represents a normal, competitive response to variations in short-run supply or demand.

Sunkist as a Withholder of Supplies

We shall first examine the evidence as to whether the Sunkist System actually systematically undershipped its members' prorate, something FTC counsel never attempted to quantity, or if he did, he did not report his findings in the FTC Trial Brief.

Our analysis follows in modified and extended form that used by Bronsteen in examining whether Sunkist had monopoly power in the California/Arizona fresh lemon market.[45] He found that Sunkist did not restrict the supply of fresh California/Arizona lemons. We extend this analysis in lemons by including additional years and variables. We also examine whether Sunkist restricted supply in the fresh California/Arizona navel and valencia orange markets. Finally, we also test whether Sunkist restricted supplies in the particular years for which the FTC said it had documented evidence that Sunkist actually engaged in limiting the supply of a particular citrus variety.

The hypothesis tested here is that Sunkist restricted supply by diverting fruit from the primary market (fresh fruit sold in the domestic market) to the secondary markets (exports and processed products). If this occurred, one would expect the rest of the industry to behave as a competitive fringe, selling relatively more fruit in the primary market.

If Sunkist consistently diverted fruit, then the percentage of Sunkist's total harvest sold for fresh consumption should be lower than the rest of the industry's percentages. As the data displayed in tables 5-1, 5-2, and 5-3 indicate, the hypothesized relationship did not hold when viewed in the aggregate from 1954/55 through 1982/83. In lemons, the market in which Sunkist held the largest share, Sunkist actually sold a higher percentage of its harvest, on average, for fresh domestic consumption than did the rest of the industry: 38.4 percent for Sunkist and 31.4 percent for the others—a statistically significant difference. As for valencia oranges, Sunkist sold 46.5 percent for fresh consumption and others sold 44.0 percent. As for navel oranges, Sunkist sold slightly less for fresh consumption than did others, 72.1 percent versus 73.1 percent. However, the differences for valencia and navel oranges were not statistically significant at the 5 percent level.

Sunkist's operations in the processed products market reflected its operations in the fresh domestic market. In lemons, where Sunkist held its largest market share, from 1954/55 through 1982/83, Sunkist sold a substantially smaller percentage of its sales in the processed products markets than did the rest of the industry, 42.6 percent versus 51.5 percent. (See table 5-1.) As for navel and valencia oranges, rates for Sunkist and the rest of the industry differed only slightly. This is not the sort of behavior to be expected of a dominant firm engaged in diverting sales to a secondary market. Clearly, the results of the above tests do not support the hypothesis that Sunkist diverted fruit from the primary markets with the result that the rest of the industry made relatively greater shipments of fresh fruit to the primary market.

We further tested the hypothesis that Sunkist's market share conferred market power. We hypothesize that Sunkist was more likely to divert fruit in those years in which it had the largest market share. Sunkist's market shares of sales in the three domestic fresh fruit markets varied quite widely over the period studied: 60 percent to 89 percent in lemons, 53 percent to 81 percent in navels, and 64 percent to 85 percent in valencias. (See tables 4-2, 4-3, and 4-4.)

Our model examines the effect of Sunkist's market share on the whole industry's sales rate. The percentage of industry harvest sold in the primary market will drop if market power is used to divert fruit into other markets. The greater the market power, the more likely is diversion to occur. Using market share as a proxy for market power, we would expect a negative relationship between Sunkist's share of the market and the percentage of industry harvest sold for fresh domestic consumption.

Another factor influencing the fresh sales rate is the overall size of the harvest. In seasons with large harvests, we expect that the marketing order would permit a smaller percentage of the crop to be sold in the primary market and vice versa.

Table 5-1
Percentage of Industry, Sunkist, and Rest of California/Arizona Lemon Industry Sales in the Domestic Fresh Market, Export Market, and Products Market, 1954/55 through 1982/83

	Percentage of Industry Sales			Percentage of Sunkist Sales			Percentage of Rest of Industry Sales		
	Domestic Fresh	Fresh Export	Products	Domestic Fresh	Fresh Export	Products	Domestic Fresh	Fresh Export	Products
1954/55	54.56%	10.55%	34.89%	56.62%	9.21%	34.17%	45.99%	16.12%	37.89%
1955/56	55.20	12.88	31.93	57.69	12.14	30.17	45.72	15.68	38.60
1956/57	47.20	12.45	40.35	49.36	11.41	39.22	40.43	15.69	43.89
1957/58	42.04	17.79	40.18	43.83	16.51	39.66	36.23	21.93	41.84
1958/59	40.78	9.58	49.64	42.58	9.30	48.12	34.93	10.50	54.56
1959/60	39.19	12.25	48.56	41.04	12.93	46.03	34.12	10.36	55.52
1960/61	49.22	17.50	33.28	51.90	18.71	29.40	41.96	14.22	43.82
1961/62	42.96	11.54	45.50	46.15	12.50	41.35	35.18	9.18	55.64
1962/63	50.36	18.88	30.76	53.97	19.90	26.13	42.34	16.61	41.05
1963/64	36.99	14.04	48.97	39.92	15.63	44.46	31.20	10.88	57.92
1964/65	45.54	16.88	37.58	47.15	18.38	34.48	41.70	13.32	44.98
1965/66	40.52	17.39	42.09	44.06	18.47	37.47	26.97	13.22	59.81
1966/67	34.59	17.21	48.21	36.75	16.80	46.45	23.30	19.33	57.37
1967/68	37.33	18.59	44.07	39.41	18.31	42.29	28.70	19.78	51.52
1968/69	39.66	16.99	43.35	41.18	17.60	41.22	32.57	14.17	53.26
1969/70	38.71	21.29	40.00	39.73	21.46	38.81	33.76	20.45	45.80
1970/71	37.34	21.24	41.42	38.52	21.83	39.65	31.50	18.28	50.22
1971/72	34.23	23.18	42.59	34.59	24.09	41.32	32.45	18.70	48.85
1972/73	28.08	22.09	49.83	28.35	23.18	48.47	26.85	17.20	55.94
1973/74	32.26	27.71	40.03	32.67	27.78	39.54	30.16	27.32	42.52
1974/75	21.33	18.27	60.40	21.87	17.90	60.23	18.02	20.54	61.44
1975/76	31.43	29.05	39.52	31.42	30.07	38.51	31.47	25.26	43.28
1976/77	25.66	25.73	48.61	27.44	27.37	45.20	20.18	20.67	59.15
1977/78	24.63	22.83	52.54	25.31	23.84	50.84	22.74	20.01	57.25
1978/79	32.42	29.21	38.37	34.63	32.07	33.31	28.30	23.89	47.81
1979/80	27.25	20.56	52.19	27.94	20.31	51.76	25.56	21.20	53.24
1980/81	21.05	15.12	63.83	22.03	15.03	62.94	19.14	15.29	65.57
1981/82	26.31	15.41	58.28	28.95	16.08	54.98	22.22	14.37	63.41
1982/83	28.28	18.69	53.02	28.70	19.13	52.18	27.68	18.06	54.26
Average	36.73	18.44	44.83	38.41	18.89	42.70	31.43	17.32	51.26

Source: Records of Sunkists Growers, Inc.

Note: Due to rounding, totals occasionally do not equal 100%.

Table 5-2

Percentage of Industry, Sunkist, and Rest of California/Arizona Valencia Orange Industry Sales in the Domestic Fresh Market, Export Market, and Products Market, 1954/55 through 1982/83

	Percentage of Industry Sales			Percentage of Sunkist Sales			Percentage of Rest of Industry Sales		
	Domestic Fresh	Fresh Export	Products	Domestic Fresh	Fresh Export	Products	Domestic Fresh	Fresh Export	Products
1954/55	51.30%	11.19%	37.51%	51.95%	10.68%	37.37%	49.48%	12.62%	37.89%
1955/56	44.05	18.64	37.31	46.39	17.01	36.60	37.79	22.98	39.22
1956/57	51.31	14.09	34.60	52.55	13.85	33.60	48.07	14.71	37.23
1957/58	70.89	8.26	20.85	75.36	6.89	17.75	57.62	12.34	30.04
1958/59	53.16	10.04	36.80	55.34	10.13	34.53	46.89	9.77	43.34
1959/60	55.21	9.36	35.42	56.00	8.61	35.39	53.26	11.24	35.50
1960/61	55.86	13.16	30.98	57.98	12.86	29.15	49.35	14.06	36.59
1961/62	52.97	13.55	33.48	55.03	12.33	32.64	47.78	16.62	35.60
1962/63	46.06	10.46	43.49	49.58	10.01	40.40	36.85	11.61	51.54
1963/64	50.41	9.86	39.73	51.17	11.00	37.83	48.57	7.14	44.29
1964/65	55.36	13.30	31.34	54.90	13.68	31.42	56.63	12.24	31.13
1965/66	47.63	13.83	38.54	47.06	13.96	38.98	51.13	13.04	35.83
1966/67	44.96	14.87	40.17	44.09	14.75	41.15	49.72	15.51	34.78
1967/68	56.47	7.24	36.29	56.75	7.00	36.25	55.12	8.42	36.46
1968/69	37.12	10.39	52.49	35.17	10.30	54.53	45.72	10.80	43.49
1969/70	43.00	12.78	44.22	41.32	13.65	45.03	48.42	9.97	41.61
1970/71	42.36	9.70	47.94	41.88	9.58	48.53	44.77	10.30	44.56
1971/72	37.91	9.53	52.55	38.10	10.17	51.73	37.19	7.11	55.70
1972/73	38.02	11.23	50.74	37.80	11.52	50.68	39.31	9.57	51.12
1973/74	44.79	17.87	37.34	43.85	19.27	36.88	48.24	12.75	39.01
1974/75	34.69	21.00	44.31	34.55	20.61	44.84	35.31	22.74	41.95
1975/76	33.18	20.23	46.59	33.80	19.90	46.29	30.92	21.42	47.66
1976/77	42.86	21.36	35.78	43.49	20.83	35.68	41.00	22.95	36.05
1977/78	41.31	18.76	39.94	39.87	18.14	41.98	45.71	20.66	33.63
1978/79	42.43	18.23	39.34	43.86	15.83	40.31	39.65	22.89	37.45
1979/80	39.97	24.45	35.59	42.50	22.68	34.82	34.36	28.37	37.27
1980/81	31.10	18.18	50.70	31.95	17.82	50.23	29.68	18.80	51.47
1981/82	50.12	26.03	23.85	53.89	24.38	21.73	44.01	28.70	27.30
1982/83	28.36	16.92	54.71	30.73	16.49	52.77	24.69	17.58	57.70
Average	45.62	14.64	39.74	46.45	14.27	39.28	44.04	15.41	40.53

Source: Records of Sunkists Growers, Inc.

Note: Due to rounding, totals occasionally do not equal 100%.

Table 5-3

Percentage of Industry, Sunkist, and Rest of California/Arizona Navel Orange Industry Sales in the Domestic Fresh Market, Export Market, and Products Market, 1954/55 through 1982/83

	Percentage of Industry Sales			Percentage of Sunkist Sales			Percentage of Rest of Industry Sales		
	Domestic Fresh	Fresh Export	Products	Domestic Fresh	Fresh Export	Products	Domestic Fresh	Fresh Export	Products
1954/55	77.77%	6.46%	15.77%	77.26%	5.94%	16.80%	79.02%	7.71%	13.27%
1955/56	82.81	4.12	13.07	82.55	3.33	14.12	83.40	5.84	10.76
1956/57	81.05	5.94	13.01	80.88	5.51	13.61	81.42	6.86	11.71
1957/58	91.25	3.17	5.58	91.73	2.41	5.86	90.00	5.17	4.83
1958/59	81.99	4.30	13.71	82.27	4.43	13.29	81.36	3.99	14.64
1959/60	81.61	4.40	13.99	81.39	4.23	14.38	82.03	4.74	13.23
1960/61	88.70	3.78	7.52	89.20	2.80	8.00	87.66	5.83	6.51
1961/62	86.02	2.93	11.05	86.63	1.91	11.47	84.70	5.16	10.14
1962/63	69.23	2.42	28.36	71.25	1.39	27.36	65.10	4.51	30.39
1963/64	79.57	3.58	16.85	80.64	3.27	16.10	77.21	4.26	18.53
1964/65	86.76	2.57	10.67	86.82	2.08	11.10	86.59	3.90	9.51
1965/66	71.75	4.11	24.13	71.27	3.56	25.16	73.84	6.53	19.63
1966/67	80.77	3.16	16.07	80.08	2.72	17.20	83.42	4.88	11.70
1967/68	57.87	3.36	38.77	58.16	2.92	38.92	56.91	4.83	38.26
1968/69	70.53	3.67	25.80	69.33	3.74	26.93	73.87	3.46	22.68
1969/70	69.06	4.05	26.89	67.18	3.95	28.87	74.08	4.33	21.58
1970/71	76.20	3.69	20.11	74.78	3.87	21.35	79.85	3.23	16.92
1971/72	68.35	4.40	27.26	66.55	4.75	28.70	72.35	3.61	24.04
1972/73	60.89	3.33	35.78	58.94	2.98	38.08	65.89	4.22	29.89
1973/74	73.77	4.15	22.08	72.19	4.45	23.36	77.00	3.52	19.47
1974/75	64.59	6.39	29.02	62.68	7.11	30.21	68.56	4.89	26.55
1975/76	63.86	7.58	29.56	62.52	8.42	29.06	66.45	5.95	27.60
1976/77	66.32	7.35	26.33	66.03	7.65	26.32	66.75	6.92	26.33
1977/78	65.09	9.06	25.85	64.83	9.23	25.95	65.46	8.83	25.71
1978/79	60.05	7.51	32.44	62.32	8.39	29.30	57.04	6.35	36.61
1979/80	58.46	6.13	35.41	58.79	6.47	34.74	58.04	5.71	36.25
1980/81	55.59	7.90	36.51	57.59	8.21	34.19	53.26	7.55	39.19
1981/82	68.99	9.22	21.79	68.18	9.69	22.13	69.98	8.64	21.37
1982/83	58.23	8.14	33.63	58.71	8.44	32.85	57.70	7.80	34.50
Average	72.31	5.06	22.62	72.09	4.96	22.95	73.07	5.49	21.44

Source: Records of Sunkists Growers, Inc.

Note: Due to rounding, totals occasionally do not equal 100%.

We posit a relation of the form:

$$PFD = b_0 + b_1 CR_s + b_2 S \qquad (5.1)$$

where

PFD is the percentage of harvest sold in the domestic fresh market,

CR_s is Sunkist's share of the fresh domestic market, and

S is the size of the harvest.

Our null hypothesis is that the coefficient for CR_s will have a negative sign (so that increasing Sunkist's market share will decrease the fresh sales rate). We hypothesize the coefficient for the control variable, *S*, to be negative. This equation was estimated using ordinary least squares regression for each of the three markets. The results are presented in table 5–4.

In each industry, the hypothesis that CR_s is negative is rejected at the 5 percent level of significance. Although the coefficient has a negative sign in the lemon equation, it is not statistically significant at the 10 percent level in a one-tailed test. The coefficient for harvest size is negative as predicted and highly significant in all equations.

We made one final analysis in which we tested the hypothesis that although Sunkist did not pursue a policy of systematic diversion, it did divert fresh fruits in the specific years for which the FTC cited evidence of alleged diversion of fruit from the primary market. The FTC Brief cited evidence of alleged fruit diversion in the following product markets and years.

lemons: 1970/71[46]

navels: 1974/75[47] and 1975/76[48]

valencias: 1975/76[49]

Table 5–4
Relationship between Percentage of Harvest Sold in Fresh Domestic Market and Sunkist's Market Share, 1954 through 1982

Dependent Variable: Percentage of Harvest Sold in Fresh Domestic Market (PFD)	Constant (C)	Sunkist's Market Share (CR_s)	Harvest Size (S)	R^2
Lemons	88.82* (8.09)	−0.14 (1.22)	−0.00093* (10.48)	.81
Navel oranges	85.12* (4.60)	0.059 (0.26)	−.0041* (3.86)	.53
Valencia oranges	76.07* (6.28)	−0.026 (0.17)	−0.00063* (7.47)	.68

Note: T-statistics in parentheses.

*1 percent level of significance using a one-tailed test.

To test whether Sunkist diverted from the primary markets in these years, we used a modified version of the preceding model. A binary variable was added to the equation to identify the varieties and seasons for which the FTC complaint counsel believed that there was clear-cut evidence of diversion. We expected a negative coefficient for this variable.

The results of this analysis are displayed in table 5–5. Although the regression coefficients have the predicted negative sign, in none of the three equations is the diversion variable, *D*, statistically significant. The regression coefficient on market share remains nonsignificant.

The various statistical analyses performed above provide no support for the FTC allegations that Sunkist engaged in *systematic* or *selective* diversion of fruit from the fresh domestic markets to secondary markets. These findings are consistent with the analysis above that, whereas Sunkist did at times undership and overship its prorate, it did not curtail the supply of fruit beyond the curtailment that may have been occurring because of the federal marketing orders in these three markets.

Alleged Monopoly Power Conferred by the Sunkist Brand

We turn now to FTC counsel's allegation that Sunkist's advertising created product differentiation conferred monopoly power on Sunkist. The differentiation allegedly created an artificial entry barrier and enabled Sunkist to obtain a monopolistic price premium.[50] FTC counsel emphasized that the commission's decisions in the *Proctor & Gamble (Clorox)*[51] and *Borden (ReaLemon)*[52] cases found that these firms' advertising achieved product differentiation created entry barriers and conferred the substantial ability to enhance prices. No comparisons were made, however, between the extent of price enhancement in those products and that existing in the Sunkist

Table 5–5
Relationship between Percentage of Harvest Sold in Fresh Domestic Market, Sunkist's Market Share, and Years Sunkist Allegedly Diverted Fresh Sales, 1954 through 1982

Dependent Variable: Percentage of Harvest Sold in Fresh Domestic Market (PFD)	Constant (C)	Sunkist's Market Share (CR_s)	Harvest Size (S)	Alleged Sales Diversions (D)	R^2
Lemons	82.7278*	−.1379	−0.00094*	−3.7323	.82
	(8.18)	(1.20)	(10.66)	(0.86)	
Navel oranges	89.5370*	0.0044	−0.00043*	−0.4215	.53
	(4.32)	(0.017)	(3.69)	(0.0714)	
Valencia oranges	73.8761*	−0.3209	−.00062*	−7.5243	.72
	(6.16)	(0.02)	(7.32)	(1.39)	

Note: T-statistics are in parentheses.

*1 percent level of significance using a one-tailed test.

brands of fresh citrus. Such a comparison reveals that while the Sunkist brand gave Sunkist somewhat higher prices than those received by competing unadvertised brands, the price enhancement was very modest. Based on our analysis, Sunkist commanded at most an average premium of about 5 percent of the average selling price. To achieve this premium, Sunkist spent about 2.8 percent of sales. In contrast, ReaLemon commanded a price premium of 42 percent over regional brands and Clorox household bleach commanded a 15 percent premium over regional brands.[53]

Finally, FTC counsel completely ignored the teaching of economic theory that a nonprofit cooperative with open membership is unable to command as high a price premium as can proprietary corporations with brands of similar strengths. Any significant price premiums resulting from a cooperative's advertising would encourage existing members to expand output and would attract new members, thereby increasing supplies that would erode the price premiums.[54] This prediction of the theory of cooperatives has empirical support. In his analysis of product differentiation by cooperatives and proprietary firms, Wills finds that cooperative price premiums from advertising are generally lower than those of similarly situated proprietary firms.[55]

Switching the Trade

FTC counsel attempted to elevate the rather ordinary business practice of changing relative prices among a product's different sizes or grades (commonly known as switching the trade) to the level of a monopolistic practice.[56] While some language used by salespersons in discussing this process may suggest that the practice involves substantial control over prices, this control clearly does not reach the level of monopoly power. Instead, it is illustrative of the numerous competitive pricing strategies engaged in by businesspeople not selling in auction markets.[57] These practices generally fall far short of monopoly pricing as that term is used by economists and in law as defined in Sherman Act cases.

Conduct evidence often lends itself to interpretations that make it consistent with alternative theories. It therefore is desirable, when possible, to develop quantitative evidence of control over price by showing actual restriction of supply by showing that prices (or profits) have actually been enhanced substantially above some competitive norm. This the FTC failed to do.

Sunkist Consultant's Report

The FTC Brief relied heavily on the so-called Bressler report to document its case that Sunkist could have exercised monopoly power over price in the fresh lemon market. A complete reading of the report shows that the FTC Brief both misrepresented Bressler's analysis and mischaracterized its significance concerning whether Sunkist had monopoly power in setting prices in the fresh lemon market. The FTC failed to acknowledge the serious question Bressler, himself, raised concerning the efficacy of his scheme should it be implemented unilaterally by Sunkist rather than through a federal marketing order. Should Sunkist, alone, carry the program, Bressler said, "Sunkist would be 'holding the umbrella' over its competition. . . . The effects of this on the competitive position of Sunkist in the field would have to be considered carefully."[58] Bressler reiterated this caveat in his conclusions, where he said that if the program cost were borne entirely by Sunkist, it "would hold the 'umbrella' for its competition—and non-Sunkist growers could have expected an increase averaging about $0.25 per carton. *Such a differential effect could have serious repercussions on Sunkist's competitive position.*"[59]

Although Bressler raised the free-rider problem, he offered no solution for it. This decision was left to Sunkist management. There is no evidence that management ever seriously considered having Sunkist adopt its own surplus disposal program. Management said that it was very sensitive to the free-rider problem, believing that it would have doomed this or any other unilateral action to raise member-grower prices by controlling supply.

In sum, the Bressler plan was designed primarily as a way of stabilizing and raising moderately lemon prices in some years. Thus, while he demonstrated that it was theoretically possible for Sunkist to implement the plan on its own, Bressler also cautioned that doing so "could have serious repercussions on Sunkist's competitive position."[60] Finally, it is not appropriate to characterize the Bressler report as "Sunkist's own economic analysis." Sunkist's own analysis led to a decision not to implement the Bressler plan.

In sum, we found no empirical support for FTC counsel's allegations that Sunkist's pricing conduct in the fresh citrus markets was that of a monopolist. On the contrary, the empirical evidence, as well as the documentary evidence addressed by the FTC, was consistent with that expected of a nonprofit marketing cooperative with open membership. Insofar as the Sunkist System acted as the industry price leader, it behaved as a competitive barometric price leader seeking to discover a competitive market-clearing price. And, while there were instances in which some Sunkist packinghouses undershipped and/or overshipped their growers' prorate, there is no evidence that they engaged in systematic or selective undershipment on an annual basis in order to maintain prices above levels contemplated by the marketing order. On the contrary, there is evidence that Sunkist Growers shipped a higher percentage of their prorate than did growers selling through competing marketers. Although Sunkist's advertising conferred a premium on the Sunkist brand, this was extremely modest compared to that commonly found for highly differentiated grocery products, falling far short of the monopolistic level. By no stretch of the imagination can the so-called practices of switching the trade be considered evidence of monopoly power. Finally, while the Bressler report demonstrated that Sunkist could raise prices unilaterally by ignoring the free-rider problem, Sunkist management, well aware of the problem, never considered implementing the Bressler plan.

Pricing Fresh-Grade Lemons in Foreign Markets

Sunkist markets both fresh lemons and oranges in foreign markets. Since exports are relatively more important for lemons than oranges and because Sunkist holds a larger market share in lemons than oranges, the discussion of foreign markets focuses on lemons. Essentially the same marketing methods apply to oranges as those discussed below for lemons. In describing the pricing of fresh-grade lemons in export markets, we distinguish between the Pacific and European markets, taking up the former first.

Weekly export sales of Sunkist lemons in the Pacific market are referred to as firm sales, in that price, grade, and sizes are negotiated and agreed upon prior to shipment. About two–and–one-half to three weeks prior to the week of shipment, personnel from the export department of Sunkist Central hold discussions with Sunkist sales agents in Pacific markets (mainly Japan) regarding market conditions. The export department relays the information thus obtained back to district exchanges; in consultation with the exchanges, the export department arrives at a price level to be quoted to foreign buyers. The quantities of fruit to be purchased by importers at the quoted prices are transmitted by sales agents to the export department. About 10 days prior to shipment, Sunkist Central offers to buy lemons for export from Sunkist packinghouses at an FOB price that equals the price paid by buyers minus transfer costs such as trucking to harbor, ocean freight, and insurance. The potential export shipment, often referred to as the export opportunity, is allocated proportionally among Sunkist packinghouses according to their levels of crop production. Importantly, the packinghouse need not agree to sell to Sunkist Central its prorate share of the total export opportunity. If a packinghouse declines to sell part or all of its share, the unused portion is distributed among remaining packinghouses. It is, of course, possible for actual exports to be less than desired by importers.

The Sunkist System exports lemons to Western European markets (mainly France, Belgium, Holland, and Great Britain) on a consignment basis. In consultation with its European sales agents and district exchanges, Sunkist Central, operating through its export department, determines potential volumes of fruit to be shipped. Prices that will be received for

Sunkist lemons sold in Europe are not known until about three weeks after loading. Shipments are based on expected prices. Sunkist purchases fruit for export from its packinghouses at pay prices determined by subtracting transfer costs from expected future prices in European markets. Weekly export opportunity is offered to Sunkist packinghouses according to their levels of crop production on a prorate basis, as in the case of the Pacific market.

Because Sunkist Central orders lemons for export on the basis of expected future prices that may differ from actual prices, a cooperative residual may result which can be either positive or negative. This residual plus any losses on sales in the Pacific market are pooled across fresh shipments every six months. Even though Pacific markets are firm sale markets, losses do occur from time to time that are not fully insured. (See, for example, note in table 5–6.) One pool runs from November through April; the other runs from May through October. The pool loss (or gain) over a six-month period is divided by the total number of cartons of fresh lemons shipped in both the domestic and foreign markets over the same period. Each packinghouse shares in the loss (or gain) depending on its volume of fresh movement.

Although the export pools could in principle be used to allow the dumping of fruit in export markets, the manner in which such pools actually operate supports the view that pooling is used to reduce risks in a market characterized by substantial uncertainty. Export pools could support dumping in European markets if initial prices paid by Sunkist Central were systematically and substantially in excess of prices that would be justified on the basis of the actual prices received at a later time. The packinghouse that did not export its share of the total opportunity would need to pay into the pool to make up for pool losses, but would not share fully in the initial gains due to excessively high export prices. To minimize

Table 5–6
Export Pool Adjustments for Lemons, 1971/72 through 1974/75
(cents per carton)

Year	November–April	May–October
1971/72	+1.63¢	+23.72¢
1972/73	–3.87	+6.91
1973/74	+1.28	–13.42
1974/75[a]	–11.25	–12.45

Source: A compilation of statistics by Sunkist on lemon marketing.

[a]The negative adjustments in 1974/75 were due mainly to a problem arising out of Japanese objections to chemical residues in California/Arizona citrus, some of which had arrived before the problem was fully understood.

carrying the burden, the individual packinghouse would need to ship its full share of the export opportunity.

The available data indicate, however, that the export pools are not managed in this way. More particularly, initial prices are based on best estimates of what prices will be in European markets upon arrival of the fruit. The data given in table 5–6 show that the export pool residual is sometimes positive and sometimes negative with no systematic tendency one way or the other.

The reason why Sunkist uses export pools is to reduce risks associated with the uncertainties associated with selling in the European market. While the data in table 5–6 suggest only a few cents per carton are involved, it must be stressed that export pool losses (or gains) are spread over total fresh movement. If expressed as cents per carton of export shipments, it can be shown that very large discrepancies (as between expected future prices and later realized prices) occur frequently.

FTC Allegations Regarding Sunkist's Operations in Foreign Markets

The Federal Trade Commission complaint charging Sunkist with monopolizing included the export market for lemons and oranges among the relevant markets. On February 7, 1978, FTC counsel eliminated from the case these relevant markets. Counsel emphasized, however, that: "We believe Sunkist employed and continues to employ export sales to hold an 'umbrella' over domestic market prices. Hence, such export activities are relevant proof of Sunkist's domestic market monopoly power." It is not clear from this statement what method FTC counsel believed Sunkist was using to create an umbrella over domestic prices, but he presumably believed Sunkist was dumping in the foreign market.

Because of the manner in which Sunkist organizes its export of lemons, dumping lemons in foreign markets at prices below alternative outlets is not feasible. Although packinghouses and district exchanges have a substantial voice in determining export potential, once the potential is established by Sunkist Central, any one packinghouse is limited as to the amount it can export. In this manner, export potential establishes an upward limit on the amounts of Sunkist exports. The individual packinghouse is under no obligation, however, to export its share of the export potential. If FOB prices for Pacific shipments (pay prices for European shipments) are low relative to other market alternatives, the individual packinghouse has both the financial incentive and freedom to refrain from selling its share of the export opportunity to Sunkist Central.

On August 1, 1979, complaint counsel articulated still another theory as to how Sunkist used exports as an alleged source of market power. Counsel asserted:

> It is our belief that the export market is used by Sunkist as a means of limiting the ability of domestic marketing organizations to increase significantly their share of domestically produced citrus.
>
> Our theory is that the export market is a necessary outlet for fresh fruit. And there has been testimony to that effect.
>
> It is our further belief that growers select a marketing organization in order to sell successfully in export sufficient volume to offer variety, depth, and continuity in shipments, thereby reducing transportation charges.
>
> Sunkist's success in export is based upon, in part, its ability to obtain a sufficient volume to move the fruit in export.[61]

When the FTC filed its Trial Brief, it neither presented evidence of dumping in foreign markets nor repeated its earlier allegation of dumping. Indeed, only one reference was made to Sunkist's operations in foreign markets. Without elaboration, the brief states that one of the two factors (the other being artificial product differentiation) giving Sunkist a price premium was "its strong export market, which as well as carrying its own premium . . . helps to support the domestic market's price premium."[62] Evidently, this premium resulted from the advantages enjoyed by Sunkist as described in the preceding statement of counsel.

FTC counsel seems to be saying that to be a successful marketer of fresh citrus in foreign markets required large-scale operations. Hence, Sunkist now was being dammed, not for restricting the domestic supply by dumping in foreign markets, but because its successful export programs resulted in higher returns for citrus sold abroad.

There are indeed some significant economies of scale in selling California/Arizona citrus in foreign markets.[63] It is generally acknowledged that, because of its size, Sunkist took the initiatives responsible for opening the Japanese markets to California/Arizona citrus. It likewise was responsible for developing a complex multilateral trade arrangement enabling it to sell lemons behind the Iron Curtain. Although Sunkist was responsible for these and other trade initiatives, other U.S. marketers subsequently exploited these opportunities.

Sunkist also enjoys significant transportation scale economies in serving foreign markets. It contracted with Salen Reefer Service Company (SRSC) in Stockholm, Sweden. The contract is annual and assures Sunkist of the services of chartered vessels for moving citrus to export markets. Sunkist advises SRSC three weeks prior to sailing of the need for a chartered vessel, indicting a firm volume of cartons to be shipped. Sunkist pays a per-carton rate established at the beginning of the season. Apparently,

75,000 cartons is a break-even point in that a lesser quantity could be more economically shipped on a liner vessel that may handle a wide variety of goods as opposed to a charter vessel specializing in citrus transport. Over 90 percent of Sunkist citrus exports move on chartered vessels.[64] There are several advantages associated with using charter vessels. These include lower rates, greater flexibility in timing shipments, and better care of fruit. Smaller citrus marketers may not enjoy these economies.

Against this short factual background, what can be made of the FTC theory that Sunkist monopolized because it enjoyed economies of scale in international markets? First, the theory once again overlooks the distinction between a federated cooperative and a profit-seeking corporation. Any savings that the Sunkist System might achieve through using charters as opposed to liner vessels would accrue to growers in the form of higher prices for citrus. Since Sunkist is an open-membership cooperative, the higher prices would cause the supply to increase until a new competitive equilibrium was reached.

Second, insofar as Sunkist enjoys certain advantages due to economies of scale and aggressive development of foreign markets, this does not constitute "the willful acquisition or maintenance" of monopoly, but, rather, success achieved "as a consequence of a superior product, business acumen, or historic accident."[65] Perhaps for the above reason, the FTC's Brief pretty well abandoned the charges that Sunkist's operations in foreign markets constituted monopolizing conduct.

Pricing Processed Lemon Products

Sunkist processes both lemon and orange products. Since processing is relatively more important in lemons than in oranges and because Sunkist holds a larger market share in lemons than oranges, this discussion is limited to lemons. In order to understand Sunkist's pricing of lemon products, one must have some appreciation of Sunkist's policy toward acceptance of product lemons from members, the temporal pattern of deliveries of such fruit to Sunkist processing plants, the nature of the supply response for product lemons, and the nature of the demand for lemon products. These topics are discussed in turn. Thereafter, we turn first to the pricing of Sunkist lemon products and then to the FTC charges.

As noted previously, all product fruit of Sunkist packinghouses is delivered to Sunkist Central. This fruit must be accepted by Sunkist Central. According to the bylaws, "Sunkist shall establish pools for the handling, processing, and marketing of all products fruit."[66] This policy was affirmed by the deposition testimony of the president of Sunkist Growers, Inc., when he said: "Yes, Sunkist's obligation to its growers is to take in and handle products that they deliver to us, whatever it may be, whatever the vagaries of nature may have been. So we don't have any control over supply."[67] The strength of Sunkist Central's commitment to market all products fruits was put to an extreme test in the 1974/75 season, when the delivery of product lemons to Sunkist Central was 174 percent of the average deliveries for the five-year period 1972/73 through 1976/77. The financial problems caused by this massive delivery will be discussed shortly.

The data on lemon production and utilization considered previously indicate that the products outlet is a residual outlet which has absorbed an increasing amount of the crop in recent years, so that since 1980, over 50 percent of the lemon crop has been processed. Weather variation and other factors cause annual lemon production to vary considerably over time. Fresh deliveries have tended, in recent years, to grow at a relatively stable rate. This has given rise to widely fluctuating supplies of product lemons delivered to Sunkist processing plants both within and among seasons. The percent change in net tons of product lemons received from one year to the next averaged 41 percent over the period 1952/53 through 1977/78, as calculated from data given in table 5–7.

The nature of supply response for product lemons reflects the manner in which packinghouses and growers are paid for lemons delivered to processing plants. The returns to the packinghouse are ordinarily determined through pools that are operated by Sunkist Central. Briefly, product lemons are accumulated in bins at packinghouses and eventually shipped to processing plants, either the lemon products division plant at Corona or the Arizona products division plant at Yuma. The quality of the fruit is determined in terms of the presence of trash, decayed fruit, and odd sizes and through approximating its acid content. (A standard ton is a poundage containing 36.5 pounds of citric acid.) Returns to packinghouses depend in specified ways on quality of fruit delivered. All fruit received from November 1 to the following October 31 is within the same pool. Separate subpools are established for juice and peel. Proceeds from the sales of juice products and peel products are credited to the respective subpools, whereas natural net tons (gross tons less decay) determine returns from peel subpools.

For several years, Sunkist adopted a policy of transferring any remaining inventory from one pool to the next pool on November 1, treating the accounting transaction as a sale. Because of an IRS ruling in 1973, each pool must now be 95 percent sold before it can be closed. Pools may be open for more than one year; multiple pools may be open at the same time. Because considerable time may elapse between the opening and closing of a pool, advance payments may be made to packinghouses at the discretion of Sunkist's board of directors.

Since final pool returns are unknown at the time of product lemon deliveries, the quantity of such deliveries must be based on expected pool returns. This may account in part for the insensitivity of deliveries in any

Table 5–7
Tonnage of Product Lemons Received and Sold
by Sunkist Growers, Inc., 1950/51
through 1977/78

Year	Product Lemons Received	Product Lemons Sold to Other Processors
1950/51	173,022[a]	NA
1951/52	152,008[a]	NA
1952/53	141,017	NA
1953/54	257,787	NA
1954/55	153,414	NA
1955/56	126,837	NA
1956/57	177,819	NA
1957/58	195,696	NA
1958/59	252,410	NA
1959/60	228,629	NA
1960/61	115,954	19,341
1961/62	181,490	31,563
1962/63	92,494	30,520
1963/64	208,008	37,856
1964/65	131,729	16,244
1965/66	181,272	12,552
1966/67	265,914	21,785
1967/68	220,646	16,577
1968/69	197,349	12,432
1969/70	190,460	12,427
1970/71	201,793	13,047
1971/72	228,656	11,946
1972/73	335,050	10,959
1973/74	232,263	11,725
1974/75	547,784	6,179
1975/76	222,521	9,226
1976/77	325,660	24,752
1977/78	372,198	NA

Source: Sunkist Growers, Inc.

NA = Not available.

[a]Gross weight.

one season to changes in the demand for lemon products during that season.

Over the long run, however, one must expect a positive response of product lemon deliveries to pool returns. With given demands for fresh lemons, higher product pool returns encourage shifting choice and standard grade lemons from the European markets to processing. Further, product pool returns account for about 15 to 20 percent or more of the total returns to total lemon production, although in recent years, over 50 percent of the total lemon crop was sold as product lemons. An increase in returns would therefore have at least a modest impact on decisions to change lemon tree acreage. Thus, to the extent Sunkist Central is able to increase the prices of lemon products, the product pool returns to growers will also increase, with a corresponding positive long-run effect on lemon production.

As we turn to the demand for lemon products, it is important to note that product lemons yield two component products in roughly fixed proportions. These are lemon juice and lemon peel. Although several juice products are manufactured by Sunkist, the percentage of juice accounted for by concentrated lemon juice, both frozen and unfrozen, tended upward starting in the early 1950s and by 1979–80 was about 90 percent.[68] The production of concentrated lemon juice is heavily dependent on product lemons processed. Regressing production of concentrated lemon juice (JP) on product lemons processed (PLP) and linear trend (T) for the years 1960/61 through 1976/77 yields the following equation:

$$JP = 67.627 + 0.0007(PLP) + 49.994(T); \qquad R^2 = 0.90 \qquad (5.2)$$
$$(4.38) \qquad\qquad (1.32)$$

where the numbers in parentheses are t-ratios. The data used in the regression, with the exception of trend, were taken from tables 5–7 and 5–8. (PLP equals lemons received minus lemons sold.) About 90 percent of the variation in concentrated lemon juice production is explained by PLP and T. The practical conclusion to be reached on the basis of this equation is that, aside from trend, the great variation in product lemons processed causes a considerable variation in the production of concentrated juice.

The basic importance of the demand for and pricing of concentrated lemon juice is derived not only from its dominance in turns of juice use, but also because of the manner in which much of the concentrated juice is marketed. Sunkist's division manager of product sales described the price discovery process as follows:

> The structure of the market for the Lemon Products Division is such that we must establish opening prices for concentrated juice, usually in October for the oncoming year. This takes place in the negotiating of supply contracts. . . . While such contracts provide some opportunity for changing prices, there isn't much doubt that once fixed they tend to establish a level that we are reluctant to move, and therefore exhibit at least a dragging force on price movement in either direction. Since many of our sales are to people who compete with each other and at least in some cases, are to people whose finished product competes with finished products that we make, there is a decided tendency for prices of most juice products to move together and to be related to the concentrate price except where differences can be justified.[69]

The short-run demand for concentrated lemon juice appears to be extremely inelastic. That is to say, within any given crop year, altering the price of juice would have a small impact on the quantity purchased. The

Table 5–8
Sunkist Concentrated Lemon Juice, Frozen and Unfrozen: Production,
Year-End Inventory, Quantity Sold in Domestic Market, and Domestic
Price, 1950/51 through 1977/78
(thousands of pounds)

Year	Production	Year-End Inventory	Domestic Sales	Domestic Price per Gallon
1950/51	185	NA	NA	NA
1951/52	274	53	NA	NA
1952/53	436	NA	NA	NA
1953/54	1,046	924	NA	NA
1954/55	634	890	NA	NA
1955/56	380	455	557	$5.72
1956/57	2,198	638	734	4.28
1957/58	2,628	464	899	4.29
1958/59	2,588	1,496	597	5.12
1959/60	3,074	1,737[a]	805	4.65
1960/61	2,370	779	1,276	5.25
1961/62	2,006	918	850	5.74
1962/63	1,399	149	997	6.31
1963/64	2,218	912	955	4.51
1964/65	1,981	540	1,404	3.50
1965/66	2,599	263	1,883	3.52
1966/67	3,134	973	2,007	3.90
1967/68	3,124	1,129	1,934	3.87
1968/69	3,305	691	2,043	3.99
1969/70	2,541	157	2,283	3.97
1970/71	2,344	387	2,294	4.45
1971/72	2,416	572	2,349	4.56
1972/73	3,951	2,123	1,858	4.55
1973/74	2,795	2,387	2,044	4.66
1974/75	5,058	6,679	1,477	4.48
1975/76	3,067	5,502[a]	3,031	3.50
1976/77	4,941	4,708[a]	3,144	3.61
1977/78	3,241	3,368	NA	NA

Source: Records of Sunkist Growers, Inc.

NA = Not available.

[a]Contains inventory owned by ReaLemon.

principle uses of concentrated lemon juice are reconstituted bottled lemon juice and soft drinks. (Limited amounts of juice are used in the manufacture of single-strength juice and lemonade.) The cost of concentrate used in bottled lemon juice and soft drinks is modest relative to the total cost of manufacture and marketing those products (perhaps 25 percent in the case of bottled juice). Sunkist sales personnel believe the demand for concentrated lemon juice is extremely inelastic.

In order to develop independent estimates, we have used regression analysis to estimate the demand for concentrated juice. The dependent variable,

DJSP, is annual quantity of Sunkist concentrated lemon juice sold (see table 5-8) divided by U.S. population in millions. The independent variables are (1) Sunkist's domestic price of concentrated juice per gallon (see table 5-8) deflated by the index of wholesale prices, *DPWP*, (2) the average raw cane sugar price, duty paid CIF, New York, deflated by the index of wholesale prices, *SPWP*, and (3) the real per capita personal income measured by dividing U.S. personal income in billions of dollars by the product of the consumer price index and U.S. population in millions, *PICP*. The wholesale price index is expressed as a ratio instead of a percentage. Price is viewed as a predetermined variable in light of the explanation of lemon juice pricing given above. The estimated equation is as follows:

$$DJSP = 6.174 - 0.7867(DPWP) - 0.4809(SPWP) + 553.84(PICP) \quad (5.3)$$
$$\quad\quad (1.29) \quad\quad\quad (2.68) \quad\quad\quad (4.31)$$

where the numbers in parentheses are t-ratios. Estimated coefficients have the correct signs in that we would expect the demand to be downward sloping, positively affected by increases in per capita income, and negatively associated with the price of the complementary good sugar. The t-ratios are high except for own price, but such ratios are based on the null hypothesis that the population parameter is zero. If the coefficient for *DPWP* were in fact zero, the demand for concentrated juice would be perfectly inelastic. Using the BLUE estimate for the coefficient for *DPWP* (viz., -0.7867) yields an estimate of the elasticity of demand evaluated at the means equal to -0.28. This means that a 10 percent decrease in Sunkist's price of concentrated lemon juice would cause their per capita sales to increase by 2.8 percent. Sunkist's sales manager's estimate of demand is confirmed by this analysis. The demand for concentrated lemon juice appears to be very inelastic.

At this juncture, it is important to point out that neither the monopolist nor the dominant firm as envisaged in economic theory would ever operate in the inelastic part of the demand curve. The reason for this, of course, is that marginal revenue is negative when demand is inelastic. Better—from the point of view of the monopolist or the dominant firm—to pour the juice down the gutter than sell it at negative marginal revenue. This suggests at the very least that Sunkist's pricing of concentrated lemon juice is heavily constrained by factors other than its market share, a conclusion consistent with the theory of a nonprofit cooperative practicing open membership.[70]

Turning from juice to peel products, we note that lemon oil is the most important of the peel products. Lemon oil is produced roughly in fixed proportion to product lemons processed. Regressing Sunkist lemon oil production on quantity of lemons processed yields a coefficient of multiple correlation equal to 0.978. (See tables 5–7 and 5–9 for the data used in the computations.) Typically, a ton of product lemons yields 7.7 pounds of lemon oil. An important point to bear in mind is that the quantity of lemon oil that must be marketed is beyond the control of Sunkist Central.

As in the case of lemon juice, Sunkist personnel with major responsibilities in the pricing of lemon oil believe that demand is inelastic. One reason for a belief of short-run inelasticity concerns the major use to which such oil is put. About 95 to 98 percent of Sunkist lemon oil is used in some

Table 5–9
Sunkist Lemon Oil: Year-End Inventory, Quantity Sold, and Average Price, 1950/51 through 1977/78
(thousands of pounds)

Year	Production	Year-End Inventory	Quantity Sold	Average Price per Pound
1950/51	774	151	702	3.66
1951/52	588	183	514	5.63
1952/53	604	151	478	6.28
1953/54	1,116	785	497	6.84
1954/55	701	925	498	5.72
1955/56	484	780	509	5.34
1956/57	812	916	631	4.09
1957/58	979	1,047	771	3.84
1958/59	1,370	1,655	658	3.58
1959/60	1,189	1,312	1,363	1.59
1960/61	729	333	1,769	1.54
1961/62	974	184	1,079	2.47
1962/63	575	134	578	5.96
1963/64	1,325	670	683	5.34
1964/65	830	571	843	4.59
1965/66	1,224	512	1,179	4.58
1966/67	1,685	714	1,357	4.55
1967/68	1,604	694	1,505	4.72
1968/69	1,436	557	1,447	4.52
1969/70	1,444	335	1,521	5.46
1970/71	1,658	734	1,215	6.47
1971/72	1,912	956	1,517	6.48
1972/73	2,613	1,054	2,204	6.55
1973/74	1,852	687	1,921	6.81
1974/75	4,086	3,038	1,597	6.63
1975/76	1,702	2,358	2,115	6.01
1976/77	2,442	2,128	2,314	6.49
1977/78	2,432	1,331	NA	7.20

Source: Sunkist Growers, Inc.

NA = Not available.

form of beverage.[71] Apparently, the cost of lemon oil used in beverages is a very small component of total costs.

Regression analysis was used to estimate the demand for lemon oil. The dependent variable (*LOSP*) equals the quantity of Sunkist lemon oil sold, in thousands of pounds, divided by U.S. population in millions. (See table 5-9 for the data.) The first of three independent variables is the price of Sunkist lemon oil per pound deflated by the index of wholesale prices, *LOWP*. The other independent variables (*SPWP* and *PICP*) also appeared in equation 5.3. The resulting equation, based on twenty-seven observations, is as follows:

$$LOSP = 1.9167 - 1.161(LOWP) - 0.0148(SPWP) + 289.41(PICP) \quad (5.4)$$
$$(4.95) \qquad\qquad (.10) \qquad\qquad (5.94)$$

where the numbers in parentheses are t-ratios. The signs are consistent with expectations and the estimated coefficient for own price, *LOWP*, is highly significant. The coefficient of multiple correlation equals 0.889. The elasticity of demand evaluated at the means equals –0.62. This means that a 10 percent decrease in price would cause quantity demanded to increase by 6.2 percent. Demand is inelastic as expected.

We now take up the pricing of Sunkist lemon products, centering attention on concentrated juice, as the pricing processes for juice, oil, and other lemon products is very similar. It has already been noted that the short-run demand for concentrated lemon juice is inelastic and that Sunkist's pricing policy is constrained by a good deal more than its market share. There are two important constraints on the pricing of concentrated juice that tend in the long run to keep Sunkist's price close to the competitive level. The first reflects the great likelihood that in the long run, demand is much more elastic than the above estimate would suggest. The reasons for this are several: First, the biggest buyers of juice are large conglomerate companies with financial resources far in excess of those available to Sunkist. Two of these companies, Borden (ReaLemon) and Philip Morris (7-Up) are already partially integrated backward into lemon processing. (Borden's ReaLemon brand controls 80 to 90 percent of the retail market for processed concentrated lemon juice.)[72] The threat of entry of new capacity is an important constraint on Sunkist's pricing decisions. As evidence for this conclusion, consider the following statement of a Sunkist official responsible for establishing prices for concentrated lemon juice.

> With ReaLemon being what they are, a contract for the oncoming year is negotiated in the fall. Once that's done, that price is set for the rest of the season, and it sets other prices, unless something really extreme were to happen. In that contract there's usually some provision for price adjustment under extreme conditions, in the latter part of the year.

In trying to establish this feel for what would be a proper price, you have to take into account what you think the crop is going to be, what the general supply situation is. In the past few years, up until perhaps just recently, you would have to try to figure what was going to happen in Florida—whether they had an inventory on hand already or whether they didn't. I know this sounds like inspired guessing, and, really, I guess that's what it is. There's no mechanical way to decide what a price is going to be. Eventually, when you get to negotiating with the customers, you find that you may have to adjust your sights too.

He further stated:

The figures I put together here and the other day show that the juice portion of the pool would run from, beginning back in 1964, between $25 and $30 clear. Within about a five-dollar range. Now with that kind of situation, you would tend to start with that level in mind and then fine-tune it. . . . You do certainly also have in mind the other side of it. What will customers pay, and particularly, what will ReaLemon pay? There's just no getting away from the fact that you must pay attention to a customer as big as ReaLemon has been.[73]

When asked whether there was anything that ReaLemon could realistically do if it decided Sunkist's price was too high, a different top Sunkist official said: "They could have gone out and bought a processing plant; they could have gone out and bought groves. . . . [A]nd when you look at some of these major companies like Borden who have the capital resources to move in any direction, this is one of the things you are always concerned about."[74] The fact that Tenneco owns substantial citrus acreage in California's central valley may explain in part the concern of Sunkist officials as to further backward integration on the part of large juice buyers. Large corporate holdings of citrus acreage are not by any means out of the realm of possibility.

A second factor that gives rise to some elasticity in the long run is the competition offered by other processors coupled with Sunkist's inability to limit membership. Smaller processors are free to undercut Sunkist prices and sell all or much of their output without bothering to maintain large inventories in seasons of high production. At one point in his discussion of juice pricing, a top Sunkist official stated, "We can establish a complete umbrella for everyone . . . and then we'll get what's left over. And this is one thing we want to avoid."[75] If Sunkist builds up inventory without prospect of selling the inventory later at a sufficiently high price to cover storage costs, then other processors are in a position to take full advantage of the umbrella, paying higher prices for product lemons than the pool returns to Sunkist packinghouses. Sunkist packinghouses would suffer a disadvantage in the competition for grower affiliation.

Other factors contributing to long-run demand elasticity include the introduction of substitutes, such as citric acid in beverages; encouraging development of synthetics; and buyers' cultivation of foreign sources of lemon juice. Italy used to be an important source of juice for domestic buyers, but, in more recent years, Argentina and Brazil have become more likely sources of supply.[76] Unfortunately, the available data do not allow a precise estimate of juice imports as a source of competition.

The major factor that forces Sunkist to charge competitive prices for concentrated lemon juice is its inability to control production. In any one season, Sunkist Central could undoubtedly raise price above the competitive level. With short-run inelastic demand, this would entail a cutback in sales of juice at the same time that pool returns to packinghouses and growers would be increased. Over several seasons, buyers would be encouraged to buy less at the same time growers would be encouraged to produce more. The implication is that Sunkist inventories would begin to accumulate with no long-run prospect that a buildup would ever cease. The position of Sunkist would become increasingly untenable.

This brings us to a central hypothesis as regards the long-run tendency of Sunkist prices for concentrated lemon juice. This hypothesis asserts that in the long run, over several seasons and allowing for production adjustments on the part of both lemon juice buyers and product lemon sellers, Sunkist must price its juice such that in a normal crop year (with average yields) all the product lemons received are marketed and the resulting concentrated lemon juice is sold to buyers rather than added to inventory. In years of ample supply, relative to normal, an inventory of juice may be accumulated, but not in such quantity as will more than allow a drawing down of inventories in years when supply is small relative to normal. In brief, Sunkist must price concentrated lemon juice to move normal production into consumption, avoiding in the process the endless accumulation of inventory. The resulting market performance is what one would expect from vigorous competition in the absence of price discrimination and the physical destruction of product lemons. We have no data to suggest that Sunkist has destroyed product lemons nor has the FTC charged that this has occurred. The question of price discrimination will be taken up at various points in the remainder of this analysis.

We turn next to a statistical analysis in order to test the central hypothesis posed above. The data given in table 5–8 show a considerable variation in the domestic price of concentrated lemon juice over time. The question to be explored is how are these prices determined given highly variable supplies from year to year, a highly inelastic short-run demand for juice, and a market structure that reflects bigness in selling (Sunkist) and substantial concentration in procurement. Four independent variables are used to explain Sunkist's domestic price of concentrated lemon juice per gallon,

LDJP, as reported in table 5–8. The first of these is inserted to reflect the hypothesis that, *ceteris paribus*, a high level of juice production relative to what is perceived by Sunkist to be the normal supply exerts a downward pressure on prices. To test this hypothesis, we insert as an independent variable current lemon juice production divided by a moving average of juice production over the past five years, *LNPJ*. A five-year moving average of production is used as a proxy for perceived normal supply.

A second variable is inserted to test the hypothesis that, *ceteris paribus*, a large carry-in of juice inventory from the previous year relative to normal supply exerts a downward pressure on juice price. To test this hypothesis, we insert the variable past year's ending juice inventory divided by a moving average of production for the past five years, *LNIJ*. (See table 5–8 for the data on both *LNPJ* and *LNIJ*.)

The index of wholesale prices, *LWPI*, is inserted as a third independent variable to account for the increasing prices of inputs used in the production of concentrated juice. Linear trend, *LPTT*, is included as a fourth independent variable in order to capture the effects of any omitted variables that may follow systematic trends over time. Examples might include technological change, a negative or positive growth in demand relative to supply, and changes in foreign markets. It should be noted that including an irrelevant variable does not bias estimates of coefficients for relevant variables. Including trend is essentially a conservative measure designed to minimize the chance of biased estimates.

The estimated equation is:

$$LDJP = 5.5473 - 0.7509(LNPJ) - 1.041(LNIJ) \qquad (5.5)$$
$$(3.49) \qquad\qquad (2.50)$$
$$+ \; 0.0418(LWPI) - 0.2566(LPTT)$$
$$(3.04) \qquad\qquad (4.13)$$

where the numbers in parentheses are t-ratios. The estimated coefficients are highly significant and the signs for *LNPJ*, *LNIJ*, and *LWPI* are as expected. The coefficient of multiple correlation equals 0.785, which means that about 79 percent of the variation in juice price is explained by the independent variables.

We believe the above statistical results shed considerable light on the intrinsically difficult question of how Sunkist prices concentrated lemon juice. Sunkist personnel stress the importance of judgment and subjective evaluation. Without doubt, judgment is important, but the above results suggest that in setting the current price, the price from the previous year is adjusted downward according to whether inventory has grown relative to normal supply and/or whether current production is large relative to normal supply.

The analysis of lemon juice prices up to this point has centered on domestic prices. The price of concentrated lemon juice moving into the foreign market is heavily dependent on prices of juice from other countries. According to one of Sunkist's former marketing executives, "We continually get quotations from people in Europe, our own people, Sunkist employees, as to what the offerings are of Sicilian and South American juice, orange, grapefruit, and lemon. And this normally constitutes an inquiry; are you willing to meet it?"[77]

We have no systematic data on export prices for Sunkist concentrated lemon juice. In any event, simple comparisons between export and domestic prices in order to assess the possiblity of price discrimination would appear to be an unsatisfactory research procedure. The reason for this is that Sunkist is committed to continuity of supplies to a much larger extent in the domestic market than in the foreign market. Over the period 1955/56 through 1976/77, exports of concentrated lemon juice as a percentage of total juice sold varied from a low of 3 percent in 1963/64 and again in 1966/67 to a high of around 20 percent in several years, with no apparent trend. In the late 1960s and early 1970s, Sunkist used up its concentrate inventories and actually imported lemon juice and oil to supply its customers. Also, in years of short supply, Sunkist has used an allocation program to spread out its sales equitably among contract customers. (In 1978/79, Sunkist sold about 75 percent of its lemon oil and 60 percent of its concentrated juice through annual contracts negotiated in late fall, prior to certain knowledge of the upcoming season's production.) Thus, at some point in a short season, remaining contract purchases might be cut by 10 percent, say, so that all regular customers get their fair share. This practice has been used instead of allowing price to rise to a level that would have allowed allocation on the basis of willingness to pay. Through carrying inventories, allocation programs, and imports, Sunkist has striven to establish a reputation as a steady source of supply to its traditional customers and to bring price stability to the domestic market. In light of these considerations, it would appear quite plausible that price premiums received by Sunkist in the domestic market, over and above export prices, might well be justified by efforts made by Sunkist to assure continuity of domestic supply.

FTC Allegations That Sunkist Monopolized Processed Lemon Products

FTC counsel's Brief charged that Sunkist used "its control of over 70 percent of raw product lemons and of primary lemon juice sales to manipulate lemon juice supply and thereby control prices."[78] This was accomplished through withholding juice suppy from the market and through prohibiting Sunkist packinghouses from selling product-grade lemons to outside processors.

The FTC Brief relied on three sorts of evidence to support its charges that Sunkist had monopolistic control over concentrated lemon juice prices. (1) Sunkist allegedly attempted in 1974/75 to manipulate the supply of lemon juice. (2) Sunkist allegedly adopted a sales incentive compensation plan in 1970/71 for the purpose of limiting the sales of lemon juice. (3) Sunkist acted as the price leader in the sale of concentrated lemon juice.

Price Leadership. The last of these charges may be dismissed in short order. There can be little question that Sunkist is a price leader. Moreover, since Sunkist owns and controls the bulk of the capacity to produce, market, and store concentrated lemon juice, it could within any one marketing year (or even several years) elevate price above competitive levels. The relevant question, however, is whether it has the capacity and incentive to elevate prices above a long-run competitive level. As we have already seen in our discussion of fresh fruit pricing, price leadership is wholly compatible with highly competitive performance. And again, we must stress that Sunkist has no control of production. Any systematic efforts to elevate price above the competitive level in one year inevitably imply an ever larger buildup of inventory.

Sales Incentive Compensation Plan. The allegations regarding Sunkist's 1970/71 sales incentive compensation plan are without merit. The plan was used for only a single year and, in that year, did not result in reduced sales as the FTC Brief claims. On the contrary, sales in 1970/71 were above those in the previous year and the five succeeding years. Finally, if Sunkist had sought to limit lemon juice sales, it could have done so more directly than through the compensation plan, which was simply a way of compensating salespeople's efforts. The plan was not used after 1970/71 because Sunkist officials did not believe it was the most appropriate means of providing incentive to sales staff.

Sunkist's Alleged Use of Special Pools to Control Supply. The bulk of the FTC's evidence regarding Sunkist's alleged monopolization of the processed lemon juice market related to Sunkist's conduct during the 1974/75 bumper crop year for lemons. As a result, Sunkist's lemon products inventory at the end of 1974/75 season was about thirteen times the normal level.[79] The FTC charged that "to deal with this extraordinarily large lemon products inventory, Sunkist implemented a plan called the 'Lemon Set-Aside Pool.' This plan created two lemon pools, a regular pool and a "set-aside" pool."[80] Sunkist assigned 270,000 tons of fruit to the regular pool and 371,000 tons to the set-aside pool. Whereas products from the regular pool were sold for normal market uses, sales from the set-aside pool were to be made in markets not traditionally supplied by Sunkist, including sales for new products that would not displace uses already served by Sunkist. It was also contemplated that in future years, regular pools would close within a year with any unsold product included in the set-aside pool.[81] The 1974/75 set-aside pool was closed in 1979.

FTC counsel argued that the set-aside pool resulted in monopolistic pricing and that Sunkist recognized that "the ability to store and finance a voluminous inventory was essential to prevent prices from falling."[82] It cited a 1975 memorandum to the Sunkist board of directors as proof that Sunkist recognized its monopoly power: "Our competitors do not have either the storage facilities nor the financial resources to carry inventory. Consequently, they will lead in cutting prices which could reduce lemon earnings to the $30-35 per ton level before current inventories are sold."[83]

Counsel further indicated that because the demand for the lemon juice withheld was "highly inelastic," Sunkist's efforts were successful: "Although prices did decline somewhat, they did not fall nearly as much as they would have if Sunkist had not deliberately withheld thirteen times its normal inventory."[84]

Because of its experience with the huge 1974/75 crop, in July 1976, Sunkist's board of directors adopted a general plan to cope with future large lemon crops. Called the "lemon contingency reserve pool," the plan provided that packinghouses were entitled to deliver up to 250,000 tons of fruit to the regular pools.[85] For deliveries in excess of this, packinghouses would pay an assessment per ton. Those not wishing to participate could sell their fruit elsewhere, but only in outlets not competing with Sunkist and with its approval.[86] The FTC alleged that the practical effect of this requirement was that those not participating in the plan had to dispose of their fruit for "cattle feed or destruction, with neither alternative providing very much money."[87]

As evidence that Sunkist created the contingency pool plan for the express purpose of "limiting supply and preventing a glut of lemon products on the market," FTC counsel cited the following: "It is in the interest of Sunkist to maintain the current demand-supply relationship; *any increase in supply would only glut the market with the resulting deterioration in prices and returns;* economic interests suggest Sunkist gears its supply management to the optimum market level."[88]

The contingency pool plan was only in operation for one-half year, but FTC counsel argued that adoption of the plan demonstrated that "Sunkist possesses the power to manipulate supply and control price and that it exercises that power when necessary."[89]

Regarding the buildup of inventory, there can be little doubt that Sunkist has the ability to withhold concentrated lemon juice from the market, thus maintaining price at a level above that which would otherwise prevail. It is clear from the record, however, that the substantial increase in the inventory of concentrated lemon juice in the 1974/75 season was the result of highly unusual climatic conditions, not the result of monopolistic pricing. The carrying of stocks from a period of relative abundance to a period of relative scarcity has been recognized as a valuable economic function since Biblical times. Such activity tends to stabilize price and producer income while assuring consumers of stable supply. Highly competitive markets, as in the case of grains, will on occasion carry large stocks of old crop into the new crop year. It is, indeed, often alleged that even competitive markets do not, on average, carry sufficiently large old crop stocks to assure optimal price stabilization, an allegation that is sometimes advanced as an argument in favor of government buffer-stock schemes of various kinds.

A major problem with the position of FTC counsel is that it offers neither theory nor evidence to suggest, much less prove, that the pricing and storage decisions of Sunkist gave rise to a noncompetitive market performance in the temporal dimension. Presumably, FTC counsel would have been less concerned with Sunkist performance if it had channeled more juice into the consumption outlet at a lower price. What levels of consumption and price would have been judged to be competitive? FTC counsel does not say. Our view, as expressed earlier, is that in the absence of control over production of lemons, Sunkist must price concentrated lemon juice to avoid the endless buildup of inventory. We believe, moreover, that the FTC counsel seriously misjudged the implications of Sunkist's handling of the 1974/75 lemon crop.

Fruits and vegetables tend to be highly perishable. Producers are rightly concerned that market outlets exist for their outputs at harvest time, that they "have a home" for their fruit in the case of western citrus. Sunkist's decision to construct and/or acquire lemon-processing facilities and to accept all product lemons produced by its members mirrors this concern of producers. Sunkist's agreement to accept all product lemons represents a substantial risk, however, a risk that an enormously large supply might put considerable strain on its processing capacity, financial situation, or both.

Importantly, there are many examples of crops that are simply not harvested in years of high yields because canners and freezers do not wish to commit their financial reserves to the carrying of large stocks. Tomatoes grown for processing in California are a notable case in point. It frequently happens that tomatoes are left to rot in the fields in years of exceptionally high yields. The essential point is that physical waste must not be interpreted necessarily as economic waste or inefficiency.

In the 1974/75 season, estimates of the size of the crop rose dramatically as the season progressed. Sunkist's agreement to accept all product fruit strained both its financial position and its ability to market fruit through normal channels. Its inventory of concentrated lemon juice rose substantially as noted. The FTC counsel admits that Sunkist's lemon juice price "declined somewhat." In fact, Sunkists's average annual juice prices fell by 25 percent over the two years 1974/75 and 1975/76 relative to the price in 1973/74. (See table 5–8.) The lemon contingency reserve pool is best seen as an effort on the part of Sunkist, ineffective in retrospect, to establish marketing relationships that would reduce the risk of insolvency in the event of very large supplies. (If a cannery contracts with vegetable growers to purchase no more than some maximum amount of production from specified acreage, does this respresent an effort to monopolize or to reduce cannery risks?) It is also of interest to note that the price of lemon concentrate for both domestic and export use rose from $37 per ton in 1975/76 to $52 per ton in 1978/79. This represents a 41 percent increase. Viewed from a later vantage point in time, the decision of Sunkist management to increase its inventory by thirteen times the normal level in 1974/75 was probably in error. They should have increased it by even more, if they had the physical capacity to do so.

Finally, there is no evidence to support the charge that Sunkist followed classic monopolistic conduct in its handling of the huge lemon crop of 1974/75. A monopolist would have been expected to curb the supply of domestic fresh lemons in such a year. Yet, whereas Sunkist members produced 86 percent of the 1974/75 lemon crop, they accounted for 88.2 percent of fresh domestic lemon marketings, an all-time high. Their share of lemons going to the processed market was 85.8 percent, just about equal to members production, as shown in table 4–4. These facts provide no support for the hypothesis that Sunkist restricted supply in its primary market (domestic fresh lemons), as a monopolist would do in a large crop year, by diverting lemons into the processed product market or export fresh market.

Notes

1. D. Greer, *Industrial Organization and Public Policy* (New York: Macmillan, 1980), 225.

2. W.F. Mueller, "The Economics and Law of Full-Supply Contracts as Used by Agricultural Cooperatives" (Proceedings of the National Symposium on Cooperatives and the Law, University of Wisconsin-Madison, April 23–25, 1974), 99–131.

3. On occasion, prorates are so large as to be nonbinding. This could happen following a severe frost, for example, such that supply is sharply curtailed.

4. See chapter 3.

5. Deposition of Robert H. Autenrieth (July 26, 1979), 36.

6. Ibid., 50.

7. Ibid., 94–96.

8. Ibid., 99.

9. See chapter 4, notes 28 to 35.

10. In the "Complaint Counsel's Statement of Its Case" (February 7, 1978), 9, it was also asserted that Sunkist manipulated auction market prices. The reasons for this assertion were not given. The decreasing importance of auction markets in the pricing of citrus cannot be taken as cogent evidence in favor of the FTC charge because the decline of auctions is not endemic to citrus. The decline is widespread throughout fresh fruit and vegetable marketing. The only way Sunkist Central could reduce Sunkist shipments to auction markets would be through selling members' fruit at higher prices through other channels. The only way Sunkist could keep independent supplies from auction market is through dumping fruit, at least occasionally, in those markets at ruinous prices. But, the decisions to ship to auction market are made by the packinghouse manager, not by Sunkist Central or the district exchange. This, plus the absence of any mechanism for accomplishing cross-subsidizing among Sunkist houses and the fierce competition among individual houses for growers, is sufficient reason for rejecting the belief that Sunkist is able to dump fruit in auction markets. The simple fact is that the Sunkist System is operationally incapable of the manipulation alleged by the FTC. In any event, in its Trial Brief, FTC counsel did not pursue the charge of manipulating auction markets. Evidently, the FTC staff felt that it had insufficient evidence to support the charge.

11. FTC Brief, 75.

12. Ibid.

13. Ibid., 123.

14. Ibid.

15. Ibid., 58.

16. Ibid.

17. Ibid.

18. Ibid., 59.

19. Ibid., 59–60.

20. Ibid., 76.

21. Ibid. Emphasis added by FTC.

22. Ibid.

23. Ibid.

24. Ibid., 77.

25. Ibid.

26. Ibid., 78.

27. Ibid.

28. Ibid.

29. FTC Brief, 73. R.G. Bressler, memo to Sunkist, "Stabilizing the Domestic Market for Fresh Lemons," August 1959.

30. Bressler, "Stabilizing the Domestic Market," 2.

31. Ibid., 25.

32. FTC Brief, 74.

33. Bressler, "Stabilizing the Domestic Market," 32.

34. FTC Brief, 74. Emphasis added by FTC counsel.

35. Ibid., 75.

36. U.S. Dept. of Justice, *Vertical Restraint Guidelines,* reprinted in Bureau of National Affairs, *Antitrust and Trade Regulation Report,* 48, no. 119 (Washington, D.C.: GPO, January 23, 1985): 10.

37. G. Stigler, "The Kinky Oligopoly Demand Curve and Rigid Prices," *Journal of Political Economy* 60(October 1947):446.

38. J.W. Markham, "The Nature and Significance of Price Leadership," *American Economic Review* 41(December 1951):891–905.

39. Ibid., 901.

40. Ibid., 898–899.

41. See chapter 4.

42. See above this chapter.

43. FTC Brief, 124. These two statements were quoted in the brief's legal analysis at 123.

44. See above this chapter.

45. P. Bronsteen, "Allegations of Monopoly and Anticompetitive Practices in the Domestic Lemon Industry" (Ph.D. diss., University of California-Los Angeles, 1981).

46. FTC Brief, 69.

47. Ibid., 57.

48. Ibid., 58.

49. Ibid.

50. Ibid., 130–31.

51. *Proctor & Gamble Co.*, 63 FTC 1465 (1963), *vacated and remanded,* 358 F.2d 74 (6th Cir. 1966), 386 U.S. 568 (1967).

52. Federal Trade Commission. *In the Matter of Borden, Inc.*, 92 FTC 669 (1978).

53. See chapter 4.

54. See chapter 3.

55. R.L. Wills, "Evaluating Price Enhancement by Processing Cooperatives," *American Journal of Agricultural Economics* 67(May 1985):183.

56. Consider the competitive pricing of several classes of a farm commodity. A structure of prices will be observed at any one point in time reflecting the demands for and the quantities of the various classes. The price of any one class will rise (fall) *relative* to other prices if the demand-supply forces are strong (weak) for that class *relative* to other classes. The entire structure tends to rise and fall depending on aggregate demand and supply. Now consider a case in which the supply of one class, (class *A*, say) is ample relative to the supplies of other classes although the aggregate quantity is scarce. It is wholly consistent with competition if the price of class *A* remains the same while the prices of other classes increase. The structure of price increases is recognition of the short aggregate supply. The price of class *A* remains the same absolutely, but declines *relative* to the prices of other classes. Thus, the brief is in need of major qualification when it asserts that, "In a truly competitive setting, a seller would have to lower the price to encourage the sale of the excess-supply item" (p. 59). If "excess-supply item" means a class in ample supply relative to other classes in a period of ample aggregate supply, then the statement appears to be correct. If "excess-supply item" means a class in ample supply relative to other classes in a period of scarce aggregate supply, then the statement is in general not true. Thus, the argument does not really come down to the matter of switching the trade as such, but rather raises the issue of whether Sunkist can control and raise the price structure above that justified by aggregate

supply and demand. Again, the brief mistakenly infers that because Sunkist exercises some leadership in achieving appropriate prices, the resulting prices must be monopolistic ones.

57. M.F. Porter, *Competitive Advantage* (New York: Free Press, 1985).

58. Bressler, "Stabilizing the Domestic Market," 32.

59. Ibid., 44. (Emphasis added.)

60. Ibid.

61. Transcript (August 1, 1979), 99–100.

62. FTC Brief, 77.

63. See chapter 4.

64. FTC Brief, 44.

65. *United States v. Grinnel Corp.*, 384 U.S. 563, 570–71 (1966).

66. Sunkist bylaws, 13.

67. Deposition of Russell L. Hanlin (1979), 185.

68. William A. Delaney, Jr., division manager of product sales, Sunkist, Inc., interview.

69. Delaney, interview.

70. See chapter 3.

71. Delaney, interview.

72. Federal Trade Commission, *In the Matter of Borden, Inc.* FTC Docket 8978, Initial Decision (Washington, D.C.: FTC, 1976).

73. Richard S. Bylin, director of the lemon products division, 1971–78.

74. Delaney, interview.

75. Ibid.

76. Bylin, statement.

77. Ibid.

78. FTC Brief, 60.

79. Ibid., 62.

80. Ibid.

81. Ibid., 62–63.

82. Ibid., 63.

83. Ibid.

84. Ibid.

85. Ibid., 64.

86. Ibid., 65.

87. Ibid.

88. Ibid., 66. Emphasis added by FTC counsel. In the same vein, the principal draftsman of the contingency plan wrote as follows on two occasions:

> There is a *consensus of opinion that curtailment of fruit receipts is necessary.* . . . The principal of the Contingency Plan satisfies [that] appraisal. (Ibid., 66.) (emphasis added by FTC counsel.)
>
> The creation of the Contingency Reserve Pool is intended to prevent the occurrence of the condition—large volume of fruit receipts—which led to the establishment of the Set-Aside Pool. From another vantage point: the Set-Aside Pool was established as a reaction to an existing and developing condition; *the Contingency Reserve Pool is being created as a preventive and deterrent measure.* (Ibid., 66–67.) (emphasis added by FTC counsel.)

89. Ibid., 68.

6
Market Conduct: Nonprice Practices

The essence of the FTC case against Sunkist was that it had a large market share and that it engaged in a variety of practices to attain and maintain that share. In the language of the law, Sunkist allegedly had willfully maintained and enhanced its monopoly power in the various relevant markets. The law draws a distinction between the willful acquisition or maintenance of monopoly power and monopoly power achieved through superior business performance. An economic counterpart to this distinction between lawful and unlawful practices is the distinction between "innocently" created entry barriers and "strategically" created entry barriers.[1] The former result from normal profit-maximizing behavior of a firm (e.g., to achieve an economy of scale), whereas the latter are purposefully pursued to erect barriers that make entry more difficult (e.g., predatory pricing).

FTC counsel identified five specific willful acts allegedly engaged in by Sunkist to secure and maintain monopoly power in the relevant markets. To achieve this goal Sunkist:

1. Adopted, first as a corporate objective and later as a policy, the maintenance of a 70–75 percent (later 65–75 percent) share of the California-Arizona citrus production;

2. Combined with commercial packinghouses specifically to maintain its share of citrus production and to prohibit competition;

3. Enforced an informal "all or nothing" policy which requires owners of multiple commercial packinghouses to combine all of their houses with Sunkist if they want any of their houses to pack citrus for Sunkist growers;

4. Acquired a competing citrus processor, thereby eliminating a major competitor, specifically to increase its processing capacity to maintain its production share and market power; and

5. Eliminated a competing non-cooperative fresh fruit marketing organization by combining with thirteen of the fourteen packinghouses which supplied the citrus it marketed.[2]

These charges reduce to three broad categories of conduct. First, Sunkist pursued a policy of seeking to maintain a large share of the market; second, it had so-called exclusive dealing contracts with commercial packinghouses, including the informal all-or-nothing requirements for commercial houses; and third, Sunkist was involved in two combinations or acquisitions. We consider these three charges in turn.

Sunkist's Deliberately Maintaining a Dominant Share

This charge asserts that for at least twenty years, "Sunkist has intentionally attempted to control a sufficiently high percentage of the citrus produced in California and Arizona, set between 65 and 75 percent, to enable it to control prices in marketing that production."[3]

In support of the charge, FTC counsel cited statements of various Sunkist officials. The statements typically said something to the effect that Sunkist should strive to attain some specified market share. For example, in 1968, an assistant general manager stated that Sunkist should actively seek to maintain a 75 percent share.[4] Not mentioned by the FTC was the fact that Sunkist's share had been 79 percent in the prior year and 74 to 75 percent in the current year.[5] The following year, when Sunkist's share had fallen further, the Sunkist board adopted the following as a corporate objective: "To establish a membership position by variety and district in the 70% to 75% range, for each variety in each district in which it is produced."[6]

Other statements like the above were frequently made in succeeding years. Such statements, standing alone, prove nothing more than that Sunkist, like all large corporations, set goals for its management. More often than not, the statements reflected what had happened in the past rather than what was subsequently achieved, being statements of hope rather than of accomplishment. Read in this context, the statements prove no more than that Sunkist set goals expressed in market shares. Whether or not these goals, if achieved, conferred monopoly power is another matter, one requiring examination of market structure and Sunkist's conduct in these markets. The crucial question, both in law and economics, is whether Sunkist engaged in willful acts as opposed to competition on its merits in achieving its goals. We therefore turn to the market conduct Sunkist engaged in that allegedly enabled it to attain and maintain market dominance.

Sunkist's Engaging in Exclusionary Contractual Arrangements

The most serious of the three categories of charges was that relating to exclusive dealing with licensed commercial packinghouses, since it challenged an integral part of the Sunkist System. Had the FTC counsel's recommended relief been granted, it would have destroyed the System as it existed at that time.[7] Also the objections to the two challenged acquisitions rested, in large part, on the same logic as that applied to Sunkist's exclusive dealing arrangements with licensed commercial packinghouses.

We therefore begin our analysis of these charges by examining the nature and purpose of the contractual arrangements joining together the Sunkist System. In doing so, we look at the contracts involving cooperative packinghouses as well as licensed commercial packinghouses affiliated with the Sunkist System. There is little economic difference between the licensed commercial packinghouses that pack member's fruit and grower-owned cooperative packinghouses. Indeed, "Complaint Counsel's Statement of Its Case," February 7, 1978, charged Sunkist with willfully maintaining its monopoly power through exclusive dealing contracts with local cooperative houses as well as licensed commercial houses.

The effects of these contracts, according to the FTC, was to result in market foreclosure in three markets.

1. Growers that are not members of Sunkist are foreclosed from the opportunity of using the packing service of Sunkist-affiliated houses.

2. Firms that compete with Sunkist in marketing fresh fruit are foreclosed from dealing directly with Sunkist-affiliated packinghouses.

3. Processors of citrus products are foreclosed from dealing directly with Sunkist-affiliated houses in the purchase of citrus products for processing.[8]

Likewise, the FTC complaint challenged the decision in 1966 of thirteen commercial packinghouses owned by or under contract to Blue Goose Growers, Inc., to affiliate with Sunkist as licensed commercial packinghouses.[9] The FTC said the effects of the "combination, contracts, or agreements" between Sunkist and these houses prohibited the houses from dealing with non-Sunkist growers. Understanding the nature, purpose, and effects of these matters requires understanding how argicultural cooperatives, especially federated cooperatives, differ from proprietary corporations.

Purpose and Types of Cooperatives

Farmers create cooperatives to improve their economic position in a capitalist market economy. The need for cooperatives has roots in the problem created by the disparity in the structure of agricultural industries and most other parts of the economy. Farming is probably the only atomistically structured industry outside the economist's textbook.

For over a century, American farmers of many products have joined in various "cooperative" efforts, recognizing that as individuals, they were powerless in an economic system where market power, not perfectly competitive markets, more often than not sets the terms of trade. The origins of

U.S. agricultural cooperatives, therefore, are not to be found in ideology but in natural responses to nineteenth and twentieth century capitalism.

Their basic objective is economic—to enhance the economic well-being of farmers. The FTC put it simply in its large-scale inquiry into U.S. income in 1937. Speaking of the early fruit and vegetable associations, the Commission said: "They grew out of dissatisfaction on the part of growers with privately owned distribution agencies which were practically the only growers' outlets for products sold in distant markets."[10]

Farmers form cooperatives as a means of performing marketing and/or processing tasks that require larger scale than can be provided by individual farmers. Even though some farms are quite large (at least relative to other farms), they generally are too small to perform their own marketing and/or processing functions. Farmers must therefore integrate horizontally, through cooperative action, in order to perform vertically integrated marketing functions.

To achieve this result, cooperatives can assume two legal stuctures: centralized and federated associations.

1. In a *centralized* cooperative, there exists a single legal entity owned by its farmer-patrons. All rights and obligations of the farmer-patron relate directly to a single cooperative corporation.

2. A *federated* cooperative association is one in which farmers have direct membership in one cooperative which, in turn, is affiliated, usually through contract, with another cooperative corporation, often called the "central" cooperative.

At one time, many large-scale cooperatives were federated associations of local cooperatives. This often reflected the fact that farmers in various areas organized separate local cooperatives. Experience taught many of these groups that they were too small to perform various production and/or marketing functions for their owner-patrons as effectively as could larger-scale cooperatives. They then had two choices: (1) merge the local cooperatives into a single "centralized" cooperative or (2) agree to band together into a "federated" cooperative in which the local cooperative partially maintained its independence while marketing through a commonly owned central cooperative. For example, the original local cooperatives might continue to manufacture butter but form a new association to market the butter. Such was the origin of Land O'Lakes Creameries, Inc., in 1924.

Various factors determine whether local cooperatives desiring to form large organizations choose the centralized or federated cooperative route. A major reason farmers prefer the federated route to large-scale cooperatives is a desire to maintain control over the initial stage of the marketing process while enjoying the economies of large-scale operations at some subsequent stage.

Through the years, as circumstances changed, many cooperatives have been transformed from federated cooperatives to centralized cooperatives. Others have incorporated features of both types of cooperatives, e.g., some farmers in an association hold ownership in local cooperatives that, in turn, hold an interest in the central unit, whereas other farmers in the cooperative hold a direct ownership in the central unit of the association.

Whether a cooperative is a centralized or federated cooperative is in part an accident of its history or stage of its evolution. In some respects, it matters little whether a cooperative is a centralized or federated association. In both cases the purpose is to provide a means of integrating farmers horizontally so that as a group they have sufficient volume to integrate vertically into one or more stages of marketing. This raises the question of how must cooperatives be structured legally in order to interpret their operations in an efficient and effective manner.

The Role of Marketing Contracts

Although a cooperative is a voluntary association, it is imperative that it employ legal devices to insure that it performs effectively. This is the *raison d'etre* for marketing contracts between growers and their cooperatives and for contracts among cooperative affiliates of federated associations. These contracts are not motivated by a desire to restrain trade nor is this their effect. Rather, they are the legal foundations of the cooperative association, spelling out the rights and duties of the parties. Operationally, such contracts are the cement that binds the association together. Such contracts are not required in a proprietary corporation in which the horizontal and vertical integrating process is accomplished through ownership.

Characteristics of Cooperative Marketing Contracts. Most discussions of cooperative marketing contracts deal only with the provisions regarding duration, delivery, and legal enforcement.[11] While important, these provisions emphasize only one of the integrating functions of marketing contracts—that of delivery. This is certainly the contract's most important function in most cases. It binds otherwise independent farmers together by guaranteeing each of the others' performance. Emphasis on this function of marketing contracts has apparently led to neglecting the study of other functions; yet marketing contracts often can and do perform other important integrating functions besides insuring patron delivery.

Successful vertical integration of farm enterprises through the cooperative method is complex. It is much more difficult than when individual business firms expand vertically. When large numbers of farm businesses unite to form a jointly owned operation, it is very difficult to coordinate their production and marketing operations. Yet close coordination may be essential to marketing efficiency for the group. When farmers form a cooperative, they must relinquish to it some sovereignty over certain of their production and marketing decisions.

The extent of such subordination depends in part on the amount of coordination between members and their association necessary to insure operating efficiency. This depends largely on the peculiarities of the commodity that the cooperative markets, the nature of the marketing functions that it performs, and the character of the markets in which it operates. For example, single-function associations may require little coordination. A livestock association whose only function is to sell at auction need not be closely integrated with its patrons. When associations perform many complicated marketing and processing functions, however, they may have to be integrated closely with their patrons.

Among the important provisions in grower–cooperative contracts are those specifying: duration, delivery and acceptance, time and place of delivery, methods of payment, termination, enforcement, crop inspection and reporting, product quality, crop harvesting, and product pooling.[12] Most of these provisions integrate, during the period of the contract, the activities of grower-members and their cooperative. The economic motive underlying such provisions is to provide a legal basis for insuring the effective functioning of the cooperative while protecting the rights of the parties. The significance of various provisions is discussed in some detail by Mueller and Tinley, and will not be reported here. Rather, we will examine only those provisions most likely to raise questions of anticompetitive effect.[13]

Duration and Delivery Requirements of Cooperative Membership Marketing Contracts. The contract provisions most likely to raise questions of anticompetitive effect are those relating to duration and to delivery and acceptance requirements. These provisions have the following potential competitive effects:

1. They confer control over supply in circumstances where a cooperative contracts with farmers supplying all or practically all of an industry's output, and
2. They result in foreclosure of other first handlers from access to the market.

For a cooperative to control supply, (1) it must be the dominant marketing outlet for a product, (2) it must have a policy of limited membership, and (3) it must be able to control its members' production. During the

1920s, long-term contracts became quite common, as the Sapiro cooperative movement sought to give farmers control over supply in various fields.[14] These efforts failed, however, in spite of the adoption of long-term "iron clad" contracts.[15]

By the 1950s, multiyear contracts had become quite uncommon. Fully 154 (80.2 percent) of a sample of 192 California cooperatives had contracts of only one-year duration.[16] Eighteen cooperatives (9.4 percent) had one-year contracts after a longer initial period of membership. Of the remaining 20 cooperatives (10.4 percent), 13 had either five- or seven-year contracts and the remainder had two- or three-year contracts. None of the multiyear contracts involved citrus cooperatives.

Most cooperatives used short-term contracts because they are quite adequate and because longer-term contracts deter membership.[17] One-year contracts usually are adequate because these cooperatives do not have "price enhancement or stabilization as a primary objective."[18] However, even long-term contracts do not necessarily confer on cooperatives significant market power:

> To raise market prices significantly, a cooperative must do two things: (1) it must have most of the producers as patrons, and (2) in the absence of production controls, it must divert part of the supply from regular market channels—either by export, dumping, or processing or diverting it to some lower price use. The immediate effect of such actions is to raise prices in the primary markets above competitive levels. This may give cooperative patrons a blended price—a weighted average of the price of the product sold in the primary and secondary market—which is higher than they would otherwise have received. But this is only part of the story. Noncooperative members may be benefited even more than members by such a program. Because they are able to sell all of their output in primary markets, nonpatrons receive net prices exceeding the blend prices of members. Cooperative members, seeing this, have a powerful incentive to desert their association in subsequent years. *Consequently, associations having price enhancement or stabilization as a primary objective must have contracts exceeding one year.*
>
> *But experience has demonstrated that even long-term marketing contracts are not enough to permit cooperatives to achieve significant market power.* As more and more members leave the association, and as production is expanded (both by members and nonmembers) in response to the noncompetitive price levels, the burden of the diversion program becomes excessive. The blend prices of cooperative members fall so far below nonmember prices that mass desertions of members occur until the association either goes out of business or changes its objectives.[19]

This study concluded that whereas during the 1920s, some California cooperatives had as their objective the attainment of monopoly power, none of these associations succeeded for long.[20] Since the 1920s, California farmers have relied primarily on federal and state marketing orders rather than cooperatives to achieve their price objectives.[21]

The FTC in its *Agricultural Income Inquiry* came to essentially the same conclusions as those cited above regarding the limited market power of agricultural cooperatives without supply control. The FTC observed:

> Even for those fresh fruits and vegetables for which the most extensive concentration of cooperative control of marketing exists, the tendency of higher prices is to foster increased production, both by members and non-members. The history of unaided efforts of cooperatives to enhance prices is that this tendency, and the fact that nonmembers are subject to no restriction as to the marketing of their products, make it practically impossible to hold members in line under any program that involves important restriction of quantities marketed. . . .
>
> Consequently, although the price object of cooperative marketing organizations is to obtain the best possible prices for the products of their members, the inherent difficulties mentioned above have been regarded as offering such an effective check to enhancement of prices that cooperatives and their members have been exempted from certain prohibitions and penalties of antitrust laws.[22]

This is not to say that cooperatives can operate effectively without any contracts requiring membership performance. If members do not agree to deliver their crop for at least one marketing season, the cooperative may lose sales to a noncooperative because the latter may offer some growers a price slightly above the going price to induce them to sell to it. The cooperative cannot meet such competition because it must pay all of its members the same price. One-year contracts are adequate to deal with this problem:

> Growers generally are unable to know at the time of signing their annual contracts whether or not supply is going to be abnormally short. Even if the grower anticipated a short supply, he might not be sure that he would be singled out by competitors for special treatment. Consequently, he would probably decide to sign a contract with his cooperative if past experience proved that it usually paid growers an average market price or better. Thus, this type of threat to member loyalty can usually be met as well by annual contracts as by longer-term ones.[23]

It has long been accepted in law as well as in economics that marketing contracts are an essential and legitimate instrument of cooperative associations. The dean of the early law and economics of cooperatives, the late Dr. E.G. Nourse, summarized over a half-century ago the three grounds upon which the courts relied in accepting the contract method of tying a cooperative together:

1. It is proper that a mutual association provide for the financing of its current operations by the assessment of their cost upon the whole body of members, who themselves adopt this provision as one feature of their by-laws;
2. That an association making capital outlays for the erection of buildings or otherwise must make definite contract arrangements for the liquidation of such long-term obligations by equitable distribution of the burden over the membership who are to be benefited by such outlays and will be the owners of the property; and
3. That the purposes of the association in providing more efficient or more economical processing or marketing services can be realized only if mutually supported by a sufficiently large number of people on a sufficiently permanent basis.[24]

Limited Acceptance Provisions of Cooperative Membership Marketing Contracts. One contract provision symptomatic of an effort to achieve market power is the right of the cooperative to limit the amount that members may deliver annually. The ability to limit deliveries is essential to the exercise of control over supply. About 18 percent of California cooperatives have the right to limit in some fashion the amount of a member's products that will be marketed. In the 1950s, most of these cooperatives were wine- and prune-drying cooperatives.[25] *No California citrus cooperatives had limited acceptance provisions in their bylaws or marketing contracts.* One reason many growers affiliate with Sunkist is that it guarantees them a "home" for their fruit.

An Addendum on the Use of Grower–Processor Contracts by Proprietary Firms. Marketing contracts are not unique to cooperatives. Indeed, most contract provisions found in cooperatives' member–grower contracts— both duration and performance requirements—are also found in contracts between farmers and proprietary firms in certain industries. Proprietary concerns and farmers dealing with them frequently have marketing contracts with essentially the same provisions as cooperatives.[26]

In canned fruits and vegetables, as with many other products, both grower and proprietary processors have strong economic incentives for entering into contracts that (1) require delivery by growers and acceptance by processors during the contract periods, (2) specify product quantity and quality, and (3) spell out the timing of deliveries.[27] Such contracts guarantee the farmers an outlet and the buyers a source of supply during the contract period, typically one year. Such contracts are viewed as a necessary means of coordinating the buyer–seller relationship at the first-handler level; they are designed primarily to increase the operating and pricing efficiency of the system.

The widespread use of grower–first handler contracts by noncooperative as well as cooperative handlers, in a broad range of industry structures, indicates that there exist common economic motives for such contracts. Indeed, Nourse observed that when, in 1892, the first citrus cooperative used contracts with growers, it was "simply carrying into a co-operative undertaking what was already the established practice of commercial concerns handling fruit."[28]

But there is an important difference between cooperatives and noncooperatives that makes contracts more important for a cooperative than for a proprietary concern. The cooperative is owned by and operated for its member patrons who have an investment in its operations. As a result, each grower-member's financial well-being depends in part on the performance of other grower-members. Each therefore has a right to expect that others will perform equally and not receive a free ride. The cooperative has a greater need for marketing contracts than does the noncooperative because the latter can buy from whomever it chooses, and growers selling to noncooperatives do so without any obligations, such as investing in marketing firms.

Use of Marketing Contracts by Federated Cooperatives. The same economic factors that make imperative the use of marketing contracts between cooperatives and growers also necessitate the use of contracts between local associations and the central unit of the federated cooperative. Nourse aptly characterized their economic form:

> In a word, then, co-operative federations are associations of associations. They permit integration of an agricultural industry horizontally by bringing together many local units of like character. They also permit integration vertically by the addition of functions, ordinarily those of central market or export selling, demand promotion, and packing or processing.[29]

The contracts' provisions serve the same integrating functions as those between growers and the cooperative. Indeed, it is inconceivable that most kinds of federated marketing cooperatives could function effectively without such contracts. Where cooperatives are free to leave the federation annually, federated cooperatives are much more loosely knit organizations than centralized cooperatives, where the local creamery or packinghouse is merely a *plant* or a *division* of the cooperative, not an autonomous legal unit. Marketing contracts among cooperatives are designed to accomplish what can be done through managerial edict in a centralized cooperative.

These facts of life were explicitly recognized in the Capper-Volstead Act of 1922. Section 1 of the act states that cooperatives "may have marketing agencies in common; and such associations and their members may make the necessary contracts and agreements to effect such purposes."[30] This language permits cooperatives to "carry on like a business corporation without thereby violating the law." This immunizing legislation was designed to accomplish the intent of the act's authors that farmers should be given the same privileges as those conferred upon corporations. As the Supreme Court said in *Maryland and Virginia Milk Producers Association v. United States* 362 U.S. 458 (1960), "Individual farmers should be given, through agricultural cooperatives acting as entities, the unified competitive advantage and responsibility available to businessmen acting through corporations as entities."

As shown above, when viewed in terms of economic purpose and effect, federated cooperatives are no different than centralized ones. However, because they must accomplish through contracts and agreements among cooperatives what centralized cooperatives can accomplish through ownership, it was necessary to permit contracts among federated cooperatives under section 1 of the Capper-Volstead Act lest they may be viewed as restraints of trade under section 1 of the Sherman Act or section 5 of the FTC Act.

To deny cooperatives the right to accomplish through federations of cooperatives what is legal in a centralized cooperative or a proprietary corporation would encourage, if not compel, all cooperatives to become centralized cooperatives. In the over sixty years since Capper-Volstead was enacted, cooperatives have been free to choose between these alternative methods of achieving larger-scale organizations. If cooperatives had been foreclosed or discouraged from forming federated cooperatives in favor of centralized cooperatives, there would have been two adverse effects: (1) insofar as it discouraged the creation of federated cooperatives, fewer efficient cooperatives would have emerged and (2) insofar as it encouraged farmers to create centralized cooperatives in situations where farmers would have preferred federations, it would have forced farmers to give up local control over their cooperatives.

Viewed in their historical context and as imperatives of the economies of federated cooperatives, contracts among members of a federated cooperative are not restraints of trade, but, rather, essential and therefore legitimate business arrangements. To argue otherwise may be to deny the right for federations to exist.

Contracts integrating the activities of cooperatives are restraints of trade in the same way as are the legal ties that bind the divisions of proprietary corporations into an integrated whole. Neither constitutes a *per se* anticompetitive effect. But there is an important distinction. The divisions of proprietary corporations are bound permanently through ownership. The legal bonds of federated cooperatives are ephemeral and typically severable annually. Their short duration bears witness that their intent is not to restrain trade but to promote effective integration. Their short lives also makes impossible long-run restraints of trade. Just as growers will leave a cooperative if they can get a free ride when the cooperative raises farm prices by actions such as dumping or other means of supply control, so will a local cooperative desert a federated cooperative. Thus a federated cooperative with short-term contracts has even less potential market power than does a similar-size centralized cooperative with short-term member contracts, for the free-rider problem can cause desertion of both member-growers and affiliated member-cooperatives.

We now turn to the grower-member and packinghouse contracts of Sunkist that the FTC characterized as exclusive-dealing contracts in restraint of trade.

Marketing Contracts of the Sunkist System

Evolution of Sunkist's Legal Structure. Sunkist Growers, Inc., (hereafter Sunkist) is the culmination of western citrus growers' efforts to market cooperatively beginning in the 1880s. The first associations were organized "cooperatively to obtain better prices for their fruit than were paid by private shippers who then constituted the only outlets for growers. The earliest associations were small, and generally were short-lived."[31] Because the individual units were too small to serve adequately their citrus grower-members, in 1893, several local associations adopted a plan of pooling and selling through a central marketing organization known as the Southern California Fruit Exchange.[32] These local associations also formed what were known as district exchanges. Members of the local associations had contracts that obligated them to sell their total production through the Southern California Fruit Exchange.[33] According to the FTC *Agricultural Income Inquiry*, "Thus, prior to 1900, the essential features of the present cooperative organization plan were developed."[34]

In 1905, the California Fruit Growers Exchange was formed as the successor to Southern California Fruit Exchange. The new association was organized much along the same lines as the present Sunkist Growers, Inc. (It was renamed Sunkist Growers, Inc., in 1952.)

The FTC in 1938 described Sunkist's federated structure as follows:

> The federated form of organization involving a three-layer pyramided structure inherited from its predecessor has been preserved. . . . At the top of the pyramid stands the California Fruit Growers Exchange which, on November 10, 1936, had 26 individual members, each designated by and

representing a district exchange. Its president and 3 vice presidents are elected from among these 26 individual members who also constitute its board of directors. Each of the district exchanges represents from 2 to 20 local cooperative associations and individual shippers in the States of California and Arizona. Of the total of 205 local growers' associations listed as members of district exchanges in November 1936, 183 were non-profit cooperatives and the balance were corporations or other large individual producers of citrus fruits. These locals have a combined membership of over 13,500 growers.[35]

The Commission then explained the contractual ties that bound together the federated structure of Sunkist at that time:

Thus the ultimate seat of authority throughout the exchange structure is the local association. Each local association binds its members by contract to market their citrus fruit production through the local. The local in turn contracts to sell through the district exchange, and the district exchange contracts to sell the production of the locals through California Fruit Growers Exchange. *Each local association or shipper reserves the right to regulate and control its own shipments as to quantities shipped, markets to which shipments are made, and except at auction points, the prices at which it will sell.* The district exchange in turn *contracts* to act as the agent for the locals in the marketing of fruit through California Fruit Growers Exchange. The California Fruit Growers Exchange in turn *binds* itself to act as the agent of the district exchange and its locals in disposing of fruit.[36]

The FTC thought it sufficiently noteworthy to mention Sunkist's "reserved rights of shippers" clause: "It is specifically stated that 'the right of free competition with all other shippers, including other members of this organization, unhampered and uncontrolled by anyone' is fully reserved."[37]

The FTC also noted that in 1937, Sunkist did not market citrus fruit of nonmembers:

In general [Sunkist] markets only the citrus fruit products of its locals through its extensive selling organization. It is important to note, however, that there is one exception to this general statement, namely, that the sales facilities of [Sunkist] in some markets have been made available to the California Fruit Exchange for the sale of their products.[38]

No fundamental changes have been made since the 1930s in Sunkist's federated structure and the contractual agreements binding it together. The major change occurred in 1968, following the U.S. Supreme Court decision in *Case-Swayne Co., Inc. v. Sunkist Growers, Inc.*, 389 U.S. 384 (1967). The

Supreme Court ruled that commercial packinghouses could not be members of Sunkist. To meet the Court's holding, Sunkist reorganized so that each grower became a direct member of Sunkist Growers, Inc., and also was a member of either a local association or a district exchange. Under this arrangement, commercial packinghouses are no longer members of Sunkist.[39] Rather, such houses are licensed by Sunkist to perform packing functions of growers, who are members of a district exchange or a local association and Sunkist.

Commercial Packinghouse Affiliations with Sunkist. In considering the 1968 change in Sunkist's legal structure, several facts should be kept in mind. The presence of licensed commercial houses as Sunkist members had dated from its origin.[40] From the outset, growers of these affiliated commercial houses (which typically were owned by some of their grower suppliers) were viewed as "Sunkist growers," enjoying most of the advantages of legal members. They were provided the same field services and publications that members received. They often displayed Sunkist grower signs on their property. Thus, both from Sunkist's standpoint and the growers', those selling to the commercial houses affiliated with Sunkist were generally considered "Sunkist growers." The 1968 contract changes made the grower–member relationship more explicit by giving it a legal basis and by depriving commercial houses of any legal interest in Sunkist.

Rather than own a cooperative packinghouse, many growers prefer to license a commercial packinghouse to perform the packing functions. With the license arrangement, it is unnecessary for growers to contribute the substantial capital funds required to build new cooperative packinghouses and to share in the risks of their operation. As in other fields of business, having other firms provide certain functions enables a firm (in this case, a farm) to avoid using its own capital to finance the purchase of plant, machinery, and other equipment and facilities.

The 1968 changes in Sunkist's legal structure made it a partially centralized association (as has happened to some other large federations) in that all growers become direct members of Sunkist Central. But while Sunkist has changed its legal structure somewhat over the past nine decades, it remains principally what it always has been, a federation of cooperatives whose functional relationships are tied together with various contractual agreements essential to its operations.

Sunkist's history demonstrates that its present organizational structure is a product of over ninety years of evolution. Throughout this period, there existed contracts between member-growers and among the cooperatives forming the federated association. We now turn briefly to some of the specific provisions of these contracts.

Nature of Marketing Agreements between Sunkist Grower-Members and Local Cooperative Packinghouses. Through its history, Sunkist has used contracts that are revocable annually. During the 1920s, Aaron Sapiro, legal counsel of the California State Market Commission, argued forcefully that one-year contracts such as Sunkist's were totally inadequate. As he put it, "a short-term contract is *hardly worth the paper it is written on.*"[41] Unlike many farmers in California and elsewhere, Sunkist growers refused to give up their independence by signing the five-year type of contracts advocated by Sapiro.[42]

The marketing obligations of Sunkist growers that are members of a local cooperative packinghouse are spelled out in the cooperative's by-laws.[43] Here we shall describe some of these obligations as they appear in the bylaws of a typical cooperative packinghouse that is part of the Sunkist System.

The bylaws spell out the members' duties in marketing their fruit. Each member agrees "to deliver to the Association for packing and marketing, and to market, through the agency association, all fruit matured during membership upon the member's land." The association, in turn, has an obligation "to receive, pack and market . . . all fruit that a member is obligated to deliver in accordance with the provisions of these bylaws."

The bylaws provide that members may withdraw from the association during the last day of December to be effective the following year. They also spell out other methods of termination, including expulsion.

Other provisions that cover the marketing of members' fruit are those relating to pooling, determination of operating expenses, determination of member net proceeds, determination of damages for breach of contract, and establishment of revolving funds.

The bylaws also include a prorate agreement, under which by majority vote the board may:

> Enter into and subscribe to and cause to be performed and observed, by and on behalf of the Association, as incidental to the conduct of its business, prorate, control, allotment and other agreements, codes, stabilization plans, conventions, . . . intended to promote and benefit the fruit industry by regulating, prorating, and/or limiting shipments, and by withholding from market, surplus low grade fruit and disposing as such surplus and low grade fruit in such manner as shall not adversely affect the sale price of other fruit.

This provision is necessary for the association to comply with marketing orders. Related to this objective, the bylaws provide that the board may "assent to marketing orders" of the state of California or the United States.

In sum, the contract between a grower-member and it's local cooperative packinghouse spells out the duties and rights of the parties during a one-year contract period. Some of these provisions are similar to those commonly found between growers and proprietary packers or processors, particularly the obligation of the grower to deliver and of the packer to market products from a specified acreage during the one-year marketing period. Provisions whereby the grower gives the packer the right to determine time and method of harvesting, etc., are also found in grower contracts of many proprietary firms.

The unique provisions are those relating to pooling, determination of method and time of payments, and revolving funds; these are essential features of the cooperative method of conducting business. (Pooling also is used by some noncooperatives.)

The proration provision is unique; it is designed to give the cooperative association authority to engage in orderly marketing methods in behalf of all grower-members. In practice, this provision permits the cooperative to carry out effectively the provisions of marketing orders.

Finally, the provision giving the cooperative board discretion in assenting to marketing orders is unique to cooperatives. This is a practice contemplated and authorized by state and federal marketing order legislation. Indeed, it is difficult to comprehend how effective grower input into marketing orders could be achieved without using cooperatives. Individual growers are simply too small to acquire the expertise necessary to provide relevant inputs in developing and administering such orders. The FTC recognized in 1937 the critical role cooperatives play in the effective functioning of marketing orders when it concluded:

> The need of fresh fruit and vegetable growers for further extension of cooperative organization and activity is great, both as a *means of improving their economic status by cooperating with Federal authorities in marketing programs*, and as a means of securing a wider distribution of their products on an increasingly efficient basis.[44]

Marketing Contracts between Local Cooperative Packinghouses, District Exchanges, and Sunkist. Each local association is required to market all of the fresh fruit under its control through the district exchange with which it is affiliated. Each district exchange is obligated to market through Sunkist Central all of the fruit under its control. Sunkist Central in turn is obligated to market all such fruit and shall determine the methods of marketing, the types of containers, and methods of packaging to be used. In this marketing arrangement, each local association and district exchange designates Sunkist Central as its agent, granting to it authority to conduct the marketing activities in such manner as it determines to be in the best interests of the members.

Although each grower and local association delegates to its district exchange the right to make price and other decisions regarding the marketing of the grower's fruit, "such Growers or Local Association *reserve* the right from time to time to terminate this delegation and to exercise such rights for such period as they may deem proper or to redelegate said reserved right to said District Exchange."

Among other significant provisions relating to marketing is one that prohibits local cooperatives and district exchanges from soliciting business from the trade. The selling function is to be provided exclusively by Sunkist Central. Sunkist Central also has authority to route fruit shipments, establish pools for processing and marketing fruit, and establish quality standards.

License Agreements between Sunkist Growers and Licensed Commercial Packinghouses. Since 1968, as noted above, licensed commercial packinghouses no longer have been members of Sunkist. Grower members of the Sunkist System, however, may enter into license agreements with commercial or licensed packinghouses that pack for such growers. Such licensed commercial houses remain proprietary enterprises. The fruit packed by them is, in turn, marketed through the Sunkist System in behalf of Sunkist's members.

The licensed commercial packinghouses agree to pack exclusively the fruit of Sunkist members. In grading, packing, and handling growers' fruit, these houses must comply with Sunkist's regulations. The licensed commercial house's function is that of packing, not marketing the fruit of growers, nor shall such houses solicit business from the trade. Thus, the members' fruit is packed by the licensed commercial house, but is marketed through the Sunkist System. Furthermore, the licensed commercial packer has an agreement with Sunkist Central that obligates the packer to return to such grower the net proceeds from the marketing of growers' fruit by Sunkist Central, after deducting the packer's costs and agreed reasonable charges.

These and other provisions spell out explicitly the licensed commercial packer's obligation to Sunkist Central and the growers for whom it packs under license. The contracts between licensed commercial houses and Sunkist Central are for one year. The licensed commercial houses also handle most of the harvesting and related matters that are performed for growers by cooperative packinghouses. The compensation they receive from growers reflects the performance of these essential services as well as those relating to packing the grower's fruit.

Competitive Significance of Sunkist's Various Contracts

The FTC complaint alleged that Sunkist's various contracts represented restraints of trade adversely affecting competition. Before turning to the specific charges, some general observations are in order.

The charges seem to rest on a fundamental misconception concerning the purposes underlying these contracts. Simply put, the FTC challenged the very legal foundations of federated cooperatives. As shown above, the various contracts employed by Sunkist are not unique; rather, they are imperative to the successful functioning of a federated cooperative. Such contracts have long been widely used by other federated cooperatives. They are the legal ties that bind the Sunkist federation into an integrated whole. Many provisions are similar to and were predated by provisions in contracts between growers and proprietary packinghouses. But even with these legal ties, the federated Sunkist association is much less securely and permanently integrated than are proprietary corporations. This is important since a fundamental purpose of the Capper-Volstead Act was to give individual farmers acting through their cooperative entities the same competitive advantages as those available to businesspeople acting through corporations. This objective can only be accomplished in a federated cooperative through the use of contractual ties among its cooperative and individual members, as permitted by section 1 of the Capper-Volstead Act. This, it seems to us, is all that Sunkist's contracts seek to do.

It should also be emphasized that if Sunkist were a centralized cooperative, some of its contracts (especially those between local packinghouses and Sunkist) would be unnecessary to accomplish the same purposes and effects.

All of the above the FTC seemed to be unaware of or chose to ignore. This is in marked contrast to the views expressed by the FTC over forty years ago, following its extensive examination of the role cooperatives played in the U.S. food system and in aiding farmers to achieve a more equitable position in the market. At that time the Commission concluded:

> Although a measure of proof in terms of dollars and cents of the value of cooperative associations is difficult to obtain, the Commission desires to add its opinion to the vast body of opinion to the effect, namely, that true cooperative associations have been a great value to producers of farm products. *These cooperatives have significantly increased the bargaining strength of producers and have reduced the spread between producers' and consumers' prices. . . . Moreover, the financial strength of the cooperative makes possible orderly marketing of crops and more favorable prices for its members.*[45]

Alleged Foreclosure of Nonmember Growers to the Use of Local Cooperatives and Licensed Commercial Packinghouses. As explained above, cooperative packinghouses are the vertical extension of their grower owners, while marketing contracts are the essential vehicle for integrating the growers and their cooperative. These contracts have many provisions, some of which spell out the delivery and acceptance responsibilities of the parties. They are of one-year duration. Local cooperative houses and licensed commercial houses *pack only for Sunkist members.* The effect of these contracts is to require the two parties to do business with one another "exclusively" for the contract period with respect to the contracted acreage. However, a Sunkist grower may, and many do, simultaneously enter into a contract with a non-Sunkist packinghouse for a specified amount of acreage. By dividing acreage between Sunkist and a non-Sunkist house, the grower can compare directly the performance of Sunkist with a competing packinghouse.

What is the competitive significance of these contracts? Are non-Sunkist growers injured by these exclusive dealing contracts?

Given Sunkist's policy of open membership, any California/Arizona grower may join Sunkist and avail itself of the Sunkist marketing system. Not only is membership open to any qualified grower, but the new grower can gain access to the Sunkist System without making any capital outlay, since Sunkist's revolving method of financing does not require a capital investment when joining. This gives the new member, without any initial investment, the benefits created by the Sunkist System's accumulated capital, reputation, and marketing expertise. It would seem that these operating procedures should be sufficient, alone, to dispel the FTC's contention that nonmembers are foreclosed from Sunkist-affiliated packinghouse facilities. To argue otherwise is to imply that cooperatives have an obligation to serve nonmembers on better terms than members, i.e., to give nonmembers a free ride. Nonmembers do not join Sunkist of their own choosing. If they are then injured by their choice, this injury also is of their own choosing, not Sunkist's. If viewed in the legal and economic context set forth above, it should not be necessary for a cooperative to make further justification for not doing business with nonmembers. Clearly, the legislative intent underlying Capper-Volstead was to give farmers the same rights acting through cooperatives as businesspeople enjoy acting through corporations. In this context, to insist that a cooperative packinghouse cannot limit its business relations solely to members is like saying one division of a corporation cannot do business solely with another vertically related division of the same company, but that it must buy from other potential suppliers. Thus, a cooperative should enjoy the right of requiring that farmers join the cooperative if they are to enjoy its benefits. Indeed, one of the reasons Sunkist has given for its policy regarding nonmember packing is to prevent outside shippers or marketing organizations from benefiting from Sunkist packinghouse facilities without the risks associated with ownership. In our view, this should be justification enough for Sunkist's policy, unless it can be demonstrated that some nonmembers have no alternative outlets (see below).

Business Justification for Not Packing Nonmember Fruit. Sunkist's concern with packing nonmember fruit goes back at least to 1915. But it apparently was not until 1918 that its board first formally adopted a policy on non-member packing, which was subsequently reaffirmed in 1937 and 1968. Among the reasons cited in support of the policy is that packing non-member fruit creates opportunities for abusing Sunkist market information and the Sunkist brand. Moreover, such a policy eases enforcement of Sunkist quality regulations and prevents diversion of fruit into and out of the Sunkist System.

Evidently, Sunkist feared strongly that houses packing nonmember fruit might use the confidential business market information they obtained from the Sunkist System to benefit nonmembers. Because this would be extremely difficult to detect, Sunkist could not effectively discipline packinghouses that pursued such practices.

The above and other marketing reasons cited are persuasive arguments that the nonmember packing policy is essential in maintaining the economic integrity of the Sunkist System. One might still ask, however, why does Sunkist not market nonmember fruit when some other cooperatives do?

There is nothing inherently uneconomical or otherwise disadvantageous in engaging in nonmember business, and the Capper-Volstead Act explicitly permits cooperatives to deal in the products of nonmembers to an amount equal to that handled by members. Most supply cooperatives and some marketing cooperatives find such a policy in their interest. For example, the California Almond Growers Exchange has had the following policy toward nonmember business: "The Exchange agrees that during the term of this contract it will not accept for sale or deal in any almonds except for the account of members of the Exchange."[46] But the exchange may make exceptions to this requirement.

> "When any almonds grown or delivered to the Exchange by members of the Exchange are insufficient in quantity or quality . . . or when for any other reasons the Board of Directors deems it appropriate, the Exchange may purchase, acquire, accept for sale or deal in almonds produced by nonmembers."[47]

Obviously, the exchange believed that there were times when its members were best served if the exchange purchased or marketed nonmember almonds. This raises the question, if such a policy was good for the exchange, why was it not also good for Sunkist? Based on our study of cooperatives, we believe one reason for this difference is that the exchange is a centralized type of cooperative whereas Sunkist is a large federation of cooperatives. Generally, a large centralized cooperative has greater flexibility than a similar-sized federation of cooperatives in exercising control over such practices as maintaining high-quality standards to achieve price premiums. Federations often have considerable difficulty in implementing certain policies because of the degree of autonomy of their local associations. Applying this to the issue of dealing with nonmembers, a centralized association (or a small federated one) very likely can handle problems relating to nonmember business much more effectively than can large federated cooperatives such as Sunkist. Management of a centralized association could more easily and objectively decide what quality and volume of nonmember business is in the best interest of the *overall* membership than could the managers of the local cooperatives and affiliated licensed commercial houses of a federation, which might put their own interests above those of the entire association, e.g., they might follow practices to obtain nonmember business that were detrimental to members. The latter would confront problems because the various members and/or management of local packinghouse cooperatives might be able to establish control procedures to ensure that local cooperatives and licensed houses would perform satisfactorily. But if the imposition of such procedures became too complex or controversial, the federation of cooperatives might decide that the most practical and effective way to deal with the problem would be a simple rule that prohibited all local cooperatives and licensed houses from engaging in packing of nonmember fruit. Although this would involve some costs for the association, these costs would be outweighed by the benefits.[48]

Competitive Consequences of Sunkist's Nonmember Packing Policy. Although there are strong business reasons for Sunkist's policy, there still remains the question as to whether it was anticompetitive. In view of Sunkist's policy of open membership, nonmembers are not likely to be injured since such growers would always have the option of joining Sunkist. The only instance in which we can visualize injury to individual nonmember growers is if Sunkist were monopsonist in a geographic area, with the result that growers would be forced to join Sunkist to have an outlet for their fruit. Whether there were, in fact, situations such as this is a matter of proof. Based on our familiarity with the facts, it appears that citrus growers in California/Arizona always had several alternative outlets available to them in addition to Sunkist. Merely because they had only a few, however, does not justify a rule that forces Sunkist to pack for them. For example, concerning fruits and vegetables sold to processors, it is quite common for a grower to face relatively few buyers or even a single buyer. But all that growers can do in these circumstances is complain, since they seldom have the option of joining freely an effective cooperative like Sunkist.

In sum, we do not believe an economic case can be made to compel Sunkist to pack for nonmembers unless Sunkist were the only effective outlet. Indeed, if Sunkist began packing nonmember fruit in situations where it had very few competitors, the effect might be to skim the cream of the proprietary firms' cutstomers, resulting in increased market shares for Sunkist and increased entry barriers for proprietary packers in such market areas.

There is evidence that Sunkist has been responsive to the requests of nonmember growers to pack their fruit in hardship cases. Practically all of the situations where Sunkist made an exception to its nonmember packing policy fell into the following categories: growers of a competing packing-house had a larger crop than normal or their packer had problems that made it impossible or uneconomical to handle a grower's crops; competing packinghouses were destroyed by fire; or a competing packinghouse had insufficient volume to operate efficiently.[49]

In each of these situations, nonmember growers would have suffered severe hardships had they not found a home for their fruit during the current marketing season. In nearly all cases, Sunkist packinghouses packed the fruit of these nonmembers for a single season. (Presumably, all or most of these growers had signed contracts to sell to another packing-house before "disaster" struck; Sunkist's action relieved the other house of its responsibilities.)

Sunkist's waiver of its nonmember packing policy in these cases illus-trates that it was not insensitive to the problems of nonmember growers. However, these were special situations that could almost always be handled by waiving for a single season its nonmember packing policy. At the end of that period, growers either found new outlets or joined Sunkist.

Effect of Sunkist's Marketing Contracts on Competing Citrus Marketers or Processors. The FTC complaint views the marketing agreements between Sunkist as exclusive dealing contracts that have the effect of depriving competing fresh fruit marketers or fruit processors access to fruit supplies. In this theory, the local packinghouses, the district exchanges, and Sunkist Central are viewed as autonomous business entities. This view of the Sun-kist System misrepresents its true economic character as it has existed for over eight decades. Sunkist was created to improve the economic welfare of its grower-members. To achieve this objective, it integrated the activities of its members horizontally and extended their activities vertically into mar-keting and processing by assuming the legal structure of a federated co-operative (modified slightly following the 1967 Supreme Court decision in *Case-Swayne*).

As a federated cooperative, economic imperatives dictated that Sunkist enter into agreements with its local packinghouses. The member-growers have invested millions of dollars in packinghouses, processing plants, a nationwide marketing organization, foreign sales offices, valuable trade-marks, research and development facilities, and other facilities or func-tions. These investments were made in contemplation of creating a large-scale marketing and processing organization to serve the interests of the ultimate member-growers. Various contractual arrangements are neces-sary to insure that these operations function in an integrated fashion that serves the interests of the growers who financed them rather than others who have no financial stake in them. It is inconceivable that Sunkist's growers would invest in these various operations unless, first, each grower made a legal commitment to use the facilities and, second, the various levels of Sunkist's tripartite system were legally bound to one another—for at least one year. The same reasons explain why all California federated marketing cooperatives use such contracts.[50]

Of course, were Sunkist a centralized cooperative, as are Sunmaid Raisins and the California Almond Growers Exchange, there would be no need for such contracts. What Sunkist must accomplish by contract, the centralized cooperative, like the proprietary corporation, can accomplish by management edict. Certainly, Sunkist should not be punished for assuming a federated legal form; nor should it be coerced into transforming itself into a centralized cooperative so that it may do legally what the courts to date have viewed as not being illegal.

It seems that this is what the Supreme Court was talking about in *Sunkist Growers, Inc. v. Winckler and Smith Citrus Products Co.*, 370 U.S. 19 (1962).

> There can be no doubt that under these statutes the 12,000 California-Arizona citrus growers ultimately involved could join together into *one* organization for the collective processing and marketing of their fruit and fruit products without the business decisions of their officers being held combinations or conspiracies. The language of the Capper-Volstead Act is specific in permitting concerted efforts by farmers in the processing, preparing for market, and marketing of their products. And the legislative history of the Act reveals several references to the Sunkist organization . . . including a suggestion by Senator Capper that this was the type of cooperative that would find "definite legalization" under the legislation. Although we cannot draw from these references a knowing approval of the tripartite legal organization of the 11,000 growers, they do indicate that a cooperative of such size and general activities was contemplated by the Act.

The Supreme Court, after reviewing the evolution of the Sunkist System, concluded that:

> In practical effect and in the contemplation of the statutes, [Sunkist's growers have created] one "organization" or "association." . . . To hold otherwise would be to impose grave legal consequences upon organizational distinctions that are of *de minimus* meaning and effect to these growers who have banded together for processing and marketing purposes within the purview of the Clayton and Capper-Volstead Acts.[51]

It is true that the contracts between local packinghouses and Sunkist's processing and marketing arms deny, in large part, direct access to these packinghouses by competing marketers and processors. But in economic theory, this is no different than the denial of access to intracompany transactions of a proprietary concern. It is in the nature of a cooperative organization that when farmers choose to join a vertically related business via the cooperative route, other businesses will lose the patronage of the cooperating farmers. This is inevitable since, by definition, the farmers had chosen to do the business themselves. Similarly, when farmers choose to enter a second stage of the marketing process, other businesses will be displaced. But it is inappropriate to analogize such loss of business with that resulting from exclusive-dealing or full-supply contracts among independent business entities. This distinction seemed self-evident to a Wisconsin court as early as 1923, when it explained the rationale underlying the Capper-Volstead Act that gave antitrust immunity to contracts between growers and their cooperatives:

> It may be and probably is true that the organization and operation of this association had a very serious effect upon defendants' business in the various respects above set forth, *but it is to be remembered that the very purpose of the legislation was to bring about a different system of marketing, which must of necessity injuriously affect middlemen* (and such is the Bekkedal firm). The effect of the operation of such associations upon business in general cannot be considered in determining the legality thereof or their operations, because the public policy which formerly condemned them now encourages their existence and operation. *If they have no effect upon business as heretofore existing and conducted, then their existence and operation as well as the legislation promoting them is futile and to no purpose.*[52]

E.G. Nourse captured the essence of this decision when he said: "In other words, the Wisconsin court, manifesting a lively appreciation of the homely fact that 'you can't make an omelet without breaking eggs,' aligned itself with those who believe there is a greater public advantage in testing out the nutritive value of the omelet than in maintaining the sanctity of eggshells."[53]

In sum, Sunkist's competitors cannot buy from local packinghouses without Sunkist's approval. Some of Sunkist's individual actual or potential competitors may be injured by this practice in the sense that they would be better off financially if individual packinghouses were forced to sell to them.

But this result is not the same as that occurring when an independent legal entity chooses to enter into an exclusive dealing contract with one firm rather than the firm's competitors. The key difference here is the word "independent" when speaking of legal entities. Each Sunkist packinghouse is not an "independent" legal entity. To force an analogy between the essential marketing contracts of local packinghouses and Sunkist and the exclusive dealing contracts between entirely independent business entitites is to deny that Sunkist is an integrated federated association and that, if its members chose, they "could join together into *one* organization for the collective processing and marketing of their fruit and fruit products."[54] To argue otherwise—to say that Sunkist uses its marketing contracts for anything but to integrate effectively its operations—is to deny ninety years of history. Thus, in equating Sunkist's contracts with those between independent business enterprises, the FTC complaint relied on superficial similarities rather than economic realities.

Sunkist's Acquisition and Affiliation Activities

The third element of the FTC's complaint concerned Sunkist's expansion within the industry. The FTC cited Sunkist's acquisition of Growers Citrus Products and the affiliation of Blue Goose Growers, Inc.

The Acquisition of Growers Citrus Products

On April 17, 1974, Sunkist acquired Growers Citrus Products (GCP) of Yuma, Arizona, a processor of orange and lemon products.[55] The FTC's Trial Brief alleged that Sunkist acquired GCP "for the specific purpose of increasing its processing capacity so it could maintain its monopoly share of fresh California-Arizona orange, lemon, and lemon juice production, and continue its monopoly power over the sale and distribution of those products."[56]

The essence of the FTC charge was that:

> The acquisition of GCP was not made to accomodate the current needs of Sunkist's existing members. Rather, Sunkist purchased GCP to increase its processing capacity to handle anticipated new members it would solicit in order to maintain its 70 percent share of California-Arizona citrus production and, consequently, its monopoly power. The acquisition also eliminated one of its major competitors and forced competing processors to incur higher transportation costs for their raw supplies.[57]

In support of its charge that the acquisition greatly augmented Sunkist's market power, the FTC stated that Sunkist's share of the lemon juice market (in dollar sales) was 80.2 percent before the acquisition and 91.0 percent the following year.[58] It provided no evidence showing that the acquisition foreclosed other growers to processing outlets.

Several facts not mentioned in the FTC Brief are particularly relevant to the analysis. First, GCP was not an independent business entity engaged solely in citrus processing. Several citrus growers owned and operated a packinghouse, Golden Y, Inc., as well as the GCP plant used to process the growers' fruit.[59]

Second, according to the uncontradicted deposition testimony of one of these growers, Golden Y, Inc., had been marketing the growers' fresh citrus through Tenneco, Inc. but decided they would be better off marketing through Sunkist as members of the cooperative. The growers intended to join Sunkist irrespective of whether Sunkist bought GCP.

Third, GCP had never been very profitable, and in the years preceding the sale, GCP was able to process only 20,000 to 30,000 tons of fruit for its own account annually despite having a rated capacity of 120,000 tons per year. Over a period of years, the owners had tried unsuccessfully to sell the plant to various parties, including Sunkist in 1970.

Fourth, when Sunkist subsequently decided to develop processing capacity in Arizona, it had four alternatives, according to Sunkist's then vice president, Russell Hanlin:

1. Expand existing plants [in California] at a cost of $2.5 million, which would have a negative earnings impact; . . .

2. Construct a satellite plant at a cost of over $3 million, which would produce an increased operating cost of $350,000;

3. Use outside processors; last year [1973] processing of 46,000 tons had an excess cost of $127,000; and

4. Acquire existing processing facility.[60]

Sunkist believed the most efficient alternative was to acquire the failing GCP plant. In view of the above, what was the probable competitive impact of the acquisition? Specifically, did it increase significantly Sunkist's market share in the fresh or processed market and/or did it foreclose a significant part of the market to non-Sunkist growers?

Sunkist could only have increased its market share by adding new growers or acquiring from nonmember growers fruit that it would not have acquired but for the acquisition of GCP. The available evidence indicates that the only new growers that Sunkist received in Arizona were the owners of Golden Y packinghouse. According to deposition testimony, the decision to join Sunkist was made independently of the acquisition.

Sunkist picked up no additional fruit for processing as a result of the acquisition. GCP had been processing the fruit of one packinghouse in addition to Golden Y. Although Sunkist has a general policy prohibiting custom packing of nonmember fruit, to avoid criticisms of foreclosure, Sunkist offered to custom pack this house's fruit; however, the packinghouse decided to go with another processor. Thus, Sunkist gained only the fruit supplied by the Golden Y growers, resulting in a much smaller market share gain than the 10 percentage points alleged by the FTC. Indeed, the FTC's claimed 10 percent share gain apparently reflected a misreading of its own exhibit.

Table 6-1
Sunkist and Growers Citrus Products's Percent
Shares of Total Lemon Juice Dollar Sales,
1970/71 through 1976/77

Year	Sunkist	GCP
1970/71	88.6%	10.1%
1971/72	86.8	9.4
1972/73	84.1	8.8
1973/74	80.2	10.9
1974/75	75.0	0.0
1975/76	91.0	0.0
1976/77	84.9	0.0

Source: Sunkist Growers, Inc.

Note: The FTC's public version of its Trial Brief does not show these percentages because the table includes proprietary information for Sunkist and other citrus processors. Sunkist Growers, Inc., has given permission to reproduce here the figures for it and GCP.

As shown in table 6-1, in the year prior to the acquisition, 1973/74, Sunkist accounted for 80.2 percent of the market and GCP 10.9 percent of sales. In the following year, Sunkist's share dropped to 75 percent.[61] Although Sunkist's share rose to 91 percent in 1975/76, the following year, it fell to 84.9 percent, which was below the level it held in the early 1970s. The various percentages cited in the FTC Brief are of questionable reliability and relevance. First, the questionnaire requesting the information asked for sales of lemon juice. Because the concentrated juice processed by buyers from their own groves or from the fruit purchased from others was not included in the figures, the figures overstated Sunkist and GCP's share of processed lemon juice.

Second, the facts shedding the most light on the question of whether the GCP acquisition had a significant and lasting effect on Sunkist's market position are its shares in the fresh and processed lemon markets. Turning back to table 4-4, we see that whereas Sunkist's share of the processed lemon market was 85.8 percent in 1974/75, thereafter it declined steadily, reaching a low of 58.4 percent in 1982/83. A similar decline occurred in the fresh lemon market.

In sum, the empirical evidence does not support the hypothesis that Sunkist's acquisition of GCP had the purpose or effect of monopolizing any relevant market. On the contrary, the facts support the inference that Sunkist acted in the interests of its members by exercising an opportunity to acquire a failing plant, which, under the circumstances, represented the most efficient of the several alternative ways of increasing processing capacity in Arizona.

The Affiliation of Blue Goose Growers, Inc.

The FTC charged that in 1966, Sunkist "combined with 13 commercial packinghouses marketing citrus fruit through the Western Fruit Sales Company (Western Fruits Sales) division of Blue Goose Growers, Inc."[62] The FTC viewed this as a "combination" and as part of Sunkist's continuing effort "to achieve the 70 percent share of California-Arizona citrus shipments it regarded necessary to maintain its monopoly power."[63] The FTC cited Sunkist documents, as it had elsewhere in the brief, indicating that Sunkist actively sought to maintain and increase its volume.[64]

Evaluating the probable competitive consequences of the alleged Blue Goose combination requires placing it in the context of the continuing mobility among citrus growers and packinghouses discussed at length in chapter 4. It is also essential to understand the nature of the Blue Goose packinghouses and the factors prompting their growers to affiliate with Sunkist.

Blue Goose was an affiliation of thirteen packinghouses that packed fruit of its owners, who were substantial citrus growers in their own right, as well as fruit of other farmers.[65] According to Sunkist, "the owners decided their own interests would be increased if they joined Sunkist and that the interests of the other growers who used their facilities would be better served by marketing through Sunkist."[66] Sunkist alleged that a major reason for this decision was that Minute Maid, which had been processing Blue Goose's product-grade fruit, announced "that it would no longer guarantee the return on the Blue Goose's product fruit, a financial commitment that had caused Minute Maid serious problems in a large crop year. At the same time, Sunkist's own product returns had been steadily improving, in large part due to an internal overhaul of Sunkist's operations."[67]

Because the individual Blue Goose houses generally were not owned by the same individuals, each made its own decision as to whether to affiliate with Sunkist. Indeed, one Blue Goose packinghouse had affiliated with Sunkist four years previously, in 1961/62, as shown in table 4-12. Moreover, one of the thirteen Blue Goose houses that joined Sunkist in 1966 disaffiliated in 1967. Lending support to Sunkist's statement that its product returns "had been steadily improving" and therefore made affiliation particularly attractive at this time is the fact that five packinghouses had affiliated in 1964/65, the year previous to the Blue Goose affiliation, three licensed commercial packinghouses in addition to Blue Goose had affiliated in 1965/66, and three had affiliated in 1966/67. (See table 4-12.)

When viewed in this broader picture of continuing affiliation and disaffiliation of packinghouses which characterized the marketing associations in the California/Arizona citrus industry, the so-called Blue Goose "combination" with Sunkist could be expected to have little impact on competition. The market share statistics support this expectation. Sunkist's performance in the early 1960s caused more growers and packinghouses to affiliate with Sunkist than to disaffiliate, reaching a peak in 1966/67, as shown in table 4–11. As a result, Sunkist's share of fresh lemon marketing reached a record of 89.2 percent in 1967. (See table 4–4.) Its share of navel and valencia oranges reached highs in 1966. (See tables 4–2 and 4–3.) After 1967, this process was reversed as disaffiliation accelerated and affiliation slowed. Thus, after 1967, Sunkist's market shares declined in all of its markets, reaching lows in the 1982/83 season.

This pattern of rise and decline largely reflects the ease of entry and exit that permeates the industry because Sunkist operated as an open-ended federated cooperative that has no long-run control over supply. (See chapter 4.) The expected benign competitive effect of the Blue Goose affiliation is further borne out by events occurring after the case was settled in 1981. In 1984, owners of all of the remaining Blue Goose packinghouses sold their houses to Castle and Cooke. This event, entirely unrelated to the FTC's legal action against Sunkist, provides further proof that the Blue Goose affiliation lacked the sort of monopoly-conferring power one might expect when a proprietary corporation with a large market share acquires a leading competitor.

Significance of Market Foreclosure Absent Monopoly Power

The FTC did not analyze the alleged foreclosure resulting from Sunkist's various marketing contracts, the acquisition of Growers Citrus Products, and the affiliation of the Blue Goose packinghouses within the theoretical framework set forth in chapter 3 or in recognition of the empirical evidence presented in chapters 4 and 5. If the analyses of structure and conduct in these chapters is correct, Sunkist lacked market power because there did not exist significant entry barriers for either nonmember growers or competing marketers or processors. On the contrary, the evidence indicated that Sunkist's organizational makeup and operating procedures lowered entry barriers, both for growers and competing marketers.[68] Thus, Sunkist did not have the monopoly power required to make these contracts anticompetitive.

In economic theory, exclusive dealing contracts constitute monopolizing only when they prevent competitors from gaining access to a market. The contracts, alone, cannot create exclusionary power. Rather, they are merely a means of implementing existing power. If the party "imposing" an exclusive dealing contract on another does not already have market power, the contracts cannot result in monopolistic market foreclosure.[69] The same reasoning is relevant in evaluation, for Sherman section 2 purposes, of alleged foreclosure resulting from acquisitions or mergers.

It is also well recognized in economics as well as law that there are a number of business reasons, based primarily on operational economies, that justify exclusive dealing arrangements.[70] Our analysis leads to the conclusion that Sunkist's contracts with growers, local cooperatives, and licensed commercial houses were "imposed" for reasons of economic efficiency rather than for reasons of economic power. The acquisition of Growers Citrus Products and the affiliation of the Blue Goose packinghouses also appears to have been motivated by a desire to achieve economic efficiency, not monopoly.

Notes

1. See chapter 4 at note 37.
2. FTC Brief, 79.
3. Ibid., 79–80.
4. Ibid., 80.
5. Sunkist Membership Committee (July 17, 1968).
6. FTC Brief, 81.
7. Complaint counsel asked that the all-or-nothing requirements be eliminated and that if this remedy were inadequate, the court should order Sunkist to sever all agreements with licensed commercial packinghouses.
8. "Complaint Counsel's Statement of Its Case," FTC Docket 9100 (February 7, 1978):4–5.
9. Ibid., 6–7.
10. Federal Trade Commission, *Agricultural Income Inquiry, Part II: Fruits, Vegetables, and Grapes* (Washington, D.C.: GPO, 1938), 30.
11. Much of the factual discussion in this section is from W.F. Mueller and J.M. Tinley, *Membership Marketing Contracts of Agricultural Cooperatives in California*, California Agricultural Experiment Station Bulletin 760 (University of California-Davis, College of Agriculture, March 1958). Although the contracts analyzed in the study are now over twenty years old, we believe that California cooperatives have not significantly changed their contracts since then.
12. The contract provisions of fruit and vegetable cooperatives in the 1930s are reported in the FTC, *Agricultural Income Inquiry*, 722–33.
13. For another discussion on the economic and legal purposes of cooperative marketing contracts, see H.H. Bakken and M.A. Schaars, *The Economics of Cooperative Marketing* (New York: McGraw-Hill, 1937), 307–13.
14. Mueller and Tinley, *Membership Marketing Contracts*, 12.
15. Ibid.
16. Ibid., 19.
17. Ibid., 21.
18. Ibid., 22.
19. Ibid. Emphasis added. Also see E.G. Nourse, *The Legal Status of Agricultural Co-operation* (New York: Macmillan, 1928), 174–75.
20. FTC, *Agricultural Income Inquiry*, 886–87.

21. Ibid.

22. Ibid.

23. Mueller and Tinley, *Membership Marketing Contracts*, 23. L. Garoyan reported, however, that in 1974, several California fruit and vegetable bargaining cooperatives had marketing agreements ranging from two to fifteen years. "Producer–First Handler Exchange Arrangements for Selected California Processed Fruits, Vegetables, and Nuts," in *Coordination and Exchange in Agricultural Subsectors*, ed. B. Marion, N.C. Project 117, Monograph 2 (Food Systems Research Group, University of Wisconsin-Madison, January 1976), 13–28.

24. Nourse, *Legal Status of Agricultural Co-operation*, 282–83. Mueller and Tinley cite three additional reasons that cooperatives use short-term contracts: (1) longer contracts deter membership, (2) cooperatives are sufficiently well established that they no longer need long-term contracts to survive in the short run, and (3) cooperatives have nonlegal ties with their members, which make it unnecessary to have long-run contracts. None of the above have anticompetitive implications. Mueller and Tinley, *Membership Marketing Contracts*, 23–24.

25. Mueller and Tinley, *Membership Marketing Contracts*, 38–39.

26. See, for example, N.R. Collins, W.F. Mueller, and E.N. Birch, *Grower–Processor Integration: A Study of Vertical Integration between Growers and Processors of Tomatoes in California*, California Agricultural Experiment Station, Bulletin 768 (University of California-Davis, College of Agriculture, October 1959), 41–54; W.F. Mueller and N.R. Collins, "Grower–Processor Integration in Fruit and Vegetable Marketing," *Journal of Farm Economics* 39 (December, 1957); Garoyan, "Producer–First Handler Exchange Arrangements," 13–28; G.R.Campbell, "Grower–First Handler Exchange Arrangements in the Wisconsin Processed Vegetable Industry," in *Coordination and Exchange in Agricultural Subsectors*, ed. B. Marion, N.C. Project 117, Monograph 2 (Food Systems Research Group, University of Wisconsin-Madison, January 1976).

27. Collins et al., *Grower–Processor Integration*, 47–54.

28. Nourse, *Agricultural Co-operation*, 185.

29. Ibid., 135.

30. This language was designed to permit the continued operations of federated cooperatives, which predated enactment of the Capper-Volstead Act of 1922.

31. FTC, *Agricultural Income Inquiry*, 678.

32. Ibid.

33. See appendix D for the views expressed in 1920 by G. Harold Powell, long-time general manager of Sunkist.

34. FTC, *Agricultural Income Inquiry*, 678.

35. Ibid., 679.

36. Ibid. (Emphasis added.) The U.S. Dept. of Agriculture's history of Sunkist makes a similar characterization of the contractual ties that bound together the federated structure: "In its earliest form, the federation involved a contractual relationship between a grower and his respective packinghouse association, its district exchange, and Sunkist Growers, Inc. *Each level in the federated structure was tied to the next by contract and by representation on the board of directors of the next succeeding level.*" (Emphasis added.) C.H. Kirkman, *The Sunkist Adventure*, Farmer Cooperative Service, Cooperative Information Report no. 94 (Washington, D.C.: U.S. Dept. of Agriculture, May 1975), 20.

37. Ibid., 680.

38. Ibid., 684. (The Fruit Exchange sold deciduous fruit and grapes.)

39. Following this reorganization in 1971, a district court in a declaratory judgment concluded: "In contrast to the organizational structure existing at the time of the Supreme Court decision in this suit, Sunkist's present structure constitutes an agricultural cooperative protected by section 1 of the Capper-Volstead Act." *Case-Swayne Co. v. Sunkist Growers, Inc.* 355 F. Supp. 408, 415 (C.D. Cal. 1971).

40. FTC, *Agricultural Income Inquiry*, 679.

41. Bakken and Schaars, *Economics of Cooperative Marketing*, 323, note 12.

42. See appendix D for the views expressed in 1920 by G. Harold Powell, long-time general manager of Sunkist.

43. It is significant that when, in 1892, the Pachappa Orange Growers Association became the first Sunkist local cooperative to employ contracts with its members, it was "simply carrying over into a cooperative undertaking what was already established practice of commercial concerns handling fruit." Nourse, *Agricultural Co-operation*, 185.

44. FTC, *Agricultural Income Inquiry*, 891. (Emphasis added.)

45. Ibid. (Emphasis added.)

46. Mueller and Tinley, *Membership Marketing Contracts*, 60.

47. Ibid.

48. Bronsteen also reasons that Sunkist adopted its policy prohibiting custom packing for reasons of efficiency rather than exclusions (Peter Bronsteen, "Allegations of Monopoly and Anticompetitive Practices in the Domestic Lemon Industry" (Ph.D. diss., University of California-Los Angeles, 1981): 144–78. His reasoning supporting this conclusion is more persuasive, however, than the empirical evidence he brings to bear on the issue. He hypothesizes that Sunkist prohibited custom packing to reduce "the cost of monitoring packinghouses' compliance with standards that exceed the USDA requirements, and this is achieved by enabling Sunkist inspectors to detect violations without having to know the identity of the grower whose lemons are being packed" (ibid., 154–55).

If the hypothesis is correct, Bronsteen reasons, one would expect packers not to engage in custom packing if they established higher grades than the USDA grades and to engage in custom packing if they need only USDA or lower grades. Bronsteen's examination of industry practices in lemons, oranges, and grapefruit reveals that Sunkist was the only packer to impose higher-than-USDA grades; other packers neither imposed higher-than-USDA grades nor did they prohibit custom packing (ibid., 155–60). Although this evidence is consistent with Bronsteen's hypothesis, it is also consistent with the FTC's that Sunkist did not engage in custom packing because it was the dominant firm in the California/Arizona fresh lemon and orange markets. Bronsteen further argues that Sunkist could not have engaged in the practice for exclusionary purposes because it used the practice in the fresh grapefruit market despite the fact that it had only a 7 percent share of this market (ibid., 162). This inference does not follow, however, since there may well be compelling practical grower relations or other business reasons necessitating that Sunkist follow a consistent policy regarding custom packing of all three citrus products regardless of its market position in each of these markets.

49. Based on an examination of Sunkist records of instances where it made an exception to its nonmember packing policy.

50. See above this chapter.

51. 370 U.S. at 29 (1962).

52. *Northern Wisconsin Co-operative Tobacco Pool v. Bekkedal*, 182 Wis. 571 (1923), cited in Nourse, *Agricultural Co-operation*, 378–79. (Emphasis added.)

53. Nourse, *Agricultural Co-operation*, 379.

54. *Sunkist Growers, Inc. v. Winckler and Smith Citrus Products Co.*, 370 U.S. 19 (1962).

55. FTC Brief, 92.

56. Ibid.

57. Ibid., 95.

58. Ibid.

59. Sunkist Growers, Inc., *Statement of Its Defense*, FTC Docket 9100 (March 22, 1979), 42.

60. FTC Brief, 94.

61. FTC Brief, 95, note 11. The FTC attributes the fall in Sunkist's 1975/76 share to its alleged withholding in that year. There is no evidence that Sunkist withheld a disproportionate share in 1974/75. See chapter 5 at note 7 and after.

62. FTC Brief, 96. The FTC also charged Sunkist with "combining" in 1978 with two Arizona packinghouses, Sun Country and Spencer & Sons, owned by the family of Charles E. Lakin (FTC Brief, 99–101). We have not discussed this matter because it differs in no significant respect from the many other affiliations and disaffiliations discussed earlier and summarized in tables 4–12 through 4–15. For the same reason, we have not discussed an FTC charge that by acquiring Spencer & Sons, Sunkist was attempting to eliminate Southland Produce Company, whose sole source of supply had been Spencer & Sons. The FTC acknowledged no competitive injury occurred because, in the FTC's words, "Fortunately, Southland was able to acquire [an interest in another packinghouse], which enabled it to enter in the business of marketing fresh lemons" (ibid., 101). Southland's experience in readily switching to another outlet provides further proof of the ease of entry in the industry. Throughout this and other discussions of alleged monopolization, the FTC Brief equates slight injury (or mere inconvenience) to competitors with injury to competition reaching the level of monopolization.

63. The FTC alleged this was part of Sunkist's effort to monopolize the markets through the price leadership conferred by a large market share. See chapter 5.

64. FTC Brief, 96–97.

65. Although Blue Goose resembled in many respects a cooperative association, it did not meet the requirements of a Capper-Volstead cooperative.

66. Sunkist Growers, Inc., "Statement of Its Defense," FTC Docket 9100 (March 22, 1979), 40.

67. Ibid.

68. See chapter 4.

69. R.D. Blair and D.L. Kaserman, *Antitrust Economics* (1985), 415–17.

70. Ibid., 408–13, 417–23.

7
Summary and Conclusions

T he preceding chapters identified and analyzed various issues raised by the Federal Trade Commission complaint charging Sunkist with monopolizing the California/Arizona citrus industry. The analysis was guided by the legal-economic frameworks developed in chapters 2 and 3. We therefore begin this summary of the analysis by reviewing briefly the legal doctrine of monopolization and then identifying the economic concepts most relevant in undertaking an empirical inquiry into whether the legal standards had been satisfied in the Sunkist case.

Monopolization in Law and Economics

The law of monopolization as applied to agricultural cooperatives is essentially the same as that applied to proprietary businesses, as set forth in judicial decisions interpreting section 2 of the Sherman Act and section 5 of the Federal Trade Commission Act. Under this law, unlawful monopolization must satisfy two tests: the possession of monopoly power and the willful acquisition or maintenance of that power as opposed to achieving it on the basis of competition on the merits. Although the Capper-Volstead Act gives agricultural cooperatives a limited exemption from the antitrust laws, the legal standards for identifying monopoly power and monopolizing conduct are generally the same for agricultural cooperatives as for proprietary corporations.

The first step in identifying unlawful monopolization is to determine whether a firm possesses monopoly power, defined as the power to control prices or to exclude competitors, in a relevant market. If a firm possesses monopoly power, the plaintiff must further establish that the alleged monopolist willfully acquired or maintained this power as opposed to achieving it by growth due to a superior product, business acumen, historic accident, or conduct compatible with what Congress authorized in the Capper-Volstead Act.

The courts generally begin their analysis of monopoly power by examining the alleged monopolist's market share in a relevant market. Although large market share is a necessary condition of monopoly power, it is not a sufficient condition. At least in other contexts, courts are giving increased attention to the question of whether there exist substantial entry barriers, recognizing that, first, without such barriers, even a seller with a large market share cannot for long elevate its prices above marginal costs; and, second, were a seller to do so, competitors would enter the industry, expanding output until prices were driven to competitive levels.

When a seller is found to have monopoly power, the court next determines whether this power was willfully acquired or maintained by such clearly predatory acts as coercion, boycotts, or pricing below average variable costs. In the absence of clearly predatory acts, exclusionary conduct looked at as a whole may include unreasonably tying up supply, interfering with buyers' access to alternative outlets or sources of supply, undermining a competitor's ability to sell, or discriminating against certain members in a given class of producers, rivals, or buyers. Conduct that is exclusionary in purpose or function tends to erect barriers to new-firm entry or to deter incumbent-firm expansion.

If analysis shows that a cooperative does not have monopoly power, it becomes unnecessary to examine the question of exclusionary conduct or intent. Without monopoly power, such practices cannot constitute monopolization, i.e., practices that were undertaken with the intent to maintain or expand a monopoly. Some courts have neglected to make a careful analysis of whether the cooperative enjoys monopoly power before turning to an examination of alleged exclusionary evidence. These courts began their analysis with the observation that the cooperative had a large market share, then noting that the mere possession of monopoly power is permissible because of the Capper-Volstead Act exemption. By focusing on market share and neglecting the entry barriers question, the courts may assume inadvertently the presence of monopoly power where none exists.

Economics can make common cause with the law in determining whether an agricultural cooperative has engaged in unlawful monopolization. This is particularly true for matters relating to monopoly power. Economists have developed a comprehensive body of economic theory identifying the necessary conditions of monopoly power, particularly the possession of large market share and the existence of significant entry barriers. The theory of the dominant firm approximates most closely the legal definition of monopoly power as control over price. This theory requires modification, however, when the alleged monopolist is an agricultural cooperative rather than a proprietary, profit-seeking firm. Most importantly, when the theory of the firm is extended to include the nonprofit cooperative as a special case, then for an open-ended cooperative (one that neither restricts the supply of its members nor limits the number of members), large market share, alone, does not confer monopoly power. When a cooperative operates on a nonprofit basis and is open-ended, the result is essentially the same as when an industry has no significant entry barriers. Even when such a cooperative markets 100 percent of a crop, prices and output will equal those in perfectly competitive equilibrium.

A cooperative could, however, attain a degree of market power if it differentiated its product, practiced price discrimination, or both. An open-ended cooperative that has differentiated its product as a result of advertising destroys the equivalence between the perfectly competitive outcome and the cooperative outcome. But even with a 100 percent market share, such a cooperative would have a larger output and lower price than would a profit-maximizing monopolist.

An open-ended cooperative that is able to practice price discrimination also may achieve some market power. Its nonprofit, open-ended nature, however, causes output to be higher and prices lower than those associated with monopoly. The potential benefits of price discrimination decline as a cooperative's share falls below 100 percent. Moreover, price discrimination gives rise to a free-rider problem which, if not solved, will ultimately make price discrimination infeasible.

Economic theory also is useful in identifying exclusionary conduct, particularly whether an alleged monopolist creates "strategic" entry barriers as opposed to "innocent" barriers resulting from normal profit-maximizing conduct such as the pursuit of economies of scale. Potentially strategic entry barriers examined in this book included alleged exclusive dealing and combinations or acquisitions that foreclosed markets to competitors. Economic analysis also is useful in distinguishing practices employed for efficiency reasons from those employed for exclusionary purposes.

Using the above legal-economic framework, various empirical analyses were made to determine whether the Sunkist System operated in a monopolistic market structure and whether it engaged in exclusionary practices to maintain and enlarge its alleged monopoly power. The results of these analyses are summarized below.[1]

Did Sunkist Possess Monopoly Power?

The threshold issue in monopolization cases is whether the defendant has monopoly power. The legal standard of monopoly power is the power to control price or to exclude competitors. The economic concept most useful in identifying the existence of such power is the structure of the market (particularly the market share of the alleged monopolist and the number and size distribution of its competitors), the barriers to entering the market, and the extent of product differentiation. Economic theory predicts and empirical evidence verifies that when entry barriers are high and a seller has a dominant market share, it has the power to both exclude competitors and exercise control over price. Although such structural evidence may be sufficient to determine whether monopoly power exists, empirical analysis of market conduct and performance may provide direct evidence of the exercise and fruits of monopoly power. Below we summarize both kinds of evidence developed in the course of this book.

A necessary first step in an examination of industry structure is the identification of the appropriate markets. For purposes of our analysis, we accepted the FTC Trial Brief's definition of the relevant markets for fresh citrus grown in California and Arizona. The relevant product markets are fresh oranges grown in California and Arizona and fresh lemons grown in California, Arizona, and Florida. The relevant geographic market is the United States and Canada.

Market Concentration

Since the turn of the century, most California/Arizona citrus has been marketed by two nonprofit agricultural cooperatives, whose current corporate names are Sunkist Growers, Inc., and Pure Gold, Inc. (Hereinafter, we shall identify the current Sunkist System as well as its predecessor associations as Sunkist.) These two cooperatives marketed over 70 percent of all California/Arizona citrus fruit in the early 1920s and marketed a record high share of 95 percent in 1933/34.

Sunkist's share of fresh orange marketings averaged just over 70 percent for the period 1954/55 through 1982/83, with the share dropping to near 60 percent in recent years. Sunkist's share of fresh lemon marketings averaged about 79 percent since 1954/55, with the share falling to about 60 percent in 1982/83.

Through the years, Pure Gold, Inc., was Sunkist's leading competitor. In recent years, however, several other citrus marketers (e.g., Sun World, Paramount Citrus, and Riverbend Farms) have grown larger than Pure Gold. During the 1970s and into the 1980s, there were about two dozen marketers of California/Arizona citrus.

In sum, for over six decades, Sunkist enjoyed a large market share in both fresh oranges and lemons. This share, if accompanied by significant entry barriers, was of a magnitude sufficient to confer monopoly power. Economists generally conclude that such power is conferred with a market share near 50 percent.

The Condition of Entry

This structural variable measures the advantages that established firms have over potential entrants. Such advantages determine the height of entry barriers protecting an industry from new competitors. When these advantages are substantial, established firms can persistently raise prices above marginal costs without attracting new firms into the industry. In law, as well as in antitrust economics, this is referred to as the power to exclude competitors. The book analyzed the following potential entry barriers: economies of scale, absolute cost advantages, product differentiation, and strategic behavior by established firms.

A minimum-optimum–scale packinghouse was estimated to require between 1.1 percent and 2.2 percent of annual California/Arizona orange shipments in the late 1970s. A specialized lemon packinghouse would require a larger market share. But, because most proprietary marketers pack both oranges and lemons in the same packinghouse, they require a smaller market share than the 1.1 to 2.2 percent figure. Even the 2.2 percent estimate constituted a low entry barrier, being well below the average minimum optimum scale commonly found in U.S. industries.

Although no significant scale economies existed at the packinghouse level, Sunkist enjoyed some multiplant economies of scale in brand advertising, research and development, and the special requirements of developing and marketing in foreign markets.

Sunkist has been the leader in R&D in the California/Arizona citrus industry. Its laboratories and engineers have produced a disproportionate share of patentable product and process inventions and innovations. These have been aimed at increasing demand for fresh and processed citrus and at reducing processing and marketing costs. While this evidence suggests that Sunkist enjoyed economies of scale in this area, there is no evidence that other actual and potential competitors were significantly disadvantaged. This has been particularly true in recent years because the greater part of all R&D in the citrus industry, as in other food-processing industries, is conducted by public and private researchers outside the industry. Because of this, new entrants are not disadvantaged in gaining access to state-of-the-art technology from food machinery manufacturers. Sunkist's leadership in R&D conferred on it greater advantages in the early decades of the industry than it has in recent decades, as the citrus industry grew and specialized firms had an incentive to develop unique equipment and services.

Another multiplant economy enjoyed by Sunkist is that it can mobilize the larger resources often required to penetrate and develop foreign markets. This explains why it has made considerable and successful efforts in opening the Japanese and East European markets. Smaller marketers would have found it excessively expensive to develop the marketing muscle and expertise to undertake these efforts.

The final multiplant economy enjoyed by Sunkist—a potentially significant one—is in advertising-created product differentiation. Since its first advertising efforts in 1907, Sunkist has spent millions of dollars to develop the well-known Sunkist brand. In the past decade, Sunkist spent about $10 million annually, or 2.8 percent of sales, in advertising, promotion, and merchandising. Sunkist's expenditures as a percentage of sales have declined in recent decades, however, indicating that Sunkist's relative advertising costs declined as it grew larger. This, combined with the fact that smaller marketers spend little on advertising and have not developed well-known brands, suggests that Sunkist enjoys some economies of scale in this area.

Absolute Cost Barriers

If new entrants must pay more for capital or other resources than established firms, they are at a disadvantage because of higher absolute costs. Potential entrants into citrus marketing do not confront sizable absolute cost disadvantages. Capital costs of a packinghouse ranged from $1 million to $3 million in the late 1970s. Even the capital cost of operating several packinghouses were quite modest by modern-day standards in U.S. industry.

A potentially important absolute cost barrier in this industry, given Sunkist's large market share, is access to fresh citrus supplies. This does not create a significant barrier because citrus growers affiliated with Sunkist are not tied to it with long-term contracts, as occurs with some cooperative and proprietary firms in other industries. Growers may leave Sunkist at the end of each market season, resulting in considerable actual or potential mobility among growers, as growers are free to move from one packinghouse to another annually.

In addition, the packinghouses affiliated with Sunkist and other California/Arizona citrus marketers have considerable mobility. Sunkist's packinghouses operate with one-year contracts. Rather than build a new packinghouse, a new marketer entering the industry may persuade an established proprietary packinghouse or an affiliated cooperative packinghouse to affiliate or merge with it. Such freedom of affiliation and disaffiliation is virtually without precedent among proprietary corporations. It is analogous to giving a new entrant in an industry freedom to buy or contract for the services of a plant from an established competitor without requiring its approval.

Because such affiliation may occur at no cost to the new marketer, this further reduces the capital entry barrier. These affiliations also enable a new entrant to avoid the "capacity effect" experienced when an entrant builds new capacity in a market, thereby causing temporary excess capacity for all marketers in the trading area, including the entrant.

Sunkist's organizational characteristics thus actually lower entry barriers confronting proprietary packinghouses as well as citrus growers. Entrepreneurs wishing to enter citrus packing may contract to serve as a licensed commercial packinghouse for Sunkist members. These so-called commercial houses pack but do not market fruit for Sunkist members. Sunkist's growers benefit from such arrangements because they need not finance the packinghouse. The entering packinghouse benefits because it need only put up the funds to build a packing facility; Sunkist Central markets a member-grower's fruit that has been packed in the licensed commercial packing-house. If the licensed commercial concern becomes successful in the packing business, it may at any time discontinue, on one year's notice, as a licensed commercial Sunkist packinghouse and become an independent operator or a licensed commercial packinghouse affiliated with another citrus coopera-tive or else it may affiliate or merge with another proprietary business. At times, when licensed houses disaffiliate with Sunkist, they take with them the growers supplying them. Thus, the use of licensed commercial houses by some of Sunkist's growers has not only made it easier for growers to become and remain Sunkist members, but it has also made it easier for new citrus packers to enter and exit the California/Arizona citrus industry.

There is abundant evidence supporting this conclusion. Through the years, dozens of houses have affiliated and disaffiliated with Sunkist. An indication of the extent to which Sunkist has facilitated entry is that as of 1979/80, fully 24 of the 43 packinghouses affiliated or owned by Sunkist's competitors originally were affiliated Sunkist houses. For example, 7 of the 12 houses packing for Pure Gold, Inc., in 1979/80 had previously been affiliated with Sunkist, as seen in table 4–14.

The extensive packinghouse mobility between Sunkist and its competi-tors has the effect of reducing considerably both entry and exit barriers. This mobility also prevents Sunkist from exercising control over supply and selling prices. Should Sunkist raise prices by withholding part of its members' fruit, nonmember growers would get a free ride. Growers and packinghouses affiliated with Sunkist also could readily participate in free riding by leaving Sunkist. These structural characteristics compel Sunkist to seek prices that approximate the long-run equilibrium price.

Product Differentiation

Product differentiation is an entry barrier when it gives an established seller a substantial advantage over its smaller rivals and would-be entrants. As discussed earlier in the context of economies of scale, Sunkist spent mil-lions of dollars over nearly eighty years advertising its brand; in doing so, Sunkist's large size enabled it to advertise more efficiently than could the smaller citrus marketers. A relevant issue here is just how much market power Sunkist has achieved from these accumulated and current advertis-ing outlays.

While these efforts created one of the United States's best-known food brands, the brand does not command the large price premiums typically enjoyed by other leading food brands. In recent years, Sunkist brand fresh citrus commanded a price premium at wholesale of about 5 percent. At least some of this premium, however, may appropriately be attributable to the superior quality of the citrus packed under the Sunkist brand compared to the top quality packed by other California/Arizona marketers. No packer but Sunkist used quality standards exceeding the top USDA grades. Further evidence that Sunkist received surprisingly small margins for its advertising is that its advertising outlays were equal to about 2.8 percent of the wholesale revenues. Thus, at most (assuming no quality differences and a 5 percent price enhancement) an entrant would face a product differentiation disadvantage of only about 2.2 percent of the selling price. This is extremely modest compared to the barriers faced in most food products characterized by extensive advertising-created product differentiation. (The average price differential between the leading advertised brand of a food product and lesser brands is over 10 percent; some dominant brands enjoy price differentials exceeding 25 percent.) The absence of a substantial product differentiation barrier despite the strong consumer franchise enjoyed by Sunkist is anomalous, a matter we return to below.

Did Sunkist Exercise Monopoly Power in Fresh Domestic Markets?

In addition to evidence of market structure, the possession of monopoly power may be identified by an empirical analysis of market conduct and performance. The FTC Trial Brief cited five kinds of such evidence that allegedly demonstrated that Sunkist possessed monopoly power: Sunkist acted as the industry's price leader; Sunkist allegedly withheld fruit supplies to control prices; Sunkist received a price premium for fresh citrus sold under the Sunkist trademark; Sunkist used a practice called "switching the trade"; and a report prepared by a Sunkist consultant purportedly demonstrated that Sunkist had monopoly power.

Price Leadership

The FTC Trial Brief stated that Sunkist's dominant market share enabled it to set the industry price in each of the relevant product markets. It presented neither an economic theory of price leadership nor empirical evidence validating its effects on price. The allegation that the price leadership led to a monopoly price rested on selected statements of Sunkist personnel to the effect that they believed prices were too low and that something should be done about raising them.

That Sunkist was a price leader of sorts seems beyond dispute. Nor is it disputed that Sunkist sought to obtain the best possible returns for its members consistent with the constraints imposed by its organizational characteristics and market forces. Because of its large market share and its superior knowledge of market conditions, Sunkist Central inevitably took some initiatives in the price discovery process. It could not have done otherwise.

But economists have long recognized that merely identifying a seller as a price leader cannot be equated with the possession of monopoly power. The relevant issue is whether the price leader is able to lead an industry to a monopolistic price, a competitive price, or a price somewhere in between. Although large market share, alone, generally is sufficient to confer price leadership potential on a seller, such a price leader will command adherence to its price only insofar as that price reflects market conditions. As such, it acts as an industry's "barometric" price leader. When the leader has a large market share and entry is restricted, the leader may set a monopoly price. In the absence of entry barriers, however, the barometric price leader must inevitably lead the industry toward the competitive equilibrium price. Especially relevant in the case of Sunkist is that despite its large market share, it was unable to restrict entry. This structural evidence supports the hypothesis that Sunkist is a competitive barometric price leader.

This conclusion is borne out by analysis of Sunkist's organizational structure and pricing practices. Sunkist's pricing actions were preoccupied with discovering the market clearing price in the fresh market. If the Sunkist prices were too high, packinghouse inventories would accumulate and the pressure to lower price would continue to grow until price was adjusted downward. If the Sunkist prices were too low, orders would go unfilled by individual packinghouses. The only way Sunkist could establish a monopoly price in the short run would be for it to sell below the prorate its members received under the California/Arizona marketing orders, diverting the supplies into the fresh foreign market or processed products market. While actual experience in this regard is discussed immediately below, it should be noted here that Sunkist lacks the mechanism for allocating sales among growers and its federation of packinghouses that would be necessary if it were to systematically withhold supplies below prorate. Moreover, if it were successful in withholding supplies from the domestic fresh market, there would arise a serious free-rider problem which would undermine the effort.

Withholding Supplies

The essence of monopoly power is the ability to control supply. For Sunkist, this would require withholding some of the fruit that its members were allowed to ship in the primary market (the domestic fresh fruit market) under the appropriate California/Arizona federal citrus marketing order. Although FTC counsel charged that Sunkist did, in fact, undership the prorate, no statistical evidence was provided to support this charge.

We tested the hypothesis that Sunkist restricted the supply by diverting fruit from the primary market to secondary markets (exports and processed products). If Sunkist had practiced such diversion, one would expect the rest of the industry to behave as a competitive fringe, selling a higher proportion of its fruit in the primary market than did Sunkist.

Several statistical approaches were used to test this hypothesis. One straightforward test is to examine whether Sunkist sold a smaller share of its total shipments in the fresh domestic market than did the rest of the industry, as would be true if Sunkist were systematically withholding in the fresh market. Concerning lemons, the market in which Sunkist held the largest market share, Sunkist actually sold a higher percentage of its harvest, on average, for fresh domestic consumption than did the rest of the industry. As for both valencia and navel oranges, there was no statistically significant difference between the shipments patterns of Sunkist and other marketers.

Another statistical analysis was based on the assumption that Sunkist would have had more market power in years when it held a large market share than in years when it held small shares. If so, Sunkist would be expected to have diverted larger amounts in years when it held the largest market shares. (Its annual share of navel oranges ranged from 53 percent to 83 percent over the 28 years studied.) Then, holding other things constant, we would expect a negative relationship between Sunkist's market share and the percentage of harvest sold in the domestic fresh market. In a multiple regression analysis testing this hypothesis, no statistically significant relationship was found between Sunkist's market share and the percentage of its total shipments that were made in the primary market.

A final statistical test involved analyzing the specific years that the FTC cited as representing clear-cut examples of Sunkist diverting sales from the primary market. Again, the statistical analysis found no support for the FTC's allegations that Sunkist diverted sales in these years.

In sum, the various statistical analyses do not support the allegation that Sunkist engaged in either systematic or selective diversion of fruit from the fresh domestic market to secondary markets. Indeed, there is evidence that Sunkist sold relatively *more* in the primary market than did its competitors, a finding directly contrary to the expectations of the behavior of a monopolist.

Price Premium for Sunkist Brand

Although the FTC charged that the Sunkist brand conferred monopoly power, it provided no evidence of the extent of price premiums or of how these premiums compared with other branded food products. Over the past eight decades, Sunkist has established one of the United States's most familiar brands. Sunkist received a premium of about 5 percent of annual sales revenue at a cost of about 2.8 percent of sales. This is modest when viewed in the context of contemporary experience. The typical advertised food product enjoys a price premium exceeding 10 percent above lesser brands. As revealed in the FTC's *Borden-ReaLemon* case, the price differential of the alleged monopolist was over 25 percent for a product that was physically identical to lesser brands. In contrast, there is evidence that some of the price premium received for Sunkist citrus is attributable to superior product quality. Thus, after adjusting for quality differences, the price premium less the cost of achieving it very likely was miniscule. In sum, by contemporary standards the price premium received for the Sunkist brand fell far short of what would be expected of a proprietary brand of equal strength. This finding is consistent with the predictions of the theory of an open-ended, nonprofit cooperative and recent empirical work.[2] Any significant price premium resulting from advertising would encourage members to expand output and would attract new members until the premiums were eroded.[3]

Switching the Trade

The FTC alleged that Sunkist "manipulated price by a practice called switching the trade." The practice involved no more than changing relative prices to better equate in the short run the supply and demand of different sizes, grades, and varieties of citrus. This is a commonplace business pricing strategy and is simply a response to changing supply and demand conditions rather than evidence of monopoly power.

Sunkist Consultant's Report

In the 1950s, Sunkist commissioned a study by an academic consultant, the late Professor Raymond Bressler, that analyzed alternative ways of increasing grower returns. The FTC focused on one part of the study that discussed a possible price support activity whereby Sunkist would remove part of the crop from commercial markets. The FTC Trial Brief alleged that the proposed scheme proved that "Sunkist possessed the power to control the price of fresh lemons in the domestic market."[4]

FTC counsel did not acknowledge the serious questions that Bressler, himself, raised concerning the efficacy of his scheme if implemented unilaterally by Sunkist. He warned that Sunkist would hold an "umbrella" over competition that "could have serious repercussions on Sunkist's competitive position."[5] And while Bressler raised the free-rider problem, he offered no way of solving it.

There is no evidence that Sunkist management ever seriously considered adopting its own surplus disposal program as discussed in the report. Sunkist management had long been very sensitive to the free-rider problem, believing it would doom the Bressler suggestion and any other unilateral action to raise member returns by diverting supply.

Did Sunkist Derive Monopoly Power When Selling in Foreign Markets?

FTC counsel equivocated on this issue. The complaint charging Sunkist with monopolizing included the export market for fresh citrus among the relevant markets. In 1978, FTC counsel eliminated from the case this relevant market, although still implying that Sunkist dumped in foreign markets to maintain domestic prices of fresh citrus. The FTC Trial Brief neither presented evidence of dumping in foreign markets nor repeated the earlier allegations of dumping. Indeed, the brief made only one reference to Sunkist's operations in foreign markets. Although presenting no evidence supporting its assertion, the brief stated that one of the two factors (the other being artificial product differentiation) giving Sunkist a price premium for fresh oranges was "its strong export market, which as well as carrying its own premium . . . helps to support the domestic market's price premium." FTC counsel had earlier implied that successful foreign marketing required large-scale operations. By claiming that Sunkist achieved a price premium because it was strong in export markets, FTC counsel seemed to acknowledge that Sunkist was not dumping in these markets. The FTC did not document or estimate the size of the alleged price premium.

Although FTC counsel ultimately abandoned the foreign market aspect of the case, we examined Sunkist's practice in this market to test the hypothesis that it diverted fresh citrus sales to foreign markets or engaged in other kinds of monopolizing conduct. Analysis of Sunkist's operations in foreign markets yielded no evidence of dumping. Although Sunkist could theoretically have diverted fresh fruit to the foreign market, its method of selling in domestic and foreign markets permitted free riding by its own members if it had engaged in price discrimination for the purpose of raising primary market prices. Moreover, statistical analysis provides no support for the hypothesis that Sunkist diverted fresh citrus from the primary market to foreign markets.

There is support for FTC counsel's claim that Sunkist enjoyed certain scale economies when operating in foreign markets. Sunkist's large size was an important factor in mobilizing the resources required to break into the Japanese market and in developing a market for lemons in Eastern European countries. Likewise, the large volume of Sunkist exports enabled it to enjoy significant economies in transportation. These facts, alone, do not support an inference that Sunkist had achieved sustainable monopoly power or had engaged in unlawful monopolization in export markets. First, because Sunkist operated as an open-ended, nonprofit cooperative, any savings the Sunkist System enjoyed because of scale economies went to the growers in the form of higher prices. These prices would have attracted additional supply, as Sunkist growers expanded and non-Sunkist growers joined Sunkist, until a new competitive equilibrium was reached. Second, under the law, any advantages that Sunkist may have enjoyed due to economies of scale in foreign operations did not constitute "the willful acquisition or maintenance" of monopoly, but, rather, success achieved as a result of superior business performance. In economics, these advantages represent "innocent" scale economies resulting from normal profit-maximizing behavior (or, in this case, cost-minimizing behavior of a cooperative).

Did Sunkist Have Monopoly Power in the Lemon Products Market?

The FTC Trial Brief charged Sunkist with using its control over 70 percent of the raw and processed lemon market "to manipulate lemon juice supply and thereby control prices." To support this charge, the FTC focused primarily on Sunkist's conduct in handling the 1974/75 lemon crop. This crop was enormous, causing Sunkist to end the season with a lemon products inventory about thirteen times the normal level. The FTC charged that Sunkist acted like a monopolist when, in dealing with the huge crop, Sunkist implemented a plan called the "lemon set-aside pool." The plan created two lemon pools, a regular pool and a set-aside pool. Whereas products from the regular pool were sold for normal market uses, sales from the set-aside pool were to be made in markets not traditionally supplied by Sunkist, including sales for new product uses that would not displace uses already served by Sunkist. Because of problems created by the huge 1974/75 lemon crop, in 1976, Sunkist adopted a general plan to cope with future large lemon crops. This plan, called the "Lemon Contingency Reserve Pool," provided that in the future, members would be entitled to deliver up to 250,000 tons to the regular pools. Those delivering in excess of their pro rata share of this amount would pay an assessment per ton on the excess.

FTC counsel argued that the set-aside pool resulted in monopolistic pricing because Sunkist recognized that "the ability to store and finance a voluminous inventory was essential to prevent prices from falling." Counsel further asserted that the Contingency Reserve Pool Plan, which was in operation for only six months, had as its purpose "limiting supply and preventing a glut of lemon products on the market."

FTC counsel was correct in the belief that the pools were designed to be ways of handling a glut on the market and to prevent disastrously low prices. The major problem with the FTC position was that it offered neither theory nor evidence that Sunkist's pricing and storage decisions reflecting monopolistic conduct or resulted in monopolistic prices. True, prices would have been lower had Sunkist not established the set-aside pool and, instead, sought to sell an amount equal to all but its normal inventory.

But, given the large size of the crop and the inelasticity of demand for processed lemon juice, this would have caused prices to drop well below marginal cost. (As it was, they dropped 25 percent over the following two years.) While such pricing behavior would have exonerated Sunkist from monopoly pricing, it may have invited a predatory pricing claim by Sunkist's smaller competitors. Current legal doctrines in the Ninth Circuit Court of Appeals, as well as other appellate courts, holds that when a dominant firm sells below marginal cost, this is presumptive evidence of predatory conduct in violation of section 2 of the Sherman Act.[6]

What conduct would one expect Sunkist to follow if it had performed as a competitive barometric price leader in this market as it did in the fresh domestic market? Once again, answering this question requires recognizing an important distinction between agricultural cooperatives and proprietary firms. Sunkist's decision to operate lemon-processing facilities reflected its growers' concerns with having assured outlets for their products at harvest time, something often not available for growers dealing with proprietary concerns. Sunkist's agreement to accept *all* lemons produced represented a substantial risk that a huge crop might someday place considerable strain on its processing capacity and financial resources, a risk that Sunkist was forced to assume with the 1974/75 crop. In the face of ruinously low prices if it sold too much of the processed product, Sunkist's most rational course was to inventory a large part of the crop. Predicting the most appropriate volume of inventory is a complicated and risky business. But the evidence indicates that Sunkist cannot be faulted for having inventoried too much. Lemon concentrate prices rose from $37 per ton in 1975/76 to $52 per ton in 1978/79, a 40 percent increase. Viewed in retrospect, Sunkist's inventoried *too little* of the 1974/75 crop, not *too much*. In sum, the inventory policy followed by Sunkist was consistent with that of a rational firm operating in a competitive but price-volatile market.

Finally, other facts contradict the hypothesis that Sunkist operated as a classic monopolist in its handling of the huge lemon crop of 1974/75. A monopolist would have diverted from the primary fresh market to secondary markets. Yet, whereas Sunkist members produced 86 percent of the 1974/75 lemon crop, they accounted for 88.2 percent of fresh domestic lemon marketings, an all-time high. In contrast, their share of the processed lemon market was 85.8 percent. This evidence does not support the hypothesis that Sunkist engaged in monopoly conduct with respect to the 1974/75 lemon crop by diverting sales to the processed market or by following an inventory policy designed to achieve a monopolistic price.

Did Sunkist Engage in Monopolizing Conduct?

To this point, we have summarized evidence of market structure and conduct bearing on the question of whether Sunkist had monopoly power.

Under the law, if this question is answered in the negative, it is not necessary to evaluate whether a defendant engaged in monopolizing conduct. Although we concluded above that Sunkist lacked monopoly power, we nonetheless summarize here our analysis of the FTC's allegations that Sunkist engaged in specific willful acts designed to achieve or maintain its monopoly. We first explain each FTC charge and then review the evidence associated with it.

Sunkist's Deliberately Maintained Dominant Share

This charge asserts that Sunkist pursued a specific policy of maintaining a sufficiently dominant market position to confer control over price. The FTC sought to support the charge by marshalling various statements of Sunkist officials to the effect that Sunkist should strive to attain some specific market share. These targeted shares varied over time. As such, the statements prove nothing more than that Sunkist, like all large business organizations, set goals in the planning process. More often than not, the statements were reflections of hope rather than of accomplishment. The crucial question, both in law and economics, is whether Sunkist engaged in willful acts as opposed to competition based on the merits in achieving its market share goals. This requires examining the nature, purposes, and effects of various specific practices that the FTC alleged to be exclusionary.

Sunkist's Exclusionary Arrangements with Licensed Commercial Packinghouses

The FTC charged that the use of licensed commercial packinghouses by Sunkist's members represented exclusive dealing arrangements unlawfully used to maintain monopoly. Indeed, in 1978, the complaint counsel, in the statement of its case, charged Sunkist with willfully maintaining its monopoly power through exclusive dealing contracts with local cooperative houses and licensed commercial houses. Analysis of this charge requires understanding the contents, goals, and results of the contractual arrangements that bind together the Sunkist System. In this connection, contracts involving cooperative packinghouses need to be compared and contrasted with contracts involving commercial packinghouses.

FTC counsel asserted that these contracts foreclosed competing growers, packinghouses, and processing plants from the market. This charge challenged the very legal foundation of federated cooperatives because the contracts Sunkist used were not unique, but were, instead, imperative to the successful functioning of a federated cooperative. The FTC charges failed to recognize certain inherent organizational differences between federated cooperatives and proprietary corporations. Recall the basic features of the Sunkist System. It is a three-tiered, federated-type cooperative consisting of local cooperatives, district exchanges, and Sunkist Central. The entire federation is called the Sunkist System. The grower-owners of the Sunkist System are either grower-members that own local cooperative packing-houses or grower-members that use licensed commercial packinghouses. All of the growers are members of the Sunkist System. Those contracting with commercial packinghouses to perform the packing function differ from other Sunkist members in only one significant respect: they find it economical to contract out the packinghouse function while in every other respect relying on the Sunkist System. The licensed commercial houses are not members of Sunkist.

The various parts of the Sunkist System are bound together and are functionally integrated by various contractual agreements. Efficient inte-gration of farm enterprises through cooperative corporations is more diffi-cult than with individual proprietary corporations. It is necessary to bind together otherwise independent farmers by guaranteeing each farmer of the others' performance. The process is even more complex in federated coop-eratives, where some or all growers also own separate legal entities—in Sunkist's case, the local packinghouses and district exchanges. A federation of cooperatives must use contracts to accomplish what can be brought about through managerial edict in a multiplant centralized cooperative or a proprietary corporation.

To prohibit cooperatives from using marketing contracts in such circum-stances is to deny farmers the same rights acting through cooperatives that businesspeople enjoy acting through proprietary corporations. To insist that a cooperative cannot limit its business relations exclusively to members is like saying one division of a proprietary corporation cannot do business solely with another division of the same company, but that it must deal as well with competing suppliers or customers. One of the reasons Sunkist has given for its policy regarding nonmember packing is to prevent outside growers from benefiting from Sunkist packinghouse facilities without sharing the risks of ownership: simply put, nonmembers would get a free ride, thereby under-mining the cooperative. Sunkist also is concerned that licensed commercial houses packing nonmember fruit might use the confidential market informa-tion they obtain from the Sunkist System to benefit nonmembers.

It appears that for reasons of business efficiency, Sunkist has not fol-lowed a policy of packing nonmember fruit. This conclusion is supported by the policies of other federated marketing cooperatives. Whereas central-ized types of marketing cooperatives frequently do business with non-members, large federated marketing cooperatives generally have not done so because they find it more difficult to exercise tight managerial control over their local marketing organizations.

Although Sunkist's contracts appear to have been adopted to promote efficiency, the question remains whether they result in exclusionary con-duct meeting the standards of monopolization. We consider, in turn, the potential competitive effects of these contracts on other growers, marketers, and processors.

The marketing contracts of the local cooperative houses and the contracts with licensed commercial houses provide that the houses will pack only for Sunkist members for a period of one year. Are non-Sunkist growers injured by these exclusive dealing contracts? Given Sunkist's policy of open membership, any grower may join Sunkist and enjoy the benefits of the Sunkist marketing system. Nonmembers that do not join Sunkist remain apart of their own choosing. To permit nonmembers access to market through Sunkist's local cooperative packinghouses and the licensed commercial houses without joining Sunkist would give them a free ride that could undermine the Sunkist System.

The contracts also require that Sunkist members' fruit be marketed exclusively through the Sunkist System. These provisions, the FTC charged, foreclosed competing fresh citrus marketers and citrus processors. According to the FTC's theory, the local packinghouses, district exchanges, and Sunkist Central are treated as separate business entities. In fact, however, the Sunkist System has invested millions of dollars in packinghouses, processing plants, a nationwide marketing organization, foreign sales offices, R&D, valuable trademarks, and other facilities and functions. It is inconceivable that Sunkist's growers would invest in such operations unless Sunkist's trilevel federated system had a legal structure binding it together into an integrated whole. Were Sunkist a centralized cooperative organization, as are such other large California cooperatives as Sun Maid Raisins and the California Almond Growers, it would not need the legal ties the FTC found offensive. Sunkist should not be penalized for assuming a federated legal form. This is essentially what the Supreme Court held in a 1962 decision sanctioning Sunkist's federated structure: "To hold otherwise would be to impose grave legal consequences upon organizational distinctions that are of *de minimus* meaning and effect to those growers who have banded together for processing and marketing purposes."

Finally, FTC counsel's entire analysis of foreclosure was flawed because it failed to examine the contracts in the structural setting in which they were used. In economic theory, exclusive dealing arrangements can only be anticompetitive when they are used by a party with market power. If the party demanding an exclusive dealing contract with another does not already have market power, the contracts cannot result in monopolization. Because our earlier analysis of market structure and conduct indicates that Sunkist did not possess monopoly power, it follows that the contracts did not represent the asserted monopoly conduct.

Acquisition of Grower Citrus Products

In 1974, Sunkist acquired Growers Citrus Products (GCP), a lemon juice processor in Yuma, Arizona. The FTC Trial Brief alleged that the acquisition increased Sunkist's share of the processed lemon juice market from 80 percent to 90 percent, resulting in foreclosure of the processed lemon juice market.

Sunkist alleged that it acquired GCP for purely business reasons: GCP was a failing company and it therefore was cheaper to buy its facilities than to expand in other ways. Among other things, there was evidence that GCP had been operating far below its capacity and had been trying to sell out for some time.

It does not seem necessary to make a judgment as to whether GCP was a failing company because other facts did not support the FTC's charge that the acquisition foreclosed the processed lemon products market. The FTC appeared to misread its own facts as to market shares. Whereas Sunkist and GCP had a combined share of lemon juice (measured in dollars) of 90 percent in the year before the acquisition, the year after, their share was only 75 percent. Moreover, Sunkist experienced a steady decline in its share of lemon products production following the acquisition, reaching a low of 58 percent in 1982/83, the last year for which data were available. This postacquisition decline in Sunkist's share undermines the FTC's charge of monopolization achieved through foreclosure of the market.

Affiliation of Blue Goose Growers, Inc.

In 1966, thirteen commercial packinghouses affiliated with Blue Goose Growers, Inc., changed their affiliation to Sunkist Growers, Inc. The growers became Sunkist members and the houses operated as licensed commercial packinghouses. At the time, there were special economic circumstances that made affiliation with Sunkist an attractive alternative to the growers owning the Blue Goose packinghouses. One immediate effect of the affiliation was to increase Sunkist members' shares of lemon production by about 8.8 percentage points and orange production by about 10 percentage points. The FTC Trial Brief charged that the Blue Goose affiliation represented a "combination" with Sunkist and was part of Sunkist's continuing effort to achieve market dominance.

Evaluating the probable competitive effect of the affiliation of these houses and growers requires viewing them in the context of the continuing process of affiliation and disaffiliation occurring in the California/Arizona citrus industry. Many citrus growers and packinghouses have changed their affiliation with marketers depending upon their perception of the benefits to be gained by doing so. The only unique feature of the Blue Goose affiliation was the decision of thirteen houses to affiliate at one time. In this respect, it is important to note that the Blue Goose packinghouses were not under common ownership and, therefore, each made the decision to affiliate with Sunkist independently. In fact, one Blue Goose house had affiliated with Sunkist four years earlier, in 1961/62, and one of the Blue Goose houses that affiliated in 1966 disaffiliated the following year. Moreover, many other houses and growers affiliated and disaffiliated in earlier and later years, reflecting the open-ended nature of Sunkist Growers, Inc.

The Blue Goose affiliations in 1966 were not sufficiently unique to sustain a charge of monopolization. First, although Sunkist's market shares rose when the Blue Goose houses affiliated, these shares eroded steadily afterward, falling well below the 1966 levels by the late 1970s. Second, in 1984, all of the remaining Blue Goose houses disaffiliated with Sunkist. Although the later event occurred after the Sunkist case was settled in 1981 and was not related to that settlement, it confirms the conclusion of our mobility analysis based on experience before the FTC settlement.

Conclusions

The conclusions of the legal-economic analysis summarized above differ on nearly every major point with those of FTC counsel. The main reason for the differences stems from a failure of the FTC to develop a well-articulated legal-economic theory of the case. And, insofar as an economic theory of monopoly and monopolizing was implicit in organizing the analysis, the FTC's theory failed to incorporate the unique organizational features of a nonprofit, open-ended marketing cooperative. These deficiencies created a flawed thread that ran through the entire FTC case.

FTC counsel's Trial Brief was preoccupied with market share in the structural analysis, ignoring almost entirely—as have most reported cooperative monopoly decisions—the issue of entry barriers. Given the increasing attention that the law of monopoly has placed on entry barriers, this failing of the FTC Brief represents bad law as well as bad economics.

Instead of testing a complete theory of monopoly power, the FTC case rested exclusively on evidence of Sunkist's large market share and evidence consisting of selected statements by Sunkist officials. FTC counsel interpreted the statements as admissions of the existence, use, and consequences of Sunkist's monopoly power. Although statements by businesspeople may provide insights into unlawful intent, they may also merely reflect a purpose to prevail over competitors based on the merits. Such statements, more often than not, support conflicting hypotheses of conduct, requiring that the statements be tested with empirical evidence. The FTC counsel failed to do this. Despite an abundance of statistical data for Sunkist and other firms in the various relevant markets, no evidence was presented in the Trial Brief indicating that Sunkist had diverted products from the fresh citrus market to secondary markets, as would be necessary were Sunkist a monopolistic price leader, as charged. No economic analysis was presented nor was evidence developed to determine whether price discrimination occurred in either the processed products or fresh export markets. Our statistical analysis of the above matters indicates that Sunkist did not behave as a monopolistic barometric price leader and did not engage in price discrimination.

The FTC Trial Brief charged Sunkist with enjoying monopoly power because of its advertising-created product differentiation. But it presented no evidence indicating whether Sunkist's modest price premium reflected artificial product differentiation, as it claimed, or whether some of the premium was attributable to real differences in product quality. Most importantly, no analysis was made to determine whether the price premium was at a monopolistic level rather than merely being somewhat above a perfectly competitive level. Again, this represents a failing in law as well as in economics, because the law does not consider every price premium due to advertising to be evidence of unlawful monopoly. Despite the FTC's long experience and involvement in matters relating to market power associated with advertised trademarks, FTC counsel failed to compare the Sunkist price premium with that of other products where the FTC has had experience with alleged monopoly price premiums attributable to strong trademarks, e.g., ReaLemon processed lemon juice and ready-to-eat breakfast cereal products. As shown by our analysis, the Sunkist premium was truly modest compared to these as well as lesser trademarks in the food industry. In our view, the reason for Sunkist's small price premium is to be found in the unique organizational characteristics of Sunkist as a non-profit, open-ended cooperative.

Finally, FTC counsel's analysis of the alleged foreclosure resulting from various Sunkist practices was flawed because the practices were not examined within a proper conceptual framework. The analysis incorrectly assumed Sunkist had monopoly power. This alone was sufficient to nullify the analysis. The analysis further erred because it failed to recognize the unique organizational characteristics of a federated cooperative. Agreements that counsel viewed as being unlawful were in fact dictated by the economic imperatives of Sunkist's three-tiered federated structure. Simply put, they were motivated by reasons of economic efficiency. In this area, again, the FTC staff may be faulted for practicing bad law as well as bad economics, since the Supreme Court has explicitly sanctioned Sunkist's organizational structure.

Notes

1. This analysis has not examined whether marketing orders confer market power on growers in the California/Arizona citrus industry. Marketing orders were not involved in the FTC case. In essence, the FTC charged Sunkist with monopolizing over and above any market power that marketing orders may have conferred on Sunkist and other California/Arizona growers.

2. Robert L. Wills, "Evaluating Price Enhancement by Processing Cooperatives," *American Journal of Agricultural Economics* 67(May 1985):183.

3. We emphasize a distinction between our findings and those of Bronsteen. Peter Bronsteen, "Allegations of Monopoly and Anticompetitive Practices in the Domestic Lemon Industry" (Ph.D. diss., University of California-Los Angeles, 1981): 162–78. While he also concluded that Sunkist received a price premium for its brand, he believed the premium occurred because Sunkist's advertising provided consumers with credible and valuable information of product quality. We do not disagree that the brand provided consumers with information of quality. But recognizing this does not settle the issue of whether the premium also reflected market power, as measured by the size of the premium compared to the cost of achieving it. We go beyond Bronsteen by demonstrating that (1) Sunkist's price premiums were small compared to other well-known food brands, (2) the premiums were raised only modestly above the cost of achieving them, and (3) the small premiums occurred because Sunkist operated as a nonprofit, open-ended marketing cooperative.

4. FTC Brief, 75.

5. Bressler, "Stabilizing the Domestic Market," 44.

6. *William Inglis & Sons Baking Co. v. ITT Continential Baking Company,* 668 F.2d 1014 (9th Cir. 1981), *cert. denied,* 459 U.S. 825 (1982).

8
Addendum: The Agreement Settling the Sunkist Litigation

O
n August 15, 1980, Sunkist and the FTC entered into an agreement settling the Sunkist litigation. (See appendix C.) The agreement was for settlement purposes only and did not constitute an admission by Sunkist that the law had been violated.

The agreement had five substantive provisions. (1) For a period of five years, Sunkist could not without prior approval of the FTC have more than thirty-nine commercial packinghouses affiliated with it. (2) Sunkist was required to divest its Arizona Products Division (APD), the successor to Growers Citrus Products (GCP), which Sunkist had acquired in 1974. (3) For four years following the divestiture, Sunkist was required to annually supply the acquirer of APD with specified amounts of citrus. (4) For a period of ten years, Sunkist could not acquire without the prior approval of the FTC any commerical citrus-processing plants in California or Arizona. (5) For a period of five years, Sunkist could not acquire without prior FTC approval any citrus packinghouses.

What was the significance of this decree as measured against the objectives of antitrust policy? Answering this question requires examining whether the relief achieved the results contemplated by the relevant statutes. The FTC complaint charged Sunkist with monopolizing the California/Arizona citrus industry in violation of section 5 of the FTC Act and with acquiring Growers Citrus Products in violation of section 7 of the Clayton Act.

The legal-economic analysis in the preceding chapters dealt with the law and economics of monopolization. Based on this analysis, we concluded that Sunkist had not engaged in monopolization as defined in the law or in economics. If our analysis is correct, the Federal Trade Commission or the courts should have dismissed the case had it been fully litigated. To what extent, then, did the settlement in this case violate the objectives of the antitrust laws?

Neither of the decree's main provisions had a significant effect on the long-run structure of the California/Arizona citrus industry or Sunkist's position in the industry. The only part of the agreement seeming to promise relief for the FTC's monopolization claim was the provision that for five years, there should not be more than thirty-nine commercial packinghouses affiliated with Sunkist. This prohibition suggests that the FTC had obtained structural relief, a suggestion amplified by the FTC staff's "Analysis of Proposed Consent Order to Aid Public Comment" found in appendix C. The staff analysis stated:

> The year before the issuance of the complaint Sunkist had affiliations with 51 commercial packinghouses. The proposed order limits that number to 39. This reduction will assure competitive access to a significant number of the industry's commercial houses without interfering with Sunkist's right, as a Capper-Volstead agricultural cooperative, to continue affiliating with cooperative packinghouses. Moreover, the five-year duration of this limitation should enable competitors to establish sound relationships with a substantial number of packinghouses to improve competition and thereby provide viable alternatives to Sunkist's marketing operations.

Those unfamiliar with the facts may infer from the staff's analysis that Sunkist had been required, if effect, to divest a substantial number of commercial houses, thereby enabling Sunkist's "competitors to establish sound relationships with a substantial number of packinghouses." Not so. What was left unsaid was that by 1980, Sunkist already had fewer than the permissible 39 houses. The number of such houses had fallen rather steadily over time, from 57 in 1966/67 to 30 in 1979/80, as seen in table 4–11. On May 5, 1986, 5 years after the agreement went in effect, Sunkist had affiliations with only 27 commercial houses. This decline largely reflected a long-term trend toward increasing size of packinghouses and had absolutely nothing to do with the requirements of the consent decree.

By including this provision in the agreement, the FTC seemed to have acknowledged that Sunkist had not monopolized in the past and was unlikely to do so in the future. Indeed, the provision seems quite meaningless, except as a peace settlement permitting the FTC to withdraw from the field without admitting defeat.

The other main provision of the decree, that requiring divestiture of Grower Citrus Products, is another matter. The FTC complaint had challenged the acquisition of GCP as a violation of section 7 of the Clayton Act as well as section 5 of the FTC Act. Our analysis concluded that the acquisition did not constitute monopolization. Whether the acquisition violated section 7 of the Clayton Act is less clear, however, since section 7 prohibits acquisitions when the effect "may be substantially to lessen competition, or to tend to create a monopoly." While our inquiry focused on the monopolization charge, suffice it to emphasize that the legal-economic standards used in applying section 7 are quite intolerant of horizontal mergers. It seems likely that the acquisition would even have violated the relaxed standards of the current Dept. of Justice[1] unless Sunkist could have prevailed under the so-called failing company defense.[2] The FTC staff seemed to acknowledge the merits of Sunkist's defense to the section 7 charge, since the Trial Brief did not allege that the acquisition of GCP violated section 7; the brief included the acquisition as part of Sunkist's alleged monopolizing conduct in violation of section 5 of the FTC Act.[3] In view of the above, Sunkist's agreement to divest GCP may best be explained as the price Sunkist was willing to pay to avoid added years of litigation, the outcome of which was uncertain.

Finally, the provision specifying that Sunkist Growers, Inc. not acquire any citrus packinghouses for five years was purely symbolic. Sunkist Growers, Inc. never acquired any packinghouses in the past nor is it likely to in the future.

In sum, the consent agreement would not have provided any relief for the asserted monopoly had any monopolization actually existed. Particularly significant, the agreement made no reference to the most important specific "contemplated relief" mentioned in the complaint (reprinted in appendix A). The agreement never mentioned prohibition of the requirement that Sunkist packinghouses not pack for others; prohibition of contracts preventing Sunkist's cooperative packinghouses or affiliated commercial packinghouses from dealing with marketers or processors in competition with Sunkist; severance of all contracts or agreements with commercial packinghouses; and a prohibition against refusing to sell fresh or product-grade fruit to competing marketers or processors. By not including in the agreement any of these contractual arrangements that long had been essential integrating features of the Sunkist System, the FTC seemed to acknowledge the legitimacy of such contracts by Sunkist under the antitrust laws. Rather than constituting restraints resulting in monopolization, the various contracts are essential in achieving the legitimate business purposes of a federated agricultural cooperative such as Sunkist. As such, these contracts meet the Supreme Court's dictum that farmers should receive, "through agricultural cooperatives acting as entities, the same unified competitive advantage—and responsibility—available to businessmen acting through corporations as entities."

Notes

1. U.S. Dept. of Justice, "Merger Guidelines," reproduced by Bureau of National Affairs (Washington, D.C.: GPO, June 14, 1984).

2. Sunkist alleged the GCP's "plant was not viable and its acquisition therefore without adverse competitive effect." (Sunkist Growers, Inc., "Statement of Its Defense," FTC Docket 9100 [March 22, 1979], 43). Sunkist argued that unless Sunkist bought GCP, GCP was "faced with the need to install extensive and expensive pollution control equipment or be shut down by . . . the Environmental Protection Agency. The improvements could not be justified in light of the current return from

the operation." (Ibid.) The owners allegedly had previously been unsuccessful in their efforts to sell the plant, and, in recent years, had been able to operate it at only about 25 percent of its capacity. Sunkist had in 1970 refused to purchase GCP when the latter had approached Sunkist concerning an acquisition. (Ibid., 43–44).

3. FTC Brief, 142.

Appendix A
Federal Trade Commission Complaint in the Matter of Sunkist Growers, Inc.

In the Matter of	DOCKET NO. 9100
SUNKIST GROWERS, INC.,	
a corporation	

COMPLAINT

The Federal Trade Commission, having reason to believe that Sunkist Growers, Inc. has violated and is now violating Section 5 of the Federal Trade Commission Act, as amended, 15 U.S.C. Section 45, and Section 7 of the Clayton Act, as amended, 15 U.S.C. Section 18, and that a proceeding by it in respect thereto is in the public interest, hereby issues its complaint charging as follows:

DEFINITIONS

PARAGRAPH ONE: For the purposes of this complaint, the following definitions shall apply:

(a) "Western citrus fruit" includes oranges, lemons, grapefruit and other varieties of citrus which are grown in California and Arizona;

(b) "Fresh-grade fruit" is citrus that is sold for fresh consumption;

(c) "Product-grade fruit" is citrus that is used for processing into juice or peel products;

(d) "Citrus products" are juice or peel products made from product-grade fruit;

(e) "Packing" means services performed by packinghouses including, among others: receiving western citrus fruit, separating it into product-grade fruit and fresh-grade fruit, shipping the product-grade fruit to citrus processing plants, washing, waxing, grading and sizing fresh-grade fruit, placing it into cartons and shipping the cartons to buyers;

(f) "Processing" means receiving western product-grade fruit and manufacturing it into citrus products;

(g) "Marketing" is the sale and distribution of western citrus fruit or citrus products to wholesale buyers.

SUNKIST GROWERS, INC.

PARAGRAPH TWO:

(a) Respondent Sunkist Growers, Inc. (hereinafter "Sunkist") is an incorporated cooperative association, without capital stock, organized under the laws of the State of California, with its principal office and place of business at 14130 Riverside Drive, Sherman Oaks, California;

(b) Sunkist engages in the marketing and processing of western citrus fruit packed by approximately 43 cooperative associations and 51 commercial citrus fruit packinghouses with which Sunkist has contracts and agreements;

(c) Sunkist markets fresh or in processed form approximately 75 percent of the total production of western oranges and lemons;

(d) Total sales for Sunkist were $482.9 million for the fiscal year ending October 31, 1975.

TRADE AND COMMERCE

PARAGRAPH THREE:

(a) The western citrus fruit industry is composed of several levels of operation, including growing, packing, processing and marketing;

(b) Total wholesale sales of western citrus fresh-grade fruit and western citrus products exceeded $500 million in the 1974–75 crop year.

PARAGRAPH FOUR:

(a) The relevant markets include the following and any submarkets thereof:

　　(1) The packing of western citrus fruit in California and Arizona;

　　(2) The trade in product-grade western oranges in California and Arizona;

　　(3) The trade in product-grade lemons in California and Arizona;

　　(4) The manufacture, sale and distribution of lemon products in the United States and Canada;

　　(5) The sale and distribution of fresh-grade western oranges to wholesale buyers in the United States and Canada;

　　(6) The sale and distribution of fresh-grade lemons to wholesale buyers in the United States and Canada;

　　(7) The sale and distribution of fresh-grade western oranges for export outside of the United States and Canada;

　　(8) The sale and distribution of fresh-grade lemons for export outside of the United States and Canada.

(b) Sunkist controls approximately 65 percent or more of each of the relevant markets or submarkets alleged herein. No other firm accounts for more than 15 percent of any of the relevant markets or submarkets alleged herein.

JURISDICTION

PARAGRAPH FIVE: At all times relevant herein, Sunkist sold and shipped western citrus fruit and citrus products throughout the United States and to various foreign countries and engaged in commerce within the meaning of Section 1 of the Clayton Act, as amended, 15 U.S.C. Section 12, and engaged in or affected commerce within the meaning of Section 4 of the Federal Trade Commission Act, as amended, 15 U.S.C. Section 44. Except to the extent that competition has been hindered, frustrated, lessened or eliminated by the acts and practices alleged in this complaint, Sunkist is in competition with other firms in the relevant markets and submarkets alleged herein.

COUNT ONE

PARAGRAPH SIX: The allegations of PARAGRAPHS ONE through FIVE are incorporated herein by reference.

PARAGRAPH SEVEN:

(a) Sunkist maintains exclusive dealing contracts and agreements with approximately 51 commercial packinghouses which prohibit these packinghouses from:

(1) Packing fruit for non-Sunkist growers; and

(2) Dealing with marketers or processors which compete with Sunkist.

(b) The effects, among others, of these contracts separately or in combination with other agreements entered into by Sunkist have been or may be to foreclose competitors from a substantial share of one or more of the markets or submarkets alleged in PARAGRAPH FOUR (a)(1)-(3) and (5)-(8).

PARAGRAPH EIGHT: The aforesaid acts and practices, considered alone or in combination with the other acts and practices alleged in this complaint, have had or may have, among other things, the tendency and capacity to increase barriers to entry or to restrain, lessen or eliminate competition or create a monopoly in one or more of the markets or submarkets alleged in PARAGRAPH FOUR (a)(1)-(3) and (5)-(8) and thus are to the prejudice and injury of the public and constitute unfair methods of competition or unfair acts and practices in or affecting commerce all in violation of Section 5 of the Federal Trade Commission Act, as amended, 15 U.S.C. Section 45.

COUNT TWO

PARAGRAPH NINE: The allegations of PARAGRAPHS ONE through FIVE are incorporated herein by reference.

PARAGRAPH TEN:

(a) In January 1966, Sunkist combined contracted, or agreed with the Western Sales Division of Blue Goose Growers, Inc. (hereinafter "Blue Goose"). Pursuant to this combination, contract, or agreement, Blue Goose ceased marketing fresh-grade western citrus fruit and Sunkist entered exclusive dealing contracts with 13 commercial packinghouses that were owned by or under contract to Blue Goose and formerly marketed through Blue Goose;

(b) The combination, contracts, or agreements alleged above resulted in prohibiting commercial packinghouses owned by or under contract to Blue Goose from dealing with growers that are not members of Sunkist or with marketers or processors that compete with Sunkist;

(c) The effects, among others, of the combination, contracts, or agreements described above have been or may be to eliminate substantial competition between Sunkist and Blue Goose, or increase entry barriers, or increase concentration or strengthen the position of Sunkist in one or more of the relevant markets or submarkets alleged in PARAGRAPH FOUR (a)(1)–(3) and (5)–(8).

PARAGRAPH ELEVEN: The aforesaid act and practice, considered alone or in combination with the other acts and practices alleged in this complaint, has had or may have, among other things, the tendency and capacity to increase barriers to entry or to restrain, lessen or eliminate competition or create a monopoly in one or more of the markets or submarkets alleged in PARAGRAPH FOUR (a)(1)–(3) and (5)–(8) and thus is to the prejudice and injury of the public and constitutes an unfair method of competition or unfair act and practice in or affecting commerce all in violation of Section 5 of the Federal Trade Commission Act, as amended, 15 U.S.C. Section 45.

COUNT THREE

PARAGRAPH TWELVE: The allegations of PARAGRAPHS ONE through FIVE are incorporated herein by reference.

PARAGRAPH THIRTEEN:

(a) In August 1974, Sunkist, which then owned two citrus processing plants, acquired the assets of Growers Citrus Products, a division of Golden Y Growers, Inc. (hereinafter "GCP"), a corporation. The assets consisted of a citrus processing plant located in Yuma,

Arizona. At the same time, Sunkist also purchased land and cold storage facilities from Southwestern Ice and Cold Storage Co. (hereinafter "Southwestern"), a corporation. The land and cold storage facilities were previously leased by GCP from Southwestern for use in connection with operation of the processing plant;

(b) Prior to the acquisition, GCP was in competition with Sunkist in the markets or submarkets alleged in PARAGRAPH FOUR (a)(3)–(4). In the years prior to the acquisition, Sunkist's share of the markets or submarkets alleged in PARAGRAPH FOUR (a)(3)–(4), exceeded 65 percent and GCP's share was approximately 5 percent.

(c) At all times relevant herein, GCP and Southwestern were engaged in commerce within the meaning of Section 1 of the Clayton Act, as amended, 15 U.S.C. Section 12, and engaged in or affected commerce within the meaning of Section 4 of the Federal Trade Commission Act, as amended, 15 U.S.C. Section 44.

(d) The effects, among others, of the acquisitions described above have been or may be to eliminate substantial competition between Sunkist and GCP, or increase entry barriers, or increase concentration or strengthen the position of Sunkist in one or more of the relevant markets or submarkets alleged in PARAGRAPH FOUR (a)(1)–(8).

PARAGRAPH FOURTEEN: The acquisitions by Sunkist alleged herein may subtantially lessen competition or tend to create a monopoly in one or more of the relevant markets or submarkets alleged in PARAGRAPH FOUR (a)(1)–(8) in violation of Section 7 of the Clayton Act, as amended, 15 U.S.C. Section 18, and Section 5 of the Federal Trade Commission Act, as amended, 15 U.S.C. Section 45.

COUNT FOUR

PARAGRAPH FIFTEEN: The allegations of PARAGRAPHS ONE through FIVE are incorporated herein by reference.

PARAGRAPH SIXTEEN: Sunkist processes approximately 75 percent of the product-grade lemons grown in the United States.

PARAGRAPH SEVENTEEN:

(a) Sunkist, as an instrumentality of its members, who are otherwise competitors of each other, stores and withholds from the market a large supply of lemon products for the purpose or with the effect of stabilizing the price of lemon products.

(b) The effects, among others, of the act and practice described above have been or may be to stabilize the price of lemon products, or to deter entry into lemon processing.

PARAGRAPH EIGHTEEN: The aforesaid act and practice, considered alone or in combination with the other acts and practices alleged in this complaint, has had or may have, among other things, the tendency and capacity to increase barriers to entry or to restrain, lessen or eliminate competition or create a monopoly in the market or one or more of the submarkets alleged in PARAGRAPH FOUR (a)(4) and thus is to the prejudice and injury of the public and constitutes an unfair method of competition or unfair act and practice in or affecting commerce all in violation of Section 5 of the Federal Trade Commission Act, as amended, 15 U.S.C. Section 45.

COUNT FIVE

PARAGRAPH NINETEEN: The allegations of PARAGRAPHS ONE through FIVE are incorporated herein by reference.

PARAGRAPH TWENTY: Sunkist has monopoly power in one or more of the relevant markets or submarkets alleged in PARAGRAPH FOUR (a)(1)–(8) above.

PARAGRAPH TWENTY-ONE: Sunkist, individually or in combination with others, has engaged in the acts and practices alleged in COUNTS ONE through FOUR, above, among others.

PARAGRAPH TWENTY-TWO: Sunkist has adopted and followed a policy of refusing to permit competing processors to purchase product-grade western oranges and lemons from cooperative associations under contract to Sunkist.

PARAGRAPH TWENTY-THREE: Sunkist has adopted and followed a policy of refusing to permit competing marketers to purchase or market fresh-grade western oranges and lemons packed by cooperative associations under contract to Sunkist.

PARAGRAPH TWENTY-FOUR: Sunkist has adopted and followed a policy of refusing to permit western citrus fruit of non-Sunkist growers to be packed in packinghouses owned by cooperative associations under contract to Sunkist.

PARAGRAPH TWENTY-FIVE: Sunkist has adopted and followed a policy of refusing to sell product-grade or fresh-grade western oranges and lemons to competing marketers or processors.

PARAGRAPH TWENTY-SIX: Sunkist has adopted and followed a policy of achieving and maintaining control of at least 70 percent of the total supply of western oranges and lemons packed by packinghouses in California and Arizona.

PARAGRAPH TWENTY-SEVEN: The effects, among others, of the acts and practices described above, have been or may be to increase barriers to entry, or stabilize, control, hinder, lessen, foreclose, or restrain competition in one or more of the relevant markets or submarkets alleged in PARAGRAPH FOUR (a)(1)-(8).

PARAGRAPH TWENTY-EIGHT: By engaging in the acts and practices alleged herein, Sunkist by itself or in combination with others has monopolized, attempted to monopolize, or maintained a non-competitive market structure in one or more of the relevant markets or submarkets alleged in PARAGRAPH FOUR (a)(1)-(8) above in violation of Section 5 of the Federal Trade Commission Act, as amended, 15 U.S.C. Section 45.

WHEREFORE, THE PREMISES CONSIDERED, the Federal Trade Commission on this 31st day of May A.D., 1977, issues this, its complaint, against said respondent.

NOTICE

Notice is hereby given to the respondent hereinbefore named that the 20th day of July A.D. 1977, at 10:00 a.m. o'clock is hereby fixed as the time and Federal Trade Commission Officies, 1101 Building, 414—11th and Pennsylvania Avenuen, N.W., Washington, D.C. 20580 as the place when and where a hearing will be had before an administrative law judge of the Federal Trade Commission, on the charges set forth in this complaint, at which time and place you will have the right under said Act to appear and show cause why an order should not be entered requiring you to cease and desist from the violations of law charged in this complaint.

You are notified that the opportunity is afforded you to file with the Commission an answer to this complaint on or before the thirtieth (30th) day after service of it upon you. An answer in which the allegations of the complaint are contested shall contain a concise statement of the facts constituting each ground of defense; and specific admission, denial, or explanation of each fact alleged in the complaint or, if you are without knowledge thereof, a statement to that effect. Allegations of the complaint not thus answered shall be deemed to have been admitted.

If you elect not to contest the allegations of fact set forth in the complaint, the answer shall consist of a statement that you admit all of the material allegations to be true. Such an answer shall constitute a waiver of hearings as to the facts alleged in the complaint, and together with the complaint will provide a record basis on which the administrative law judge shall file an initial decision containing appropriate findings and conclusions and an appropriate order disposing of the proceeding. In such answer you may, however, reserve the right to submit proposed findings and conclusions and the right to appeal the initial decision to the Commission under Section 3.52 of the Commission's Rules of Practice for Adjudicative Proceedings.

Failure to answer within the time above provided shall be deemed to constitute a waiver of your right to appear and contest the allegations of the complaint and shall authorize the administrative law judge, without further notice to you, to find the facts to be as alleged in the complaint and to enter an initial decision containing such findings, appropriate conclusions and order.

NOTICE OF CONTEMPLATED RELIEF

Should the Commission conclude from the record developed in any adjudicative proceeding in this matter that the respondent is in violation of Section 5 of the Federal Trade Commission Act, as amended, 15 U.S.C. Section 45, or Section 7 of the Clayton Act, as amended, 15 U.S.C. Section 18, as alleged in this complaint, the Commission may order such relief as is necessary or appropriate including, but not limited to, one or more of the following:

1. Prohibition of requirements that packinghouses under contract to Sunkist not pack for others;

2. Prohibition of contracts preventing packinghouses or cooperative associations under contract to Sunkist from dealing with marketers or processors in competition with Sunkist;

3. Severance of all contracts or agreements with commercial packinghouses;

4. Prohibition on entering into contracts or agreements with, or acquiring or financing the acquisition of any additional packinghouses for 10 years without the prior approval of the Federal Trade Commission;

5. Divestiture of the processing plant acquired from Growers Citrus Products, a division of Golden Y Growers, Inc., and land and cold storage facilities acquired from Southwestern Ice and Cold Storage Co.;

6. Prohibition of the acquisition of any citrus processing plant without the prior approval of the Federal Trade Commission;

7. Prohibition against refusing to sell fresh or product-grade fruit to competing marketers or processors;

Appendix B
Sunkist Growers, Inc.
Amended Articles of Incorporation and Bylaws

AMENDED ARTICLES OF INCORPORATION
SUNKIST GROWERS, INC.

FIRST: THE NAME OF THIS CORPORATION (HEREIN-AFTER REFERRED TO AS "SUNKIST") IS:

SUNKIST GROWERS, INC.

SECOND: The primary purpose for which Sunkist is formed is to furnish facilities and agencies through which citrus fruits of its members and other producers may be marketed or processed and marketed, and to return to said members or other producers the proceeds of sales, less necessary operating and marketing expenses, on the basis of the quantity or value of citrus fruits marketed for such member or other producer.

In carrying out said primary purpose, Sunkist shall have every power, privilege, right and immunity now or hereafter author-ized or permitted by law to a corporation organized or existing pursuant to the provisions of Chapter 1 of Division 20 of the Agricultural Code of the State of California and amendments thereto and substitutions therefor and continuances thereof. Nothing herein contained shall be deemed to limit the right or power of Sunkist to do any lawful act that the board of directors shall determine.

THIRD: Sunkist is organized and exists as a nonprofit co-operative marketing association, without capital stock, pursuant to the provisions of Chapter 1 of Division 20 of the Agricultural Code of the State of California.

FOURTH: The principal office for the transaction of busi-ness of Sunkist is located in the County of Los Angeles, State of California.

FIFTH: The number of directors shall be thirty-two (32); provided, that bylaws may be adopted whereby a different num-ber of directors may be fixed, in which event the number of directors shall be as provided in said bylaws.

SIXTH: As stated in the original articles, the names and ad-dresses of the persons who were to serve as the first directors were:

NAME	RESIDENCE
F. Q. Story	Alhambra, California
W. E. Sprott	Porterville, California
A. P. Harwood	Upland, California
H. E. Cheseboro	Covina, California
W. R. Powell	Glendora, California
P. J. Dreher	Pomona, California
S. J. Beals	Orange, California
W. G. Fraser	Riverside, California
A. P. Johnson	Riverside, California
Frank Scoville	Corona, California
E. F. Van Luven	Colton, California
W. H. Young	Duarte, California
D. Felsenthal	Los Angeles, California

SEVENTH: To provide funds for corporate purposes of Sun-kist, revolving funds, capital credits, and other allocated reserves may be established. Such revolving fund, capital or allocated reserve credits shall not be deemed to evidence, create or estab-lish any present property rights or interests, as such terms are herein used, but such credits shall be deemed to evidence an indebtedness of Sunkist payable only as provided in the bylaws. In the event the membership of any member shall terminate for any reason whatsoever, such member shall not thereupon become entitled to demand or receive any interest in the prop-erty and assets of Sunkist as herein defined, but shall be entitled only to receive payment of its revolving fund or capital credits and its interest, if any, in other allocated reserves as and when same would have been paid had it remained a member.

EIGHTH: Sunkist is a membership corporation, without shares of stock. It shall have three classes of members, as more particularly defined in the bylaws: (1) Growers, (2) Local Asso-ciations, which shall be nonprofit cooperative associations of Growers, and (3) District Exchanges, which shall be nonprofit cooperative associations composed of Growers and Local Associ-ations. In order to be eligible for membership in Sunkist, Local Associations and District Exchanges shall provide voting and property rights consistent with this Article Eight.

The voting power and property rights and interests of each said class of members of Sunkist shall be as follows:

1. *Voting Power*—The voting power of members of Sunkist shall be unequal. All voting power shall ultimately be exercised by Growers, through the representative channels of their respective Local Associations and District Ex-changes. Growers shall have the sole voting power in, and control of, their Local Associations, including the power to elect the boards of directors thereof. The Local Associ-ations and direct Grower members shall elect the board of directors of their respective District Exchanges. The Dis-trict Exchanges shall elect the directors of Sunkist. In the election of directors, each District Exchange shall be enti-tled to as many votes as the number of directors it is enti-tled to nominate, multiplied by the number of directors to be elected. Each District Exchange shall be entitled to nominate one (1) director. Additional directors may be nominated by District Exchanges, on the basis of the vol-ume of all fruit marketed through Sunkist as shown by its records for the average of the three (3) preceding fiscal years, in accordance with the following formula:

   Each District Exchange shall be entitled to nominate one (1) additional director for each whole four per-cent (4%) increment of such volume which such Dis-trict Exchange has in excess of two percent (2%) of such volume.

   Commencing in 1976, each District Exchange having less than two percent (2%) of such volume, as reflected in any two of the three most recent compilations of such volume approved or accepted by the board of directors, shall, for the purpose of nominating directors as specified above, combine its volume with one or more other District Exchanges in such manner as shall allow such combination of District Exchanges to nominate not less than one (1) director in accordance with the above formula as though they were a single District Exchange, and such combination of District Exchanges may so nominate a director or directors as though they were a single District Exchange.

Other than in the election of directors of Sunkist, the voting rights of the Growers shall be exercised by and through their respective Local Associations or their representative or representatives on the board of directors of their District Exchange, on the basis of one (1) vote for each one thousand (1,000) cartons or equivalent (or major fraction thereof) of citrus fruit, fresh and products, marketed through Sunkist during the average of the three (3) preceding complete fiscal years of Sunkist.

2. *Property Rights—* The property rights and interests of the members of Sunkist shall be unequal. The District Exchanges and Local Associations, as such, shall have no property rights or interests. The property rights and interests of Growers in Sunkist at any time shall be such part of the entire property rights and interests as the amount of citrus fruit, fresh and products, marketed by each member Grower through the Sunkist System, during the six (6) preceding completed years bears to the total of such citrus fruit shipped by all member Growers through the Sunkist System during the same six (6) years.

In the event of dissolution or liquidation, any residue that may remain after payment in full of all indebtedness, including that evidenced by revolving fund or capital credits and other allocated reserves, shall be distributed among those member Growers who were members at the time of commencement of proceedings for liquidation or dissolution, in proportion to the property rights held by each such Grower at the time of commencement of proceedings for liquidation or dissolution.

In the event Sunkist shall at any time determine to transfer the property and assets of Sunkist to a successor association and shall designate such association as the successor association of Sunkist, then the transfer of said property and assets by Sunkist to such successor association shall not be considered a dissolution or liquidation within the meaning of the foregoing paragraph. Such association may be formed or exist under state or federal laws, provided only it shall be in substance a farmers' nonprofit cooperative marketing association. Such successor association may be an association formed or recognized for such purpose, or it may be formed by merger, consolidation, or any corporate reorganization. Property rights and interests of the members of Sunkist shall be recognized and preserved in an equitable manner in such successor association.

NINTH: Sunkist shall have perpetual existence.

AMENDED BYLAWS
SUNKIST GROWERS, INC.

GENERAL

1.1 *Articles of Incorporation* — The articles of incorporation of Sunkist are hereby made a part of these bylaws and all matters hereinafter contained in these bylaws shall be subject to such provisions in regard thereto, if any, as are set forth in the articles of incorporation. All references in these bylaws to the articles of incorporation shall be construed to mean the articles of incorporation as from time to time amended. The name and purposes of the corporation shall be as set forth in the articles of incorporation.

1.2 *Definitions* — As used in these bylaws, the following terms have the following meanings:

(a) "Fresh fruit" means fruit destined only for fresh consumption and moving in normal fresh fruit channels. The board of directors may from time to time specify other and more detailed definitions not inconsistent herewith.

(b) "Products fruit" means all fruit other than that defined as fresh fruit.

(c) "Fruit" or "citrus fruit" means both fresh and products fruit of all varieties.

(d) "Variety" means any one of the following: Navel oranges, Valencia oranges, miscellaneous oranges (including Tangerines), lemons, grapefruit or limes.

(e) "Carton" means the quantity of the particular fruit involved which is contained in the standard carton in common use for fresh shipments of such fruit, or the equivalent thereof, as determined from time to time by the board of directors. The board may from time to time establish the relationship or ratio between the carton and other units of weight or quantity.

(f) "Market" or "marketing" means the sale or shipment for purposes of sale as fresh fruit or as products fruit, utilization for products, or other disposition.

(g) "Volume marketed through Sunkist as shown by its records" means the volume, in terms of one thousand (1,000) cartons or equivalent (or major fraction thereof), of the particular fruit involved, marketed through Sunkist during the average of the three (3) preceding completed fiscal years, on which assessments or deductions for capital or revolving funds and Sunkist charges and expenses have been collected. As soon after the close of a fiscal year as such volume records can be compiled, the average volume of the three (3) preceding completed fiscal years shall be reported to the board of directors and, when approved or accepted by the board, shall be the basis for determination of volume whenever pertinent under these bylaws. Any fruit exempted from the requirement of delivery as provided in Bylaw No. 9.3(b) shall not be included in volume as herein defined. In determining such average volume, appropriate adjustments may be made in such manner as determined by the board of directors upon evidence satisfactory to it, in the case of transfers of Growers and Growers who have marketed through Sunkist for less than three (3) years.

MEMBERSHIP

2.1 *General Organization* — Throughout California and Arizona since the 1880s citrus growers have formed themselves into cooperatives or have constructed or contracted for facilities to pick, pack and market their fruit in fresh or products form. Local nonprofit cooperative packing house organizations have been known and will in these bylaws be referred to as "Local Associations." The Local Associations created regional marketing agencies in common generally known, and in these bylaws referred to, as "District Exchanges." In addition to those growers who formed Local Associations, some growers have become direct members of their respective District Exchanges for marketing purposes, preferring to contract individually for packing services. Sunkist was, in turn, formed by the Growers, Local Associations and their District Exchanges, in order to furnish additional facilities and agencies in maintaining, extending and making more efficient the marketing of the Growers' citrus fruit. Sunkist and its member District Exchanges, Local Association and Growers constitute the cooperative marketing system sometimes referred to as the "Sunkist System."

The fundamental purpose of the Sunkist System is to market the Growers' citrus fruit in the form received, or in processed, or other form at the highest return to such Growers, consistent with their long-term interests. In carrying out such purpose, Sunkist shall act as a nonprofit cooperative marketing association. Sunkist may, at the discretion of the board of directors, also market, in the form received or in processed or other form, the fruit or products thereof, of nonmembers who are producers, or of any nonprofit cooperative association of such producers, insofar as the same may be done in compliance with federal and state laws and regulations applicable to farmers' marketing cooperatives; but such nonmember business shall not exceed fifty percent (50%) by value of the total marketing business and shall be handled on the same basis as that transacted for members.

2.2 *Classes of Members* — There shall be three (3) classes of members:

(a) "Growers" who shall be persons engaged in the production of citrus fruit to be handled by or through the Sunkist System. The word "person," as used herein, includes individuals, fiduciaries, corporations, partnerships, and associations. Such Growers must also be members of a Local Association or District Exchange; and

(b) "Local Associations" which shall be nonprofit cooperative associations of Growers. Each Local Association must also be a member of a District Exchange; and

(c) "District Exchange," each of which shall be a nonprofit cooperative association composed of Growers and Local Associations.

2.3 *Agreements of Local Associations and District Exchanges With Their Growers* — Each Local Association and District Exchange shall maintain appropriate written agreements between itself and its Growers which will provide for the delivery to such Local Association or District Exchange of all the fruit covered by such agreements. Each such agreement shall specify that such Grower is and shall be a member of Sunkist, so long as said Local Association or District Exchange shall be a member thereof, and subject to the Growers' right to withdraw from Sunkist, the District Exchange and Local Association. Each Local Association and District Exchange shall furnish to Sunkist, upon request, a list of Growers then affiliated with said Local Association or District Exchange and a copy of its agreement with Growers.

No Local Association or District Exchange shall release any of its Growers from such Grower agreement (except upon termination of such agreement in accordance with its terms) without giving to Sunkist ten days' notice of such proposed release. At any time within the varietal season that such releases individually or collectively shall total more than five percent (5%) of the volume of the District Exchange by variety, any releases in excess of such percentage must be approved by Sunkist.

2.4 *Representative of Member* — If any member is other than a natural person, such member may be represented by any individual, associate, officer or manager or member thereof, duly authorized in writing filed with the secretary of Sunkist.

2.5 *Membership Contract* — Persons qualified under Bylaw No. 2.2 may become members of Sunkist by submitting an application for membership, in a form prescribed by the board of directors. When accepted by Sunkist, such application shall constitute a contract between the member and Sunkist, for the benefit of each and every other member of Sunkist. The board of directors shall have the right, in its sole discretion, to refuse to accept such application for membership.

2.6 *Membership Certificate* — As evidence of acceptance by Sunkist of said membership contract Sunkist shall issue a membership certificate to each member in a form to be adopted by its board of directors.

2.7 *Nontrasferability of Membership* — No membership shall

be assigned or transferred either voluntarily or involuntarily or by operation of law, nor shall any membership or membership rights of a member be assigned, transferred, alienated or encumbered in any manner or by any means whatsoever; provided, however that nothing herein contained shall be deemed to impair the transferability of capital credits as herein provided in Bylaw No. 10.9.

2.8 *Termination of Membership* — Any membership in Sunkist shall be terminated upon occurrence of any of the following events:

(a) If the member ceases to be a producer or cooperative association of producers within the meaning of applicable federal and state laws and regulations; or

(b) By death, disbanding or dissolution of the member; or

(c) As to a Grower member, by termination of his membership in his Local Association or District Exchange, or

(d) As to a Local Association or District Exchange, by notice of termination as provided in the membership contract; or

(e) By expulsion as provided in Bylaw No. 2.9.

2.9 *Expulsion* — Any member may be expelled by a majority vote of the authorized number of the board of directors for failure to comply with the bylaws or rules and regulations issued thereunder, or by a two-thirds (2/3) vote of the authorized number of directors if termination of such membership is judged to be in the best interests of other members. Before vote upon a proposal to expel any member, such member shall be given notice and a fair and reasonable opportunity to be heard at a regular or special meeting of the board. Any action of the board hereunder shall be final and conclusive. Upon expulsion, all voting and property rights of the member so expelled shall cease and terminate except that such member shall be entitled to receive payment of any outstanding revolving fund, capital or other allocated reserve credits (less any indebtedness to Sunkist) to be paid in the manner and at the time such payment would have been paid had such membership been continued.

VOTING RIGHTS

3.1 Growers — All voting power within Sunkist shall ultimately be exercised by Growers, through the representative channels of their respective Local Association or District Exchanges. Growers shall have the sole voting power in, and control of, their Local Associations and District Exchanges, including the power to elect the boards of directors thereof.

3.2 *Local Associations and Voting Units of Growers* — For purposes of voting, Growers who are not members of Local Associations shall be grouped with relation to packing facilities preparing their fruit for market, in accordance with the bylaws of the respective District Exchanges. Such grouping is herein called a "voting unit" of Growers. Each voting unit of Growers shall exercise its voting right in Sunkist through the person or persons it nominated on the board of directors of its District Exchange. Local Associations and the District Exchange director or directors nominated by each voting unit of Growers shall exercise their Growers' vote upon all questions requiring membership action except the election of directors. All such voting shall be based on volume of fruit marketed and each Local Association or voting unit shall be entitled to one (1) vote for each one thousand (1,000) cartons or equivalent (or major fraction thereof) of the volume of citrus fruit, fresh and products, marketed by Local Association or voting unit through Sunkist during the average of the three (3) preceding completed fiscal years of Sunkist, as shown by its records, as provided in Bylaw No. 1.2(g). In the event any question requiring concurrence of directors representing a specified percentage of volume for board action is submitted to a vote of members, a majority vote thereon to be effective must include the votes of members representing a like percentage.

3.3 *Varietal Voting* — It is recognized that certain questions may from time to time arise relating solely to the promotion of a particular variety of fruit and the assessment relating thereto. To the extent that such questions, as herein more particularly specified, are referred to the members for vote under this bylaw, either at a meeting of members or by mail, the following provisions shall apply:

(a) *Procedure* — At the request of Local Associations or voting units of Growers representing one fifth (1/5) of the voting power of a particular variety or at the request of one-third (1/3) of the authorized number of directors, any question subject to varietal voting shall be submitted to a vote of Local Associations and voting units of Growers on a varietal basis. The affirmative vote of three-fourths (3/4) of the voting power represented by such variety shall be binding upon all members insofar as it concerns the promotion of the variety involved and the assessment relating thereto.

(b) *Varietal Questions* — Voting by Local Associations and voting units of Growers shall be on a varietal basis on any question relating to the appropriation or use of funds for advertising, promotion or research to be raised solely by assessing a single variety but nothing herein contained shall be construed to authorize varietal voting on assessments resulting from an allocation between varieties of the general cost of maintaining any department or facility of Sunkist for the use of more than one variety.

3.4 *District Exchanges* — District Exchanges shall have the exclusive power to nominate and elect directors, but shall have no other voting rights. Each District Exchange shall nominate only as many directors as it shall be entitled to under Bylaw No. 5.2. Each District Exchange shall be entitled to cast votes for election of directors in accordance with the following formula: The number of directors which it is entitled to nominate under Bylaw No. 5.2 multiplied by the number of directors to be elected.

3.5 *Proxies* — Any District Exchange, Local Association or District Exchange director nominated by a voting unit of Growers entitled to vote at a membership meeting or execute consent shall have the right to do so either in person or by proxy, which proxy shall be in writing executed by the member or its duly designated representative and filed with the secretary of Sunkist. No proxy shall be valid after the expiration of ninety (90) days from its date.

3.6 *Voting by Mail* — Whenever so authorized by these by-laws or by the board of directors, a membership vote may be conducted by mail, without the necessity of a meeting. To be effective, the total vote cast by mail on any question shall be not less than the number required to constitute a quorum had such vote been taken at a meeting of members.

MEETING OF MEMBERS

4.1 *Place of Meetings* — All meetings of members shall be held at the principal office of Sunkist or at such other place as may be designated by the board of directors.

4.2 *Regular Annual Meeting* — A regular annual meeting of all Sunkist members shall be held at 10 o'clock a.m. on the third Wednesday in January of each year, or such other hour (within normal business hours) on that day as may be designated by the board of directors. At such meeting directors shall be elected, reports of the affairs of Sunkist shall be considered and any business may be transacted which is within the power of the members.

4.3 *Notice of Regular Annual Meeting* — Ten days' notice of each regular meeting of the members shall be given as provided in Bylaw No. 11.2. Such notice shall state the place, the day and the hour of the meeting and that the purposes thereof are the election of directors and the transaction of such other business as may come before the meeting.

4.4 *Special Meetings* — Except in those instances where a particular manner of calling a meeting or obtaining a vote of members is prescribed by law or in these bylaws, a special meeting of all members or of the members of any class may be called at any time by the chairman of the board, or on demand of one-third (1/3) of the directors, or by members entitled to exercise one-fifth (1/5) of the voting power. No business shall be transacted at a special meeting other than such as is included in the purposes stated in the notice.

4.5 *Notice of Special Meeting* — Notice of each special meeting shall be given in the same manner as for annual meetings. Notice of any special meeting shall specify the purposes of the meeting, in addition to the place, the day and the hour of such meeting.

4.6 *Adjournment and Notice* — Any members' meeting, whether or not a quorum is present, may be adjourned from time to time by a vote of the majority of the voting power of the members present in person or by proxy, but in the event there is not a quorum initially present at any members' meeting, no other business may be transacted. When any meeting of members is adjourned for thirty (30) days or more, notice of the adjourned meeting shall be given as in the case of an original meeting. Otherwise it shall not be necessary to give any notice of adjournment other than by announcement at the meeting at which adjournment is taken nor shall it be necessary to give any notice of the business to be transacted at an adjourned meeting.

4.7 *Quorum* — At any meeting of all members, or of any class of members, the presence in person or by proxy of persons entitled to vote a majority of the voting power entitled to vote at such meeting shall constitute a quorum for the transaction of business, except as otherwise may be required by law. The members present at a duly called and held meeting at which a quorum is present may continue to do business until adjournment, notwithstanding the withdrawal of enough members to leave less than a quorum.

4.8 *Consent of Absentees* — The transactions of any meeting of members, either regular or special, however called and noticed, shall be as valid as though had a meeting duly held upon regular call and notice, if a quorum be present either in person or by proxy, and if, either before or after the meeting, each of the members entitled to vote, not present in person or by proxy, signs a written waiver of notice, or a consent to the holding of such meeting, or an approval of the minutes thereof. All such waivers, consents or approvals shall be filed with the corporate records or made a part of the minutes of the meeting.

DIRECTORS

5.1 *Number and Qualification* — The authorized number of directors of Sunkist shall not be fewer than twenty-eight (28) nor more than thirty-one (31). Until changed by the board of directors within the foregoing limits, the authorized number of directors shall be thirty (30). A director must be a person engaged in the production of citrus fruit to be handled by or through the Sunkist System.

5.2 *Election of Directors* — Each District Exchange shall be entitled to nominate one (1) director. Additional directors may be nominated by District Exchanges, on the basis of the volume of all fruit marketed through Sunkist as shown by its records for the average of the three (3) preceding fiscal years, as provided in Bylaw No. 1.2(g), in accordance with the following formula:

Each District Exchange shall be entitled to nominate one (1) additional director for each whole four percent (4%) increment of such volume which such District Exchange has in excess of two percent (2%) of such volume.

Commencing in 1976, each District Exchange having less than two percent (2%) of such volume, as reflected in any two of the three most recent compilations of such volume approved or accepted by the board of directors, shall, for the purpose of nominating directors as specified above, combine its volume with one or more other District Exchanges in such manner as shall allow such combination of District Exchanges to nominate not less than one (1) director in accordance with the above formula as though they were a single District Exchange, and such combination of District Exchanges may so nominate a director or directors as though they were a single District Exchange. If such combination of District Exchanges is not achieved by mutual consent, the board of directors shall specify such combination. Within each such combination of District Exchanges the nominee or nominees of such combined District Exchanges shall be determined between or among such District Exchanges by a vote on the basis of their respective amounts of such volume.

5.3 *Election and Term of Office* — The directors shall be elected annually by District Exchange members at the time of the regular annual meeting of the members, but if any such annual meeting is not held, or the directors are not elected thereat, the directors may be elected at any special meeting of District Exchange members held for that purpose. Any Director shall hold office until his successor is elected.

5.4 *Vacancies* — Vacancies in the board of directors shall be filled by the other directors in office upon nomination and certification by the appropriate District Exchange; and such person shall hold office until his successor is elected. At any time, the number of standing nominations certified by a District Exchange, for the filling of vacancies in the board of directors, shall not be greater than the number of directors such District Exchange is entitled to nominate under Bylaw 5.2, plus one.

5.5 *Place of Meetings* — Meetings of the board of directors shall be held at the principal office of Sunkist, or at any other place within or without the State of California which has been designated by the board or by written consent of all members of the board.

5.6 *Organization Meeting* — Immediately after each annual election of directors, the newly elected directors shall hold a regular meeting for the purpose of organization, election of officers, and the transaction of other business. Notice of such meeting is hereby dispensed with.

5.63 *Regular Meetings* — In addition to the regular organization meeting, regular meetings of the board of directors shall be held at the time appointed for them by the board.

5.65 *Special Meetings* — A special meeting of the board of directors shall be held whenever called by the chairman of the board, or by any vice chairman of the board in the absence of the chairman of the board, or by one-third (1/3) of the directors. Any and all business may be transacted at a special meeting.

5.7 *Notice of Meetings of Directors* — No notice of regular meetings of the directors need be given. Notice of each special meeting shall be given pursuant to Bylaw No. 11.2, showing the time and place, at least two (2) days prior to the time of such meeting.

5.75 *Adjournment* — Notice of the time and place of holding an adjourned meeting need not be given to absent directors, if the time and place be fixed at the meeting adjourned and the adjournment is for a period of not more than seven (7) days.

5.8 *Waiver of Notice* — The transactions of any meeting of the board of directors however called and noticed or wherever held, shall be as valid as though had a meeting duly been held, after regular call and notice, if a quorum be present, and if, either before or after the meeting, each of the directors not present signs a written waiver of notice, a consent to holding such meeting, or an approval of the minutes thereof. All such waivers, consents or approvals shall be filed with the corporate records or made a part of the minutes of the meeting.

5.85 *Quorum* — A majority of the authorized number of directors shall be necessary to constitute a quorum for the transaction of business. However, in the absence of a quorum of directors who have been previously regularly seated, a quorum for the purpose of accepting resignations of directors and filling such vacancies shall be one-third (1/3) the authorized number of directors.

5.9 *Fees and Expenses* — Directors shall not receive any stated salary for their services as directors, but by resolution of the board, a fixed fee, plus expenses may be paid for attendance at any meeting of the board or at any committee meeting.

POWERS OF DIRECTORS

6.1 *General Powers* — Subject to the limitations of the articles of incorporation, of the bylaws and of the statutes of the State of California relating to action which shall be authorized or approved by members, all corporate powers shall be exercised by or under the authority of, and the business and affairs of Sunkist shall be controlled by, the board of directors. Without prejudice to such general powers, but subject to the same limitations, it is expressly declared that the board of directors shall have the following powers, to wit:

(a) To appoint and remove, at pleasure, all officers, agents and employees of Sunkist, prescribe their duties, fix their compensation, and require from them, if deemed advisable, security for faithful service.

(b) To conduct, manage and control the affairs and business of Sunkist and to make rules and regulations not inconsistent with the laws of the State of California, the articles of incorporation or bylaws, for the guidance of its officers and the management of its affairs.

(c) To borrow money and incur indebtedness for the purposes of Sunkist, and to cause to be executed and delivered therefor, in the corporate name, promissory notes, bonds, debentures, deeds of trust, mortgages, pledges, hypothecations and other evidences of indebtedness and securities therefor, and to do every act and thing necessary to effectuate the same.

(d) To establish grades for fruit and for products with rules and regulations pertaining thereto, and to prescribe the standards of quality for fruit and products to be marketed under such grades, and permit Local Associations and District Exchanges to pack or deliver their fruit under such grades upon compliance with such prescribed standards and with all rules and regulations established pursuant hereto.

(e) To prescribe rules and regulations in connection with the use of any trademarks, trade names, brands, patents or copyrights owned or controlled by Sunkist and any such rules or regulations may be changed from time to time.

6.2 *Charges and Expenses*

(a) *Assessments or Deductions* — All charges and expenses of Sunkist, including deductions for such reasonable reserves as may from time to time be prescribed by the board of directors and including a subscription to "The California Citrograph," shall be met by assessments or deductions upon District Exchanges or Local Associations. The method, amount, manner and time of assessment or deduction shall be fixed and determined from time to time by the board of directors. Each District Exchange or Local Association shall pay to Sunkist when due the amount of any assessments or deductions hereunder.

(b) *Refunds* — Any amount by which the marketing or other assessments or deductions hereunder exceed the actual cost (including in such cost any reserves prescribed as provided in these bylaws) shall be refunded to the persons from whom collected as promptly as accounting procedure permits.

(c) *Set-off* — Any amount due Sunkist from any member or other producer as an assessment, deduction or otherwise may be set off against any amount which Sunkist is or may become obligated to pay such person.

COMMITTEES OF THE BOARD

7.1 *Products Executive Committee* — A Products Executive Committee is hereby established. It shall be composed of fifteen (15) directors but in no event to exceed one-half (1/2) of the authorized number of directors.

There are hereby delegated to said Products Executive Committee all of the functions and powers of the board relating to or directly affecting products operations, including products sales, subject to the direction and control of the board. It is the purpose of these bylaws to afford substantial autonomy to said committee in the operation of the products portion of Sunkist business.

7.2 *Other Committees of the Board* — Other committees may be established by resolution of the board specifying the number of members and prescribing the committee functions and duties. Such other committees may include individuals who are not members of the board.

OFFICERS AND MANAGEMENT

8.1 *Corporate Officers* — The officers of Sunkist shall be elected by the board of directors and shall be a chairman of the board, one or more vice chairmen of the board, a president, one or more vice presidents, a secretary and a treasurer. The board may also appoint one or more assistant secretaries or assistant treasurers and any other corporate officers which the board of directors may see fit in its discretion to designate. The chairman of the board and vice chairman or vice chairmen shall be elected by the directors from their number. The chairman of the board may not be elected to that office more than five successive times. One person may hold two or more offices except that the offices of president and secretary may not be held by the same person.

8.2 *Election and Term of Office* — Officers shall be elected annually at the organization meeting of the board of directors following the annual meeting of members, or at such other time as the board of directors shall determine. Unless sooner removed by the board of directors, or unless they resign or become disqualified, all officers shall hold office until their successors are chosen and have qualified. Any officer, whether elected or appointed by the board of directors, may be removed at any time by a majority vote of the authorized number of directors.

8.3 *Powers and Duties* — Subject at all times to the control and direction of the board of directors, each officer shall have and exercise the powers and duties usual to his office. The chairman of the board shall, if present, preside at all meetings of members and of the board of directors. In the absence of the chairman of the board, a vice chairman of the board designated by the board of directors shall assume the powers and duties of the chairman of the board.

8.4 *Management* — The president shall be the chief executive officer of Sunkist and shall, subject to the control and direction of the board of directors, have general and active management, direction and control of the business, officers (other than the chairman of the board and any vice chairman of the board), and employees of Sunkist. He shall conduct the business operations and affairs of Sunkist in accordance with the policies and directives of the board of directors, and according to his own discretion whenever not expressly guided by such policies and directives.

MARKETING

9.1 *Marketing Obligation* — Each Local Association shall market all of the fresh fruit subject to its control through the District Exchange with which it is affiliated. Each District Exchange shall market through Sunkist all of the fruit subject to its control. Each Local Association and District Exchange shall deliver to Sunkist all of the products fruit subject to its control. Sunkist shall market all of said fruit both fresh and products and shall determine the methods of marketing to be adopted in any or all markets, and the types of containers and methods of packaging to be used. Each Grower shall have his fruit graded and packed by a packing facility of a Local Association or by a packing facility licensed by Sunkist to perform such service.

9.2 *Marketing Agency Created* — Each Local Association and District Exchange designates and appoints Sunkist as its agent and the agent of its Growers in all matters concerning the marketing of its fresh fruit, and the processing and marketing of its products fruit. Full power and authority are conferred upon Sunkist as such agent to conduct its marketing activities in such manner as it, in its sole discretion, determines to be for the best interests of all of its members. As such agent, Sunkist may inspect any records pertaining to the disposition of fruit maintained by or for any member, including any or all records maintained by any federal or state marketing committee or board pertaining to such member. Also, as requested by Sunkist, each Local Association and District Exchange shall furnish Sunkist with detailed information concerning the amount, volume, and value of all fresh and products fruit marketed by each Grower member or patron of such Local Association or District Exchange. Information concerning the amount, volume and value of fruit marketed by any Grower member or patron of a Local Association or District Exchange shall be used by Sunkist only for appropriate corporate purposes.

9.3 *General Marketing Plan* — In carrying out the basic purpose of marketing the Growers' citrus fruit at the highest return to the Growers, the Sunkist System has adopted the following general marketing plan.

(a) *Fresh Fruit* — Sunkist shall develop and determine the market opportunities for each variety of citrus fruit to be marketed by its members. Sales shall be made through the facilities and agencies furnished by Sunkist.

(b) *Products Fruit* — Products fruit shall be delivered to Sunkist f.o.b. the packing house. Thereafter Sunkist shall market such products fruit either in the form received or in processed form.

9.4 *Regulations Relating to Marketing Fresh Fruit* — The following provisions relate and are applicable with regard to the marketing of fresh fruit by Sunkist:

(a) *Reserved Right* — Each Grower and Local Association hereby delegates to its District Exchange the right to determine to what markets it shall ship, where its fruit shall be sold, and, subject to auction practices, the price it is willing to receive; provided, however, that each Local Association and each voting unit of Growers affiliated directly through a District Exchange and packing fruit other than as a nonmember of a Local Association, may through the director or directors representing such Growers or Local Association, reserve the right from time to time to terminate this delegation and to exercise said rights for such period as they may deem proper or to redelegate said reserved right to said District Exchange.

(b) *Quotas and Allocation* — Sunkist may, by a majority vote of the authorized number of directors, determine the maximum amount of fresh fruit to be marketed currently and allocate the opportunity to ship equitably among its members; provided, however, that said majority includes directors representing eighty-five percent (85%) of the volume marketed through Sunkist, as shown by its records, of the variety (both fresh and products) under consideration. Such allocation shall be binding upon District Exchanges and Local Associations.

(c) *Contact With Buyers* — District Exchanges and Local Associations shall not solicit business from the trade or employ any solicitor or agent, or correspond with any buyer for the purpose of promoting the sale of their fresh fruit. All prices, quotations and allowances shall be issued and distributed solely by Sunkist. Copies of correspondence with district managers in the markets by any District Exchange must be sent to Sunkist; and by any Local Association to Sunkist and to the District Exchange with which it is affiliated. District Exchanges shall be entitled to receive, upon request, copies of Sunkist correspondence relating to their fruit.

(d) *Transportation*

(1) *Routing* — Sunkist shall have authority to specify the route of all shipments of fresh fruit. Any Local Association or voting unit of Growers affiliated directly through a district Exchange and packing fruit other than as nonmembers of a Local Association may at any time and from time to time

(c) *Delivery of Fruit and Freight Regulations* — Sunkist may establish, maintain, and enforce an inspection for quality, and reject such products fruit as is not acceptable for products purposes, and may charge back freight thereon to the shipper. Sunkist shall govern the collecting and assembling of products fruit for shipment to Sunkist and may prorate shipments if supply exceeds capacity of available facilities. Sunkist shall provide for the equitable handling of freight charges on products fruit in order that no shipper may be at a disadvantage by reason of his location with reference to the location of the processing facilities of Sunkist.

(d) *Obligation to Return Net Proceeds* — All proceeds of sales, less necessary operating and marketing expenses, shall be returned to the persons entitled thereto on the basis of the quantity or value of products fruit furnished. Such proceeds shall be so returned as promptly as the collection thereof, the financial position of Sunkist and accounting procedure may permit; provided, however, that any amounts assessed or deducted on the basis of the quantity or value of fruit furnished as additions to reserves (other than so-called valuation reserves, such as reserves for depreciation, bad debts, etc., which in accordance with recognized accounting practices are deductions under Section 161 of the Internal Revenue Code of 1954) in any fiscal year shall be apportioned on the books of Sunkist, to the persons contributing thereto and an appropriate certificate or notice of such assessment or deduction (including the dollar amount thereof) shall be issued and delivered to each such person within the period specified by law following the close of each fiscal year.

9.6 *Power Conferred by Statutes* — Sunkist shall have and in its discretion may exercise on an equitable basis on behalf of District Exchanges, Local Associations and Growers any and all powers relating to the marketing of fruit and products that Sunkist, District Exchanges, Local Associations and Growers are or may be hereafter authorized by state or federal statutes or by order or regulations based thereon to exercise. Any Growers, Local Association or District Exchange may, as to it at any time and from time to time, terminate the authority conferred upon Sunkist by this bylaw or again give such authority to Sunkist. Sunkist shall be notified immediately in writing of any such termination of said authority, and unless so notified, Sunkist may exercise any of the powers referred to in this bylaw.

9.7 *Warranty* — Each Local Association and each District Exchange warrants to Sunkist that it has the right to receive, pack and deliver for marketing and to market through Sunkist all of the fruit which it may deliver. Each of said members further warrants that said fruit and the disposition thereof shall comply with all state and federal statutes and regulations applicable thereto.

9.8 *Liquidated Damages for Member's Breach* — In the event that any member shall sell, market or dispose of any of the fruit that is to be marketed by or through Sunkist under the provisions of these bylaws other than through the agency of Sunkist, such act will injure Sunkist and its members in an amount that is, and will be impractical and extremely difficult to determine and fix. The said damages are, therefore, fixed at fifty cents (50¢) per carton on all fresh fruit and fifty dollars ($50) per ton for all products fruit that is sold, marketed or disposed of contrary to the provisions of these by-laws. The member so violating the bylaws agrees to pay, and shall pay, said amount to Sunkist as liquidated damages, and in default of payment thereof to Sunkist upon demand. The same may be recovered in an action in any court of competent jurisdiction in the name of Sunkist, in which case Sunkist shall recover from the member in addition to said liquidated damages, all costs, premiums for bonds, expenses and fees, including attorneys' fees, in such action.

9.9 *Governmental Marketing Regulation* — Any action taken by Sunkist with respect to any governmental marketing regulation affecting a particular variety shall be determined by a majority vote of the authorized number of directors including directors representing eighty-five percent (85%) of the volume marketed through Sunkist as shown by its records, of the variety (both fresh and products) under consideration.

CAPITAL CREDITS

10.1 *Capital Requirements* — A capital fund continuing that heretofore known as the "Sunkist Revolving Fund" shall be maintained for the purpose of providing permanent, non-revolving capital required to operate the business of Sunkist, through capital contributions by members and patrons in proportion to their respective use of the facilities and services furnished by Sunkist. The total amount of capital so required shall be determined from time to time by the board of directors. The proportionate share of such amount to be provided by each member or patron shall be based on volume or value of both of fresh fruit and products fruit marketed through Sunkist during a representative period of years, all as determined by the board of directors. In any such determination, members and patrons shall be treated on an equal basis in respect of each variety, but rates or weighting factors may differ for the several varieties and as between fresh and products fruit.

10.2 *Member's Capital Obligation* — Whenever the capital obligation of a member or patron is determined, as a proportionate share of the total capital requirements for that year, pursuant to Bylaw No. 10.1, the computation shall be on the basis of a formula to be prescribed by the board, taking into account the volume or value or both of fruit by varieties marketed for such member or patron with appropriate rates or weighting factors to reflect the varying capital requirements of the several varieties and the differences in capital requirements of fruit for fresh shipment and fruit for products. Such formula may be modified or amended by the board from time to time, before, during, or within eight and one-half months after, any fiscal year to which such change is applicable.

terminate such authority or again give Sunkist such authority. Sunkist shall be notified immediately in writing through the District Exchange with which such Local Association or Growers are affiliated of any such termination of such authority, and unless so notified Sunkist may exercise the same.

(2) *Facility* — Sunkist may, by a majority vote of the authorized number of directors, which majority shall include directors representing seventy-five percent (75%) of the volume marketed through Sunkist, as shown by its records, of the variety (both fresh and products) under consideration, determine the transportation facility — whether by rail, by water or otherwise.

(3) *Pooling of Charges* — Transportation costs, including but not restricted to costs of refrigeration and other protective services, incurred in connection with the movement of fresh fruit destined for points outside the state of origin, may in the manner and to the extent determined by a majority vote of the authorized number of directors, which majority shall include directors representing seventy-five percent (75%) of the volume marketed through Sunkist, as shown by its records, of the variety (both fresh and products) under consideration, be pooled equitably in relation to the different types of refrigeration and other protective services and paid by charges or assessments levied and apportioned as the board of directors may determine.

(e) *Losses and Customer Claims* — The only losses for which Sunkist shall be responsible to District Exchanges or Local Associations are losses arising from the financial failure or default of purchasers after having positively accepted the fruit, which default is not due to complaint of the buyer concerning the quality, condition or grade of the fruit. Such losses shall be charged as part of the general marketing expense and paid in the method, amount and manner determined by the board of directors. In case of any controversies with customers wherein, in the judgment of the board of directors, the collective interest of members is involved, the judgment of said board as to settlement of such dispute shall be final and binding upon the Local Association or District Exchange which furnished the fruit.

(f) *Pooling* — Pools for fresh fruit may be established by the board of directors on a varietal basis and may include fruit produced in or destined for any particular geographical section, or fruit conforming or not conforming to specified standards of quality and/or size or fruit for Government use. Each Local Association and District Exchange director for his voting unit of direct Growers, other than those packing fruit as nonmembers

of a Local Association, shall have the right to determine whether or not it will provide fruit for each such pool. Sales of fruit eligible for any such pool shall not be made in competition with pool fruit, except under marketing programs specifically approved by the board of directors. The rights reserved under Bylaw No. 9.4(a) shall be limited to the extent provided in this Bylaw No. 9.4(f). Any pool so established shall be pursuant to a pooling plan to be prescribed by the board of directors. Such plan shall specify the conditions of eligibility of fruit, the methods of operation and all rules and regulations in connection therewith, which shall include provision for equitable allocation of the marketing opportunity among those desiring to participate. Such pools may be established only by a majority vote of the authorized number of directors, which majority must include directors representing seventy-five percent (75%) of the volume marketed through Sunkist, as shown by its records, of the variety or varieties (both fresh and products) in the producing area under consideration.

(g) *Obligation to Distribute Proceeds* — All proceeds of sales of fresh fruit, after deduction of freight and other charges directly allocable, and after any deductions authorized pursuant to Bylaw No. 6.2, shall be remitted to the appropriate District Exchanges and by them to the appropriate Local Associations and Growers or their authorized agents as rapidly as collection and accounting procedures permit.

9.5 *Regulations Relating to Marketing Products Fruit* — The following provisions relate and are applicable with regard to the marketing of products fruit by Sunkist:

(a) *Power and Control of Sunkist in Handling Products Fruit* — Sunkist may sell and market the products fruit of its members and other producers or the products produced therefrom, pledge or otherwise hypothecate the same or any part thereof, transfer title thereto, and collect and receipt for the proceeds in its own name exclusively, or in the name of any subagent. No member by virtue of having furnished any fruit shall exercise any control over Sunkist with regard to either the processing or marketing of said fruit, or the conduct of the business of Sunkist, in all of which matters Sunkist may, in good faith, use its own discretion and judgment, free from any direction by such member. The member shall not be directly liable under any rules of agency on account of any contract, or contracts, made by Sunkist in carrying on its business of marketing products fruit.

(b) *Pooling* — Sunkist shall establish pools for the handling, processing and marketing of all products fruit. Each products fruit pool shall include such varieties or portions thereof as Sunkist may determine. Any pool so established shall be pursuant to a pooling plan to be prescribed by the board of directors.

10.3 *Adjustment of Member Shares* — Whenever the capital share of a member or patron for any fiscal year, computed pursuant to Bylaw No. 10.2, exceeds the amount of capital credits attributed to him at the beginning of such year, as reflected by Sunkist records, the amount of such excess shall be assessed to such member or patron and may be withheld or retained from proceeds of sales, patronage dividends or any other amount otherwise due such member or patron for such year. In the event such share for such year is less than the capital credits attributed to such member or patron at the beginning of such year, the difference may be refunded to such member or patron or to the holder of credits attributed to him at such time or times and in such manner as the board may determine, provided that all members and patrons be treated alike in this respect for any one fiscal year.

10.4 *Contributions by Growers in Voting Units* — The following principles shall apply to Growers in a voting unit of Growers whose fruit is packed by a packing house other than a Local Association:

(a) The aggregate capital obligation of each such voting unit of Growers shall be computed on the same basis as if such voting unit of Growers was a Local Association. The proportionate share of such amount to be provided by each Grower in such voting unit shall be based on volume or value or both of fresh fruit and products fruit marketed by each such Grower in the same manner as the proceeds of marketing such fruit are apportioned cooperatively between such Growers.

(b) For the sole purpose of determining the obligation to contribute to the capital fund described herein, any contribution previously made to the Sunkist Revolving Fund or Capital Fund with respect to production of a Grower during the representative period of years may, with the consent of the person entitled to receive repayment of such capital credits, be attributed to such Grower even though such contribution was made with respect to such production by another person. Thus, in computing the obligation to make contributions for the fiscal year 1967-68 and subsequent years, contributions in prior years by a packing house which was formerly a member of Sunkist may be attributed to the Growers who produced the fruit with respect to which such prior contribution was made. Such attribution shall be based on the volume or value or both of the fruit produced by each such Grower in the same manner as the proceeds of marketing such fruit have been apportioned cooperatively between such Growers.

(c) Each packing house which agrees that prior contributions may be attributed to the Growers who produced the fruit with respect to which such prior contribution was made shall furnish Sunkist with detailed information concerning the volume and value of all fruit marketed by each such Grower during the representative

period of years so that Sunkist may establish a record of the capital credits attributable to the production of each such Grower.

(d) Whenever Sunkist capital credits are attributed to a Grower solely for the purpose of computing the obligation of such Grower to contribute to the Sunkist capital fund but such capital credits represent indebtedness to another person, the following special rules shall apply: (i) the attribution of such credits to the Grower shall cease if the Grower ceases to be affiliated with the packing house that originally made the contribution, and (ii) whenever the capital obligation of such Grower is less than the capital credits attributable to such Grower, the difference to be refunded shall be applied to repay such capital credits in the order in which they were credited on the books of Sunkist, so that the oldest credits are repaid first.

(e) Each accounting agent for such a voting unit of Growers shall annually furnish Sunkist with the detailed information concerning the volume or value or both of all fruit delivered by each Grower in the voting unit, so that Sunkist may compute the capital obligation of each such Grower in the voting unit, make appropriate assessments and withholds or retains, give appropriate notices and maintain appropriate records of capital credits.

10.5 *Nature of Capital Credits* — All such capital credits shall constitute indebtedness of Sunkist to the respective persons to whom credited, but such indebtedness shall be paid solely upon the conditions and at the time and times hereinafter provided. No interest shall be payable on any such credits. Such capital credits shall be subordinated to all other indebtedness of Sunkist, secured or unsecured, as provided in Bylaw No. 10.10.

10.6 *No Segregation of Funds* — The monies representing the capital credits may be commingled with and used for corporate purposes as other monies belonging or coming to Sunkist are used. Nothing herein contained shall be deemed to require that any specific monies or funds be segregated, or designated, or marked, or set apart, or held for the capital fund, nor shall the capital fund be deemed a trust fund held for the owners of capital credits.

10.7 *Losses Chargeable Against Credits* — In the event Sunkist sustains a substantial loss, from any cause whatever, the board of directors, may in its sole discretion, charge all or any part of said loss to any one or more of the following accounts:

(a) Current operating expenses;

(b) Any unallocated reserves;

(c) Capital credits and/or other allocated reserve credits for the fiscal year in which such loss was incurred or to which the loss was attributable;

(d) All capital credits and/or other allocated reserve credits for all years.

In the event said loss is charged to capital credits or other allocated reserve credits, the same shall be charged ratably and proportionally against all credits in the varietal or other class charged. Notice of such charge against capital credits or other allocated reserve credits shall be given within the period specified by law after the close of the fiscal year in which such loss is charged, to the persons in whose names the credits stand on the books of Sunkist. Anything in these bylaws to the contrary notwithstanding, there shall be payable in respect to capital credits and other allocated reserve credits only the difference between the amount of the credits originally entered and the portion of such loss charged thereto.

The board of directors shall have the power to determine when a substantial loss has occurred, and its determination shall be conclusive. In making such determination, the board may consider among other factors, losses from bank suspensions, uncollected accounts, fire, explosion, accident or other calamity, unforeseen marketing conditions, excessive or high manufacturing, operating or overhead costs due to crop failure or below normal production, inadequate depreciation charges, and unusual or unforeseen expenses, including taxes, assessments, fines, penalties and claims arising under any present or future law.

10.8 *Capital Fund Statement* — Within the period specified by law after the close of each fiscal year, Sunkist shall furnish each member and patron of Sunkist during said fiscal year with a statement showing the dollar amount of capital credits standing on the books of Sunkist in the name of such member or patron, being in such form and containing such other information as the board may prescribe. In the event of a loss chargeable against capital credits pursuant to Bylaw No. 10.7, the same shall be reflected on the capital fund statement, which shall be furnished to all holders of capital credits affected by such loss, whether or not they were patrons during said fiscal year.

10.9 *Assignment or Transfer* — Capital credits may be assigned or transferred at any time by execution of a written assignment thereof, on a form to be provided by Sunkist, and delivery thereof to the secretary of Sunkist; provided, however, that no such transfer shall be complete until entered upon the books of Sunkist.

10.10 *Payment on Dissolution* — In the event of dissolution or liquidation of Sunkist, all unpaid capital credits and other allocated reserve credits shall be deemed due but shall not be paid in any part until all other indebtedness of Sunkist has been paid or adequately provided for. In the event funds are insufficient to cover all such credits and reserves, payment of capital credits and other allocated reserve credits shall be on a pro rata basis.

10.11 *Tax Treatment* — Every person who hereafter applies for and is accepted to membership in Sunkist and each member of Sunkist on the effective date of this bylaw who continues as a member after such date shall, by such act alone, consent that the amount of any distributions with respect to his patronage occurring after November 1, 1967, which are made in written notices of allocation or per-unit retain certificates (as defined in 26 U.S.C. 1388) and which are received by him from Sunkist will be taken into account by him at their stated dollar amounts in a manner provided in 26 U.S.C. 1385(a) in the taxable year in which such written notices of allocation or per-unit retain certificates are received by him. This bylaw is effective November 1, 1967. For tax treatment for prior years refer to prior bylaw.

MISCELLANEOUS

11.1 *Principal Office* — The principal office for the transaction of business of Sunkist is hereby fixed and located at 14130 Riverside Drive, Sherman Oaks, California.

11.2 *Method of Giving Notices* — Whenever in these bylaws notice is required to be given it may be given by one (1) or more of the following methods:

(a) Delivered personally; or

(b) Written notice either deposited in the mails postage prepaid or sent by telegraph, addressed to the residence or place of business of the member or director, as the same shall appear on the books of Sunkist.

11.3 *Effect of Holiday* — If the time designated herein for any meeting should fall upon a legal holiday, then any such meeting shall be cancelled unless another date is fixed by the board of directors and notice thereof given in the manner provided for a special meeting.

11.4 *Indemnity* — District Exchanges and Local Associations shall severally indemnify and save Sunkist harmless against all loss, damage, injury, liability, cost and/or expense of whatsoever nature suffered or to be suffered by Sunkist by reason of any claim or claims asserted or made to or against Sunkist by reason of any act of commission or omission of such member.

11.5 *Fiscal Year* — The fiscal year of Sunkist extends from November 1 to October 31, following.

11.6 *Seal* — The board of directors shall provide a suitable seal containing the name of Sunkist, the date of its incorporation and other appropriate words, and may alter the same at pleasure.

11.7 *Amendments* — These bylaws may be amended or repealed or new bylaws adopted as follows:

(a) By vote or written assent of members entitled to exercise two-thirds (2/3) of the voting power, except that an amendment of repeal of the following bylaws shall require the greater percentages of such voting power as follows:

Bylaw No.		Percentage Required
9.4(d)(2)	(Transportation—Facility)	75
9.4(d)(3)	(Transportation—Pooling of Charges	75
9.4(f)	(Pooling)	75
7.1	(Products Executive Committee)	80
9.4(b)	(Quotas and Allocation)	85
9.4(a)	(Reserved Right)	90
11.7	(Amendments)	90

or

(b) By vote of two-thirds (2/3) of the authorized number of directors: except that the board may not amend Bylaws No. 3.1, 3.2, 3.3, or 3.4 (relating to voting rights of members), 5.1 or 5.2 (relating to number, qualification and selection of directors) except that the board may amend Bylaw No. 5.1 solely for the purpose of establishing the exact authorized number of directors within the limits therein prescribed, such exact authorized number to be computed solely in accordance with the formula contained in Bylaw No. 52, or any of the bylaws specified in Bylaw No. 11.7(a) as requiring a percentage of voting power greater than two-thirds (2/3); provided, however, that the power of the board of directors to adopt, amend or repeal bylaws may be revoked at any time by vote or written assent of members entitled to exercise a majority of the voting power.

NOTIFICATION AND SIGNIFICANCE OF BYLAW PERTAINING TO TAX TREATMENT OF DISTRIBUTIONS

Bylaw No. 10.11 of Sunkist Growers, Inc., effective November 1, 1967, reads as follows:

10.11 *Tax Treatment* — Every person who hereafter applies for and is accepted to membership in Sunkist and each member of Sunkist on the effective date of this bylaw who continues as a member after such date shall, by such act alone, consent that the amount of any distributions with respect to his patronage occurring after November 1, 1967, which are made in written notices of allocation or per-unit retain certificates (as defined in 26 U.S.C. 1388) and which are received by him from Sunkist will be taken into account by him at their stated dollar amounts in a manner provided in 26 U.S.C. 1385(a) in the taxable year in which such written notices of allocation or per-unit retain certificates are received by him. This bylaw is effective November 1, 1967. For tax treatment for prior years refer to prior bylaw.

The effect of such Bylaw No. 10.11, as amended effective November 1, 1967, is that each member agrees to include both patronage dividends and per-unit retains issued with respect to patronage occurring after November 1, 1967, in income at their face amount for federal·tax purposes in the taxable year when the member receives a written notice stating the amount of such patronage allocation. This is true even though the allocation is not paid in cash until a later year.

RULES AND REGULATIONS GOVERNING FRUIT PACKED FOR MARKETING BY SUNKIST GROWERS, INC., UNDER ITS TRADEMARKS SUNKIST, SGI, EXCEL, SK AND RED BALL AND UNDER ASSOCIATION NON-ADVERTISED BRANDS

Revised as of June 19, 1974

PURPOSE

The trademarks Sunkist, SGI, Excel, SK and Red Ball are the property of Sunkist Growers, Inc. The right of affiliated shippers to have their fruit marketed under these trademarks through the facilities provided by Sunkist Growers, Inc. is dependent on the shippers conforming to the rules and regulations concerning the grading and packing of the fruit as defined by the Board of Directors of Sunkist Growers, Inc. which establishes the specifications for grade and condition of the fruit which Sunkist Growers, Inc. markets under these trademarks. These rules and regulations are necessary, not only to preserve the legal rights of Sunkist Growers, Inc. in the Sunkist, SGI, Excel, SK and Red Ball trademarks, but to assure a continuing reputation of high quality which now attaches to them. This is the only way in which these famous trademarks can be used to derive the maximum benefits and returns for those marketing their fruit through Sunkist Growers, Inc. In adhering to these rules the strength and value of the trademarks will not only be maintained but will continue to increase.

Grade Regulations

(1) *Compliance with Federal and State Laws*—No fruit will be marketed by Sunkist Growers, Inc. under any brand or grade, or at all, unless the same shall in all respects conform to the laws of the State of California or the State of Arizona, and, if the sale is made in Interstate Commerce, to Federal laws and to the laws of the place where the fruit is sold. The Field Department shall inspect all grades of citrus fruits marketed through Sunkist Growers, Inc. and shall in every way endeavor to make uniform the enforcement of the regulations and laws concerning the marketing of California or Arizona citrus fruits.

Oranges

(2) *Specifications for "Sunkist"*—Oranges packed for marketing under the trademark Sunkist shall be mature; of one variety; of good eating quality and flavor; of good juice content; well grown specimens of normal form, picked from the tree; of good color for the variety; of good texture; practically free from scale or other insect pests, fungus diseases, splits, or defects of any kind that cause fruit to decay. The following classes of fruit shall be excluded: rough; coarse; more than slightly puffed; more than slightly scarred; more than slightly sunburned; misshapen

fruit; dirty fruit unattractive to the consumer; fruit showing effects of frost or which cuts dry for any reason; immature fruit; fruit insipid in flavor; fruit deficient in juice content; and fruit green or very pale in color. Soft fruit or fruit showing marked evidence of aging or shriveling shall be excluded. Fruit of extra good texture and color may properly carry more scars than fruit possessing only the minimum of color and texture required under these "Sunkist" specifications. Oranges packed for marketing under the trademark Sunkist shall not vary more than 5 percent below foregoing specifications except that decay within this tolerance shall not exceed 1 percent.

(3) *Specifications for "Excel"*—Oranges packed for marketing under brands listed in the Sunkist Growers, Inc. brand list and/or manifested as "Excel" shall meet specifications for "Sunkist," except that as to interior defects, the minimum requirements of the State Agricultural Code shall apply. In the case of damage from frost, the determination shall be made by examination of the segment walls until that time when the interior drying process has developed sufficiently so as to furnish sufficient evidence of the degree of damage by this means. The tolerance for frost damage as evidenced in damage to the segment walls shall be 15 percent of the fruits, by count. When frost damage can be determined by drying, the amount of damage will be determined volumetrically by three equidistant cuts of the fruit. The tolerance for frost damage as evidenced by drying shall be 15 percent, by count, of the fruits showing a drying or dessication in 20 percent or more of the volume of the individual fruits, except that only 5 percent of fruits, by count, may show a drying or dessication in 40 percent or more of the volume of the individual fruits.

(4) *Specifications for "Red Ball"*—Oranges packed for marketing under the trademark Red Ball shall be mature; of one variety; of good eating quality and flavor; of good juice content; well grown specimens of fair form, picked from the tree; of fair color for the variety; of fair texture; practically free from insect pests (other than scale), fungus diseases, splits, or defects of any kind that cause fruit to decay. The following classes of fruit shall be excluded: very rough; very coarse; badly sunburned; badly scarred; badly puffed; very scaly or very dirty fruit; fruit showing effects of frost or which cuts dry for any reason; immature fruit; fruit insipid in flavor; fruit deficient in juice content; and fruit very green in color. Soft fruit or fruit showing marked evidence of aging or shriveling shall be excluded. Fruit of extra good texture and color may properly carry more scars than fruit possessing only the minimum of texture and color required under these "Red Ball" specifications. Oranges packed for marketing under the trademark Red Ball shall not vary more than 5 percent below foregoing specifications with the following exceptions: Decay within this tolerance shall not exceed 1 percent; as to fruit showing effects of frost or which cuts dry for any reason, the total tolerance shall be 10 percent, but not more than half of this tolerance shall be allowed for serious drying or freezing damage as defined in the State Agricultural Code.

(5) *Specifications for "SK"*—Oranges packed for marketing under the trademark SK shall be of good eating quality and flavor, fair form, fair color, fair texture and be of good condition. They shall be practically free of pests, diseases, dirt or defects which cause fruit to decay. Fruit of extra good texture and color may carry more scars than fruit possessing only the minimum of texture and color as required under these specifications. The following classes of fruit shall be excluded: very rough, badly sunburned, badly scarred, soft fruit, overmature fruit, fruit showing evidence of aging and fruit badly puffed. Oranges packed as SK shall not vary more than 50 percent below these specifications except that decay shall not exceed 1 percent. For fruit showing frost damage, or which cuts dry for any reason, the minimum requirements of the agricultural laws of the state shall apply.

(6) *Maturity of Valencia Oranges*—In addition to the 8 to 1 maturity test, valencia oranges to be eligible for marketing under the trademarks Sunkist and Red Ball must have a Brix reading of not less than 9.0.

(7) *Storage Limitations for Oranges*—Oranges, subject to all other regulations as to inspection, etc., will not be marketed under the trademarks Sunkist, Excel, or SK, except as herein provided, if they have been off the trees more than 28 days, except that, after the following dates—January 1 on Central-Northern California and Arizona navels; March 1 on Southern California navels and miscellaneous, and Arizona valencias and miscellaneous; June 15 on Central-Northern California valencias; and August 1 on Southern California valencias—the storage limitation shall be 21 days. Associations, at the conclusion of the above dates, may only ship after those dates by certification by the Field Department at time of shipping, such certification to consist of grade, pack, condition, injury and flavor certification, i.e., inspection with "B" grade and pack, "2" condition and injury, and satisfactory flavor classifications as minimum requirements for certification.

Should disagreement ensue between the association and Field Department inspector as to flavor acceptability, the association may appeal to a panel, which the Field Department will appoint, whose judgement will be final. Cost of the panel inspection will be borne by the "loser."

Each shipper must furnish the Field Department accurate and positive information of the date fruit has been picked; and further, all containers must be marked with a code or date indicating the date packed. Failure to comply with these requirements will disqualify all fruit concerned for marketing under the Sunkist, SGI, Excel or SK trademarks for association account. Should association ship fruit beyond the storage limitation without Field Department certification, association will be assessed $1.00 per carton as liquidated damages, in addition to any other penalties provided for or allowed in these rules and regulations or in the bylaws of Sunkist Growers, Inc.

The Sales Division and Field Department shall have authority to make equitable adjustments on fruit picked during the first 30 days of any varietal season in any area when during that period domestic prorate allotments have not been sufficient to permit shipment of sizes not wanted in export markets.

Grapefruit

(8) *Specifications for "Sunkist"*—Grapefruit packed for marketing under the trademark Sunkist shall be mature; of good eating quality and flavor; of good juice content; well grown specimens of normal form, picked from the tree; of good color for the variety; of good texture; practically free from scale or other insect pests, fungus diseases, or defects of any kind that cause fruit to decay. The following classes of fruit shall be excluded: rough; coarse; more than slightly scarred; more than slightly sunburned; misshapen fruit; offcolored; soft, spongy fruit; dirty fruit unattractive to the consumer; fruit showing effects of frost or which cuts dry for any reason; pear-shaped fruit; fruit having rind of more than medium thickness; immature fruit; fruit with off-flavor or fruit deficient in juice content. Fruit of extra good texture and color may properly carry more scars than fruit possessing only the minimum of texture and color required by these "Sunkist" specifications. Grapefruit packed for marketing under the trademark Sunkist will not vary more than 5 percent below the foregoing specifications except that decay within this tolerance shall not exceed 1 percent.

(9) *Specifications for "Excel"*—Grapefruit packed for marketing under brands listed in the Sunkist Growers, Inc. brand list and/or manifested as "Excel" shall meet specifications for "Sunkist," except that as to interior defects the minimum requirements of the State Agricultural Code shall apply.

(10) *Specifications for "Red Ball"*—Grapefruit packed for marketing under the trademark Red Ball shall be mature; of good eating quality and flavor; of good juice content; well-grown specimens of fair form, picked from the tree; of fair color for the variety; of fair texture; practically free from insect pests (other than scale) and fungus diseases, or defects of any kind that cause fruit to decay. The following classes of fruit shall be excluded: very rough; very coarse; very thick-skinned; very soft; very spongy; very scaly; very dirty; badly sunburned; badly off-colored; badly scarred; badly misshapen; fruit showing effects of frost or which cuts dry for any reason; immature fruit; off-flavored fruit; and fruit deficient in juice content. Fruit of extra good texture and color may properly carry more scars than fruit possessing only the minimum of color and texture required under these "Red Ball" specifications. Grapefruit packed for marketing under the trademark Red Ball shall not vary more than 5 percent below foregoing specifications with the following exceptions: Decay within this tolerance shall not exceed 1 percent; as to fruit showing effects of frost or which cuts dry for any reason, the total tolerance shall be 10 percent, but not more than half of this tolerance shall be allowed for serious drying or freezing damage as defined in the State Agricultural Code.

(11) *Specifications for "SK"*—Grapefruit packed for marketing under the trademark SK shall be of good eating quality and flavor, fair texture and be of good condition. They shall be practically free of pests, diseases, dirt or defects which cause fruit to decay. Fruit of extra good texture and color may carry more scar or rind blemishes than fruit possessing only the minimum of texture and color as required under these specifications. The following classes of fruit shall be excluded: very rough, fruit with sunseald, badly sunburned, badly scarred, badly rind blemished, soft fruit, fruit showing evidence of aging, badly misshapen including sheepnose or very thick skinned. Grapefruit packed as SK shall not vary more than 5 percent below these specifications except that decay shall not exceed 1 percent. For fruit showing frost damage, or which cuts dry for any reason, the minimum requirements of the agricultural laws of the state shall apply.

(12) *Method of Extracting Juice for Testing Grapefruit for Maturity*—The juice used for making maturity tests for grapefruit to be packed for marketing under the trademarks Sunkist, Excel, and Red Ball must be extracted with a reamer.

(13) *Thickness of Rind in Grapefruit*—The thickness of the rind in grapefruit packed for marketing under the trademarks Sunkist and Excel shall not exceed the following average thicknesses: 7/16 of an inch on sizes 48s and smaller, 1/2 of an inch sizes 40s to 27s, and 9/16 of an inch sizes 23s and larger.

The thickness of the rind in grapefruit packed for marketing under the trademark Red Ball and SK shall not exceed the following average thicknesses: 1/2 of an inch on sizes 48's and smaller; 9/16 of an inch, sizes 40's to 27's; and 10/16 of an inch, sizes 23's and larger.

The average thickness shall be determined by measurement of the rind from midway of the outer edge of the segments after a transverse cut has been made through the center.

Tangerines, Mandarins or Tangelos

(14) *Specifications for "Sunkist"*—Tangerines, mandarins or tangelos packed for marketing under the trademark Sunkist shall be mature; of one variety; of good eating quality and flavor; of good juice content; well grown specimens of normal form for the variety, picked from the tree; of good color and texture for the variety; practically free from scale or other insect pests, fungus diseases, splits or defects of any kind that cause fruit to decay. The following classes of fruit shall be excluded: very rough; very coarse; badly puffed; more than slightly scarred; more than slightly sunburned; misshapen fruit; dirty fruit unattractive to the consumer; fruit showing effects of frost or which cuts dry for any reason; immature fruit; fruit insipid in flavor; fruit deficient in juice content; soft fruit or fruit showing marked evidence of aging or shriveling shall be excluded. Fruit of extra good texture and color may properly carry more scars than fruit

possessing only the minimum of color and texture under these "Sunkist" specifications. Tangerines, mandarins or tangelos packed for marketing under the trademark Sunkist shall not vary more than 5 percent below foregoing specifications except that decay within this tolerance shall not exceed 1 percent.

(15) *Specifications for "Choice"*—Tangerines, mandarins or tangelos packed for marketing under brands listed in the Sunkist Growers, Inc. brand list and/or manifested as "Choice" shall be mature; of good eating quality and flavor; of good juice content; well-grown specimens of fair form for the variety, picked from the tree; of fair color and texture for the variety; practically free from insect pests (other than scale), fungus diseases, splits or defects of any kind that cause fruit to decay. The following classes of fruit shall be excluded: badly sunburned; badly scarred; very badly puffed; very scaly; very dirty fruit or fruit showing marked evidence of aging or shriveling. Tangerines, mandarins or tangelos packed for marketing under brands listed in the Sunkist Growers, Inc. brand list and/or manifested as "Choice" shall not vary more than 5 percent below foregoing specifications with the following exceptions: as to interior defects and decay, the minimum requirements of the State Agricultural Code shall apply.

(16) *Specifications for "Extra Choice"*—Tangerines, mandarins or tangelos packed for marketing under brands listed in the Sunkist Growers, Inc. brand list and/or manifested as "Extra Choice" shall meet specifications for "Sunkist" as to exterior defects, except that the tolerance shall be 20 percent instead of 5 percent, by count, of which not over one-fourth (or 5 percent) shall be below specifications for "Choice" as to exterior defects. As to interior defects and decay, the minimum requirements of the State Agricultural Code shall apply.

(17) *Specifications for "Orchard Run"*—Tangerines, mandarins or tangelos packed for marketing under brands listed in the Sunkist Growers, Inc. brand list and/or manifested as "Orchard Run" shall meet specifications for "Sunkist" as to exterior defects, except that the tolerance shall be 50 percent instead of 5 percent, by count, of which not over one-tenth (or 5 percent) shall be below specifications for "Choice" as to exterior defects. As to interior defects and decay, the minimum requirements of the State Agricultural Code shall apply.

Lemons

(18) *Specifications for "Sunkist"*—Lemons packed for marketing under the trademark Sunkist shall be well-grown specimens of normal form, picked from the tree; of good juice content; of good uniform color; of good texture; practically free from scale, other insect pests, fungus diseases, red blotch, membranous stain, peteca, or defects of any kind that cause fruit to decay. The following classes of fruit shall be excluded: Fruit with abnormally long necks; fruit more than slightly sunburned, or more than slightly green in color; rough, coarse fruit; fruit with deep or dark scars; dirty fruit unattractive to the consumer;

fruit more than slightly spongy or with more than slightly hollow core; fruit affected with internal decline; fruit showing effects of frost or which cuts dry for any reason; very immature fruit, or fruit deficient in juice content; aged fruit for its class or color; fruit with dark buttons except fruit of good vitality that has been forced into color; and fruit from lots showing heavy decay out of storage. Lemons packed for marketing under the trademark Sunkist shall not vary more than 5 percent below the foregoing specifications except that Alternaria and other decay within this tolerance shall not exceed 1 percent.

(19) *Specifications for "SGI"*—Lemons packed for marketing under the trademark SGI shall meet the specifications for Sunkist except that as to interior defects one-half the tolerance for serious damage as defined by the agricultural laws of the state for freezing, internal decline, sunburn or drying due to any cause shall apply.

(20) *Specifications for "Excel"*—Lemons packed for marketing under brands listed in the Sunkist Growers, Inc. brand list and/or manifested as "Excel" shall meet specifications for "Sunkist," except that as to interior defects the minimum requirements of the State Agricultural Code shall apply.

(21) *Specifications for "SK"*—Lemons packed for marketing as "SK" shall be well-grown specimens of fair form, picked from the tree; of good, uniform color; of fair texture; practically free from scale, other insect pests, peteca, red blotch, fungus diseases, or defects of any kind that cause fruit to decay. The following classes of fruit shall be excluded: Fruit more than slightly sunburned which affects the juice content or with more than slight membranous stain; more than slightly green in color; very rough; very coarse; badly scarred; dirty and scaly fruit; fruit more than slightly spongy or with more than slightly hollow core; fruit affected with internal decline; fruit showing effects of frost, or which cuts dry for any reason; very immature fruit or fruit deficient in juice content; aged fruit for its class or color; fruit with dark buttons except fruit of good vitality that has been forced into color; and fruit from lots showing more than an occasional decay out of storage. Lemons packed for marketing as "SK" shall not vary more than 5 percent below the foregoing specifications except that Alternaria and other decay within this tolerance shall not exceed 1 percent. As to fruit showing effects of frost, sunburn, internal decline, or which cuts dry for any reason, the minimum requirements of the State Agricultural Code shall apply.

(22) *Specifications for "Red Ball"*—Lemons packed for marketing under the trademark Red Ball shall be well-grown specimens of fair form, picked from the tree; of good juice content; of fairly uniform color; of fair texture; practically free from insect pests (other than scale), fungus diseases, or defects of any kind that cause fruit to decay. The following classes of fruit shall be excluded: Fruit more than slightly sunburned which affects the juice content or with more than slight membranous stain; very green in color; very rough; very coarse; badly

scarred; very dirty and very scaly fruit; very spongy or badly hollow core fruit; fruit affected with internal decline; fruit showing effects of frost, or which cuts dry for any reason; very immature fruit or fruit deficient in juice content; aged fruit for its class or color; fruit with dark buttons except fruit of good vitality that has been forced into color; and fruit from lots showing heavy decay out of storage. Lemons packed for marketing under the trademark Red Ball shall not vary more than 5 percent below the foregoing specifications except that Alternaria and other decay within this tolerance shall not exceed 1 percent. As to fruit showing effects of frost, sunburn, internal decline, or which cuts dry for any reason, the total tolerance shall be 10 percent, but not more than half of this tolerance shall be allowed for serious drying or freezing damage as defined in the State Agricultural Code.

(23) *Tolerance for Indications of Alternaria Development in Lemons*—Lemons showing indications of the development of Alternaria appearing as a staining of the tissue (on a cross cut), under the button, in the core or in the fibrovascular bundles, shall not be marketed under the trademarks Sunkist, SGI, SK or Red Ball. A maximum tolerance of 5 percent shall be allowed for indications of Alternaria development including the 1 percent allowable for Alternaria decay.

(24) *Minimum Juice Content of Lemons*—Lemons packed for marketing under the trademarks Sunkist, Excel, SGI, SK and Red Ball for domestic shipments shall have a minimum juice content of 30 percent by volume. The determination is made as follows: The volume of a representative sample of at least twelve lemons from the packing bin to be measured by water displacement into a graduate. The juice is then extracted by reaming, screened by pressing through cheesecloth, and its volume measured in the graduate. The percent of juice by volume is found simply by dividing the juice volume by the fruit volume and multiplying by 100. Export lemons, except to Canada, shall be excluded from this requirement, but when packed for marketing under "SK" shall have a minimum juice content of 28 percent by volume.

(25) *Storage Limitation for Lemons*—No lemons shall be eligible for marketing under the trademarks Sunkist, SGI, Excel, SK and Red Ball that have been in storage longer than six and one-half months.

All Varieties

(26) *Liners*—*"Sunkist," "Excel," "SGI," "SK" and "Red Ball"*—Liners are the minimum for the grade specified after the tolerance has been removed, whether "Sunkist," "SGI," "Excel," "SK" or "Red Ball." There shall be permitted only 15 percent of liners in a grade that carries the full 5 percent tolerance for errors; 20 percent of liners in a grade that carries not to exceed 2½ percent tolerance for errors; and a maximum of 25 percent of liners in a grade that carries no tolerance for errors; in the latter case any tolerance for errors in grading must come within the 25 percent and not in addition thereto.

(27) *Universal Pack Date and Lot Coding*—All containers of oranges, grapefruit, tangerines and lemons marketed under the trademarks Sunkist, SGI, Excel and SK must be marked in legible form with a code or date indicating month and day packed. In addition to the date code, a lot number, or code, must be used so that each lot may be identified within a block of fruit. Lemons must be marked with the storage color in lieu of a lot number. Shippers will have the option of selecting a date code using the calendar month of the year plus the day of the month, or may use a universal date code issued by the Field Department. Failure to comply with these requirements will disqualify all fruit concerned to be marketed by Sunkist Growers, Inc.

(28) *Mixing Fruit Prohibited*—It shall be contrary to these regulations to blend or mix lots of fruit being packed for marketing under the trademarks Sunkist, SGI, Excel, SK and Red Ball where any one lot, if graded alone, would not comply with the minimum requirements of the specifications for "Sunkist," "SGI," "Excel," "SK" or "Red Ball," respectively.

(29) *Policy Relative to Keeping Quality and Condition of Fruit*—It is implied in the above specifications that fruit packed for marketing under the trademarks Sunkist, SGI, Excel, SK and Red Ball shall have reasonable keeping quality and be in such condition as to give satisfaction under normal conditions of handling and distribution.

(30) *Tolerance for Defects that Develop in Transit*—The tolerance for fruit packed for marketing under "Sunkist," "SGI," "Excel," "SK" and "Red Ball" on defects that develop in transit, such as pronounced scalding, pitting, or aging, granulation, Alternaria or other interior decays, shall be 10 percent except on fruit destined for export shipments. (Note: Blue or green mold or brown rot developing in transit does not come under this regulation.)

(31) *Packing Fruit for Marketing Under the Trademarks Sunkist, SGI, Excel, SK and Red Ball*—To be eligible for marketing under the trademarks Sunkist, SGI, Excel, SK and Red Ball, fruit must be in standard cartons or in bags as adopted or approved by Sunkist; except that citrus fruit conforming to the appropriate specifications may be marketed under the Sunkist, SGI, Excel, SK or Red Ball trademarks in other than such standard carton or approved bag when no standard container requirements are imposed on the shipment in question by the State laws of California or Arizona, as the case may be, and Sunkist has not adopted or approved a standard carton or bag applicable to such shipment.

(32) *Grade Specifications for "Extra Choice," "Orchard Run" and "Choice"*—Extra Choice Grade: Oranges, grapefruit or lemons packed for marketing under brands listed in the Sunkist Growers, Inc. brand list and/or manifested as "Extra

Choice" shall meet specifications for "Sunkist" as to exterior defects, except that the tolerance shall be 20 percent instead of 5 percent, by count, of which not over one-fourth (or 5 percent) shall be below specifications for ,'Red Ball" as to exterior defects. As to interior defects and decay, the minimum requirements of the State Agricultural Code shall apply.

Orchard Run Grade: Oranges, grapefruit or lemons packed for marketing under brands listed in the Sunkist Growers, Inc. brand list and/or manifested as "Orchard Run" shall meet specifications for "Sunkist" as to exterior defects, except that the tolerance shall be 50 percent instead of 5 percent, by count, of which not over one-tenth (or 5 percent) shall be below specifications for "Red Ball" as to exterior defects. As to interior defects and decay, the minimum requirements of the State Agricultural Code shall apply.

Choice Grade: Oranges, grapefruit or lemons packed for marketing under brands listed in the Sunkist Growers, Inc. brand list and/or manifested as "Choice" shall meet specifications for "Red Ball" as to exterior defects, except that the tolerance shall be 10 percent instead of 5 percent, by count. As to interior defects and decay, the minimum requirements of the State Agricultural Code shall apply.

(33) *Registration of Brands*—All brands being marketed through Sunkist Growers, Inc. shall be listed on the Sunkist Growers, Inc. brand list with their proper grade designation. The grade designated for any brand shall apply to all varieties shipped under that brand. The grade designation shall remain in effect until changed, authority for such change to be secured from the office of the Secretary of Sunkist Growers, Inc., upon recommendation by the Field Department.

(34) *Bags for Oranges, Grapefruit, Lemons and Tangerines*—The use of bags is to be handled under rules set up by the Field Services Division, Advertising Division and Sales Division jointly. Rules and regulations have been given in circulars sent out by the Field Services Division and will be withdrawn, modified or supplemented by circulars in case of change. Rules and regulations relating to size, design and marking of bags are found under the Trademark Application and Container Regulations.

(35) *Enforcement*—The Field Department of Sunkist Growers, Inc., is charged with the enforcement of these grade regulations; shall determine whether the fruit complies with the specifications; and is authorized to cause packing of fruit to cease immediately when compliance with these regulations is in question.

In addition to inspection of fruit at time of packing, the fruit shall be subject to reinspection before and/or at the time of shipment, to determine compliance of such fruit with the respective specifications.

The Field Department furthermore is charged with the authority to compel repacking or reconditioning of the fruit in case it is not up to the specifications contained in these regulations. If any member of the Field Department finds fruit that i his opinion is below the specifications adopted, he shall immediately take up the matter with the shipper or manager of the ass ciation. If they cannot agree, then the manager of the district exchange and the supervising inspector shall be called into consultation. In case these cannot agree, the manager of the Field Department shall be called in, and his decision shall be final. It understood, of course, that if any shipper feels the manager of the Field Department erred in his judgment, he may properly bring the matter before the management of Sunkist Growers, Inc.

(36) *Method of Procedure at Shipping Point Where Fruit is Found to be Below Specifications*—The Field Department inspector has the full responsibility of definitely ascertaining th disposition of the fruit ordered repacked or reconditioned. Up finding in any packing house fruit that has to be ordered repacked or reconditioned he shall make an immediate and separate report to the Field Department, on a form provided fo this purpose, of the quantity ordered repacked, reconditioned, or sent to by-products, giving date and reasons for action taken

This report shall be signed by the manager or the foreman o the packing house involved. A carbon copy of this report shall b retained by the inspector, to be sent in later, advising the result of the reconditioning as well as the final disposition of all fruit involved in the first report.

The shipper shall be required to recondition the lot before shipment in such a manner as to segregate the fruit eligible for the specifications in question from that which is not. After such segregation, the fruit shall be submitted for reinspection before shipment as fresh fruit. Any fruit which has been stamped with the Sunkist, SGI, Excel, SK or Red Ball trademark which does meet the specifications therefor shall not be permitted to be sol or distributed as fresh fruit and may be utilized for by-product purposes only, in accordance with directions given by the Field Department inspector.

(37) *Method of Procedure in the Markets Where Fruit is Found to be Below Specifications*—Whenever citrus fruit packed for marketing under the trademarks Sunkist, SGI, Excel, SK or Ball arrives in any market and is reported by the inspector as falling below the specifications therefor, the fruit in at least twenty-five containers of each brand shall be thoroughly examined personally by the district manager and a detailed record kept on each of the twenty-five containers examined. In the case of Sunkist, SGI, SK or Red Ball, if the fruit shows evide of tree frost injury, granulation, or cuts dry for any reason, at least one hundred fruits, taken equally and blindly from the twenty-five containers, shall be cut for inspection and results recorded according to photos furnished with the instruction book. If the examination confirms the inspector's report, the

district manager shall confer with his division manager as to the results of the inspection. Then the division manager, through the Los Angeles office, shall advise the shipper of the brands of fruit that are below the specifications, and the shipper shall then direct disposal in accordance with the following options:

1. Sell the fruit for by-product purposes under the safeguards established by Sunkist Growers, Inc.

2. Return to shipping point in California or Arizona for re-conditioning under the supervision of the Field Department.

(38) *Penalties for Violating Regulations for "Sunkist," "SGI" "Excel," "SK" and "Red Ball"*—In cases of willful or persistent violation by an association or shipper of the rules and regulations governing fruit packed for marketing under the trademarks Sunkist, SGI, Excel, SK, or Red Ball, the Field Department shall place an inspector in the packing house to supervise the grading of fruit being packed under the trademarks Sunkist, SGI, Excel, SK and Red Ball for a period up to 30 days, at the expense of the association or shipper violating the regulations. Any association or shipper refusing to pay the salary or other expenses in connection with the maintenance of such inspector for the period above defined shall not be permitted to pack fruit for marketing under the trademarks Sunkist, SGI, Excel, SK and Red Ball until such indebtedness is paid.

It is further provided that it is the policy of Sunkist Growers, Inc., as owner of the trademarks Sunkist, SGI, Excel, SK and Red Ball, that in case of the continued persistent misgrading of fruit for marketing under these trademarks, Sunkist Growers, Inc. will not market or permit the marketing of any fruit of such association under these trademarks and all shippers, division managers, district managers, and the Advertising Division shall be notified to such effect.

(39) *Penalty Regulation—Exports*—All varieties of citrus fruits packed under Sunkist, SGI, Excel, SK or Red Ball trademarks destined for export markets will be subject to penalties if the fruit fails to meet certain grade and condition specifications as set forth by the Field Department and authorized by the Board of Directors of Sunkist Growers, Inc.

Penalty assessments will be made against the associations whose brands fail to meet grade and condition specifications. Determination of violation of grade and condition specifications will be based on sample inspection of fruit at all harbor points of departure prior to or during the cargo loading aboard vessels, and on valid inspection at arrival points in overseas markets.

All fruit will be subject to the usual inspection at packing houses but will not be certified at those points, although it may be rejected at packing houses. Failure to reject does not constitute exemption from subsequent penalties at points of departure or market arrivals.

A panel, composed of the Export Sales Manager or his representative and two supervisory members of the Field Department, will be the final judge of all penalties.

TRADEMARK APPLICATION AND CONTAINER REGULATIONS

Property Right

Placing or displaying the trademarks Sunkist, SGI, Excel, SK or Red Ball upon or adjacent to, and with reference to, any buildings, premises, or other property, or upon the letterheads of any district exchange, association, or grower affiliated therewith, shall be done only with the permission of Sunkist Growers, Inc. and as authorized by the Board of Directors thereof and for the purpose solely of calling attention to the fact of such affiliation, and shall not create in said district exchange, association, or grower, or any of them, any property right in any of said trademarks or any colorable imitation thereof and shall not give or be deemed to give to said district exchange, association, grower or others either the right to continue such display of said trademarks or the right to make any use thereof, or reference thereto.

The Advertising Division of Sunkist Growers, Inc. is charged with the responsibility of interpreting the following regulations as pertain to the application of the trademarks Sunkist, SGI, Excel, SK and Red Ball to the fruit or package and to the application of any trademark or any other word or words used in association with the corporate name, Sunkist Growers, Inc., subject to review by the Executive Office in event of disagreement.

Proofs of all new label designs must be submitted by the association originating such design for final approval of the Advertising Division of Sunkist Growers, Inc. before production is authorized.

Design, Color and Size

The trademarks Sunkist, SGI, Excel, SK and Red Ball, respectively, shall be displayed and imprinted on fruit in uniform design, color and size as prescribed by the Advertising Division of Sunkist Growers, Inc.

Trademarks on Fruit

Oranges, grapefruit and lemons which are to be marketed under the Sunkist and SK trademark, and lemons which are to be marketed under the SGI trademark, in addition to meeting the respective specifications therefor, must carry the mark "Sunkist," "SGI," or "SK," as the case may be, on the skin. The trademark Excel or Red Ball may be stamped on oranges and lemons and grapefruit conforming to the specifications for "Excel" or "Red Ball" respectively, established for that variety.

Varieties conforming to the specifications for "Sunkist," "SGI," or "SK," which are required to carry their respective trademark on the skin, and varieties for which the shipper may elect, and does elect, to trademark Excel or Red Ball will satisfy the trademarking regulation if 90 percent of the fruits in a representative sample, composed of 100 or more fruits, carry a trademark which can be identified as being the intended mark with 80 of the 90 percent being classified as "good." Fruit not meeting the above requirement will not be accepted as a passing grade unless, in the opinion of the field inspector, the failure was temporary and related to mechanical or operational difficulties.

Grapefruit conforming to the specifications for "Sunkist" must be stamped "Sunkist" and if the fruit originates in Arizona or the desert areas of California it may also be stamped with a name indicating the area of origin. The area name to be used and the size and style of type shall be approved by the Advertising Division of Sunkist Growers, Inc.

The stamping of association brands or other marks shall not be permitted on fruit carrying the imprint "Sunkist," SGI, "Excel," "SK" or "Red Ball," except as specified for "Sunkist" grapefruit. Oranges packed for brands registered as "Excel" in the Sunkist Growers, Inc. brand list and/or manifested as "Excel" but not carrying the "Excel" mark will not be permitted to bear any other mark.

Fruit not bearing the Sunkist, SGI, SK or Red Ball trademark may be stamped with an association brand or other designation on approval of the Advertising Division of Sunkist Growers, Inc. Approval will not be given to stamp fruit with any brand or other designation which, in the opinion of the Advertising Division, consumers are likely to confuse with Sunkist, SGI, SK or Red Ball trademarks.

Trademarks on Labels

The trademarks Sunkist, SGI, Excel, SK or Red Ball may be reproduced on containers of all fruit conforming to regulations established for fruit to be marketed by Sunkist Growers, Inc. under the trademarks Sunkist, SGI, Excel, SK or Red Ball. The privilege of employing, with the Sunkist, SGI, Excel, SK or Red Ball trademark, a private brand owned by an association to indicate the origin of the fruit with that association or packer and shipper is granted by Sunkist Growers, Inc., provided all of the requirements of the regulations are complied with in respect to the Sunkist, SGI, Excel, SK or Red Ball trademarks under which the fruit is to be marketed by Sunkist Growers, Inc.

Consumer-Size Bag Regulations

(1) *Size of Bags*—The various sizes of bags shall be determined jointly by the Sales and Advertising Divisions and Field Department.

(2) *Design—*

a. *Sunkist, SK and Excel Trademarked Fruit.*

Oranges, Lemons and Tangerines. Only approved Sunkist, Excel or SK trademarked bags shall be used for oranges, lemons and tangerines packed by shippers in bags when the fruit bears the Sunkist, Excel or SK trademark.

These will be the "A" bag, the official stock Sunkist, Excel and SK bag; "B" bag, carrying a standard Sunkist, Excel or SK panel identification when a customer's trademark is involved.

Specifications as to wording, size and type of letters, and color combinations shall be established by the Advertising Division and furnished bag manufacturers by Fruit Growers Supply Company.

Grapefruit. Sunkist or Excel trademarked grapefruit may be packed in consumer-size bags showing the association trademark or buyer's trademark, but the bag must carry a panel or circle designating the contents as Sunkist or Excel brand fruit and the bags must be approved by the Sales and Advertising Divisions. Stock Sunkist and Excel grapefruit "A" bags have been established under the same regulations as apply to Sunkist and Excel orange and lemon bags.

b. *Fruit not Bearing Sunkist, Excel or SK Trademark (All Varieties).* Other brands may be used on bags containing other than Sunkist, Excel or SK trademarked fruit, but each design must be submitted for approval of Sales and Advertising Divisions.

(3) *Shipper's Identification*—All Sunkist, Excel and SK "A" bags must bear either the name and location of the district exchange or individual shipper that packed the fruit, or the legend "Marketed by Sunkist Growers, Inc., Main Office, Los Angeles, California." All other bags must bear either this legend, or the name and address of the shipper or buyer sufficient to permit ready identification.

(4) *Master Containers.* When no individual shipper's identification appears on consumer bags, this information must be shown on fibreboard master containers, and when fruit is sold by size, the size must be shown on the master container. No other markings are required, but printing of shipper labels, Sunkist, Excel or SK (when otherwise permitted under these Rules and Regulations) or other side panels is permissive. Shippers must use a master container of a size and construction approved by the Field Department.

(5) Basis for Conversion for Assessments and Records. All shipments in bags will be converted to packed equivalent cartons, the basis for each size of bag for each variety to be established by the Treasurer. All shipments in bags shall be considered as packed fruit.

Wrapper Regulations

The relatively small volume of fruit of any variety packed in tissue wraps is mostly packed in Sunkist wraps or "stock" wraps already produced. It is permissible to use "stock" wraps on "Sunkist" or "Excel" trademarked fruit when this is acceptable to buyer.

Special Regulations

Materials promoting, publicizing or describing processes, materials, supplies, services or any other project or product shall not be inserted in, imprinted on or made a part of any package, of any grade or variety of fruit, except on the shipper's label or tag affixed or attached to such package. Reference or notice on labels or tags shall not be made without supporting copy or claims and shall be subject to approval of Sunkist Growers, Inc.

The only exception to this regulation is material required by Federal or State regulatory agencies.

Container Regulations

The reproduction of the trademarks Sunkist, SGI, Excel, SK, Extra Choice and Choice, on fibreboard cartons is fully covered in bulletins which have been furnished by Sunkist Growers, Inc., to field personnel and to all local associations and district exchanges affiliated with Sunkist, and by Fruit Growers Supply Company to carton manufacturers.

These bulletins give full details of size of type, colors for each variety and placement of the trademark and all other copy on cartons.

As provided in these bulletins, before the printing of any new label design or redesign of an existing label, proof thereof shall be sent to Fruit Growers Supply Company for submission to and approval of Sunkist Growers, Inc.

Appendix C
Agreement between the Federal Trade Commission and Sunkist Growers, Inc.

In the Matter of SUNKIST GROWERS, INC., a corporation.	Docket No. 9100 AGREEMENT CONTAINING ORDER TO DIVEST AND OTHER RELIEF

The agreement herein, by and between Sunkist Growers, Inc., a corporation, hereafter sometimes referred to as Sunkist, by its duly authorized officer and its attorney, and counsel for the Federal Trade Commission, is entered into in accordance with the Federal Trade Commission's Rules governing consent order procedures. In accordance therewith the parties hereby agree that:

1. Respondent Sunkist Growers, Inc. is a corporation organized, existing and doing business under and by virtue of the laws of the State of California with its principal offices located at 14130 Riverside Drive, Sherman Oaks, California.

2. Sunkist has been served with a copy of the complaint issued by the Federal Trade Commission charging it with violation of Section 7 of the Clayton Act, as amended, 15 U.S.C. Section 18, and Section 5 of the Federal Trade Commission Act, as amended, 15 U.S.C. Section 45, and has filed answers to said complaint denying said charges.

3. Sunkist admits all of the jurisdictional facts set forth in the Federal Trade Commission's complaint in this proceeding.

4. Sunkist waives:

(a) Any further procedural steps;

(b) The requirement that the Federal Trade Commission's decision contain a statement of findings of fact and conclusions of law; and

(c) All rights to seek judicial review or otherwise to challenge or contest the validity of the Order to Divest and Other Relief, sometimes referred to hereafter as the order, entered pursuant to this agreement.

5. This agreement shall not become a part of the public record of the proceeding unless and until it is accepted by the Federal Trade Commission. If this agreement is accepted by the Commission, it will be placed on the public record for a period of sixty (60) days and information in respect

in respect thereto publicly released. The Commission thereafter may either withdraw its acceptance of this agreement and so notify Sunkist, in which event it will take such action as it may consider appropriate, or issue and serve its decision in disposition of the proceeding.

6. This agreement is for settlement purposes only and does not constitute an admission by Sunkist that the law has been violated as alleged in the complaint.

7. If this agreement is accepted by the Federal Trade Commission, and if such acceptance is not subsequently withdrawn by the Commission pursuant to the provisions of Section 3.25(f) of the Commission's Rules, the Commission may without further notice to Sunkist (1) issue its decision containing the following Order to Divest and Other Relief in disposition of the proceeding, and (2) make information public in respect thereto. When so entered, the order shall have the same force and effect and may be altered, modified or set aside in the same manner and within the same time provided by statute for other orders. The order shall become final upon service. Delivery by the U.S. Postal Service of the decision containing the agreed-to order to respondent's address as stated in paragraph 1 of this agreement shall constitute service. Sunkist waives any right it might have to any other manner of service.

8. This agreement contemplates that the complaint and Prehearing Order No. 1, dated October 28, 1977, may be used in construing the terms of the order, and that no agreement, understanding, representation, or interpretation not contained in the order or in this agreement may be used to vary or to contradict the terms of the order.

9. Sunkist has read the order contemplated hereby and understands that once the order has been issued, Sunkist will be required to file one or more compliance reports showing that it has fully complied with the order. Sunkist further understands that it may be liable for civil penalties in the amount provided by law for each violation of the order after it becomes final.

ORDER

DEFINITIONS

For the purpose of this order, the following definitions shall apply:

(a) "Sunkist" means Sunkist Growers, Inc.; its divisions and subsidiaries; its officers, directors, representatives, agents and employees acting as such; and its successors and assigns.

(b) "Affiliated packinghouse" or "packinghouse affiliated with" means a citrus packinghouse authorized by Sunkist to pack citrus for Sunkist grower-members. It does not include a packinghouse which packs citrus for Sunkist members only on a temporary, ad hoc, emergency basis.

(c) "Arizona Products Division" means (1) all facilities and assets located in Yuma, Arizona, owned by Sunkist which are used in connection with the conversion of citrus fruit into citrus products; (2) the cold storage facilities and assets, acquired by Sunkist, which previously had been part of the Southwestern Ice and Cold Storage Company; and (3) all agricultural lands used for effluent disposal from the above-described facilities. The facilities, assets and agricultural lands listed above shall include, but are not limited to, all land, buildings, equipment, supplies and machinery used by Arizona Products Division, together with any other additions and improvements thereto.

(d) "Citrus Packinghouse" means any facility which packs lemons, navel oranges, valencia oranges, grapefruit or tangerines for fresh fruit shipment on a regular basis, but does not include a facility which packs those varieties only on an auxiliary and overflow basis.

(e) "Commercial Packinghouse" means a citrus packinghouse located in California or Arizona which is not a packinghouse owned or operated by an association of growers meeting the requirements of Section 1 of the Capper-Volstead Act, or by one or more growers packing only their own citrus fruit.

(f) "Commercial Citrus Processing Plant" means a processing plant, used or equipped to be used, in whole or in part, to process whole citrus fruit into juice, peel or oil products, which is not owned or operated by an association of growers meeting the requirements of Section 1 of the Capper-Volstead Act.

(g) "District III" means the prorate district established pursuant to the Agricultural Marketing Agreement Act of 1937, 7 U.S.C. §§601 et seq., as amended, and as specified in regulations thereunder, 7 C.F.R. §§907.66(c), 908.66(c) and 910.64(c), as of the date this order becomes final.

(h) "Lemon Administrative Committee" means the Lemon Administrative Committee established pursuant to the Agricultural Marketing Agreement Act of 1937, as amended, and regulations thereunder.

(i) "Orange Administrative Committees" means the Navel and Valencia Orange Administrative Committees established pursuant to the Agricultural Marketing Agreement Act of 1937, as amended, and regulations thereunder.

(j) "Product-grade citrus" means citrus which is received by processing plants for processing into citrus products.

I

IT IS ORDERED that within eighteen (18) months from the date this order becomes final, Sunkist shall divest as a unit, absolutely and in good faith, all properties and assets constituting the Arizona Products Division ("APD") of Sunkist in order to establish APD as a viable competitor in the citrus processing business. The divestiture shall be subject to the prior approval of the Federal Trade Commission. Pending divestiture, Sunkist shall take all measures necessary to maintain APD in its present condition and prevent any deterioration, except for normal wear and tear, of any of the assets to be divested which may impair their present operating abilities or market value.

II

IT IS FURTHER ORDERED that for each of the four (4) complete District III citrus seasons (approximately September–August) after the divestiture of APD or the four (4) years (twelve-month periods) beginning on the date of divestiture, whichever the acquirer of APD ("acquirer") shall elect, Sunkist shall offer to sell to the acquirer for processing by the acquirer a mixed supply of product-grade citrus grown in District III in the manner described below, unless otherwise modified by mutual agreement between Sunkist and the acquirer:

(a) The total volume of citrus to be offered for sale in the first three (3) seasons or years shall be determined as follows:

Sunkist's total seasonal or yearly tons of product-grade citrus from District III	Total tons Sunkist shall offer to sell to the acquirer of APD
0–100,000	45% of Sunkist's product-grade citrus from District III
100,001–150,000	45,000
150,001–170,000	50,000
170,001 and above	55,000

(b) The total volume of citrus to be offered for sale in the fourth (4th) season or year shall be one-half (1/2) of the amount determined in accordance with subparagraph (a) of this paragraph.

(c) The volume of such citrus shall consist of a mix of varieties grown in District III that is equal to the proportion that each such variety bears to Sunkist's total District III volume of those varieties.

(d) Sunkist's total seasonal or yearly obligation to offer to sell citrus to the acquirer shall be reduced by an amount equal to any amount of citrus the acquirer obtains in that season or year for processing at APD from any citrus packinghouse affiliated with Sunkist on the date this order becomes final and not affiliated with Sunkist at the time the citrus is obtained from the packinghouse. In calculating Sunkist's obligation to offer to sell citrus under this order, the amount of citrus purchased by the acquirer from such a packinghouse shall be included in the total tons of Sunkist's product-grade citrus from District III computed on a yearly or seasonal basis, consistent with the acquirer's election referred to above.

(e) The amount of citrus which the acquirer agrees to buy from Sunkist shall be specified in a yearly contract. Sunkist shall make the citrus available in daily quantities of not less than 100 tons and not more than 600 tons until Sunkist has met its total requirements specified in the yearly contract. If Sunkist's District III tonnage on any day is less than 100 tons Sunkist shall make all its District III citrus tonnage available to the acquirer, and the acquirer shall give reasonable notice to Sunkist whether the acquirer will take such tonnage. The contract shall be in accord with usual and customary industry terms and conditions, including reasonable terms and conditions to assure timely removal of the citrus from Sunkist's affiliated packinghouses.

(f) To determine Sunkist's obligations in paragraphs II (a), (b) and (c) of this order, the seasonal crop projections of the Orange Administrative Committees for oranges, the Lemon Administrative Committee for lemons, and Sunkist's regular seasonal projections for grapefruit, tangerines and other varieties shall be used. If during the season or year the crop projection or the actual crop production for any season or year varies from the projections establishing Sunkist's initial requirements for that season or year, the total amount and mix of citrus that Sunkist must sell under its contract or offer to sell under this order shall be adjusted to conform to the revised projections or to actual production as appropriate.

(g) The price Sunkist shall charge the acquirer for the citrus shall be no less favorable than the price at which Sunkist makes comparable sales of that variety of product-grade citrus to any other processing customer. If Sunkist has no such sales to any other processing customer, then the price shall be the prevailing market price for comparable sales of that variety.

III

IT IS FURTHER ORDERED that for a period of five (5) years after the divestiture of APD, if Sunkist uses a non-Sunkist processing plant to process the citrus of Sunkist growers packed in Yuma County, Arizona, it shall first offer to the acquirer the opportunity to process that citrus, provided the product will be processed to meet Sunkist's specifications and the charge for processing is commercially reasonable.

IV

IT IS FURTHER ORDERED that for a period of ten (10) years from the date this order becomes final Sunkist shall not directly or indirectly acquire, without the prior approval of the Federal Trade Commission, any stock interest in or assets of any commercial citrus processing plant in the states of California or Arizona.

V

IT IS FURTHER ORDERED that for a period of five (5) years from the date this order becomes final, there shall not be more than thirty-nine (39) commercial packinghouses affiliated with Sunkist unless prior approval of the Federal Trade Commission is obtained.

VI

IT IS FURTHER ORDERED that for a period of five (5) years from the date this order becomes final, Sunkist shall not directly or indirectly acquire, without the prior approval of the Federal Trade Commission, any stock interest in or assets of any citrus packinghouse in the states of California or Arizona, except for an interest resulting from foreclosure by Sunkist, in which case Sunkist shall divest such interest in the packinghouse within one year of the foreclosure.

VII

IT IS FURTHER ORDERED that within sixty (60) days after the date this order becomes final, and every sixty (60) days thereafter until Sunkist has fully complied with the provisions of paragraph I of this order, Sunkist shall submit to the Federal Trade Commission a verified written report setting forth in detail the manner and form in which it intends to comply, is complying with or has complied with that provision. All compliance reports shall include, among other things that are required from time to time, a full description of contacts or negotiations with any party for the properties specified in paragraph I of this order and the identity of all such parties. Sunkist shall furnish to the Commission copies of all written communications to and from such parties, and all internal memoranda, reports and recommendations concerning divestiture.

On the date Sunkist divests APD and on every anniversary date of the divestiture thereafter for the following five years, Sunkist shall submit to the Commission a verified written report setting forth the manner and form in which it is complying or has complied with paragraph II of this order.

On the first anniversary of the date this order becomes final and on every anniversary date thereafter for the following five years, Sunkist shall submit to the Commission a verified written report setting forth the manner and form in which it has complied with paragraphs III, V and VI of this order.

On the first anniversary of the date this order becomes final and on every anniversary date thereafter for the following nine (9) years, Sunkist shall submit to the Commission a verified written report setting forth the manner and form in which it has complied or is complying with paragraph IV of this order.

VIII

IT IS FURTHER ORDERED that Sunkist notify the Commission at least thirty (30) days prior to any proposed change in the corporate respondent, such as dissolution, assignment or sale resulting in the emergence of a successor corporation, or any other proposed change in the corporation, including but not limited to changes in the corporate by-laws or membership contracts, which may affect compliance obligations arising out of this order.

Signed this 15th day of August, 1980.[1]

Analysis of Proposed Consent Order
to Aid Public Comment

The Federal Trade Commission has accepted an agreement to a proposed consent order from Sunkist Growers, Inc.

The proposed consent order has been placed on the public record for sixty (60) days for reception of comments by interested persons. Comments received during this period will become part of the public record. After sixty (60) days, the Commission will again review the agreement and the comments received and will decide whether it should withdraw from the agreement or make final the agreement's proposed order.

The complaint, as modified by Pre-Hearing Order No. 1 (October 28, 1977), alleges that Sunkist has monopolized or attempted to monopolize, in the United States and Canada, the sale and distribution of fresh California-Arizona oranges, the sale and distribution of fresh lemons, and the manufacture and sale of lemon products.

In general the proposed order provides that Sunkist must: (1) divest its citrus processing plant located in Yuma, Arizona within 18 months; (2)

This agreement between Sunkist and the staff of the Federal Trade Commission was accepted by the Commission May 5, 1981.

offer substantial supplies of citrus to the divested plant for processing for four years (or seasons) following the divestiture; (3) give the divested plant for five years following the divestiture a right of first refusal to process the citrus of Yuma-area Sunkist members when Sunkist does not process the citrus in its own facilities; (4) refrain for 10 years from acquiring any commercial citrus processor located in California or Arizona without prior approval of the Federal Trade Commission; (5) limit its commercial packinghouse affiliations for 5 years without prior approval of the Federal Trade Commission; (6) refrain for 5 years from acquiring any stock interest in or assets of any citrus packinghouse located in California or Arizona, except for a possible interest resulting from foreclosure which must be divested within one year, without the prior approval of the Federal Trade Commission; (7) file periodic verified written compliance reports setting forth its compliance with the provisions of the order; and (8) provide the Federal Trade Commission at least 30 days notice prior to effecting changes in the corporation which may affect its compliance obligations arising from the order.

Paragraph I of the proposed consent order requires Sunkist to divest the Arizona Products Division (APD), one of its three processing divisions. APD, located in Yuma, Arizona, consists of a citrus processing plant, cold storage facilities, a waste-water treatment system and land. The division was acquired in 1974 by Sunkist. Before that acquisition, APD, then known as Growers Citrus Products, (GCP), was the second largest (Sunkist was, and is, the largest) processor of primary lemon products in the United States and the only non-Sunkist lemon and orange processor in Arizona.

The proposed order requires Sunkist to divest the plant and all post-acquisition improvements, together as one unit, in order to reestablish APD as a viable competitor in the citrus processing business. As a direct result of this provision, competition in the lemon products market should increase and Sunkist's dominance thereof should decrease. The provision may also indirectly increase competition in the fresh citrus markets. Sunkist's bylaws require Sunkist to market all the citrus produced by its growers. Since the divestiture of APD will reduce Sunkist's processing capacity, Sunkist may be required to limit the total volume of fresh and processed citrus it will agree to market. Thus, a larger percentage of citrus production may be available for competitors.

To further insure that the divested plant will be a viable competitor immediately upon divestiture, the proposed order provides for a supply contract, a right of first refusal for certain contract-processing, and a ten year ban on Sunkist's purchases of additional processing plants without prior Commission approval.

Paragraph II requires Sunkist to offer to sell the acquirer of APD a supply of product-grade citrus for four years (or seasons) following the divestiture. The subparagraphs establish the methods of calculating the total annual amounts of citrus to be offered, the varietal mix, the price and the volume of daily deliveries, and provide for an annual contract defining the terms and conditions of sale.

Subparagraph II(a) requires Sunkist to offer APD for three years (or seasons) between 45,000–55,000 tons of citrus, depending upon its total volume of District III production. (District III, as defined, means the prorate district established pursuant to the Agricultural Marketing Agreement Act of 1937 7 U.S.C. §§601 et seq., as amended, and regulations thereunder.) Subparagraph II(b), which applies only to the fourth year (or season), reduces the amount Sunkist must offer by one-half. The reduction in the volume Sunkist must offer in the fourth year creates an economic incentive for the acquirer of the plant to seek out sources of supply apart from that provided by Sunkist, thereby further contributing to the objective of establishing a viable competitor after the supply requirement expires.

Subparagraph II(c) provides the method for determining the varietal mix of citrus that Sunkist is obligated to supply. Each variety is to be supplied in the same ratio that Sunkist's total production of each variety bears to Sunkist's total production of all varieties in District III. The varietal mix recognizes that the APD plant is capable of processing more than just lemons and serves to lengthen its processing season.

The remaining subparagraphs of paragraph II provide further specifics for calculating Sunkist's supply obligation under the schedule in subparagraphs II(a) and (b), for determining the daily amount to be supplied, and the price Sunkist may charge for the supplies provided.

Subparagraph II(d) provides for a "set-off" to be applied in calculating the total amount of citrus Sunkist must supply in accordance with the schedule in II(a) and (b). This provision recognizes that to the extent that packinghouses disaffiliate from Sunkist and sell their product grade citrus to the acquirer of the APD plant during the term of Sunkist's supply obligation, the plant's need for supply from Sunkist correspondingly decreases. This subparagraph is operative only if a Sunkist packinghouse subsequently disaffiliates from Sunkist and sells citrus to APD. If this sequence of events occurs then the total amount of citrus Sunkist must supply the plant under the schedule is reduced by the same amount that the disaffiliated packinghouse(s) sells to the plant. However, the schedule provides that the amount of product grade citrus Sunkist must supply decreases as its production decreases. To prevent a double count of the set-off, the amount that Sunkist is entitled to set off from its obligation must first be added to its production figure to determine the amount of its obligation before the set-off.

Subparagraph II(e) provides both for a written supply contract between Sunkist and the acquirer and for the daily amounts in which the citrus will be supplied. While the proposed consent requires Sunkist to make available a certain amount and mix of citrus to APD, it does not obligate the plant to buy all or any of the citrus. A contract specifying the amounts APD intends to purchase will provide a degree of certainty for Sunkist and allow Sunkist to rationally anticipate its own processing needs. Sunkist must also offer to supply the citrus in daily quantities to 100 to 600 tons. These figures correspond to the plant's minimum and maximum operating capacity (including storage). The remaining contract terms are to be negotiated between Sunkist and APD in accord with usual and customary industry terms. This flexibility will enable the plant to negotiate a contract accounting for its business needs.

Since exact total citrus production figures are not available until after the season is over, subparagraph II(f) provides for use of industry-recognized estimates in determining, at the beginning of the season, Sunkist's obligation under subparagraphs II(a), (b) and (c). As actual figures become available the subparagraph allows for modification of the initial obligation to conform with the schedule of amounts and varietal mix required by subparagraphs II(a), (b), and (c). Subparagraph II(g) assures that the acquirer will be charged a price no less favorable than that charged by Sunkist to other processors. In the absence of sales by Sunkist to others, the prevailing market price is to be charged.

Paragraph III is intended to further assure that the divested plant will become a viable competitor by providing that the plant will have a right of first refusal if Sunkist uses a non-Sunkist processor for the product citrus fruit of its grower members packed in Yuma, Arizona.

Paragraph IV will prevent Sunkist from diminishing competition in the citrus processing industry by banning it for 10 years from acquiring any commercial citrus processing plant located in California or Arizona without prior approval of the Federal Trade Commission.

Paragraph V limits, for five years, the number of Sunkist affiliations with commercial packinghouses. Packinghouses are the vital link between growers, marketers and processors. Without packinghouse affiliations, fresh citrus marketers and processors do not have access to citrus supplies. A substantial number of the industry's approximately 135 packinghouses are commercially owned and operated. Access to those houses by Sunkist's competitors is critical to the competitive health of the western citrus industry.

The year before the issuance of the complaint Sunkist had affiliations with 51 commercial packinghouses. The proposed order limits that number to 39. This reduction will assure competitive access to a significant number of the industry's commercial houses without interfering with Sunkist's right, as a Capper-Volstead agricultural cooperative, to continue affiliating with cooperative packinghouses. Moreover, the five-year duration of this limitation should enable competitors to establish sound relationships with a substantial number of packinghouses to improve competition and thereby provide viable alternatives to Sunkist's marketing operations.

Paragraph VI prevents Sunkist for 5 years from acquiring any stock interest in or assets of any citrus packinghouse, without prior approval of the Federal Trade Commission, except for a temporary interest resulting from foreclosure which must be divested within one year. This provision is intended to prevent Sunkist from evading the limitation on commercial packinghouse affiliations specified in paragraph V.

Paragraphs VII and VIII are intended to assure compliance with the order by requiring Sunkist to file periodic, written, verified compliance reports and to provide advance notice of any change in the corporation which may effect compliance obligations arising out of the order.

The purpose of this analysis is to facilitate public comment on the proposed order, and it is not intended to constitute an official interpretation of the agreement and proposed order or to modify in any way their terms.

Appendix D
G. Harold Powell's
Comments on Marketing
Contracts

No form of contract will hold the membership together indefinitely unless the benefits of the organization justify its continuance but the human side of some men has not yet evolved to that ideal state in which a temporary advantage offered them may not blind them to the permanent values of their own association. Therefore, voluntary membership is not always practicable. Always, too, there are opportunists who take no interest in the real problems of agriculture and do not see their position as part of a great working whole, i.e., they have little consciousness of the larger factors influencing the disposition of crops, and, in their disposal, are rampant speculators. The opponents of the cooperative system, understanding this psychology, tempt the speculative farmer with offers of high prices as a means of strengthening themselves in the community and, unless this type of producer has formally bound himself to his association by a contract to handle all of his produce through it for a given time, the buyers may draw heavily from the membership and thereby weaken its financial and business stability. A large proportion of the failures in cooperative marketing have been due to the irresponsibility of the membership when an association has been subjected to competitive fire. Then if the association has incurred liabilities, based on the expected loyalty of its members, it finds itself not only with a reduced membership but also with a correspondingly reduced income with which to meet its liabilities. Though the contract is essential to stabilize an association, it is clearly apparent that the best success will only follow when a majority of its members are convinced that the cooperative principle is most beneficial, ultimately. This conviction will be strong enough to hold them together when their opponents attack them—providing it is reenforced by the successful returns of the association itself in the management of its business.

Powell was the long-time general manager of Sunkist. This quote originally appeared in G.H. Powell, *Fundamental Principles of Cooperation in Agriculture*, California Agricultural Experiment Station Circ. 222 (1920), 11-12, cited in H.H. Bakken and M.A. Schaars, *The Economics of Cooperative Marketing* (New York: McGraw-Hill, 1937), 313-14.

References

"The Agricultural Cooperative Antitrust Exemption—*Fairdale Farms Inc. v. Yankee Milk, Inc.*" *Cornell Law Review* 67 (January 1982).

"Agricultural Cooperatives—The Clayton Act and the Capper-Volstead Act Immunize the Concerted Price-Bargaining Activities of Two Agricultural Cooperatives from Antitrust Liability." *Texas Law Review* 53 (1975).

"Antitrust Law—*Fairdale Farms, Inc. v. Yankee Milk, Inc.:*—The Right of Agricultural Cooperatives to Possess Monopoly Power." *Journal of Corporation Law* 7 (1982).

Areeda, P., and D. F. Turner. "Predatory Pricing and Related Practices under Section 2 of the Sherman Act." *Harvard Law Review* 88 (1975).

Bain, Joe S. *Industrial Organization.* New York: Wiley, 1959.

Bakken, H.H., and M.A. Schaars. *The Economics of Cooperative Marketing.* New York: McGraw-Hill, 1937.

Baldwin, William L. *Antitrust and the Changing Corporation.* Durham, N.C.: Duke University Press, 1961.

Blair, R.D., and D.L. Kaserman. *Antitrust Economics.* Homewood, Ill.: Richard D. Irwin, 1985.

Bok, Derek. "Section 7 of the Clayton Act and the Merging of Law and Economics." *Harvard Law Review* 74 (December 1960).

Bronsteen, Peter. "Allegations of Monopoly and Anticompetitive Practices in the Domestic Lemon Industry." Ph.D. diss. University of California-Los Angeles, 1981.

Bunje, R. *Cooperative Farm Bargaining and Price Negotiations.* Cooperative Information Report no. 26. Washington, D.C.: U.S. Dept. of Agriculture, July 1980.

Campbell, G.R. "Grower–First Handler Exchange Arrangements in the Wisconsin Processed Vegetable Industry." In *Coordination and Exchange in Agricultural Subsectors,* ed. B.W. Marion. Monograph 2. Food Systems Research Group, University of Wisconsin-Madison, January 1976.

Collins, N.R., W.F. Mueller, and E.N. Birch. *Grower–Processor Integration: A Study of Vertical Integration between Growers and Processors of Tomatoes in California.* California Agricultural Experiment Station, Bulletin no. 768. University of California-Davis, College of Agriculture, October 1959.

Connor, John M. "Competition and the Role of the Largest Firms in the U.S. Food and Tobacco Industries." Working Paper no. 29. Food Systems Research Group, University of Wisconsin-Madison, February 1979.

Connor, J.M., R.T. Rogers, B.W. Marion, and W.F. Mueller. *The Food Manufacturing Industries: Structure, Strategies, Performance and Policies.* Lexington, Mass.: Lexington Books, 1985.

"Establishing Bargaining Units in Agricultural Marketing." *Virginia Law Review* 68 (September 1982).

Federal Trade Commission. *Agricultural Income Inquiry, Part II: Fruits, Vegetables, and Grapes.* Washington, D.C.: GPO, 1937.

———. *In the Matter of Borden, Inc.* FTC Docket 8978, Initial Decision. Washington, D.C.: FTC, 1976.

———. *In the Matter of Sunkist Growers, Inc.* FTC Docket 9100. Washington, D.C.: FTC, May 31, 1977.

———. *In the Matter of Sunkist Growers, Inc.* FTC Docket 9100. "Agreement Containing Order to Divest and Other Relief." Washington, D.C.: FTC, August 15, 1980.

Folsom, Ralph H. "Antitrust Enforcement Under the Secretaries of Agriculture and Commerce." *Columbia Law Review* 80 (1980).

French, B.C. "The Analysis of Productive Efficiency in Agricultural Marketing: Models, Methods, and Progress." In *A Survey of Agricultural Economics Literature,* vol. 1, ed. L. Martin. Minneapolis: University of Minnesota Press, 1977.

Gardner, K.B., and A.W. McKay. *The Citrus Industry and the California Fruit Growers Exchange.* Farm Credit Administration Circular C-121. Washington, D.C.: U.S. Dept. of Agriculture, June 1940.

Garoyan, L. "Producer–First Handler Exchange Arrangements for Selected California Processed Fruits, Vegetables, and Nuts." In *Coordination and Exchange in Agricultural Subsectors,* ed. B.W. Marion. Monograph 2. Food Systems Research Group, University of Wisconsin-Madison, January 1976.

Greer, Douglas F. "A Critique of Areeda and Turner's Standard for Predatory Practices." *Antitrust Bulletin* 24 (1979).

———. *Industrial Organization and Public Policy.* New York: Macmillan, 1980.

Helmberger, P.G. "Cooperative Enterprise as a Structural Dimension of Farm Markets." *Journal of Farm Economics* 46 (August 1964).

Helmberger, P.G., and S. Hoos. *Cooperative Bargaining in Agriculture: Grower-Processor Markets for Fruits and Vegetables.* Berkeley: University of California Division of Agricultural Sciences, 1965.

———. "Cooperative Enterprise and Organization Theory." *Journal of Farm Economics* 44 (May 1962).

———. "Economic Theory of Bargaining in Agriculture." *Journal of Farm Economics* 45 (December 1963).

Hoos, S. "Economic Possibilities and Limitations of Cooperative Bargaining Associations." In *Cooperative Bargaining,* Farmer Cooperative Service Report no. 113. Washington, D.C.: U.S. Dept. of Agriculture, August 1970.

Jesse, E.V., and A.C. Johnson. "Defining and Identifying Undue Price Enhancement." In *Antitrust Treatment of Agricultural Marketing Cooperatives,* ed. E.V. Jesse. Monograph 15. Food Systems Research Group, University of Wisconsin-Madison, September 1983.

Jesse, E.V. and A.C. Johnson. "Marketing Cooperatives and Undue Price Enhancement: A Theoretical Perspective." Working Paper no. 46. Food Systems Research Group, University of Wisconsin-Madison, October 1980.

Joskow, P.L., and A.K. Klevorick. "A Framework for Analyzing Predatory Pricing Policy." *Yale Law Journal* 89 (December 1979).

Kamien, M.I., and N.L. Schwartz. "Market Structure and Innovation: A Survey." *Journal of Economic Literature* 13 (March 1975).

Kirkman, C.H. *The Sunkist Adventure.* Farmer Cooperative Service, Cooperative Information Report no. 94. Washington, D.C.: U.S. Dept. of Agriculture, 1975.

Knutson, R. "What Is a Producer?" In *Proceedings of the National Symposium on Cooperatives and the Law.* University of Wisconsin-Madison Center for Cooperatives, 1974

Lande, Robert H. "Wealth Transfers as the Original and Primary Concern of Antitrust: The Efficiency Interpretation Challenged." *Hastings Law Journal* 34 (September 1982).

Leading National Advertisers, Inc. *Ad $ Summary.* New York: Leading National Advertisers, 1981.

———. *Company/Brand$.* New York: Leading National Advertisers, 1979.

Leibenstein, H. "Allocative Efficiency vs. 'X-Efficiency'." *American Economic Review* 56 (1966).

Markham, Jesse W. "The Nature and Significance of Price Leadership." *American Economic Review* 41 (December 1951).

Masson, Robert T., and Philip Eisenstat. "Capper-Volstead and Milk Cooperative Market Power: Some Theoretical Issues." In *Agricultural Cooperatives and the Public Interest,* ed. B.W. Marion. Monograph 4. Food Systems Research Group, University of Wisconsin-Madison, September 1978.

McKay, A.W. and W.M. Stevens. *Organization and Development of a Cooperative Citrus-Fruit Marketing Agency.* USDA Bulletin no. 1237. Washington, D.C.: U.S. Dept. of Agriculture, May 1924.

Mighell, R., and L. Jones. *Vertical Coordination in Agriculture.* Agricultural Economics Report no. 19. Washington, D.C.: U.S. Dept. of Agriculture, February 1963.

Mueller, W.F. "Alleged Predatory Conduct in Food Retailing." Working Paper no. 78. Food Systems Research Group, University of Wisconsin-Madison, September 1984.

———. "The Economics and Law of Full-Supply Contracts as Used by Agricultural Cooperatives." Proceedings of the National Symposium on Cooperatives and the Law, University of Wisconsin-Madison, April 23–25, 1974.

———. "The Enforcement of Section 2 of the Capper-Volstead Act." In *Antitrust Treatment of Agricultural Marketing Cooperatives,* ed. E.V. Jesse. Monograph 15. Food Systems Research Group, University of Wisconsin-Madison, September 1983.

Mueller, W.F., and N.R. Collins. "Grower–Processor Integration in Fruit and Vegetable Marketing." *Journal of Farm Economics* 39 (December 1957).

Mueller, W.F., J. Culbertson, and B. Peckham. *Market Structure and Technological Performance in the Food Manufacturing Industries.* Monograph 11. Food Systems Research Group, University of Wisconsin-Madison, February 1982.

Mueller, W.F., and R.T. Rogers. "Changes in Market Concentration of Manufacturing Industries." *Review of Industrial Organization* 1 (Spring 1984).

Mueller, W.F., and J.M. Tinley. *Membership Marketing Contracts of Agricultural Cooperatives in California.* California Agricultural Experiment Station Bulletin 760. University of California-Davis, College of Agriculture, March 1958.

Nourse, E.G. *The Legal Status of Agricultural Co-operation.* New York: Macmillan, 1927.

Paterson, T.W., and W.F. Mueller. "Agricultural Marketing Cooperatives and Section 1 of the Capper-Volstead Act: Conditioning (Limited) Antitrust Immunity on Capper-Volstead Policy." Working Paper no. 84. Food Systems Research Group, University of Wisconsin-Madison, December 1984.

Porter, Michael F. *Competitive Advantage.* New York: Free Press, 1985.

Posner, Richard. *Antitrust Law: An Economic Perspective.* Chicago: University of Chicago Press, 1976.

Preston, L.E. "Predatory Marketing" In *Regulation of Marketing and the Public Interest,* Frederick Balderston, J.M. Carmen, and F.M. Nicosia. Pergamen, 1981.

Salop, Steven C. "Strategic Entry Deterrence." *American Economic Review* 69 (May 1979).

Scherer, F.M. *Industrial Market Structure and Economic Performance.* 2d ed. Chicago: Rand McNally, 1980.

———. "Predatory Pricing and the Sherman Act: A Comment." *Harvard Law Review* 89 (1976).

Scherer, F.M., A.R. Beckenstein, E. Kaufer, and R. D. Murphy. *The Economics of Multi-Plant Operation.* Harvard Economic Studies, vol. 145. Cambridge, Mass.: Harvard University Press, 1975.

Shepherd, William G. *The Economics of Industrial Organization.* 2d ed. Englewood Cliffs, N.J.: Prentice-Hall, 1985.

Stigler, George. "The Kinky Oligopoly Demand Curve and Rigid Prices." *Journal of Political Economy* 60 (October 1947).

Stocking, G.W., and W.F. Mueller. "The Cellophane Case and the New Competition." *American Economic Review* 45 (March 1955).

Sullivan, Lawrence. *Handbook of the Law of Antitrust.* St. Paul: West, 1977.

Turner, D.F. "Antitrust Policy and the Cellophane Case." *Harvard Law Review* 70 (1956).

U.S. Dept. of Agriculture. Farmer Cooperative Service. *Farmer Cooperative Statistics, 1982.* Cooperative Information Report no. 1. Washington D.C.: U.S. Dept. of Agriculture, 1984.

U.S. Dept. of Justice. *Merger Guidelines.* Reprinted by Bureau of National Affairs. Washington, D.C.: GPO, June 14, 1984.

———. *Vertical Restraints Guidelines.* Reprinted in Bureau of National Affairs. *Antitrust and Trade Regulation Report* 48, no. 119. Washington, D.C.: GPO, January 23, 1985.

Vitaliano, Peter. "The Theory of Cooperative Enterprise: Its Development and Present Status." In *Agricultural Cooperatives and the Public Interest,* ed. B.W. Marion. Monograph 4. Food Systems Research Group, University of Wisconsin-Madison, September 1978.

Warlich, Eugene M., and Robert S. Brill. "Cooperatives vis-a-vis Corporations: Size, Antitrust and Immunity." *South Dakota Law Review* 23 (Summer 1978).

Weiss, L.W. "The Structure-Conduct Performance Paradigm and Antitrust." *Pennsylvania Law Review* 127 (1979).

Wills, Robert L. "Evaluating Price Enhancement by Processing Cooperatives." *American Journal of Agricultural Economics* 67 (May 1985).

Youde, J.G., and P.G. Helmberger. "Marketing Cooperatives in the U.S.: Membership Policies, Market Power, and Antitrust Policy." *Journal of Farm Economics* 48 (1966).

Index

About the Authors

Willard F. Mueller is William F. Vilas Research Professor of Agricultural Economics, Professor of Economics and Professor in the Law School, University of Wisconsin-Madison. During 1961–1969 he was Chief Economist and Director of the Bureau of Economics of the Federal Trade Commission; and during 1968–1969 he was Executive Director of the President's Cabinet Committee on Price Stability. He also has taught at the University of California-Davis, the University of Maryland, Michigan State University, and American University. He has written extensively in the areas of industrial organization and public policy and has been involved in many antitrust proceedings.

Peter G. Helmberger is Professor of Agricultural Economics at the University of Wisconsin-Madison. He has been on the faculty at both Pennsylvania State University and the University of California-Berkeley. He is a leading authority in the theory of cooperatives, industrial organization, and agricultural policies, and he has received several professional awards for distinguished research in these areas.

Thomas W. Paterson is an attorney with Susman, Godfrey & McGowan in Houston, Texas, where his practice focuses on complex commercial litigation. In 1984, he received a J.D., magna cum laude, from the University of Wisconsin Law School and a Ph.D. in Agricultural Economics from the University of Wisconsin-Madison. His Ph.D. dissertation addressed legal-economic issues in the industrial organization of the U.S. food system. Upon finishing graduate studies at the University of Wisconsin, Mr. Paterson clerked for the Honorable Thomas Gibbs Gee on the United States Court of Appeals for the Fifth Circuit.